BILINGUAL SPEECH
A TYPOLOGY OF CODE-MIXING

PIETER MUYSKEN

CAMBRIDGE
UNIVERSITY PRESS

CAMBRIDGE UNIVERSITY PRESS
Cambridge, New York, Melbourne, Madrid, Cape Town, Singapore, São Paulo

Cambridge University Press
The Edinburgh Building, Cambridge CB2 2RU, UK

Published in the United States of America by Cambridge University Press, New York

www.cambridge.org
Information on this title: www.cambridge.org/9780521771689

First published 2000
This digitally printed first paperback version 2005

A catalogue record for this publication is available from the British Library

ISBN-13 978-0-521-77168-9 hardback
ISBN-10 0-521-77168-4 hardback

ISBN-13 978-0-521-02391-7 paperback
ISBN-10 0-521-02391-2 paperback

BILINGUAL SPEECH
A TYPOLOGY OF CODE-MIXING

This book provides an in-depth analysis of the different ways in which bilingual speakers switch from one language to another in the course of conversation. This phenomenon, known as code-mixing or code-switching, takes many forms. Pieter Muysken adopts a comparative approach to distinguish between the different types of code-mixing, drawing on a wealth of data from bilingual settings throughout the world. His study identifies three fundamental and distinct patterns of mixing – 'insertion', 'alternation' and 'congruent lexicalization' – and sets out to discover whether the choice of a particular mixing strategy depends on the contrasting grammatical properties of the languages involved, the degree of bilingual competence of the speaker or various social factors. The book synthesises a vast array of recent research in a rapidly growing field of study which has much to reveal about the structure and function of language.

PIETER MUYSKEN is Professor of Linguistics and Latin American Studies at Leiden University. He is co-editor, with Lesley Milroy, of *One Speaker, Two Languages* (1995) and has published widely on Andean linguistics, creole studies and language contact.

CONTENTS

FIGURES

vi

TABLES

PREFACE

This book is an attempt to analyse the recent work on code-mixing and code-switching from a single grammatical perspective and to relate it to the general study of grammar contact. Since code-mixing research is being carried out in many different places and by many different researchers, by necessity my book cites many studies by others. Rather than mostly reporting on my own data, I discuss a great many data sets (many of which were gathered in recent master's and doctoral dissertations in the Netherlands) and analyses. The reason for this is that I feel this is the only way to advance at the present stage, which is characterized by a proliferation of case-studies in many locations. Thus I want to use this occasion to gratefully acknowledge my indebtedness to all researchers in the field of language contact studies, and apologize beforehand for remaining errors in the interpretation of their data and views.

In early 1981 I was working with two colleagues in Montreal: Anna-Maria DiSciullo, who had participated in a study of the Italo-Quebecois speech community and is also a member of this community, and Rajendra Singh, expert on Hindi/English code-mixing and an accomplished switcher himself. We applied the theory of grammatical government to bilingual speech data and proposed that language mixing was structurally constrained by the government relation, just then being introduced into generative linguistics. In later research this constraint turned out to make the wrong predictions, but the insight behind it still has some value, independent of the theoretical framework adopted. Here I will try to use notions that are as little theory specific as possible, although I cannot eradicate my background in theoretical generative linguistics. This book could not have been written without my participation in the Network on Code-Switching and Language Contact of the European Science Foundation (1990–1992). This network involved a number of meetings which did much to stimulate interest in this area and to bring together interested researchers. For me it was an intense learning experience. I want to thank all participants with whom I had the opportunity to discuss the issues at hand, Penelope Gardner-Chloros and Georges Lüdi for setting up the network, and Wouter Hugenholtz and Pat Cosgrove for keeping it intact.

I want to dedicate this work to my students. A number of students in Amsterdam wrote master's and doctoral theses that have been important for me both because of the insights gained and for the rich data sets made available. In chronological order these include:

- Sita Kishna worked on Sarnami (Hindustani) and argued in detail that there is no difference between insertional code-mixing and borrowing;
- Rob Crama and Heleen van Gelderen studied Dutch/English code-mixing and underlined the importance of homophonous diamorphs in facilitating mixing;
- Jacomine Nortier, in her careful study of Moroccan Arabic/ Dutch code-mixing tested many constraints in the literature against her data and demonstrated the complete empirical inadequacy of the government constraint;
- Jeanine Treffers-Daller showed the importance of peripherality in Brussels Dutch/French code-mixing: many instances turned out to involve the margins of the clause rather than core elements;
- Liesbeth Adelmeijer focussed on Dutch/English code-mixing and argued for the importance of looking at surface rather than underlying word order in accounting for mixing possibilities;
- Peter Bakker showed in his study of Michif, the language of Cree–French *métis* that emerged in the early nineteenth century in Canada, that out of mixing a whole new language can emerge;
- Silvia Kouwenberg, in her description and analysis of Berbice Dutch Creole, showed the importance of surface convergence patterns in language change;
- Jette Bolle demonstrated how diverse the patterns of mixing become when two languages in contact – Surinamese Dutch and the version of Sranan creole spoken in Amsterdam – are very similar;
- Rosita Huwaë, in her work on Moluccan Malay/Dutch language contact underlines the historical dimension: different layers of contact varieties coexist in this very complex bilingual community;
- Vincent de Rooij studied Swahili/French mixing patterns and carefully analysed the French discourse markers in Swahili

bilingual speech, arguing that saliency contributes to the switching of French conjunctions through paratactic adjunction.

Their work is more explicitly cited in the text and referenced in the bibliography. I have tried to give detailed citations for examples of code-mixing cited from various studies, except where I was fortunate enough to be able to use some of the raw data collected by various researchers. In these cases I have cited the main publication coming out of that research. Here I want to thank particularly Rosita Huwaë, Sita Kishna, Vincent de Rooij, and Jeanine Treffers-Daller for making their data available to me.

I should also mention the work of several fellow researchers from other Dutch universities: Herman Giesbers (Nijmegen) carefully collected and analysed materials on Dutch dialect/standard code-switching; Rik Boeschoten (Tilburg) pointed to the importance of asymmetry in mixing patterns, particularly of first generation migrants; Ad Backus (Tilburg) was the first to explore the variety of mixing patterns found in a number of different networks among several generations of Turkish migrants; Henk de Wolf (Utrecht) initiated the modern study of Frisian/Dutch code mixing; finally Louis Boumans (Nijmegen) studied the dynamics in the evolving Morccan Arabic/Dutch bilingual community.

Other names of colleagues that immediately come to mind for special thanks include René Appel, Hugo Baetens-Beardsmore, Abdelâli Bentahila, Lynne Drapeau, Penelope Gardner-Chloros, François Grosjean, Helena Halmari, Roeland van Hout, Annick De Houwer, Georges Lüdi, Jürgen Meisel, Lesley Milroy, Carol Myers-Scotton, Carol Pfaff, Petr Pitha, Shana Poplack, Henriëtte Schatz, Andrée Tabouret-Keller. In addition I want to thank a number of generations of undergraduate students at the Linguistics Department of the University of Amsterdam for suffering through a series of confused lectures and seminars full of half-baked ideas. Vincent de Rooij, Jeanine Treffers-Daller, Carol Myers-Scotton, Rik Boeschoten, Suzanne Romaine, Martin Haase, and various anonymous readers for the publisher commented on earlier versions of this manuscript.

Finally, I want to thank the Netherlands Institute for Advanced Studies (NIAS) for making it possible to complete a first draft of this book during the academic year 1995/96 in an atmosphere both relaxing and inspiring, and Pilar van Breda-Burgueño for helping with corrections of the manuscript. Citi Potts of Cambridge University Press caught a great number of the remaining errors.

ABBREVIATIONS

A   adjective
ABL   ablative case
AC   accusative case
ADV   adverb
AF   affirmative
AG   agentive
agr   agreement
ALL   allative
APPL   applicative
ASP   aspect
AUX   auxiliary
BEN   benefactive
C   clause
CAU   causative
CIS   cislocative (near or toward speaker)
CONJ   coordinating conjunction
COMP   complementizer, subordinating conjunction
CONN   connective
CONSEC   consecutive
COP   copula
CPR   co-preterite
DA   dative
DEF   definite
DEM   demonstrative
DET   determiner
DIM   diminutive
DO   direct object
DUB   dubitative
DUR   durative
EL   embedded language

EMPH	emphatic
ESS	essive case
Excl	exclusive
F	feminine
Fr	formative
FOC	focus
FU	future tense
GE	genitive
HAB	habitual
I-	internal (language)
IA	intransitive action
ILL	illative
IM	imperative
IMPF	imperfective
IND	indicative
INDEF	indefinite
INF	infinitive
INFL	inflection (node)
INS	instrumental
INT	intensive
IO	indirect object
IP	inflection phrase
LO	locative
M	masculine
ML	matrix language
N	noun
NC1, 2, . . .	noun class 1, 2, . . .
NEG	negation element
NOM	nominalizer
NON-PST	non-past (often present) tense
O	object
P	adposition
PAR	partitive
PART1, 2, . . .	participle 1, 2, . . .
PERF	perfective aspect
PL	plural marker
POSS	possessive
pp	past participle
PP	adpositional phrase
PR	progressive aspect

PRD	predicate
PREP	proposition
PRES	present tense
PRET	preterite
PST	past
Pron	pronoun
Q	quantifier
RC	root change
RE	reflexive
REL	relative clause marker
REP	repetition
RES	resultative
S	subject
SD	sudden discovery tense
SUB	adverbial subordinator
TA	transitive action
TO	topic
V	verb
VP	verb phrase
W	word
Y/N	yes/no question
1ex	first person plural exclusive
1pl	1plural
1sg	1singular

I
The study of code-mixing

This book is about intra-sentential code-mixing and how it can help us understand language interaction as the result of contact, yielding a new perspective on central aspects of the human linguistic capacity. The question discussed here is: how can a bilingual speaker combine elements from two languages when processing mixed sentences? I am using the term **code-mixing** to refer to all cases where lexical items and grammatical features from two languages appear in one sentence. The more commonly used term **code-switching** will be reserved for the rapid succession of several languages in a single speech event, for reasons which will be made clear. However, sometimes the terms **switch**, **switch point**, or **switching** will be used informally while referring to the cooccurrence of fragments from different languages in a sentence. Of course, it will also be necessary to separate cases of code-mixing from **lexical borrowing**. The term **language interaction** will be used occasionally as a very general cover term for different, frequently highly innovative, results of language contact, both involving lexical items (as in code-mixing) and otherwise (e.g. phonological or syntactic interference).

In most models portraying the functioning of the speaker/listener, pictures we carry in our minds or see portrayed in a textbook, a single grammar and a single lexicon are embedded in the network of relations that constitutes the model. This is so commonplace that the essential enrichment of having several grammars and lexicons participate in it at the same time is often seen as a threat, a disruption, a malady. This is particularly the case in the structuralist tradition in linguistics. Ronjat (1913) and Leopold (1939–1949) formed the basis for the single parent/single language approach to bilingual child rearing – bilingualism in the family is ok, but it should remain tidy. Weinreich (1953: 73) thought that intra-sentential code-mixing was a sign of lack of bilingual proficiency and interference. An ideal bilingual 'switches from one language according to appropriate changes in the speech situation (interlocutor, topics, etc.) but not in an unchanged speech situation and certainly not within a single sentence.' A growing number of studies have demonstrated, however, that many bilinguals will produce mixed sentences in ordinary conversations. What is interesting to me, as it has been to many others in recent years, is that such sentences are produced with great ease and complete fluidity. Indeed, for some speakers it is the unmarked code in certain circumstances (Myers-Scotton 1993a). Neither does it reflect limited proficiency in either of the languages involved. Rather, speakers who code-mix fluently and easily tend to be quite proficient bilinguals (Poplack 1980, Nortier 1990). Finally, we cannot assume either that it is word-finding difficulties or specific cultural pressures that lead to the mixture (even if language contact itself is culturally conditioned). Often, the element introduced corresponds to a household word.

In the last fifteen years, a large number of studies have appeared in which specific cases of intra-sentential code-mixing are analysed from a grammatical perspective. These cases involve a variety of language pairs, social settings, and speaker types. It is found that intra-sentential code-mixes are not distributed randomly in the sentence, but rather occur at specific points. Where much less agreement has been reached is with respect to general properties of the process.

This book is an attempt to present a general account of the very complex intra-sentential code-mixing phenomena that have been discovered. By now the amount of material collected for different language pairs is both diverse and substantial, and it is time to attempt a first synthesis. Rather than introducing one single data set, I will try to integrate the results of a great many different studies, some still unpublished. The present work is grounded both in structural linguistics and in sociolinguistics. Many of the characteristics of the mixing patterns are determined by the structural features of language; I will adopt the general tools and concepts of generative grammar in accounting for these (while trying to stay clear of highly specific formalisms and analyses). Structural analysis along generative lines will be combined with quantitative analysis as in the work of Labov and Sankoff, and comparative typological work. Occasionally, I will try to relate my interpretations to notions from psycholinguistics such as activation and processing. I will only infrequently have recourse to pragmatic and conversational analysis, partly because of my own lack of expertise, and partly because the wide-ranging comparative approach I am adopting here necessarily relies on data gathered by others less suited for detailed textual analysis, and often taking the form of isolated mixed sentences and tables.

The work reported on here could be considered to represent a taxonomic phase in the discipline, an attempt to tie together a set of intermediary results rather than giving a conclusive account. I feel the results from current studies are so diverse that some tidying up is called for. Although the focus of the present work is grammar, it does not mean attention will not be given to the crucial role of psycholinguistic and sociolinguistic factors influencing code-mixing, such as degree of bilingual proficiency, mode of bilingual processing, political balance between the languages, language attitudes, and type of interactive setting. However, these factors are considered in so far as they are related to or manifest themselves in the grammatical patterns of code-mixing encountered. Indeed, any synthesis at present must depart from the enormous variation in code-mixing patterns encountered, variation due to language typological factors in addition to sociolinguistic and psycholinguistic factors such as those mentioned.

I do not propose a single 'model' of code-mixing, since I do not think there is such a model, apart from the general models provided by grammatical theory and language processing. The challenge is to account for the patterns found in terms of general properties of grammar. Notice that only in this way can the phenomena of code-mixing help refine our perspective on general grammatical theory. If there were a special and separate theory of code-mixing, it might well be less relevant to general theoretical concerns.

Different processes

The patterns of intra-sentential code-mixing found are often rather different from one another. Much of the confusion in the field appears to arise from the fact that several distinct processes are at work:

- **insertion** of material (lexical items or entire constituents) from one language into a structure from the other language.
- **alternation** between structures from languages
- **congruent lexicalization** of material from different lexical inventories into a shared grammatical structure.

These three basic processes are constrained by different structural conditions, and are operant to a different extent and in different ways in specific bilingual settings. This produces much of the variation in mixing patterns encountered. The three processes correspond to dominant models for code mixing that have been proposed.

Approaches that depart from the notion of **insertion** (associated with Myers-Scotton 1993b) view the constraints in terms of the structural properties of some base or matrix structure. Here the process of code-mixing is conceived as something akin to borrowing: the insertion of an alien lexical or phrasal category into a given structure. The difference would simply be the size and type of element inserted, e.g. noun versus noun phrase.

Approaches departing from **alternation** (associated with Poplack 1980) view the constraints on mixing in terms of the compatibility or equivalence of the languages involved at the switch point. In this perspective code-mixing is akin to the switching of codes between turns or utterances. This is the reason I avoid using the term **code-switching** for the general process of mixing. Switching is only an appropriate term for the alternational type of mixing. The term code-switching is less neutral in two ways: as a term it already suggests something like alternation (as opposed to insertion), and it separates code-mixing too strongly from phenomena of borrowing and interference.

The distinction I make here between alternation and insertion corresponds to Auer's distinction between code-switching and transfer (1995: 126). Some authors have used the term 'switching' for language interaction between clauses, and 'mixing' for intra-clausal phenomena. This distinction parallels my distinction between alternation and insertion, but does not coincide with it, since in my framework alternation often takes place within the clause as well.

The notion of **congruent lexicalization** underlies the study of style shifting and dialect/standard variation, as in the work of Labov (1972) and Trudgill (1986), rather than bilingual language use proper. The exception is the bilingual research by Michael Clyne (1967) on German and Dutch immigrants in Australia. This comes closest to an approach to bilingual language use from the perspective of congruent lexicalization.

In this book I am claiming that these different models or approaches in fact correspond to different phenomena: there **is** alternation between languages, insertion into a matrix or base language, and congruent lexicalization, in the code-mixing data reported in the literature. In chapters 3, 4, and 5 criteria are proposed, both structural and quantitative, for giving substance to the three-way distinction.

In some cases, a single constituent is **inserted** into a frame provided for by the matrix language:

> (1) kalau dong tukan bikin dong tukan bikin
>   when they always make they always make
>   *voor acht personen* dek orang cuma nganga dong makan
>   for eight persons and then people only look they eat
>   'When they [cook], it is always for eight people, and then they only look at it, they eat . . .'
>
> (Moluccan Malay/Dutch; Huwaë 1992)

While in (1) this is an entire Dutch prepositional phrase inserted into a Moluccan Malay sentence, in (2) it is a single English verb stem used in a complex Navaho verbal structure:

(2) na'iish-*crash* lá
1sg:pass out-crash EMPH
'I am about to pass out.'   (Navaho/English; Canfield 1980: 219)

In (3) the temporal expression *por dos días* is clearly related to the verb *anduve*, encapsulating the inserted *in a state of shock*:

(3) Yo anduve *in a state of shock* por dos días.
'I walked in a state of shock for two days.'   (Spanish/English; Pfaff 1979: 296)

With insertion, there is embedding. The English prepositional phrase is inserted into an overall Spanish structure. Insertion is akin to (spontaneous) lexical borrowing, which is limited to one lexical unit. There is considerable variation in what is or can be inserted: in some languages this consists mostly of adverbial phrases, in others mostly single nouns, and in yet others again determiner + noun combinations. Insertion and the distinction between code-mixing and borrowing are taken up again in chapter 3.

In other cases, it seems that halfway through the sentence, one language is replaced by the other. The two languages **alternate**:

(4) maar 't hoeft niet   *li-'anna ida šeft ana . . .*
but it need not   for when I-see I
'but it need not be, for when I see, I . . .'
(Moroccan Arabic/Dutch; Nortier 1990: 126)

(5) Les femmes et le vin, *ne ponimayu.*
'Women and wine, I don't understand.'   (French/Russian; Timm 1978: 312)

(6) Andale pues *and do come again.*
'That's all right then, and do come again.'
(Spanish/English; Gumperz and Hernández-Chavez 1971: 118)

In the case of alternation, there is a true switch from one language to the other, involving both grammar and lexicon. Thus in (6) there is no reason to assume that the Spanish first segment is embedded in the English second segment or vice versa. Alternation is just a special case of code-switching, as it takes place between utterances in a turn or between turns. In chapter 4 alternation is studied in more detail.

In a third set of cases, it appears that there is a largely (but not necessarily completely) shared structure, lexicalized by elements from either language, **congruent lexicalization**. Consider the following examples:

(7) Weet jij [*whaar*] Jenny is?
'Do you know where Jenny is?' (Dutch: waar Jenny is)
(English/Dutch; Crama and van Gelderen 1984)

The sequence *where Jenny is* could as easily be English in structure as Dutch. Furthermore *where* is close to Dutch *waar* (particularly when pronounced by bilinguals), *Jenny* is a name in both languages, and *is* is homophonous.

5

A similar example is:

(8) En de partij dy't hy derby blaasde,   (Frisian)
en de partij die hij erbij blies   (Dutch)
And the part that he thereby blew

is net [**foar** *herhaling vatbaar*].   (Frisian)
is niet voor herhaling vatbaar   (Dutch)
is not for repetition handable.
'And the song he sang then is not fit to be repeated.'
(Frisian/Dutch; Wolf 1995: 12)

Here, Frisian *foar* 'for' is sufficiently similar to Dutch *voor* 'for' to be an ambiguous switchpoint; Dutch *herhaling vatbaar* is not a constituent, but two words that form an idiom together with *voor*.

While English/Dutch and Frisian/Dutch are two closely related language pairs with many cognates, we may find something similar to these examples in the English/Spanish material analysed by Poplack (1980) as well:

(9) (A) Why make Carol *sentarse atrás* *(B)* *pa'que* everybody
sit at the back so that
has to move (C) *pa'que se salga.*
so that [she] may get out.   (Spanish/English; Poplack 1980: 589)

Here sentence fragment (B) is a complement to (A), and (C) is a complement to (B). Notice that the first Spanish fragment here contains both a verb phrase, *sentarse atrás* and a purposive complementizer, *pa'que*. There is no particular grammatical relation between the two English fragments nor between the Spanish ones. The example could perhaps be analysed as backfire insertions within insertions. However, this is rather counter-intuitive, both because the switched fragments are not unique constituents and because they do not appear to obey rules specific to the supposed matrix constituent, but rather rules common to both languages.

Consider a final example:

(10) Bueno, *in other words*, el *flight* [que sale de Chicago *around three o'clock*].
'Good, in other words, the flight that leaves from Chicago around three o'clock.'   (Spanish/English; Pfaff 1976: 250)

In (10) *que sale de Chicago* 'that leaves Chicago' or even *el flight que sale de Chicago* (assuming *Chicago* to be part of the Spanish stretch for the sake of the argument – in fact it may be the trigger for the subsequent switch to English) is a constituent, but not a unique one, since it also includes the English fragment *around three o'clock*.

The term congruent lexicalization refers to a situation where the two languages share a grammatical structure which can be filled lexically with elements from either language. The mixing of English and Spanish could be interpreted as a combination of alternations and insertions, but the going back and forth suggests that there may be more going on, and that the elements from the two languages are inserted, as constituents or as words, into a shared structure. In this perspective, congruent lexicalization is akin to style or register shifting and monolingual linguistic variation. The latter would be the limiting case of congruent lexicalization.

I want to explore these three separate patterns of intra-sentential code-mixing and study them through the systematic exploration of bilingual corpora, in addition to the detailed structural analysis of individual examples (van Hout and Muysken 1995).

The structural interpretation of these notions is as follows. Consider the following trees, in which *A, B* are language labels for non-terminal nodes (i.e. fictitious markers identifying entire constituents as belonging to one language), and *a, b* are labels for terminal, i.e. lexical, nodes, indicating that the words chosen are from a particular language.

(11)   **insertion**

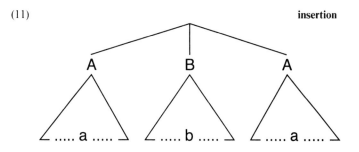

In this situation, a single constituent *B* (with words *b* from the same language) is inserted into a structure defined by language *A*, with words *a* from that language.

(12)   **alternation**

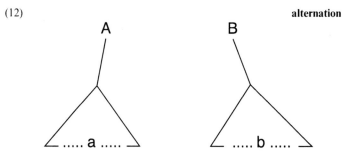

In this situation, a constituent from language *A* (with words from the same language) is followed by a constituent from language *B* (with words from

7

that language). The language of the constituent dominating *A* and *B* is unspecified.

(13)   **congruent lexicalization**

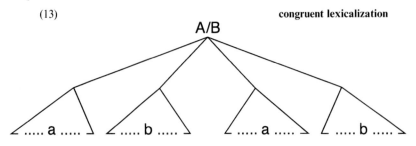

Finally, in (13) the grammatical structure is shared by languages *A* and *B*, and words from both languages *a* and *b* are inserted more or less randomly.

Having presented the three processes, insertion, alternation, and congruent lexicalization, I will try to suggest a number of diagnostic features which may be used to distinguish these three patterns in chapters 3, 4, and 5. There are a number of criteria I would like to consider, and I will illustrate their application with concrete cases. The criteria are rarely knock-down criteria by themselves, but should be used conjointly to characterize a sentence or a bilingual speech sample as a case of alternation, insertion, or congruent lexicalization.

In addition to the **structural** interpretation of the three patterns, in terms of labels in tree configurations, there can also be a **psycholinguistic** and a **sociolinguistic** one. The **psycholinguistic** interpretation of the three-way distinction made here could be in terms of different degrees of activation of components of both languages in speech production. In the case of alternation, activation would shift from one language to another, and in the case of insertion, activation in one language would be temporarily diminished. For congruent lexicalization, the two languages partially share their processing systems. Psycholinguistic factors determining the choice between these different processes include bilingual proficiency, level of monitoring in the two languages, the triggering of a particular language by specific items and the degree of separateness of storage and access systems.

The interpretation of the three patterns can also be **sociolinguistic**, in terms of bilingual strategies (an example would be Sankoff, Poplack, and Vanniarajan's (1990) distinction between equivalence and insertion). The sociolinguistic embedding of these three patterns, i.e. their use as bilingual strategies, can be described as follows. The process of alternation is particularly frequent in stable bilingual communities with a tradition of language separation, but occurs in many other communities as well. It is a frequent

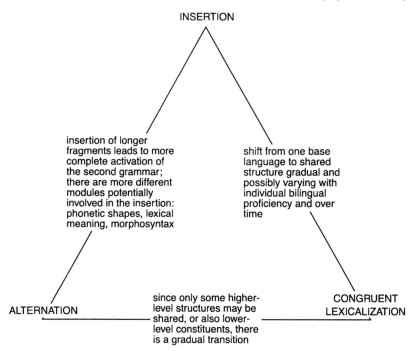

INSERTION

insertion of longer
fragments leads to more
complete activation of
the second grammar;
there are more different
modules potentially
involved in the insertion:
phonetic shapes, lexical
meaning, morphosyntax

shift from one base
language to shared
structure gradual and
possibly varying with
individual bilingual
proficiency and over
time

ALTERNATION

since only some higher-
level structures may be
shared, or also lower-
level constituents, there
is a gradual transition

CONGRUENT
LEXICALIZATION

Figure 1.1 Schematic representation of the three main styles of code-mixing
and transitions between them

and structurally little intrusive type of code-mixing. Insertion is frequent in
colonial settings and recent migrant communities, where there is a considerable asymmetry in the speakers' proficiency in the two languages. A language
dominance shift, e.g. between the first and third generation in an immigrant
setting, may be reflected in a shift in directionality of the insertion of
elements: from insertion into the language of the country of origin to the
presence of orginally native items in the language of the host country.
Congruent lexicalization may be particularly associated with second generation migrant groups, dialect/standard and post-creole continua, and
bilingual speakers of closely related languages with roughly equal prestige
and no tradition of overt language separation.

The three types of code-mixing can be conveniently viewed in terms of a
triangle, an image to which I return in chapter 8 when I discuss the various
factors that help determine which type of mixing occurs in a specific setting.
The differences between the three types are gradual rather than absolute, as
can be seen in figure 1.1.

Between **insertion** and **alternation** there is a transition zone since insertion of longer fragments leads to increasingly more complete activation of the second grammar. There are different modules potentially involved in the insertion: phonetic shapes, lexical meaning, morphosyntax, which involve activation of the second grammar to different degrees.

Since only some higher-level structures may be shared between languages, there is a gradual transition as well between **alternation** and **congruent lexicalization**: alternation when only the top node (the sentence node) is shared, and congruent lexicalization when all or most nodes are shared between the two languages.

Finally, there can be a gradual shift from one base language to shared structure and on to the other base language, possibly varying with individual bilingual proficiency and over time. This implies particularly that in many immigrant communities, **insertion** of new items and expressions into the home language can evolve into **congruent lexicalization** and then possibly into **alternation** (with set phrases and expressions from the ethnic language interspersed in the new language).

The literature abounds both with proposals for various specific constraints on code-mixing, and with claims that general constraints do not hold. Romaine (1989, 1995) takes an intermediate position, namely that none of the constraints covers all cases. A similar position is taken by Clyne (1987). I want to argue against too much relativism, however, both because it is overly pessimistic of the relevance of linguistic structure, and because I believe it only portrays a limited picture of the often quite regular array of code-mixing patterns to be found. Rather, a particular constraint can only be assumed to hold for a specific type of mixing.

The role of a dominant research experience in shaping one's vision: the development of code-mixing research

It has been said somewhat maliciously that an Indo-Europeanist will tend to make reconstructed Proto-Indo-European look like the language that she or he thoroughly studied early on. If the scholar starts out with Albanian, her or his version of the proto-language will have many features of Albanian, and so on. This subjectivism (if the observation is at all valid) may seem reprehensible, but I think there are many ways in which research that one does early on shapes one's vision of a certain domain. This does not mean one is condemned to the one perspective, but rather that this perspective is the frame of reference onto which later ideas are often grafted. In this way, research on code-mixing has been shaped by the language pairs encountered by researchers, and the key notions were introduced one by one on the basis of the data encountered.

10

Two scholars started with code-mixing research in the 1960s: ¹ Lehtinen and Michael Clyne. Thirty years ago Meri Lehtinen wrote, in study of the recorded Finnish–English bilingual corpus of one speaker:

> In order for any intra-sentence code-switching to be possible at all, there must exist in the two languages some constructions which are in some sense similar, so that certain syntactic items from each language are equivalent to each other in specific ways. Further reflection, supported by an examination of the corpus, shows that the similarities must exist in what is known as the 'surface grammar' of sentences (1966: 153)

And further on: 'It would seem, then, that switching at words which belong to a closed class is not allowed by the code-switching rules, except in cases where such a switch is forced by structural considerations' (1966: 177). The three notions of **syntactic equivalence**, **surface linear order**, and **closed class items** are still at the core of our view of intra-sentential code-mixing. In this sense, everything written since is a comment on and elaboration of Lehtinen's work. Where we have progressed enormously since Lehtinen is in the empirical scope of the research and in the level of explanation advanced. Explaining why these notions are important in accounting for bilingual speech also makes it possible to study the relation between them and their relative weight in an explanatory model.

Earlier work by Michael Clyne has helped shape the view of code-mixing as something relatively unconstrained, like congruent lexicalization. Clyne has worked in Australia, particularly with the German and Dutch immigrant communities. His best-known books in this area are *Transference and triggering* (1967) and *Perspectives on language contact* (1972). In his work he places the phenomenon of code-mixing in the context of a complex set of other language contact processes: **lexical triggering**, **transference**, and **convergence**. The perceived similarities between the languages bilinguals speak facilitate code-mixing, and in the bilingual setting the languages will tend to converge. The use of a word from another language may easily trigger other material from that language, either in anticipation of that word or subsequently. The picture dominant in Clyne's work then is neither that of alternation nor of insertion, but of congruent lexicalization. Consider examples such as:

(14) Wan ik komt *home from school.*
      'When I come home from school.' (English/Dutch; Clyne 1987: 759)

Here English *when* appears as a Dutch-like word *wan* (cf. Du *wanneer*), the Dutch word order is adapted to English (cf. Du *wanneer ik thuis* ('home') *kom*), and the inflected form of the verb is not correct. Similarly:

11

(15) That's what *Papschi mein-*s to say.
That's what Papschi means to say.   (German/English; Clyne 1987: 756)

The use of a German name, *Papschi*, triggers a German verb *mein*, which is quite close semantically to English *mean*, to be sure, and inflected with English third person -*s*.

Recognizing the sociolinguistically determined nature of code-mixing, a considerable part of the research since 1970 has focussed on the syntactic properties of code-mixing: where in the sentence do we find it, and when is it impossible? In other words, what are the constraints on code-mixing? This research has undergone three stages (Appel and Muysken 1987; Bhatia and Ritchie 1996): (a) an early stage in which grammatical constraints specific to particular constructions were focussed on; (b) a stage which has produced the classical studies in which universal constraints on code-mixing were explored, from around 1980 onward; (c) the present stage, which may be characterized by the search for new perspectives: what alternative mixing strategies are there and are constraints perhaps relative to a particular strategy?

Particular grammatical constraints

Most of the code-mixing studies from the 1970s drew on Spanish–English data recorded from conversations by Mexican Americans and Puerto Ricans, and proposed construction-specific constraints. Gumperz and Hernandez-Chavez (1971) noted that mixing was easily possible in some contexts, but not so much in others. Contexts allowing a switch included:

(16) Between a head noun and a relative clause:
those friends are friends from Mexico *que tienen chamaquitos* (that have little children)   (Spanish/English; Gumperz and Hernández-Chavez 1971: 118)

(17) Between a subject and a predicate in a copular construction:
An' my uncle Sam es *el más agabachado.* (is the most Americanized)
(Spanish/English; Gumperz and Hernández-Chavez 1971: 119)

Switches as in (18), with the verb in English, are not allowed, however:

(18) * que *have* chamaquitos

In a more systematic treatment Timm (1975) proposed the following restrictions:

(19) Subject and object pronouns must be in the same language as the main verb:
* *Yo* (I) went.
* Mira (look at) *him*

(20) An auxiliary and a main verb, or a main verb and an infinitive must be in the same language:

* They want *a venir* (to come).

* ha (he has) *seen*

In the studies of Gumperz and Hernandez-Chavez and Timm just cited two methodologies are combined: the analysis of recorded conversations and grammaticality judgements. The stars in the above examples reflect judgements of bilinguals about possible switches, but that these judgements do not always correspond to actual mixing behaviour is clear when we compare the two observations by Lipski (1978) in (21) and (22) with findings of Pfaff (1979):

(21)   It is difficult to switch inside a prepositional phrase:
         ?? in *la casa* (the house)

(22)   It is impossible to switch between the article and the noun:
         ?? I see the *casa* (house).

Both observations contrast with a large number of cases of precisely these switches found in the corpus analysed by Pfaff (1979). Mixing internal to prepositional phrases (PPs), i.e. of English nouns into Spanish PPs occurs far more often than mixing at PP boundaries. We also find more cases of a switch between the article and the noun than switches between article + noun combinations and the rest of the sentence. Clearly it is difficult if not impossible to rely on judgement data.

The studies of code-mixing carried out in the 1970s provide us with a large body of analysed data, with a number of inductive generalizations, and with insights into the type of constraints on code-mixing to expect. An overall theoretical perspective was lacking, however, and this is what the studies of the early 1980s have tried to contribute.

Poplack's Equivalence and Free Morpheme constraints

Although many of the ideas voiced in the current code-mixing literature were informally proposed earlier, the major impetus for a more systematic exploration of bilingual data came with Poplack (1980). I will take that date and reference as the starting point for my discussion of different models.

In her work on Spanish/English code-mixing in the Puerto Rican community (1980), Poplack discovered that code-mixing occurred largely at sites of equivalent constituent order. She is the principal exponent of the alternation perspective, and stresses the importance of **linear equivalence** between the languages involved at the point of the switch.

> The order of sentence constituents immediately adjacent to and on both sides of the switch point must be grammatical with respect to both languages involved simultaneously . . . The local co-grammaticality or equivalence of the two languages in the vicinity of the switch holds as

long as the order of any two sentence elements, one before and one after the switch point, is not excluded in either language.

(Sankoff and Poplack 1981: 5)

Underlying this constraint is a particular definition of code-switching, which embodies the idea of alternation, phrased by Poplack (1993) as follows: 'Code-switching is the **juxtaposition** [emphasis SP] of sentences or sentence fragments, each of which is internally consistent with the morphological and syntactic (and optionally, phonological) rules of the language of its provenance.' An example of Spanish/English code-mixing illustrating this juxtaposition is:

(23)   (A) *Se me hace que* (B) I have to respect her (C) *porque 'ta* . . . older.

'It appears to me that I have to respect her because [she] is . . . older.'

(Spanish/English; Poplack 1980: 591)

Fragment (B) is a complement to (A), and (C) modifies (B). Notice that *porque 'ta* 'because [she] is' does not form a unique constituent, excluding other elements, in this case *older*. It is clear that this type of data (see also example (9) above) cannot be handled very well in a model which takes insertion into a matrix and a dependency relation between matrix and inserted material as its primes. Rather, it has led to the idea that order equivalence across the switch point is what constrains code-mixing here.

The constituent order equivalence constraint is illustrated with the following example:

(24) I   told **him** that so that he would bring **it** fast

      | X | | | X |

  (Yo) **le** dije eso pa' que (él) **la** trajera rápido

(Spanish/English; Poplack 1980: 586)

Mixing is impossible where there is a difference in word order between Spanish and English. Here this is particularly the case around the object pronouns.

In her 1980 paper, Poplack proposed an additional principle, the **Free Morpheme Constraint**, which holds that:

(25)   Codes may be switched after any constituent in discourse provided that constituent is not a bound morpheme.   (Poplack 1980: 585–6)

Presumably switches both **before** and **after** a bound morpheme are prohibited by this constraint.

Soon, a number of criticisms were raised with respect to both the Equivalence Constraint and the Free Morpheme Constraint, often involving typologically more different language pairs, where code-mixing appeared to violate both constraints at the same time. Partly in response to this, Poplack has developed a more elaborate typology of code-mixing phenomena in later work, always taking as the starting point the issue of whether a given code-mixing pattern conforms to the equivalence constraint. She has argued that many cases that appear to violate both the Free Morpheme Constraint and the Equivalence Constraint were actually inflected **(nonce)** borrowings. Other cases violating the Equivalence Constraint are analysed as cases of constituent insertion. In subsequent papers, some written in collaboration with David Sankoff and others, Poplack developed methods and criteria for characterizing the contrasts between nonce borrowing and code-mixing, and equivalence-based mixing versus constituent-insertion. These studies have met with some criticism, and will be discussed in detail in chapter 3 on insertion. I should say that personally I am sympathetic to Poplack's attempt to separate the different types of mixing, even though I am not in agreement with the precise boundaries she draws between these types.

The typology of language contact phenomena developed by Poplack, Sankoff, and co-workers has focussed on four types of mixing so far:

(26)   code-switching under equivalence
       (nonce) borrowing
       constituent-insertion
       flagged switching

Flagged switching will be discussed in chapter 4 as indicative of alternation.

The Matrix Language Frame model

The data on which the perspectives taken by scholars such as Clyne and Poplack were based contrast rather sharply with the cases of Swahili–English mixing that have been the basis for Myers-Scotton's work, which exemplifies the insertion approach (1993b). Carol Myers-Scotton is best known for her research on Swahili–English bilingualism in eastern Africa, which she has approached from a number of perspectives: strategies of neutrality, and code-mixing as a marked or unmarked choice, and a comprehensive psycho-linguistically embedded linguistic model for intra-sentential code-mixing. Myers-Scotton (1993a: 4) gives the following definition: 'Code-switching is the selection by bilinguals or multilinguals of forms from an embedded language (or languages) in utterances of a matrix language during the same conversation.' This definition, which differs from that of Poplack cited before, is in line with the author's structural work and fits much of the African material discussed (characterized by insertions). It makes it necessary, however, to assume a going back and forth between different matrix languages where e.g. Spanish–English code-mixing in New York is discussed.

15

Neither is it clear that the central notion of 'unmarked code-switching' requires the concept of a matrix language.

Consider some of the cases that form the basis of Myers-Scotton's analysis, which are representative of the data reported on in her work:

> (27) Na kweli, hata mimi si-ko *sure* lakini n-a-*suspect* i-ta-kuwa *week* kesho.
> 'Well, even I am not sure, but I suspect it will be next week.'
>
> (Swahili/English; Myers-Scotton 1993b: 81)

Here the elements *sure*, *suspect*, and *week* are single elements inserted into a Swahili sentence.

The proto-typical type of example cited by Myers-Scotton corresponds directly to her view of the processes of code-mixing as a whole. Nishimura (1986: 126) also notes the tendency for researchers working on typologically similar languages such as Spanish or German and English to adopt symmetrical models (involving alternation or congruent lexicalization), and researchers working on typologically dissimilar language pairs such as Marathi or Swahili and English to adopt asymmetrical, insertional, models.

It is obvious that the kind of material analysed by Clyne gives rise to a quite different perspective on the phenomenon of code-mixing than the data from Spanish/English and Swahili/English that were the starting point of Poplack's and Myers-Scotton's research experiences.

For code-mixing of the insertional type a theoretical framework is provided by Myers-Scotton's Matrix Language Frame model (1993b, 1995), in which the matrix language constituent order and matrix language functional categories are assumed to dominate a clause. The model proposed, the Matrix Language Frame model, crucially incorporates the idea that there is an asymmetrical relation between the **matrix** and the **embedded** language in the mixing situation. Furthermore, **content** and **function** morphemes behave differently in Myers-Scotton's model: the former can be inserted into mixed constituents, when congruent with the matrix language categories, while the latter cannot. Finally, no essential difference is made between mixing and borrowing at the level of morphosyntactic integration, as it is in Poplack's work. The model proposed rests on the assumption that mixed sentences have an identifiable base or matrix language (ML), something that may or may not hold for individual bilingual corpora. There is always an asymmetry between the ML and the embedded language (EL).

I will primarily rely on the presentation of Myers-Scotton and Jake (1995), also citing Myers-Scotton (1993b) where necessary. The model makes the following claims:

(a) The ML determines the order of the elements in mixed (ML + EL) constituents (**Morpheme Order Principle**; Myers-Scotton and Jake 1995: 983):

> In ML + EL constituents consisting of singly occurring EL lexemes and
> any number of ML morphemes, surface morpheme order (reflecting
> surface syntactic relationships) will be that of the ML.

(b) There is a fundamental difference in distribution of functional elements
and content words in mixed sentences: functional elements in mixed ML +
EL fragments can only be drawn from the ML. The ML provides the 'system
morphemes' (functional categories) in such constituents (the **System Morpheme Principle**; Myers-Scotton and Jake 1995: 983):

> In ML + EL constituents, all system morphemes that have grammatical
> relations external to their head constituent (i.e. participate in the
> sentence's thematic role grid) will come from the ML.

(c) In mixed constituents only certain EL content morphemes may occur
(the **Blocking Hypothesis**; Myers-Scotton 1993b: 120):

> In ML + EL constituents, a blocking filter blocks any EL content
> morpheme which is not congruent with the ML with respect to three
> levels of abstraction regarding subcategorization.

Here **congruence** refers to 'a match between the ML and the EL at the lemma
level with respect to linguistically relevant features' (Myers-Scotton and Jake
1995: 985). The three levels of abstraction are: having the same status in both
languages, taking or assigning the same thematic roles, and having equivalent
pragmatic or discourse functions. Researchers have often stressed that there
needs to be some kind of categorial equivalence or congruence (Myers-
Scotton's term) between the constituent inserted and the matrix language
node into which it is inserted (e.g. Sebba 1998). The question is how to define
this notion across languages, and whether strict identity of features is
assumed, only compatibility, or translation equivalence. I return to this in
the next chapter.

The two languages are separately processed in units called islands. Three
types of constituents are listed: EL Islands, ML Islands, and Mixed EL +
ML constituents. In the Matrix Language Frame model insertions correspond to mixed EL + ML constituents, alternations to EL islands combined
with ML islands, and congruent lexicalization is akin to a notion that Myers-
Scotton is developing in as yet unpublished work on the possibility of a
'composite ML'.

A recent development in the work of Myers-Scotton and Jake (e.g. Jake
and Myers-Scotton 1997), building on Myers-Scotton and Jake (1995) has
been the attempt to explain the incidence and patterning of code-mixing
through the notion of compromise strategies, strategies meant to avoid a
clash in congruence between the properties of an inserted lemma (mental

17

representation of a lexical item) and properties of the matrix language. Several strategies are suggested, including: the creation of larger EL islands encapsulating the non-congruent lexical item, and the use of bare forms. These strategies run parallel to the approach taken here and outlined at the end of this chapter. It is an empirical question, however, whether all relevant examples can be explained in terms of the avoidance of a lexical congruence clash. Another development is the further refinement of the content word/ system morpheme distinction, e.g. in Myers-Scotton (1999). This will be taken up in more detail in chapter 6.

Myers-Scotton's work has been criticized on a number of counts: the notion of ML is often too rigid, the definition of system morphemes is problematic, it is difficult to find an appropriate definition of congruence, and the psycholinguistic processing model assumed is not fully explicit. Nonetheless, Myers-Scotton has drawn together psycholinguistic, sociolinguistic, and structural perspectives on code-mixing for the first time, and thus brought its study to a deeper explanatory level.

System morphemes (= functional elements) will be discussed in chapter 6. What is the role of functional categories in code-mixing processes? Do they determine the matrix language frame? Does (lack of) equivalence between functional categories in different languages play an important role? How do we define and identify functional elements?

One of the sources of inspiration for the Matrix Language Frame model lies in the work of Joshi (1985). Joshi has come up with an asymmetrical model on the basis of data from Marathi/English code-mixing and considerations from the mathematical theory of syntactic parsing. Crucial to Joshi's work is the notion of closed-class item, which cannot be switched. Doron (1983) has expanded his model, arguing on the basis of considerations involving left-to-right parsing that the first word of a sentence or a constituent determines the host or base language. Properties of the host language determine, in Joshi's perspective, whether mixing is possible or not, including the selection of closed class items or function words.

Another model closely related to the Matrix Language Frame model is presented in Azuma's work (1993). Departing from Garrett's (1982) speech production model, Azuma formulates the Frame-Content Hypothesis, in which the frame-building stage, 'where closed-class items are accessed and retrieved' (1993: 1072) precedes a content-word insertion stage. Though much less elaborate than Myers-Scotton's work, Azuma's model seems to be making roughly the same predictions.

Myers-Scotton's original model has been criticized on a number of grounds: the definition of matrix language, the distinction between system and content morphemes, and the relation between code-mixing and language processing. I will address these criticisms in more detail in chapters 3, 6, and 9, respectively.

Dependency, coherence, and sentence organization

I should perhaps make clear how my own research in the area of language contact started. In 1977 I had already been doing eight months of fieldwork on the Andean Amerindian language of Quechua in a community in central Ecuador, where both Quechua and Spanish were spoken. In the middle of the night I heard my hosts at the time speak yet a third language among themselves. Upon enquiry the next morning I found out that this language, which had sounded entirely strange to me, was really a highly innovative mixture of Quechua and Spanish. It was often referred to as Media Lengua 'half(way) language', or Utilla Ingiru 'little Inca-ese (Quechua)' (Muysken 1981a, 1996). In the following example the Media Lengua (MeL) original is given along with both its Quechua (Qe) and Spanish (Sp) equivalents.

(28) MeL   *Chicha*-da-ga *xora*-mi *irbi*-chi-*ndu*, *ahi*-munda-mi chicha-AC-TO
            corn-AF boil-CAU-SUB there-ABL-AF
      Qe   Aswa-da-ga sara-mi yanu-sha, chay-munda-mi
      Sp   Chicha, haciendo hervir jora, después

      MeL   *sirni*-nchi, *ahi*-munda-ga *dulsi*-da *poni*-nchi.
            strain-1pl there-ABL-TO sweet-AC put-1pl
      Qe   shushu-nchi chay-munda-ga mishki-da chura-nchi.
      Sp   la cernimos, y después la ponemos dulce.
      'As to chicha, having boiled corn first we strain it and then we put in
      sugar.'   (Media Lengua; Muysken, fieldwork data)

An inspection of this recorded sentence and its equivalents will reveal that all lexical bases in Media Lengua are Spanish, the affixes all Quechua (with the exception of the gerundive marker -*ndu*, <Sp -*ndo*), and the general word order and syntax Quechua.

A number of the questions raised by Media Lengua turn out to be the same as the questions that started to intrigue me about code-mixing in subsequent years. These include the role of morphology in language mixing; the importance of syntagmatic and paradigmatic coherence; the interaction of the lexicon and the morpho-syntax; the role of typological differences between the languages involved; and finally, simultaneous rather than sequential operation of properties of the languages involved in the mix.

The work led to a third type of approach that stresses **dependency** rather than equivalence, assuming that code-mixing obeys a general constraint of lexical dependency. The basic idea was that there cannot be a mix between two elements if they are lexically dependent on each other. A first implicit statement of this restriction is given in Shaffer (1978), but a more explicit formulation appeared in DiSciullo, Muysken, and Singh (1986), in terms of the **government** model. In this model, the relation between a head and its syntactic environment, as circumscribed by government, was assumed to constrain possible code-mixes.

Proposals similar to the one by DiSciullo, Muysken, and Singh (1986) have been put forward by Bentahila and Davies (1983) and by Klavans (1985). Klavans argues that it is the language of the inflected main verb or the auxiliary of a clause that determines the restrictions on code-mixing in that particular clause, since those elements in some sense constitute the syntactic head of the clause and govern the rest.

Bentahila and Davies (1983) propose that the **subcategorization** properties of a word determine what elements, including elements of another language, may appear within the phrase syntactically headed by that word. The following contrasts illustrate their approach.

(29) a. * *cette* l xubza   'this the loaf'
          * *un* l fqi   'one the teacher'
      b. *cette* xubza   'this loaf'
          un fqi   'one teacher'

(30) a. * had *pain*   'this loaf'
          * wahed *professeur*   'a teacher'
      b. had *le pain*   'this loaf'
          wahed *le professeur*   'a teacher'

(Moroccan Arabic/French; Bentahila and Davies 1983: 109)

The mixes in (29a) and (30a) are ungrammatical, in their view, because the French determiners in (29) subcategorize for a simple noun without the article *l* (as shown in (29b)), and the Arabic determiners in (30) subcategorize for a noun with an article (as shown in (30b)). In neither case is there a violation of the word order of either language. Something like the notion of government is at play: for Bentahila and Davies' proposal to work, they have to assume that the determiner and the rest of the noun phrase are in the government relation of selection.

Government is a traditional grammatical notion which has received several formulations within the theory of Government and Binding, e.g. as in Chomsky (1981: 164):

(31) α governs γ in $[_\beta \ldots \gamma \ldots \alpha \ldots \gamma \ldots]$, where:
      (i) $\alpha = X^0$
      (ii) α and γ are part of the same maximal projection.

Typical cases of government would be case assignment, as in the Latin example (32a), or subcategorization, as in (32b). The maximal projection of *ad*, the prepositional phrase, contains *urbem*:

(32)   a. ad urbe*m*
           'to the city'
       b. to wait *for* somebody

The Latin preposition *ad* takes an accusative complement (*-m*), and the verb *wait* subcategorizes for the preposition *for*.

In the government perspective on code-mixing the relation between a lexical element and its syntactic environment thus plays an important role. A lexical item will often require specific other types of elements in its environment, and this requirement may be language-specific. These requirements can be formulated in terms of the head–complement relations of X-bar theory.

The traditional assumption behind **X-bar theory** is that syntactic constituents are endocentric, i.e. that their properties derive from those of their head. Thus a noun phrase is characterized by many of the same features as the head noun; the internal constituency of a verb phrase in terms of number of objects derives from the properties of the verb. Another way of saying this is that the head noun or head verb project their features within the phrase, but not beyond it. The central notions involved here are exploited in the code-mixing literature under the government constraint: not only the categorial and semantic features of a lexical head are projected in the constituent, but also its language index. The language index was assumed to be something specified in the lexicon, since a lexicon is a language-specific collection of elements.

For code-mixing the government constraint was formalized in DiSciullo, Muysken, and Singh (1986) as follows:

(33)   *$[\, X_p \quad Y_q\,]$, where X governs Y, and p and q are language indices

The nodes in a tree must dominate elements drawn from the same language when there is a government or selection relation holding between them.

The government restriction on code-mixing predicts that ungoverned elements, such as tags, exclamations, interjections, and most adverbs can easily be switched. This prediction is supported by the available evidence. It also predicts that mixes of the following type are ungrammatical:

(34)   a. verb/object
       b. preposition/NP-complement
       c. verb/clausal complement

Indeed we find many mixes which do not involve these configurations. However, the government constraint fails badly for a large number of cases such as:

(35) a. sempre vicino a quella *machine*
          'always near to that machine'
      b. ha ricevuto il *diplôme*
          'has received the diploma'
          (Italian/French; DiSciullo, Muysken, and Singh 1986: 13–14)

unless we take the noun phrases *quella machine* and *il diplôme* to be Italian (even though *machine* and *diplôme* are French), on the basis of the Italian demonstrative *quella* and article *il*. DiSciullo, Muysken, and Singh (1986) claim that there can be a neutralizing element, such as a determiner, intervening between the governor (e.g. *ricevuto* 'received') and governed element (e.g. *diplôme*). Thus they introduce the notion of **language index carrier**. Adding this to the analysis predicts the following contrast in acceptability for Spanish/English:

(36) a. Veo las *houses*.
      b. * Veo *the houses*.
          'I see the houses.'

The mix in (36a) would be acceptable, since the Spanish determiner *las* would make the whole noun phrase Spanish, as far as the government restriction is concerned, and (36b) would be an impossible mix because the whole noun phrase, even though governed by a Spanish verb, would be English. The large number of mixes between the determiner and the noun found, among others, by Pfaff (1979) were interpreted in DiSciullo, Muysken, and Singh (1986) as suggesting that something like the contrast between (36a) and (36b) may be relevant. An alternative explanation for Pfaff's findings of course is at least equally plausible: the large number of single alien nouns could as well be borrowings, as in Poplack's work.

The language index carrier was defined as in (37):

(37) The highest (non-lexical) node in a tree determines its language index
          (DiSciullo, Muysken, and Singh 1986: 4)

On the basis of this notion, the first element in the constituents in (38) determines the language index of the whole constituent:

(38) a. [determiner – noun]
      b. [quantifier – noun]
      c. [subordinator – clause]

It turns out, however, that the definition of government in (33) still has a number of undesirable consequences, even for the original data considered by DiSciullo, Muysken, and Singh (1986), and even adopting a notion like language index carrier. First, a definition of government in which the noun governs the whole noun phrase, its maximal projection (Aoun and Sportiche

1983), would rule out cases like (39), which are extremely common, of course, and would be incompatible with the notion of language index carrier just defined. In (39a) French *cheques* would govern the Italian plural article *i*. The same holds for the relation between *maquillage* and *tanto* in (40b).

(39) a. Io posso fare [i *cheques*].
          'I can make the cheques.'
      b. Mettava [tanto *maquillage*] sulla faccia.
          'She put so much make up on her face.'

(Italian/French; DiSciullo, Muysken, and Singh 1986: 13–4)

Similarly with adverbs, which often are within the verb phrase, albeit not direct complements of the verb. At the same time, switched adverbs are extremely frequent:

(40) La [$_{VP}$ lascia *toujours* sulla tavola].
      'She leaves it always on the table.'

(Italian/French; DiSciullo, Muysken, and Singh 1986: 15)

Therefore a limited definition of government, involving only the immediate domain of the lexical head, including its complements but not its modifiers, was needed.

Second, in the configurations in (39) one might want to say that the determiner governs the noun, etc., particularly in the view that became popular in the mid-1980s holding that determiners, quantifiers, and subordinating complementizers are (functional) heads themselves. Similarly, the auxiliary or the finite tense marking on the main verb is often assumed to govern the subject, assigning nominative case to it. Finally, an auxiliary selects a participle or complement verb. Still, there are subject/verb phrase (41a) or auxiliary/participle (41b) mixes:

(41) a. La plupart des canadiens *scrivono* 'c'.
          'The majority of Canadians write 'c'.'
      b. *No*, parce que *hanno* donné des cours.
          'No, because they have taught courses.'

(Italian/French; DiSciullo, Muysken, and Singh 1986: 15)

Taking all these cases into account, a more limited definition of government, restricting it to the relation between a lexical head (i.e. N, V, A, P, and excluding functional heads such as determiners and auxiliaries) and its immediate complements, was adopted for code-mixing in Muysken (1986b). A convenient term for this relation is given in Chomsky (1986a), **L-marking**. Thus the constraint could be reformulated as in:

(42) * [X_p Y_q], where X L-marks Y, and p and q are language indices

L-marking is a more restricted notion of lexical government by a non-function word of its complements. The domain of lexical dependency is a proper subdomain of the domain of structural dependency: government, in exactly the way required. The notion of L-marking has the theoretical attraction that the language indices are induced from the lexicon. In this revised view code-mixing is possible where the chain of local dependencies resulting from L-marking is broken. If we assume that inflection (INFL) does not L-mark, that determiners (Det) and quantifiers (Q) are heads (hence DetP and QP) but not L-markers, and that V does not L-mark time adverbs, then it accounts for the cases listed.

As it turns out, however, even this restricted version runs into grave difficulties, due to abundant more recent **counter-evidence**. Particularly damaging for the government constraint are the data presented by Nortier (1990), who studied Dutch–Moroccan Arabic code-mixing in detail. Her findings are completely in contradiction to the government constraint. First of all, we get a large number of cases of mixing internal to the verb phrase (the number of cases is given in parentheses):

(43) a. Žib li-ya *een glas water of zo.*   V IO/DO (7)
        'Get for-me a glass of water or so.'

      b. Anaka-ndir *intercultureel werk.*   V/DO (14)
        'I I-am-doing intercultural work.'

      c. Wellit *huisman.*   COP/PRD (10)
        'I-became houseman.'   (Moroccan Arabic/Dutch; Nortier 1990: 131)

We get 7 cases of mixing between indirect and direct object (43a), no less than 14 cases of mixing between verb and direct object (43b), and 10 cases involving a predicate after a copula-type verb, (43c). I should also mention the occurrence of 97 mixes of object noun phrases involving a single noun.

The data in (44) are particularly damaging since mixing between subject and verb is, if anything, less frequent in Nortier's corpus than mixing between object and verb. Compare the following cases:

(44) a. Humaya *vergelijken de mentaliteit met de Islam.*   (3)
        'They compare the mentality with the Islam.'

      b. L-'islam kŭll-u *is echt liefde.*   (3)
        'The-islam all-of-it is truly love.'

      c. Le-mġarba *strak hè, stroef.*   (17)
        'The-Moroccans tight, huh, rough.'
        (Moroccan Arabic/Dutch; Nortier 1990: 135–6)

In (44a) a Moroccan Arabic subject is combined with a Dutch verb phrase (three cases), and in (44b) with a Dutch copular predicate (three cases). Quite frequent are examples where a Moroccan Arabic subject appears with a Dutch non-verbal predicate without a copula, as in (44c) (17 cases).

24

We also find 15 cases where a Dutch full noun phrase is the complement of a Moroccan Arabic preposition:

(45) a. u dewwezna [PP f-*zelfde tijd*]
   'and we-spent in same time'
  b. muwaḍḍafa [PP kama *maatschappelijk werkster*]
   'appointed as social workers' (Moroccan Arabic/Dutch; Nortier 1990: 139)

In addition, there are 101 cases of a mix between a preposition and a single noun. These data clearly show that the government constraint, even in the revised form of Muysken (1989b), cannot be maintained for this language pair. The distribution of noun phrases is much wider than predicted.

Given all these counter-examples, the government constraint as formulated is clearly inadequate. The main reason is that categorial equivalence undoes the effect of the government restriction. In Moroccan Arabic/Dutch code-mixing situations, apparently, a Dutch nominal complex counts as equivalent to a Moroccan Arabic one, with respect to an external governor. Thus we need to incorporate a notion of categorial equivalence or congruence, along the lines of Sebba (1998).

A second reason is that the focus of the government constraint on content words ignored the crucial role of functional categories, in contrast with e.g. Bentahila and Davies (1983), Joshi (1985), and Myers-Scotton (1993b). Functional categories impose quite specific restrictions on their structural environment and are thus responsible for most specific properties of individual languages, as I will argue in the next chapter.

On the basis of these considerations, the government constraint would need to be reformulated as:

(46) * [X_p Y_q] , where X governs Y, p and q are language indices, and where there is no equivalence between the categories Y in the languages p and q involved.

If we adopt (46) and incorporate functional elements as governors, then many of the empirical problems with the government constraint as originally formulated disappear. This is also argued by Halmari (1993, 1997) in her analysis of Finnish/English code-mixing. Functional elements appear also in Belazi, Rubin, and Toribio (1994), one of the last of the 'single model' proposals.

The latter model constitutes a further elaboration of the government model. Its principal component is the idea that functional heads determine the overall structure, and that switching is not possible for elements governed by functional heads (the **Functional Head Constraint**):

The language feature of the complement f-selected by a functional head,

> like all other relevant features, must match the corresponding feature of
> that functional head. (Belazi, Rubin, and Toribio 1994: 228)

Supplementing the Functional Head Constraint, Belazi, Rubin, and Toribio (1994: 232) propose the **Word Grammar Integrity Corollary**, stating that:

> A word of language X, with grammar G_x, must obey grammar G_x.

As shown by Mahootian and Santorini (1996), the predictions made by the Belazi, Rubin, and Toribio (1994) proposal can easily be shown to be incorrect on the basis of published data from the code-switching literature. The main reason is again that categorial equivalence undoes the effect of the government (here f-selection, selection by functional categories) restrictions.

The 'Null Hypothesis' by Mahootian and Santorini (1996) and the model of Pandit (1990) can be placed in the same tradition, but these models implicitly adopt the notion of categorial equivalence. Pandit (1990: 43) formulates the following constraint:

> Code-switching must not violate the grammar of the head of the
> maximal projection within which it takes place.

This constraint, of course, also has the property of being a natural consequence of general well-formedness principles. It is comparable to Mahootian's (1993) Null-hypothesis, which states that:

> The language of a head determines the phrase structure position of its
> complements in codeswitching just as in monolingual contexts
> (Mahootian and Santorini 1996: 466).

Recently, Boumans (1998: 89) has proposed the Monolingual Structure Approach, which assumes that 'each matrix structure originates in the grammar of only one language'.

The difference between Pandit's and Boumans', on the one hand, and Santorini and Mahootian's approach, on the other, lies in the restriction to complements (excluding adjuncts) in Mahootian's approach. My own work is closer to Mahootian's position, since the notion of alternational code-mixing also assigns a special status to adjuncts (alternational) as opposed to complements (insertional). Notice finally that Pandit's and Mahootian's approaches are closer to Myers-Scotton's System Morpheme Principle and Morpheme Order Principle than might appear at first sight.

Working within the general framework of government or dependency models, Treffers-Daller (1994) stresses the importance of peripherality in the clause as a factor favouring code-mixing, and she provides statistical evidence from Brussels Dutch/French code-mixing for this position. In chapter 4, I will take up this line, which concords with the distinction made by Mahootian and Santorini (1996) between adjunction and complementation or insertion.

Recently, Boeschoten and Huybregts (1997) and MacSwan (1997) have discussed code-mixing in the minimalist framework (Chomsky 1995). In this perspective, 'mechanisms for monolingual grammar (UG-Principles and Parameters) are necessary and sufficient for bilingual grammar (including Code switching)' (Boeschoten and Huybregts 1997: 1). In other words, 'nothing constrains code switching apart from the requirements of the mixed grammars' (MacSwan 1997: 162). The way this is achieved follows the tradition in much of the work just cited, relying heavily on the requirements that lexical items put on their environment.

Summary

All appearances to the contrary, there is much agreement within the code-mixing research community, not so much by all researchers on all issues, as by different subgroups on different issues. It turns out that the many constraints in the literature, often proposed as unique, fall into only a few categories, definable in terms of four primitives. These are:

- the potential role of word order equivalence
- the potential role of categorial equivalence
- peripherality in the clause: is code-mixing favoured in adjoined or peripheral positions?
- restrictions on function words, both as selected and as selective elements

Cross-cutting these four primitives is the distinction proposed here between insertion, alternation, and congruent lexicalization. There are asymmetrical (matrix-based) insertion, symmetrical alternation, and congruent lexicalization models. There can be unidirectional compatibility checking (Bentahila and Davies; Joshi; DiSciullo, Muysken, and Singh; Myers-Scotton) in terms of categorial equivalence or bidirectional compatibility checking (Poplack; Woolford) in terms of linear equivalence.

These themes are schematically represented in terms of some of the major researchers in the field in table 1.1.

Constraints: absolute, probabilistic, tendential

Many models propose principles or constraints ruling out a certain type of mixing. What is the nature of the constraints proposed, the predictions made? Poplack (1980), working in the variationist framework, proposes general constraints which are supposed to hold for the majority of cases.

Table 1.1. *Classification of code-mixing theories in terms of the notions of asymmetry, word order, categorical equivalence, peripherality, and functional elements*

	type	word order equivalence	categorical equivalence	peripherality	function word
Lehtinen	(ins)	+	+		+
Lipski		+			
Clyne	cl				
Poplack cs	alt/cl	+	±		
Poplack fl	alt			+	
Poplack bo	ins	−	±		
Poplack ci	ins		±		
Bentahila	ins		+		+
Woolford	alt	+			
Joshi	ins				+
DiSciullo, Muysken, and Singh	ins		−	±	
Myers-Scotton	ins	−	+	−	+
Pandit	ins		+		
Treffers-Daller	ins/alt			+	
Mahootian	ins/alt		+	+	
Sebba	ins		+		
Belazi et al.	ins		−	+	

Note: cs = switching under equivalence, bo = (nonce) borrowing, fl = flagged switching; ci = constituent insertion, ins = insertion, alt = alternation, cl = congruent lexicalization.

DiSciullo, Muysken, and Singh (1986) make absolute, all or nothing, claims, as do other researchers working in the generative tradition. In more recent work exploring the implications of the theory of government for code-mixing, however, by Treffers-Daller (1994), a probabilistic perspective is taken. Rather than just trying to predict which mixes are disallowed, an attempt is made to establish which kinds of mixes are the more frequent ones. Sankoff and Poplack (1981) explored this direction as well, but interpreted the results as showing that there were no fundamental differences in probability for any mixing site, and did not return to it in later work. Myers-Scotton (forthcoming) proposes to account for the unmarked cases of code-mixing, allowing the socially marked cases to fail the predictions made.

In my view, the evidence seems to point towards probabilistic statements, linked to different language pairs and contact settings. Absolute constraints, that could be invalidated by a single or a few counter-examples, are less appropriate for bilingual speech production data, in my opinion. Consider a case such as:

(47)   Damals haben die [mir [*biraz* Kartoffel(n)] [geben *yaptılar*]].
       at that time have those me a few potatoes give do-PRET-pl
       'At that time they have given me some potatoes.'

(Turkish/German; Treffers-Daller and Yalçin 1995: 16)

Here the sentence starts with one structure, and ends up in a different language with another one.

Statements in terms of markedness as a yes/no factor, as in the work of Myers-Scotton (1993a, b) also seem somewhat unsatisfactory to me, for three reasons: (a) it is hard to argue for the (un)markedness of any single instance of mixing; (b) so far there is little indication that the patterns of code-mixing in communities where code-mixing is not an unmarked choice are highly unusual, as we would expect if social markedness were a factor influencing the structural properties of mixing; (c) suppose the restrictions on code-mixing are in part due to factors determined by our grammatical competence. Then we should look to what extent rules of our grammar are violated in stylistically marked registers of the monolingual speech mode. The answer is: not a great deal. There are specific stylistically marked syntactic patterns, but they do not depart from our grammar as a whole in significant ways. Hence there is no immediate reason to expect this to be the case for code-mixing. It should be stressed that unusual types of code-mixing may be pragmatically marked, as they are unexpected.

The relation between qualitative structural and quantitative distributional analysis is very complicated. Intuitions about code-mixing are not always reliable and we do not know when they are and when they are not. The role of conventionalization of mixing has not been studied yet. Finally, psycholinguistic experimental techniques to study grammatical factors in code-mixing are not yet well developed, and we have to work with natural speech data. Since we do not know how the grammar and the lexicon interact with other psychological faculties to produce actual speech, we clearly cannot ignore phenomena such as frequency of occurrence and regularity. This would lead us to take the frequent types of mixes as the main body of evidence, and to consider the infrequent ones as possibly fluke phenomena, performance errors, and the like. Two (possibly related) complications arise, however. First, frequency may result from the conventionalization of a certain type of mixing pattern, rather than from a crucial grammatical factor. Second, we do not yet know enough about the relation between frequency distributions of specific grammatical patterns in monolingual speech data and properties of the grammar to handle frequency in bilingual data with any assurance.

Unification and the escape hatch model

Now that I have surveyed the grammatical properties of the different kinds of constraints it is fair to ask to what extent they can be unified. The field has become so confusing because everyone proposing constraints is right as well as wrong. The reason that this odd situation occurs is, in my view, that code-mixing is impossible in principle, but that there are numerous ways that this fundamental impossibility can be circumvented.

Hence, in different contact situations different mixing patterns are found. The differences are related, at least in part, to typological characteristics of the languages involved. At the same time, sociolinguistic and psycholinguistic factors play an important role. Different reactions are possible to this state of affairs. At the two extremes, there are quite different approaches to dealing with these observations:

(A) Some kind of global theory makes a more limited set of mixing sites available in specific instances than would be desirable (for whatever reasons that induce speakers to code-mix in the first place). In those cases, escape hatches are available, making additional mixing sites possible.

(B) Different mixing strategies are identified: flagging, constituent insertion, etc. governed by constraints specific to those strategies. There is no specific relation between linguistic properties of the languages involved and the choice of the strategy.

What unifies the two approaches is that both end up with a series of different language mixing patterns or strategies. However, model A is possibly explanatory, model B is primarily descriptive. At the same time, model A may be wrong in its empirical predictions, in not allowing for variation within the code-mixing patterns that hold for a given language pair and speech community. Model B may be correct, but not very interesting theoretically in itself.

A general way of approaching constraints in code-mixing research following model A is through the notion of **neutrality** (Muysken 1987). If we take a strong system-oriented view and conceive of the juxtaposition of material from different languages in one domain, e.g. the clause, as excluded in principle, then we can imagine there to be various strategies to neutralize mixing and make it less offensive. Something that should be ruled out by the very coherence imposed by the requirements of a lexical item within its syntagmatic unit is made possible in different ways, thus neutralizing the system conflict. Suppose we define the basic impossibility as:

(48)   *   A   B

One escape hatch from this is **categorial equivalence** in insertional mixing,

30

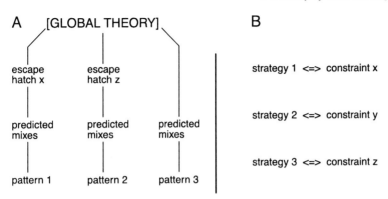

Figure 1.2 Schematic representation of two ways of conceptualizing the relation between various mixing patterns

studied in chapter 3. Mixing is then assumed to be possible under categorial equivalence, i.e. when the switched element has the same status in the two languages, is morphologically encapsulated, shielded off by a functional element from the matrix language, or could belong to either language.

(49)   A   [$_A$ B]

In the case of (49) the element in code B behaves externally as if it were in code A. Categorial equivalence may develop over time.

In chapter 4 a second escape hatch will be analysed: **alternation, adjunction, or juxtaposition**. Mixing is possible when there is no tight relation (e.g. of government) holding between two elements, so-called paratactic mixing or alternation:

(50)   A . . . B

Alternation strategies include extraposition, the suspension of syntax, fronting, adverbial constructions, pauses, flagging, fillers, and, morphologically, agglutination. In the case of (50), there is no direct link between A and B.

The third escape hatch involves direct grammatical mapping of the two languages involved; they are basically treated as the same language:

(51) $A_1 . . . A_n \sim B_1 . . . B_n$

For **congruent lexicalization**, treated in chapter 5, it is quite possible that there are no structural constraints, since all that is involved is insertion of words into one single syntactic structure (Clyne 1987; Giesbers 1989).

Viewed in this way, the complex issue of constraints on code-mixing reduces to the study of (49)–(51). Neutrality, then, may be achieved in

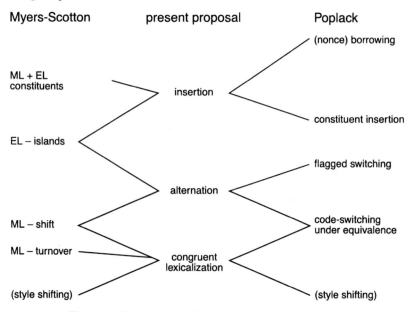

Figure 1.3 The present classification of language interaction phenomena as compared with that of Myers-Scotton and Poplack.

different ways, depending on the structures of the languages involved and on sociolinguistically motivated choices within bilingual communities. Equivalence is one form of neutrality. If you cannot have equivalence, adopt another form, by bending the rules of the systems a bit.

Roughly, the proposal in this book can be compared to some of the major current models, those of Poplack and Myers-Scotton, as follows, with style shifting added to make these models comparable to the one proposed in figure 1.3. We notice that roughly the same empirical ground is covered by these models, but that they emphasize different distinctions between specific phenomena.

Structure and scope of this book

This book has the following general structure, built up around the three approaches of alternation, insertion, and congruent lexicalization. Chapter 1 presents my main contribution, that the process of code-mixing is not unitary, but consists of three main mixing strategies: insertion, alternation, and congruent lexicalization. A systematic presentation is also given of the theoretical code-mixing literature, the grammatical constraints proposed, and how these constraints relate to the proposed three strategies.

In chapter 2 the theoretical background to the issue of language differences and similarities is discussed: typology, structural parameters, lexical differences, equivalence. In the interaction of competence and performance during bilingual speech production and perception, different modules (particularly the morpho-syntax and the content word lexicon) may be activated to a different degree.

Chapters 3, 4, and 5 present systematic presentations of the main code-mixing strategies distinguished: insertion, alternation, and congruent lexicalization. Each of these chapters illustrates the diagnostic characteristics of these three mixing patterns on the basis of a specific case, and tries to relate these characteristics to the properties of the process involved. Insertion can involve both single elements, and be akin to borrowing, and more complex constituents. I thus analyse borrowing as a special type of insertion.

Alternation resembles switching between clauses or utterances, and is related to the traditional notion of parataxis (adjunction in more recent frameworks), and insertion to syntaxis (selection in more recent frameworks). At this moment much more is known about the properties of selection than of adjunction. One theoretical issue raised by many of the cases of alternation therefore is the status of adjunction in sentences.

Congruent lexicalization resembles, in its extreme form, style shifting and intra-system variation. In the model developed by Lipski (1978) though most directly associated with Poplack (e.g. 1980), there is a bidirectional linear compatibility checking procedure in bilingual speech production, but explicitly within each language only the grammar of that language is operant.

In chapter 6 functional elements are focussed upon, since these play a role both in language typology and in language contact studies. I will argue that the restricted distribution of functional elements in mixed clauses is due to their non-equivalence across languages rather than to their special role in language production.

Chapter 7 deals with bilingual verbs, and argues that these can take several shapes, corresponding to three main strategies of insertion, alternation, and congruent lexicalization. The most important case analysed involves the foreign main verb + native helping verb construction, and I argue that here often an adjunction, i.e. an alternation, analysis is called for. Insertion is found with single verb stems, and congruent lexicalization with verb/particle combinations.

Chapter 8 relates the different mixing patterns to various sociolinguistic and psycholinguistic factors, and attempts to characterize different bilingual communities in terms of these patterns. Several factors are argued to play a role in the selection of a specific mixing strategy: structural resemblance of the languages, stage in the process of language shift, level of bilingual proficiency, attitude towards code-mixing, fixedness of language norms.

In chapter 9 the different processes of contact-induced language change are related to the mixing patterns: borrowing, shift, genesis of new languages, relexification, convergence through prolonged bilingual contact. Most recent models accounting for intra-sentential code-mixing are based on an on/off view of the languages participating in the mix: at any one point either one language is active or the other. If we conceive of the contrast between the three processes distinguished in this book in terms of the activation of either language in bilingual speech processing a rather different picture emerges. The dual structure is then seen as relative: to what extent are both languages active? Alternation presumably resembles monolingual discourse in the one languages and is assumed to be active to the exclusion of the other one, but even here at least at the point of the mix the other language must be active as well. As to insertion, here the matrix language must be assumed to remain active at the point of utterance of the inserted material, since it provides the frame for interpretation of this material. Similarly, the inserted language must be active in order to account for the amount of structure inserted. In congruent lexicalization, the two languages are seen as partly non-distinct: large components are shared. In some cases of code-mixing, components of both languages are not active in sequence, but simultaneously. Part of chapter 9 consists of evidence for simultaneous representations, from mixed verbal complexes, from the phenomenon of delayed lexicalization, from the non-linear interaction of the two grammars, and from cases of interference. The implications of the findings of this book for bilingual production and perception research are discussed, and the merits and limitations of the code-mixing research paradigm. It is tentatively suggested that the taxonomic stage of the gathering of large bilingual corpora has reached the limits of its usefulness, and that new, both historical and experimental techniques are needed in subsequent code-mixing research.

2
Differences and similarities between languages

What can the study of code-mixing contribute to grammatical theory? What makes code-mixing so special that it warrants relatively complex and time-consuming, and hence costly, research? Perhaps the most important contribution of the study of code-mixing to linguistic theory concerns the division of labour between the lexicon and the grammar of a language in defining it as a unique system. Bilinguals reach across into the other language to find something equivalent, and establish the newly found item as neutral with respect to the first language. When sentences are built up with items drawn from two lexicons, we can see to what extent the sentence patterns derive from the interaction between these two lexicons. Do speakers rely on properties of individual words when producing and comprehending sentences, or on general rules of the language they speak, triggered by more abstract categories? How are these categories determined and lexically instantiated?

Related to this question – and for many researchers the same question really – is: can we reduce the differences between languages to lexical differences? If so, all that is specific about a language is its lexicon, and the lexicon plays a very major role in sentence production and comprehension. In the latter case, there *are* no rules specific to a language independent of lexical items and the morpho-syntactic features that characterize them.

This can best be illustrated first with a phonological example. Languages differ in their vowel inventories. Thus we say that Quechua has three vowels (/i/, /u/, /a/), Spanish five (/i/, /e/, /u/, /o/, /a/), and Dutch nineteen. The Dutch vowels can be divided into:

(1)   tense vowels (long)
      lax vowels (short)
      diphthongs
      schwa
      long lax vowels

All sets, except the schwa, can be divided into front unrounded, front rounded, and back rounded vowels. The last set, long lax vowels, only occurs in a handful of loans from French:

(2) œ: oeuvre, freule 'unmarried noblewoman'
ɛ: serre 'glazed verandah', frêle 'fragile', beige
ɔ: roze 'rose (colour)', zone, colonne 'column', compôte

The set of long lax vowels poses a dilemma: do we say that the Dutch lexicon contains a few (loan)words, in turn containing these sounds, or that the Dutch phonological system contains a set of (loan)phonemes, that happen to occur only in a few words? Shifting the burden to the phonological system we lose sight of the fact that the sounds would not be there if these words were to disappear or if they had never been borrowed. Shifting the burden to the lexicon we lose sight of the fact that these three vowels constitute a semi-regular subsystem (including the distinction between front unrounded, front rounded, and back rounded vowels), and that non-Dutch sounds in other loanwords invariably get adapted to Dutch, e.g. the first [g] in *garage* becomes a /x/.

These loans constitute a dramatic example, which could be treated in a special 'loan phonology', but the same holds really for other vowels as well, such as the Dutch high front rounded vowel /ü/, as in *vuur* 'fire'. You could imagine a version of Dutch where all the words with that vowel either have disappeared from the language or undergone a phonological change. We do not speak of vowel systems, generally, where a specific vowel is in the system, but not attested in the lexicon. So the question remains: does e.g. Spanish have a five-vowel system because in all Spanish words just five vowels occur, or are Spanish words licensed by a five-vowel system of the language, somehow mentally represented independently of the lexicon?

Similar questions can be asked in syntax. Is English an SVO language because all verbs govern rightward, or is rightward government defined independently of the lexicon and imposed on all verbs in the language? The abandonment of explicit phrase structure rules, Stowell's research program (1981), then taken up in Minimalism (Chomsky 1995), forces us to reconsider the way projections in natural languages are constituted. Stowell has proposed to derive all properties of phrase structure of individual languages through the interaction of principles of X-bar structure with features of lexical items.

Schematically and with enormous oversimplification, the modularization alluded to has yielded the following picture:

(3)

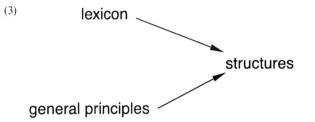

lexicon

structures

general principles

What has disappeared is the reference to language-specific grammars. A stretch of French discourse is characterized by the insertion of French lexical items, not by any rules specific to French grammar. The fact that texts often consist of lexical items from one single language is both a result of conventions of language use and of potential cooccurrence restrictions of items in specific local contexts. We may have recourse to the notion of lexical redundancy rule to account for the regularities involved. Surely it is no accident that each individual verb in English governs rightward.

In the study of the lexicon we see a curious paradox: the lexicon gives a language its shape, and at the same time words fit into a specific mould to be part of a lexicon. Thus there is a symbiotic relationship between the lexicon and the syntax and phonology. Some syntactic differences are triggered by lexical differences, while properties of lexical items conform to the syntactic possibilities of the language involved. Similarly, phonological inventories and phonotactic patterns are instantiated by the lexical items of the language, while the shape of these items is circumscribed by the phonological possibilities of the language involved.

This complicated cluster of questions has produced much research and an inconclusive debate in the linguistic literature. I think the study of code-mixing and language contact can uniquely contribute to elucidating and perhaps ultimately resolving these issues. I therefore want to explore the implications of the study of code-mixing for a central hypothesis:

> All differences between languages are ultimately lexical in nature. A particular language results from the interaction between the specific properties of a particular lexicon and a set of universal linguistic principles. All parameters can be derived from lexical properties, and in many cases these are properties of functional categories.

This hypothesis, derived from linguistic theory, is congruent with results from the study of the neurolinguistic embedding of bilingual systems (e.g. Paradis 1987). The tentative results from this latter research are that different languages are not stored in the brain entirely separately, but rather in part conjointly, in part separately. The part stored and accessed separately primarily involves the lexical items of the language. With respect to code-mixing, they point to a particular view of the constraints on the process: mixing is sensitive to the lexical restrictions imposed by either function words or content words. In addition, since in code-mixing modules from different languages are often simultaneously active, these modules must be able to operate separately.

In this chapter I will explore the theoretical background to the issues of language differentiation and the division of labour between the lexicon and the syntax. As a backdrop to the discussion, I begin with two concrete illustrative examples from Spanish/English code-mixing. They show how differences between categories of the two languages are related to functional categories.

Spanish/English code-mixing and the interaction of categorial equivalence with other factors

In the Spanish/English code-mixing literature, several interesting cases of possible non-equivalence come to the fore, relatable to morpho-syntactic elements or functional categories. One concerns definite human objects. In Spanish, the preposition or case marker *a* is obligatory with these:

(4) a. * Veo la mujer.
    b. Veo a la mujer.
       'I see the woman.'

In English no such stricture is present. Thus we may wonder what happens in code-mixing: is *a la mujer* viewed as equivalent with *the woman*? In principle, four patterns could be found, and in (5) I have indicated which ones occur in the published sources on Spanish/English code-mixing. The patterns (5a) and (5b) correspond to the cases where the language of the verb determines the pattern found. The starred patterns are unexpected from this perspective:

(5) a. V(Eng) NP(Sp)   2
    b. V(Sp) a NP(Eng)   1
    c. * V(Eng) a NP(Sp)   3
    d. * V(Sp) NP(Eng)

The predicted pattern *V(Eng) NP(Sp)* occurs twice:

(6) Any way, *yo creo que las personas* who support *todos estos grupos como los* Friends of the Earth *son personas que* are very close to nature.
    'Anyway, I believe that the people who support all these groups like the Friends of the Earth are people who are very close to nature.'
    (Gibraltar Spanish/English; Moyer 1992: 437)

(7) No creían en Jesús *and then he sent* este hombre, y
     '[They] did not believe in Jesus and then he sent this man, and'
(Spanish/English; Lance 1975: 151)

Only one example is mentioned in the published literature of (5b), *V(Sp) a NP(Eng)*:

(8) Por qué no llevas a *this lady* que cura eso?
     'Why don't you take this lady that cures this?'
(Spanish/English; Lance 1975: 144)

There are several cases of the – not predicted – pattern *V(Eng) a NP(Sp)*:

(9) He accused *a Mister Bigote de doble lenguaje.*
     'He accused Mister Bigote of double talk.'
(Gibraltar Spanish/English; Moyer 1992: 127)

(10) They invite *a El Boss* and then they don't keep their word.
      'They invite El Boss and then they don't keep their word.'
(Gibraltar Spanish/English; Moyer 1992: 208)

(11) Tú lo *underestimate* a Chito.
      'You underestimate Chito.'   (Spanish/English; Timm 1975: 478)

Notice that in this last case we also have the Spanish object clitic *lo*, which almost suggests that *underestimate* is treated like a Spanish verb (see below), while (5d) is not documented.

Given the paucity of published data, it is hard to draw any conclusions. If we were to take the absence of the (5d) pattern as significant, the conclusion would be that the *a* marker is disregarded, in terms of equivalence checking, when the verb is English, but not when the verb is Spanish. Moyer (1992) draws the conclusion from examples (9) and (10) that sometimes the lexically English verb behaves as if it were Spanish on the syntactic level. I will return to this possibility in chapter 9 as part of a discussion of mismatches between lexicon and syntax.

The example, already cited in chapter 1, of how to apply the word order equivalence constraint (Poplack 1980) also clearly illustrates the issue of the relation between linear and categorial equivalence, and the theoretical issues involved:

(12) I   told him   that   so that   he   would bring it   fast
      | X | | | X |
      (Yo)   le dije   eso   pa' que   (él)   la trajera   rápido

Notice that in this example the possible violations involve pronouns, and this is problematic. Spanish clitic pronouns are phonologically dependent, while English pronouns are not. Thus the clashes in (12) could be interpreted in terms of lack of categorial equivalence.

Consider the following monolingual examples:

(13)	Spanish	English
	a. Maria **lo** ve.	Mary sees **him**.
	b. Maria quiere ver**lo**.	Mary wants to see **him**.

In (13a) we have both a word order and a status conflict, but in (13b) only a status conflict. In mixed clauses, we have the following possibilities:

		linear	categorial
(14)	a. Maria **him** ve.	−	?
	b. Maria ve **(a) him**.	−	+
	c. Mary **lo** sees.	−	−
	d. Mary sees **lo**.	−	−
(15)	a. Maria quiere ver **(a) him**.	+	+
	b. Mary wants to see **lo**.	+	−

From the point of view of linear equivalence, all forms in (14) are blocked, while the categorial approach allows (14b), which would appear to be the correct option. The linear equivalence constraint allows both forms in (15), while categorial equivalence only allows (15a), again the correct option (Pfaff 1979: 303).

In this case categorial equivalence has the same effects as some version of the already mentioned Free Morpheme Constraint, which holds that:

(16) Codes may be switched after any constituent in discourse provided that constituent is not a bound morpheme   (Poplack 1980: 585–6)

If we reformulate this as 'code-mixing may involve any constituent', needed in any case to exclude disallowed examples such as *eat-iendo*, we can look at the effects of word order and bound/free status along the lines sketched. Where the Free Morpheme Constraint and a categorial equivalence constraint make different predictions is when two languages have (roughly) equivalent sets of bound morphemes, such as Portuguese and French. I will return to this in chapter 6.

Other reasons for pronouns being a problematic test case for linear equivalence are that they are functional elements, and may thus be restricted for independent reasons (Myers-Scotton 1993b). However, the relation between functional elements and categorial equivalence may be quite complex, as I will argue in chapter 6.

If Chomsky (1993) is correct that word order differences between languages result from differences in features of functional elements (which may be differently specified for 'strength' in different languages), then we predict that potential violations of the equivalence constraint will be related to the (in)compatibility of functional elements in different languages.

The language fortress: languages as entities

Many people, laymen and linguists alike, cherish the image of a language as a closely guarded separate unit, a fortress, with clearly defined boundaries. Languages may be fortresses in at least two senses:

Firstly, languages are perceived by their speakers as separate and expressive of a particular identity. For this reason many speech communities have developed mechanisms to maintain the boundaries between themselves and others. Speakers often keep different languages they know separate when speaking, correcting themselves when they accidentally mix, etc. The first way then in which a language is a fortress is as the bastion of a single identity.

Secondly, the set of cognitive modules which interact and interlock in highly complex and structured ways to produce and perceive sentences may be thought of as constituting a fortress. In the Chomskyan paradigm the language system is itself seen in this way: modules are tightly connected and the whole system is separate from various other cognitive systems or modules. Much of language is highly structured, and this very structure may be thought of as a cognitive bastion. While people can and do mix their languages, this may be a strain on language production and perception, in short on the processing system.

The question then is how code-mixing breaks into these fortresses (in a double sense), and how strong the fences are around a given language, both those deriving from language as an identity carrier and from it being embedded in a processing system. The latter question has aroused much debate, often phrased as: are the restrictions or constraints on mixing processes social or structural in nature?

There is one general, biologically given, language capacity, but many, perhaps 6,000, different languages in actual use. These should be thought of, in the biological perspective of generative linguistics, as rather trivial variations upon a single genetic theme. Nonetheless, they are perceived by speakers as quite separate languages. Seen against the perspective of the single biological language, the existence of separate languages is in itself rather surprising. However, what it is in the language system that allows for or indeed causes the existing typological differentiation is a vexed issue. If we think of languages as separate fortresses, the question is what keeps these fortresses intact.

The two factors conspiring in the building and keeping of fortresses may be conveniently tagged as I-language (internal) and E-language (external) phenomena (Chomsky 1986b). I will first discuss the distinction and then return to the question of the separateness of individual languages.

Chomsky (1986b: 19) defines E-language as the 'totality of utterances that can be made in a speech community,' and I-language as 'some element of the mind of the person who knows the language, acquired by the speaker, and used by the speaker-hearer' (Chomsky 1986b: 22).

I-language phenomena are thus determined by cognitive principles and parameter settings. However, the grammars associated with I-languages are defined strongly enough to constitute the basis for what speakers perceive as a separate language.

The following quote from Chomsky (1986b) contrasts code-mixing with the conception of I-language adopted by him:

> The language of the hypothesized speech community, apart from being uniform, is taken to be a 'pure' instance of UG [univeral grammar] in a sense that must be made precise, and to which we will return. We exclude, for example, a speech community of uniform speakers, each of whom speaks a mixture of Russian and French (say, an idealized version of the nineteenth century Russian aristocracy). The language of such a speech community would not be 'pure' in the relevant sense, because it would not represent a single set of choices among the options permitted by UG but rather would include 'contradictory' choices for certain of these options.
>
> (Chomsky 1986b: 17)

From the perspective taken here, there is no theoretical need to adopt an unmixed perspective on I-language, as Chomsky appears to do (perhaps unconsciously importing thinking in terms of E-language into the I-language domain). The options permitted by UG are tied to the use of specific sets of lexical items, and if bilinguals draw upon two sets, the resulting system will, to some extent, be characterized by different options from the set allowed by universal grammar. The question I address in this book is to what extent this is allowed.

E-language phenomena are social in nature, and involve norms and identity. They have been the concern of sociologists of language and socio-linguists, and a particularly coherent perspective on them is given in *Acts of Identity*, written by LePage and Tabouret-Keller (1986). In their study of the bilingual language use of different social groups in Belize they rely on concepts such as ethnicity and focussing – the concentration of a group of speakers around a single norm – to explain a complex linguistic mosaic of choices made among different languages and language varieties. In their perspective, the existence of languages perceived as being more or less homogeneous and stable is a historical accident. It is characteristic of nation-states which have a tradition of language standardization.

Thus from both perspectives, two extremes in current linguistics, languages are seen as fortresses: the E-language leads to separateness of outer form, to use Humboldt's term, and the I-language to a clearly distinct inner form. A strong fortress indeed that is buttressed from such opposite sides. A separate outer form is defined by vocabulary, pronunciation and morphology – the concerns of the self-appointed guardians of language; the separate inner form is manifest in the syntax and semantics – the concerns of formal linguists.

However, I would like to argue that the fortress may be built on quicksand, in that the two ways the fortress is constructed do not always correspond. In fact, there are many cases where the perfect matching between E- and I-language breaks down. The asymmetries involve a number of different types:

A Several E-languages correspond to a relatively coherent I-language

(17)
$$
\begin{array}{l}
\nearrow E_1 \quad \text{Hindi} \quad | \quad \text{Serbian} \quad | \quad \text{Quechua} \\
\text{I} \qquad\qquad\qquad\qquad \text{Bosnian} \\
\searrow E_2 \quad \text{Urdu} \quad | \quad \text{Croatian} \quad | \quad \text{Media Lengua}
\end{array}
$$

Here two languages share almost all of their grammar and much of their lexicon, but are perceived as separate languages by their speakers, and associated with different religions, nationalities, ethnic identities, etc. The separateness is sometimes underlined by separate writing systems, spelling conventions, etc. Classic examples of this are Hindi and Urdu, as well as Serbian, Bosnian, and Croatian.

A related set of cases involves languages which are identical in their grammar and morpho-syntax, but differ widely in their content vocabulary. One has emerged out of the other through relexification. An example is given from Media Lengua (Muysken 1981a):

(18) intonsi lindu radiyu-da trayi-shka. (MeL)
then nice radio-AC bring-SD
shina k'uilla radiyu-da apa-mu-shka. (Qe)
resultó que trajeron un radio lindo entonces. (Sp)
'Then it turned out they'd brought a nice radio.'

In these examples the Media Lengua (MeL) sentences and forms are closely modelled on the Quechua (Qe) forms, but with a different content word vocabulary. Two language varieties share their syntax but not their vocabulary. It is an extreme case of a more general situation in which several registers exist in a language with separate vocabularies.

Gumperz and Wilson (1971) describe a situation in northern India in which a number of languages coexist in a village and are perceived as distinct by the speakers, many of whom are multilingual, but which share their basic grammar.

B *Several I-languages correspond to something perceived as one E-language*

(19) I_1 ⟍
       ⟩ E   'patois', 'dialect', 'quechua'
   I_2 ⟋

This situation sometimes arises in cases where there is a dominant official language, and in addition there are other varieties, which are not publicly differentiated. Again, several subtypes may be distinguished.

First of all, there may be a continuum of varieties going from something close to the dominant language to language systems which have an entirely different structure. An example is a creole-speaking community like Jamaica, where the term 'patois' will cover for some speakers anything ranging from a variety close to the standard language to structurally quite different varieties associated with the 'deep' or 'basilectal' creole (Bailey 1966; DeCamp 1971; Akers 1981). The term 'patois' (the alternative to 'English') is a relative one. Creole continua have been studied particularly in the English-lexifier creoles; Bickerton (1975) and Rickford (1987) are both studies of the situation in Guyana.

Another subtype is represented by Sranan (the English lexifier creole of Surinam). The case of Sranan is interesting because the dominant language is Dutch here, and not English. The 'upper' varieties of Sranan resemble Dutch only in some subtle ways. An example is preposition stranding. The following expressions differ only in that (20) is a case of stranding (perhaps due to Dutch influence), and (21) is not, while (22) is a case of pied-piping:

(20) a man   [*di* mi go luku a kino *nanga*]
       the man [REL I go look the movies with]

(21) a man   [*di* mi go luku a kino *nanga en*]
       the man [REL I go look the movies with him]

(22) a man   [*nanga suma* mi go luku a kino]
       the man [with who I go look the movies]
       'The man I go to the movies with.'

(Sranan; Bruyn 1995 citing Lilian Adamson, p.c.)

For different groups of speakers, any of these three expressions is the preferred form. Contemporary Sranan contains a whole series of constructions which are quite variable between different speaker groups. Nonetheless, all varieties of the language are labelled and perceived as 'Sranan'.

A different set of cases where several I-languages correspond to one E-language involves a single dominant (often colonial or ex-colonial) language and an undifferentiated set of indigenous languages and language varieties which have a generic label such as 'patois' or 'dialect'. Sometimes the label is really one of the indigenous languages, such as 'quechua', often used for 'Indian language' in the Andes. To be fair, this second case is weakened by the fact that the subjugated speakers may have specific labels for their languages simply unknown to the colonizers. However, this is not necessarily the case.

C   *Dialect continua within a language family may be arbitrarily*
     carved up into E-languages, which do not directly correspond to I-
     language borders (if we can conceive of these):

(23)

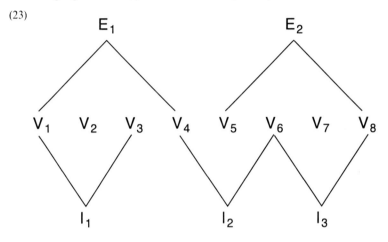

Thus we could imagine a situation where a large number of varieties in a dialect continuum (e.g. the West Germanic continuum) are divided up into two E-language varieties (e.g. Dutch and German), due to the historical accident of national borders, but correspond structurally to three I-languages. Presumably, an I-language is defined in terms of a specific combination of parameter settings.

D   *Bilingual language use involves the combination of modules from*
     different languages. Thus, if we take bilingual use as an E-
     language, it corresponds to components from various I-languages.
Bilingual language use will be the focus of this book. Chambers distinguishes the degree to which E-languages, in Chomsky's terms, are monolithic in terms of the mobility of the speakers involved (1995: 220): 'Human social groups range along a continuum between the polar extremities of global mobility and local insularity. Sociolinguistically, the effects of high mobility

include multilingualism, code-switching, diglossia, accommodation, style shifting.' Thus, bilingual language use affects our view of the language fortress as well.

Accounting for language differentiation

Long before Wilhelm von Humboldt wrote his *Über die Verschiedenheit des menschlichen Sprachbaues*, scholars had realized that languages differed considerably among each other, and language differences remain subject to debate. However, there is little agreement about the nature of the differences. A central issue is to what extent the categories in one language are equivalent to those in another. Categorial equivalence is problematic in linguistic theory. In the rationalist tradition typified by the Port Royal grammarians categories were generally assumed to be equivalent in different languages. This is also the position taken in much generative research. However, both the tradition initiated by Saussure, wherein languages are viewed as self-contained systems of oppositions, and the tradition associated with Boas of describing non-Indo-European languages strictly in their own terms, lead in the opposite direction: true equivalence is rarely found and perhaps even theoretically impossible. Present-day linguistics is torn between these two views.

Dimensions of typological differentiation

Typological research shares with language contact research the preoccupation with both similarities and differences between languages. Typology, now a fast-growing field, has focussed on a number of dimensions for interlinguistic variation. I will list some of these.

- **Word order** differences have received considerable attention, both in absolute terms (OV vs. VO, AN vs. NA) and in terms of the contrast between free word order and fixed word order languages.
- Connected but logically independent are issues of constituency and **configurationality**: to what extent is the constituent structure of a language free or rigidly defined?
- Again connected but to some extent separate are issues of **topicality** and **discourse configurationality**: to what extent are syntactic positions defined in terms of **topic** and **focus**?
- As mentioned above, there is discussion about the universality of **syntactic categories** and **word classes**.
- Related to this is considerable work on **semantic** and **morpho-**

syntactic distinctions (e.g. deixis, gender, animacy, case). In particular, evidentiality and tense/mood/aspect have been studied.

- There is a long tradition of work on **lexical** and **morphological typology**, involving notions such as 'analytic' and 'synthetic'.
- A syntactic reflex of this is the typological distinction between **head** and **dependent marking** languages. The 'head' here is the predicate, and the 'dependents' are the arguments.
- Languages differ considerably in the way in which **verbal morphology** marks **valency** on the predicate. Typological research in this area has been concerned with causatives, reflexives, benefactives, and applicatives.
- Some of this research has also been concerned with the more general subject of **grammatical relations**, a topic brought to the fore in Relational Grammar.
- In the area of **subordination** and **relativisation**, a large number of differences between languages have been documented and analysed. Topics studied include nominalization, serial verbs, and noun phrase accessibility in relativization.
- In phonology, a central concern has been **phoneme inventories**. It appears that there are clear hierarchies in the distribution of particular vowels and consonants across languages.
- A second area of study in phonological typology concerns **stress**, **tone**, and **syllabicity**.

I will try to argue that many of these differences can be viewed theoretically as categorial differences. Before that, however, I need to look at the generative perspective on interlinguistic differences.

A brief history of the generative approach to language differences

Let us consider the recent accounts of language differentiation in the generative paradigm more generally and trace their recent history. Such accounts should be able to provide answers to three questions:

(a) Why is there differentiation at all, given the supposed biological foundation for language?

(b) How are individual language systems acquired, given the tremendous potential differentiation in the input that the child is faced with, and its limited ('impoverished') character?

(c) What are the limits of linguistic differentiation? How different can languages be?

Models proposed to account for differentiation between languages, often no more than metaphors, have been developed in the generative tradition since the 1970s. Approaches from this period often included an invariant UG-core and a variant periphery. A good early example is the proposal by Emonds (1973) that grammars are invariant with respect to more **global**, large-scale phenomena such as long-distance question-word movement, and that differences between languages are **local** in nature, such as Romance clitic placement and verb/complement order. While this early proposal was limited in its scope (meant to deal mostly with English and French), later proposals took up the idea that local differences should provide a clue to linguistic differentiation for the child acquiring language.

In the early 1980s the **parameter** model was introduced (Chomsky 1981; Rizzi 1982). In this perspective universal grammar specifies a set of options, parameters, which the child acquiring a language should 'fix' or 'set', on the basis of fairly specific evidence, that can be gathered from simple sentences. A few simple examples: is it a adposition/complement (**pre**positional) or a complement/adposition (**post**positional) language? Is it a null-subject (**pro-drop**) language or not? It was assumed that there was not an unlimited number of parameters, but rather that one specific parameter setting would imply a number of more complex properties for a language, so that the many actual grammatical differences between languages are only the manifestations of a few parametrized options. Outside the invariant core and differentiation structured through parameters the space for unstructured differentiation is limited in these models.

There are several versions of parameter theory. In one version, the different options are in a subset/superset relation, so that one option is more specific than the other. Either multiple choice or binary choice models are considered, and finally parameter settings are sometimes viewed as having a marked or unmarked value.

The parameter model is quite attractive in that it both yields an answer to the acquisition problem and sets a principled limit on the differentiation allowed by universal grammar. It fares less well in explaining why there is differentiation at all. The principles and parameters model is conceptually rather unexpected under a reasonable interpretation of Chomskyan biological determinism (Baker 1995). In this sense, it is descriptive rather than explanatory, and does not answer the question why there is so much differentiation between languages.

Since the conceptual basis for it is rather weak, we must wonder how strong the empirical basis is. The empirical results from parameter theory so far have been the fracturing into 'partial typologies'. No clear cases of parameters accounting for a wide range of separate phenomena have survived scrutiny. To give but one example: the original pro-drop parameter proposed by Rizzi (1982) yielded some elegant predictions for a set of differences between Italian and English. No other group of languages turns out to pattern like either Italian or English, however. To my knowledge, there is no published and unchallenged example of a parameter which accounts for a cluster of differences between two languages or language groups. The acquisition results are at best weakly compatible with the parameter model, but do not strongly support it.

The reasons for this failure of parameter theory could be manifold: inadequate technology for storage and retrieval of typological data, absence of a clear notion of what a parameter is, and data analysis problems due to the rapid theoretical developments in the field.

A quite different approach to linguistic differentiation from the parameter perspective was taken in work initiated by Hale (1983), where it was suggested that it is the different patterns of **interaction** of the linguistic and non-linguistic **modules** in the cognitive system that yield linguistic differentiation. If we think of the human linguistic capacity as a highly modular system, we may expect the modules to interact in different ways. Thus, syntactic principles may be involved in word formation in one language, yielding highly complex agglutinative systems, but not in another one.

One virtue of viewing linguistic differentiation in terms of module interaction lies in the possibility of an answer to the question of why there is differentiation at all. It does not help much with the issue of acquisition, nor does it give an indication, at this stage, of the limits of differentiation between languages.

In the recent models for inter-linguistic differentiation that go under the name of **lexical learning** (Borer 1983; Borer and Wexler 1987) the claim is made that all differences between languages are ultimately lexical in nature. In Borer's model there is a large role for morphology. While there is considerable evidence for this view it still begs the question because it postulates a symbiotic relationship between lexicon and syntax/phonology. This type of approach may thus be useful for explaining acquisition facts, but not the causes and limits of differentiation.

Chomsky's (1993) **minimalist program** is rather vague about differentiation, but follows the lexical learning model. 'So it [the grammar of a language] is constituted of invariant principles with options restricted to functional elements and general properties of the lexicon. A selection σ among these options determines a language' (Chomsky 1993: 4). And just above:

> Variation must be determined by what is 'visible' to the child acquiring
> language, that is, by the PLD [primary linguistic data]. It is not
> surprising, then, to find a degree of variation in the PF component, and
> in aspects of the lexicon: Saussurean arbitrariness (association of
> concepts with phonological matrices), properties of grammatical
> formatives (inflection, etc.), and readily detectable properties that hold
> of lexical items generally (e.g. the head parameter) . . . beyond PF
> options and lexical arbitrariness (which I will henceforth ignore),
> variation is limited to nonsubstantive parts of the lexicon and general
> properties of lexical items.   (Chomsky 1993: 3)

In a footnote Chomsky wants to 'restrict variation to elements of morphology' (1993: 44). More generally, the account is formulated in terms of
'strong' features of functional categories visible at PF and 'weak' features
invisible at PF but visible at LF. With this distinction Chomsky goes on to
explain the differences between SVO/SOV languages and VSO languages: in
the former the subject moves to preverbal position in PF, and in the latter
only at LF.

The most ambitious recent attempt to deal with language differentiation is
Baker (1995): rather than micro-parameters becoming more and more
minute or than a lexical learning approach, **macro-parameters** are proposed,
formulated as visibility parameters (see also Chomsky 1981 for the notion of
visibility). However, Baker's approach runs into a number of the empirical
problems sketched above.

Typological differences in generative research

Comrie (1987) has explored various avenues for linking typological differences to parameter setting models. Here I will explore the link of the
typological differences listed earlier in this chapter to lexical and categorial
differences.

- **Word order variation** involving OV/VO contrasts can be interpreted in terms of the directionality of case and theta-marking
  and hence the head-first/head-last parameter (Baker 1995: 444),
  which accounts for many word order differences:
  A phrase X is visible for θ-assignment from a head Y only if it is
  coindexed with a position to the {left}/{right} of Y.
- Free word order and discourse **configurationality** have been
  linked to a larger inventory of functional elements marking focus
  etc. (Kiss 1995).
- **Topic-drop** in languages like Chinese has been analysed in terms

of operator-binding, something originally subsumed under the
pro-drop parameter (Huang 1982).

- Much of the differentiation we find is in some sense **lexical**. First,
  of course, there is the obvious fact that languages differ not only
  in the outer shapes of words, but also in the organization of the
  lexicon and the concepts expressed in it.

- Many differences appear to involve **categorial inventories**, particularly of functional elements. This is in line with recent work
  of e.g. Ouhala (1989), who suggests that differences between
  languages reside primarily in the types and features of functional
  categories in those languages. The work on the emergence of
  functional elements in grammaticalization research can be linked
  to theorizing about the inventories of functional categories
  (cf. N. Vincent 1993).

- The possibility of lexically unrealized subjects and objects, i.e.
  pro-drop may be linked to their being marked on the verb or the
  auxiliary. In other languages, this is impossible, as is the case in
  English. Pro-drop extends into argument drop and head
  marking, the marking of relations on the predicate itself.

- Many differences have to do with case-marking and verbal
  morphology, or more generally speaking, with **head/dependent
  marking**. The requirement that arguments be overtly expressed
  on the predicate (head marking) can be accounted for through
  the Morphological Visibility Condition (Baker 1995: 12), which
  states that a 'phrase X is visible for θ-role assignment from a
  head Y only if it is coindexed with a morpheme in the word
  containing Y via: (i) an agreement relationship, or (ii) a movement relationship'.

- **Case-marking** (dependent marking) has been analysed in terms of
  visibility parameters for abstract and morphological case.

- The categorial status of AGR, INFL and assignment domain of
  case for subjects (ergativity, Austronesian voice) (Bittner and
  Hale 1996).

Module interaction and the lexicon

My working hypothesis is that the differentiation between languages results
from differences in the interaction of the different autonomous modules that
together constitute the language capacity. Specifically, the main differences
between languages can be found in the way information is either lexically or
grammatically encoded. In other words, differentiation results from the

51

different ways in which two autonomous modules, the lexicon and the grammar, interact. This is not an arbitrary matter, given the differences between these components.

When we consider the lexicon as such, we notice that many word meanings within the content lexicon are relatively constant across languages and that linking rules governing the mapping of specific semantic relations onto grammatical functions are not exceedingly varied. Nonetheless, there are great differences in the degree of lexicalization and grammaticalization of semantic distinctions as functional categories, and lexical forms are rather varied.

The lexicon is basically a semiotically constituted system that relies on both phonological and grammatical principles but is independent of these. There is a lexical phonology and a lexical syntax, modelled upon, derived from, but not identical to postlexical phonology and syntax.

I will illustrate the ways in which a particular morphological pattern concretely shapes the syntactic expressions in a language with two examples from my own work on Quechua (Muysken 1988a). The first involves causative–reflexive interactions. Both notions are expressed morphologically in Quechua, and the suffixes expressing them may occur in two orders:

(24) a. riku-chi- ku- n   (Southern Peruvian Quechua)
         see   CAU RE 3
         'he causes himself to see y'
      b. * riku-ku- chi-   n
         see   RE CAU 3
         'he causes y to see himself'

In (24a) the subject and the causee are linked, and (24b) is blocked for a specific reason in the southern Quechua dialects: in these reflexive *ku* may not precede causative *chi*, and the meaning in (24b) cannot be expressed directly. In Central Peruvian Quechua the order *ku – chi* is allowed, and the meaning in (24b) is expressible. This set of examples illustrates two things. First, syntactic principles can be operant within the lexicon. Second, restrictions quite specific to the lexicon can block certain syntactically well-formed structures.

The second example involves subordination through the use of the verbal nominalizing suffixes *na* and *sqa*:

(25) a. Riku-wa- sqa-   n-ta   yacha-ni
         see   1O NOM 3 AC know 1
         'I know (s)he has seen me.'
      b. Riku-wa- na-   n-ta   yacha-ni
         see   1O NOM 3 AC know 1
         'I know (s)he is to see me.'

In these nominalized clauses we find an aspectual distinction which resembles

52

a (dependent) tense distinction and is made possible by grammaticalized properties of the nominalizing morphology. However, the possibility of nominalization as such is quite independent of the syntax and tense system, and what can be expressed through nominalization is limited by the availability of a specific set of nominalizers. Again, syntax is operant within lexical structures, but is constrained by their possibilities.

Typological differences and comparative code-mixing research

It is clear that some mixing patterns have to do with the **linguistic typology** of the languages concerned. Dimensions of differentiation considered in the code-mixing literature so far include:

- The order of constituents and linear equivalence between languages. I return to this in chapter 4.
- The inventory of morpho-syntactic categories, to be discussed below.
- Morphological typology (agglutination, etc.), dealt with below and in chapter 3.
- Marking of the relation predicate/arguments: case and agreement. Possibly quite interesting but as yet not fully explored in the code-mixing literature (an exception is MacSwan 1997), is pro-drop. We do find some references to it in the Spanish/English literature, e.g. in Woolford (1983). How do bilingual sentences fare with respect to this: does the language of the verb or the auxiliary determine omissibility of the main arguments, or some other feature? Are subject and object frequently omitted, or do we find a tendency towards their realization as pronouns?

The degree of linguistic kinship and the lexical and morphosyntactic similarity between the languages involved are quite important.

Exploiting typological differences can lead to new, more directed research strategies in code-mixing research. Rather than comparing any two language pairs, I think it is more profitable to do comparisons keeping one element of the set constant. An example involves Moroccan Arabic and Turkish in contact with Dutch. In a study of over 600 mixes, Nortier (1990) found less than a handful of counter-examples to the Free Morpheme Constraint (Poplack 1980) for Moroccan Arabic/Dutch mixing:

(26) dak š-ši   lli t - *bezig* fi – h
      that the thing that 2sg busy with it
      'that thing that you are busy with'

(Moroccan Arabic/Dutch; Nortier 1990: 144)

Nonetheless, in a much more limited study of Turkish/Dutch mixing, Backus (1992) found violations of the constraint to be the dominant pattern:

(27) Bu bir sürü   *taal* – lar – ı *beheersen* yapıyor-ken.
DEM one string language PL AC control do-PR-3-though
'though he controls a whole string of languages'

(Turkish/Dutch; Backus 1996: 232)

The typological differences between Arabic and Turkish are highly relevant to help explain this type of contrast.

Lexical and morphological typology

We thus need to look at the lexical and morphological typology: how do words differ in the various languages? I will now turn to an issue that has not yet been discussed: the morphological integration of mixed-in elements. To consider this fully, we have to take **morphological typology** into account. Morphological typology plays a role in code-mixing in so far as we consider the type of word-internal mixing involved in morphologically integrated borrowing to be a type of code-mixing. This I will attempt to do below. Consider first a by now classical example from Poplack (1980):

(28) * eat – *iendo*
'eating'

The stated reason for the impossibility of this form, the Free Morpheme Constraint, is not without problems, since we do find morphological material from one language attached to a word from another one:

(29) Misis K. oli housekeeper*ina*.
Mrs. K. was   ESS
'Mrs. K. was housekeeper.'

(Finnish/English; Poplack, Wheeler, and Westwood 1987: 38)

Here the Finnish essive case marker is attached to an English noun. However, what makes (28) not well-formed, is the fact that the Spanish gerund ending -*iendo* is specific to a Spanish verbal conjugation class, to which *eat* does not belong. Thus we may find *eat-eando* instead. For the Finnish agglutinative case marker -*iina* no such restriction holds. This brings us to selectiveness of affixes, and hence back to government, as the grammatical notion behind selection. The element governed by -*iendo* has to conform to very specific requirements, and thus cannot be easily replaced, while the requirements for the element governed by -*iina* are quite general, if not universal.

In chapter 3 I will illustrate the issues involved in trying to unify the grammatical constraints on borrowing with those on code-mixing, in terms of the notion of local coherence imposed by language indices. The unified perspective adopted allows us to link the ways in which elements are borrowed to the morphological typology of languages.

We find differences in borrowing patterns, for instance, between languages with respect to verbs (Nortier and Schatz 1992); in the mixed language Michif, for instance, French verbs are very rare (Bakker 1997), while in some varieties of Quechua 35 per cent of all Spanish borrowed items are verbs (37.6 per cent of the tokens).

In my view this type of finding should not be taken to negate the value of borrowability hierarchies, but rather to suggest that they should be treated as diagnostic yardsticks: given overall general patterns, deviations call for specific explanations. In Michif, for instance, Cree verbal morphology practically precludes the integration of French elements. In Quechua, the highly regular agglutinative morphology facilitates incorporation. How this is accomplished will be discussed in the next chapter.

What is needed, then, is a general perspective on morphological typology. Some elements for this include (Anderson 1985) the observation that typology is no longer mono-dimensional, i.e. no longer only covers the range [isolating/analytic – fusional – agglutinative – polysynthetic], as in earlier studies. Furthermore, typology cannot be formulated of whole languages but only of sub-components of languages.

At first sight, five dimensions of morphological typology can be distinguished that are relevant to language contact research:

> *Dimension 1*: What type of concept can be expressed by morphemes (Sapir 1921)? Sapir distinguished four types:
> - concrete concepts
> - pure relational concepts: subject/object, etc.
> - derivational concepts: plural, diminutive
> - concrete relational concepts: agreement
>
> *Dimension 2*: To what extent are words complex? I have already illustrated this briefly with examples from Quechua.
>
> *Dimension 3*: To what extent are there morphophonological relations between the components of a word? Are there relations of allomorphy and fusion, for instance? In this respect Semitic systems such as Hebrew and Arabic will have vastly different properties from systems such as Turkish or Swahili. Here the distinction between compounding and affixation is relevant as well.
>
> *Dimension 4*: To what extent are there selectional restrictions

between the components of a word, in terms of declension class or the lexical specification of a given affix. A language like Quechua has no declension classes, in contrast with e.g. French or Spanish.

Dimension 5: To what extent are the meanings of complex forms paradigmatically rather than syntagmatically defined (Matthews 1972; Anderson 1992).

The characterization of a morphological subsystem in terms of these dimensions is crucial to its role in language contact. Paradigmatically determined, highly selective, and fusional systems or subsystems are quite opaque, for instance, to morphological mixing, while agglutinative systems are quite open.

Categorial equivalence

Insertion has been argued to take place under **categorial equivalence**: speakers can only insert a constituent or element from another language if it is somehow perceived as equivalent to a host constituent or element. The power of equivalence is such that the structural restrictions on code-mixing appear most clearly in typologically divergent languages. However, how do we know when there is equivalence? The study of code-mixing can help considerably to elucidate this problem.

In much work on language contact, at least since Weinreich (1953), and including e.g. the tradition of contrastive grammar research, the notion of equivalence plays an important role (Flege 1988; Wode 1990): the guiding assumption is that equivalence between the grammars of two languages facilitates bilingual usage, be it second language learning, lexical borrowing, or code-mixing.

There can be equivalence of categories (lexical elements, phonemes, phrase structure nodes, morphosyntactic features) or of relations between categories, in structuralist terms. The latter are either syntagmatic (e.g. word order or agreement rules) or paradigmatic (equivalent oppositions). I will limit myself here to categorial equivalence. Notice that linear equivalence logically presupposes categorial equivalence, but not vice versa. We can only say that the order between V and NP is equivalent in two languages (e.g. a VO constituent order) if we assume that the Vs and NPs are equivalent in the two languages. In the Sankoff and Poplack (1981) and Sankoff and Mainville (1986) formalizations there is the preliminary idealization of categorial equivalence: there is assumed to be a match between both the terminal and the non-terminal nodes of the languages involved in the mix. It has been pointed out before that this idealization is not unproblematic; in fact there is no exact match between categories in different languages. Poplack (1980: 587) discusses the case where Spanish has a subjunctive complement and English an infinitival complement, and considers them to be non-equivalent structures.

Typologically, there are many cases where languages do not correspond exactly. In fact, Steele et al. (1981) shift the burden of proof to the need to demonstrate correspondence or equivalence cross-linguistically, in a discussion of auxiliaries.

Categorial typology is rather open at present as a field of study. Hengeveld (forthcoming) suggests that the only universal category, present in all languages, is verb; other authors have assumed that noun and verb are the universal categories. It is clear that all other categories, including adjective, adverb, adposition, and conjunction, cannot be viewed as universal. Hengeveld argues that there are strict implicational relations governing the differentiation of categories across languages. Clearly, this is a field urgently in need of further research.

In the generative literature the problem of subcategories is solved through the mechanism of subcategorization features, which specify in which context a category can occur. Thus the difference between intransitive, transitive, and ditransitive verbs is marked in the following way:

intransitive   +V
transitive   +V, [__ NP]
ditransitive   +V, [__ NP NP]

The unspoken assumption behind this solution is of course that all subcategorial differences can be reduced to such distributional differences. In fact, languages may differ from each other in the very inventories of their categories. This brings us to the issue of categorial equivalence between languages.

Well-documented problem-areas in categorial equivalence mentioned in the typological literature include:

- full pronouns (West-Germanic) versus clitics (Romance). Jake (1994) has commented on the implication of this difference for code-mixing;
- auxiliaries (Modern English) versus main verbs (Old English, Dutch);
- predicate adjectives (Indo-European) versus stative verbs (Kwa, Caribbean Creoles)
- finite clauses (Indo-European) versus nominalizations (e.g. Turkish)

- cases (e.g. Turkish, Finnish) versus adpositions (e.g. English). In chapter 3 I will discuss work on Finnish/English code-mixing which directly refers to this distinction.

All oppositions in this list correspond to notional equivalents with different categorial realizations. The list can be extended once we get into determiner systems etc., as was argued by Bentahila and Davies (1983) for the difference between Moroccan Arabic and French demonstratives.

There are four conceivable ways in which categorial non-equivalence can be dealt with, ordered here on a scale of permissiveness:

(a) We could assume that constraints are simply suspended in cases of categorial non-equivalence. Any time that there is that type of non-equivalence, mixing is possible.

(b) There is an automatic interlingual translation mechanism, triggered by notional equivalence, so that non-equivalent categories are treated as if they are equivalent.

(c) We could assume a kind of tolerant checking mechanism that establishes equivalence if there is a partial overlap of features. For instance, suppose Modern English Aux-elements have the features [+V, +Aux] and Dutch auxiliary-like elements are simply [+V], then the mechanism could still treat the elements from the two languages as equivalent.

(d) We could assume that categorial non-equivalence is taken seriously, so that mixing is not allowed.

The difference between (b) and (c) is that there may be notional equivalence without feature-sharing. The choice between these four options, and indeed of any interpretation of code-mixing constraints, must be made in part on the basis of a careful evaluation of the empirical evidence, and in part on the basis of a reasonable view of what happens psycholinguistically when speakers mix their languages.

We need to conceive of equivalence as a grammatical notion embedded in the bilingual's processing system, and hence from a psycholinguistic perspective. This allows us to treat processes of code-mixing in diachronic and sociolinguistic terms (Sebba 1998). Assume that one bilingual speech community does not recognize the categories from different languages as equivalent, and another one does. This may be due to frequency of use, degree and kind of bilingualism, and language attitudes. In any case, this will have an immediate impact on code-mixing patterns, of course. We can think then of the recognition of categorial equivalence as the first step in the process of syntactic convergence. A category often recognized as equivalent may be 'noun', and frequently also 'noun phrase' will be recognized as such, whereas conjunctions are perhaps less likely to be interpreted as equivalent. In addition, morphological (e.g. similar paradigms) and phonological factors (e.g. lexical similarities) may be involved in furthering the recognition of equivalence.

Meechan and Poplack (1995), in their analysis of data from Wolof/French and Fon/French code-mixing, discuss the issue of categorial non-equivalence. How do speakers solve the problem of matching two languages when there is no equivalence? They conclude that categorial equivalence is indeed a major factor in code-mixing.

3
Insertion

This chapter discusses the grammatical dimensions of insertion. My first claim will be that the phenomena of borrowing, nonce-borrowing, and constituent insertion all fall within the same general class and are subject to the same conditions. My second claim will be that a version of the type of approach exemplified by the government model (DiSciullo, Muysken, and Singh 1986) and related models, incorporating categorial equivalence and functional elements as syntactic heads, appropriately accounts for insertional mixing. I will begin by discussing the main diagnostic features of insertional code-mixing, on the basis of Spanish–Quechua data. Subsequently, two problems are focussed upon: first, how do we define a base or matrix language? This question is crucial of course to insertional code-mixing, since insertion always occurs with respect to a base language. Second, what is the relation between lexical borrowing and insertion?

Then the discussion turns to some of the issues that follow from this with respect to the behaviour of noun phrases in mixed sentences. These include the following.

Can we maintain the distinction made between nonce-borrowing (in the Tamil case) and constituent insertion (in the Arabic case) in work by David Sankoff and Shana Poplack (Nait M'Barek and Sankoff 1988; Sankoff, Poplack, and Vanniarajan 1990; Poplack and Meechan 1995)?

How do we explain the differences found between Dutch/Moroccan Arabic code-mixing (Nortier 1990) and French/Moroccan Arabic code-mixing (Bentahila and Davies 1983)?

Are nouns in different languages truly equivalent in principle? This will be discussed in connection with Papiamentu/Dutch code-mixing data.

What is the relation between categorial and linear equivalence, and which notion explains the distribution of noun phrases best? This issue will be discussed in relation to Finnish/English code-mixing.

The central hypothesis I will explore is that there are insertions of several types of constituents (limiting myself here to nominal constituents):

N insertion:	only nouns	many languages
NP insertion:	adjective + noun	Tamil, Turkish,
	noun + complement	Quechua, Arabic/Dutch
DGNP insertion	noun phrases marked	Arabic/French
	for number, gender,	
	and definiteness	
DP insertion	full determiner phrases	Spanish/English

Separating these four cases will help considerably to clarify the issue of categorial equivalence, and the role of functional categories such as determiners and case markers in defining equivalence. Note that in this account instances of full DP (determiner phrase) insertions are fairly rare. It is important for the analysis to note that I assume at least a four-level nominal complex, schematically presented as:

(1)

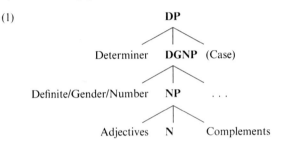

As noted in the previous chapter, languages may differ in the precise constituency of the DP and the features expressed.

Features of insertional code-mixing

A good starting point for our analysis is *constituent structure*, a central notion in the analysis of the sentence. One interpretive principle for code-mixing research has rarely been made explicit (an exception is Annamalai 1971, 1989a) but is implicit in many analyses, and may be termed the **Adjacency Principle**:

> If in a code-mixed sentence two adjacent elements are drawn from the same language, an analysis is preferred in which at some level of representation (syntax, processing) these elements also form a unit.

To apply this principle, we need to establish constituency. A constituent can be any syntactic unit, either a lexical item (e.g. a noun) or a phrase (e.g. a prepositional phrase). This principle is not absolute, but it can be used as an evaluation measure for analyses and is presupposed in what follows. Consider an example such as:

(2) Ni-ka-*wash all the clothes.*
   1sg-PST-wash all the clothes
   'I washed all the clothes.'   (Swahili/English; Myers-Scotton 1993b:80)

Here the principle would predict *wash all the clothes* to be a single switch (e.g. an entire switched VP), even though the element *wash* by itself receives Swahili prefixes and could be treated as an incorporated borrowing.

In insertional code-mixing what is inserted is a constituent. Sometimes several constituents in a row do *not* form a *unique* constituent. When these are switched insertion is not plausible, and alternation or congruent lexicalization are serious possibilities. A number of elements form a unique constituent if that constituent contains no other elements. With several constituents, we would have to assume multiple contiguous insertions.

In contrast, when the switched element is a single, well-defined constituent insertion is a plausible option; this holds *a fortiori* for single words. When several words are switched which do not form one or more constituents together, congruent lexicalization is plausible, as we will see in chapter 5.

However, analysis of actual speech data is not always straightforward. The following example illustrates the problem of constituency, *in casu* whether or not we should analyse *of zo* 'or so' as part of the previous constituent:

(3) Žib li-ya   *een glas water of zo.*
   get for-me   a glass water or so
   'Please get me a glass of water or something.'
                                       (Moroccan Arabic/Dutch; Nortier 1990: 131)

Examples like these illustrate the occasional difficulty of giving a definite structural interpretation to spoken sentences. Generally speaking code-mixing involving noun phrases is clearly of the insertional type, however. Noun phrases are well-defined constituents and tend to be syntactically inert and hence easily insertable.

Consider the following example from (Bolivian) Quechua/Spanish data. Alien elements may, but need not, be marked for Quechua case:

(4) *catch-as-can*-ta phujlla-rqo-y-ta-wan
   AC play-INT-INF-AC-with
   'after playing catch-as-can'

(5) Chay-pi-qa nuqayku-qa *catch-as-can* bati-yku-yku
   That LO TO 1pl-TO
   beat-INT-1pl
   sonso ind-itu-s-wan-qa.
   stupid indian-DIM-PL-with-TO
   'There we played catch-as-can with the stupid little Indians.'
                                       (Quechua/Spanish: Urioste 1964: I, 3)

In (4) the accusative case marker -*ta* is present, though absent in (5). It needs to be seen to what extent such a distribution reflects, in specific language pairs, a general optionality of case marking (as in Bolivian Quechua) and to what extent a specific zero strategy for borrowings, or the maintenance of Spanish patterns. This type of issue is typical in the study of noun phrase insertion.

In the Bolivian Quechua material a number of Spanish fixed expressions are inserted, such as *a ver* 'let's see', and *en fin* 'finally'. We also find compound subordinating expressions such as *así que* 'thus' and *quizás que* 'perhaps that' and combinations such as *mal criado* 'badly raised'. Most of the (very numerous) Spanish elements are single words, however (Van Hout and Muysken 1994). Thus the vast majority of the Spanish insertions are **single constituents**, the first diagnostic feature of insertions.

A second feature of insertions is that they tend to exhibit a **nested a b a structure**. The fragment preceding the insertion and the fragment following are grammatically related. An example is:

(6)   Chay-ta *las dos de la   noche*-ta chaya-mu-yku.
      that-AC the two of the night-AC arrive-CIS-1pl
      'There at two in the morning we arrive.'

Here the locative/directional expression *chay-ta* 'there' and the verb *chaya-mu-yku* 'we arrive' are clearly part of the same clause.

A third property is that the switched elements tend to be **content words** rather than function words (Van Hout and Muysken 1994). Out of 363 borrowed Spanish types, 338 are content words. Of the 25 borrowed non-content words (types) many are part of fixed expressions rather than loose elements. Inserted elements are mostly nouns, adjectives, and verbs. Typical examples are:

(7)   *Paga*-wa-y uj qolqe *duro*-wan willa-sqa-yki-taj.
      pay-1O-IM one silver hard-with say-PST-2-EMPH
      Se había comprometido **pagar**le con plata **dura**.
      'You had promised to **pay** him with **hard** cash.'

A fourth feature is that many Spanish insertions are **selected elements** (objects or complements) rather than adjuncts. Notice the many cases where the Spanish insertions receive Quechua case markings such as -*ta* 'accusative' or -*wan* 'instrumental'.

This automatically leads to another diagnostic feature of insertions, **morphological integration**, which is particularly striking in the case of verbs in (8) and (9), but also occurs with quantifiers as in *entero-n* 'whole' in (10):

(8) *Desmaya*-chi-pu-ni nuqa-pis.
faint-CAU-BEN-1sg I-also
'I also let (him) faint.'

(9) *A ver, trompea*-ku-na.
let's see, mistake-RE-NOM
'Let's see, we will be wrong.'

(10) Suchu-rpari-wa-sqa-nku, *entero*-n orqo-rpa-sqa-nku.
drag-INT-1O-SD-3pl, whole-3 take-INT-SD-3pl
'They started to drag me, and they took all of it.'

Sometimes, we also find telegraphic mixing, as in the following example, where *de verdad* is part of a more complete expression:

(11) Sut'i *de verdad*-manta capunita-pi rua-rqa-ni chay-ta-qa.
name in truth-ABL Capunita-LO do-PST-1 that-AC-TO
'For sure, I did that in Capunita.'

Thus insertions tend to be single, nested, often selected, often morphologically integrated constituents, often content words. A matrix language is maintained, and the grammar of this matrix language determines the overall structure. The issue I want to turn to now is the nature of the matrix language.

Base or matrix language

How can one determine the base or matrix language of an utterance? If there is a base or matrix language in a mixed sentence, how do we determine which one it is? The answer to this question is in part empirical – on the basis of diagnostic criteria – in part theoretical in nature.

To determine a matrix language empirically and independently of structural criteria is not unproblematic. A number of diagnostic criteria have been proposed. In Myers-Scotton (1993b: 3) the matrix language is termed 'the main language in CS [mixed] utterances in a number of ways'. However, there is no single independent criterion, besides a structural one, to determine the matrix language.

A **discourse**-oriented way of determining the base language would be in terms of the language of the conversation. An example of this is the analysis presented by Berk-Seligson (1986: 323) for Hebrew/Spanish code-mixing. She mentions the following dialogue:

(12) A. Ke dixo el *rav*?
'What did the rabbi say?'
B. La misma *paraša* ke avía en *šabat*.

'The same scriptural portion that there was on Sabbath.'

Ával parašá, tefilá ke se áze al *beyt aknéset,*

'But [the] scriptural portion, the prayer that is done in the synagogue,'

al kal, *az* todos ya saven kwalo es.

'in the synagogue, so everybody knows what it is.'

(Hebrew/Spanish; Berk-Seligson 1986: 323)

Berk-Seligson analyses the Hebrew fragments in italics as separate insertions from Hebrew into the Spanish base or matrix language, determined by the discourse, which is generally Spanish. This is possible, but it conflicts with other criteria. The sequence *Ával parašá, tefilá* is not a constituent, and this suggests we should analyse it as a brief total switch to Hebrew, since it is not plausibly a single insertion (cf. the Adjacency Principle).

Consider now a stretch of more extended Swahili–English discourse, for which again Swahili is taken to be the matrix language:

(13) A: Bwana O., niambie kuhusu mpango wa posta wa *save as you earn.*

'Mr. O., tell me about the postal plan of "save as you earn."'

B: Mpango huu ni *the customer fills the forms and* plan this is

surrenders kiasi fulani ch-a pesa   *say like 200*

amount some NC7–of money

shillings every month for two years. The interest paid is good and the customer can collect it after the expiration of the agreed period.

Tuna *customers* we-ngi sana kwa mpango huu.

we have customers NC2–many very in plan this

'The plan is [that] the customer fills the forms and surrenders some amount of money, say like 200 shillings every month for two years. The interest paid is good and the customer can collect it after the expiration of the agreed period. We have very many customers in this plan.'

(Swahili/English; Myers-Scotton 1993b: 72)

It is hard to see what purpose is gained and what criteria can be used to assume that Swahili is the matrix language throughout. Yet, this is what Myers-Scotton (1993b: 72) is implying in her analysis of this fragment.

A second approach is in terms of **left-to-right parsing**. In a model that attaches great importance to a parsing procedure from left to right, the first word or set of words in the sentence determines the base language (such a model is reported on in Doron 1983), triggering a set of grammatical rules. Whatever insights this yields, care should be taken that switched left-peripheral interjections, exclamatives or adverbial adjuncts are not taken as the first element. These elements do not in any way determine the structure of the rest of the sentence. Still, this model would suggest that the sentence starting with *Ával parašá, tefilá* 'But the scriptual portion, the prayer' is in fact a Hebrew sentence.

A third possibility is **morpheme-counting**. A discourse-oriented base model can be given a statistical interpretation, such that the base language is the language in which most words or morphemes are uttered. In Myers-Scotton (1993b: 68) an 'ML criterion' is proposed, leading to the definition of ML as 'the language of more morphemes in interaction types including intra-sentential CS'. It must be based on a discourse sample and the count must exclude cultural borrowings and words for new concepts. This is tricky as an independent measure because morpheme frequency is dependent on the typology of the languages involved: an agglutinative language like Swahili encodes many grammatical concepts (which are crucial structurally) with an overt morpheme, while isolating languages often do not. A case in point is Moluccan Malay/Dutch mixing, studied by Huwaë (Huwaë 1992). In all three examples below, Malay pronouns, auxiliaries, negators, and determiners suggest that the sentences constitute Malay structures in a grammatical sense. Consider (14), where two single Dutch constituents are present in a Malay structure:

> (14) *Nou* ini *laatste avond.*
> now DEM last evening
> 'Now this is the last evening.'   (Moluccan Malay/Dutch; Huwaë 1992)

However, notice that *nou* 'now' is more like an adjoined element, while *laatste avond* 'last evening' is inserted.

> (15) *Volgens mij* a su *verslaafd aan die pijnstillers.*
> according-to me I PERF addicted to those painkillers
> 'I think I have become addicted to those painkillers.'

> (16) Ini tong *nog* ada *bedanken.*
> DET we still be / have give thanks
> 'That is we are still saying thanks here.'

Nonetheless, the number of Malay morphemes is equal to or smaller than the number of Dutch morphemes.

Considering this definition, take an example like (17), cited in isolation:

> (17) Ni-*check all that particular day's constructions.*
> 'I should . . .'   (Swahili/English; Myers-Scotton 1993b: 146)

Since Swahili *ni* 'first person subject clitic' is a function morpheme (and hence is supposed to be part of the matrix language), we must take the author's word for it that the sentence was taken from a discourse that was mostly Swahili, since the matrix language in (17) is taken to be Swahili. A similar example is (18), again cited in isolation:

(18) *It's only essential services*   amba-zo zi-na
                               COMP-NC10 NC10-PRES-
      -function right now.
      'It's only essential services that function right now.'

(Swahili/English; Myers-Scotton 1993b: 103)

Here the sequence *function right now* is not a single constituent, and thus not plausibly analysed as inserted into a Swahili matrix.

We might define the matrix language in **psycholinguistic** terms as the language most activated for the speaker, but we have no independent way to establish this. Neither can **proficiency** in a language in itself be a reliable indicator because a speaker may switch over to the weaker language entirely. Similarly, sometimes speakers will perceive a bilingual conversation as having taken place exclusively or primarily in one language. This might then be the basis for identifying the conversation as having a single matrix language. However, perceptions can be deceptive.

Given the difficulties with all of these criteria, we may turn to a structural definition of matrix language as determined by some element or set of elements. Often the **main verb**, which is the semantic kernel of the sentence, assigning the different semantic roles and determining the state or event expressed by the clause, is taken to determine the base language. Plausible though adoption of the main verb as determining the base language may be, in many languages there is a strategy to incorporate alien verbs (see chapter 7), e.g. through prolitic elements, as in Swahili, or through an auxiliary verb like 'do', as in Hindi. In these cases, taking that borrowed verb as determining the base language is clearly not correct.

A more theoretical approach departs from the constituent structure. In the perspective of the government model (DiSciullo, Muysten, and Singh 1986), there need not be a single base or matrix language for the clause. Still, there is a notion of base or matrix present in that model: each governing element (e.g. verb, preposition, auxiliary) creates a matrix structure, namely its maximal projection. If the chain of government were unbroken, the highest element in the tree would determine the language for the whole tree; this would often be the inflection on the **finite verb**, as in the theory proposed by Klavans (1985) and taken up by Treffers-Daller (1994). In subordinate clauses, this would be the **complementizer**.

These criteria are compatible with Myers-Scotton's model, since both verbal inflections and the complementizer are functional elements, system morphemes and hence should stem from the matrix language. However, the purely structural definition is somewhat circular if the matrix language thus determined is then invoked to explain the origin of system morphemes such as the verbal inflections and the complementizer.

While in insertion the notion of matrix language is called for, in alternation it plays no role. In the string of words of a sentence, some elements have a syntactic relationship, others are simply juxtaposed. There are numerous gaps in the grammatical edifice, which make it possible for e.g. dislocated elements, appositions, interjections and tags, predicative elements, and adverbial phrases to differ in their language index from the matrix without having to be equivalent to a constituent of the matrix language: alternational or paratactic switches. In addition, there may be such structural parallelism between the languages that we have congruent lexicalization and in that case a matrix language is shared by both codes and hence impossible to determine.

A related issue is the relation between the definition of matrix language used by Myers-Scotton (1993b) and the notion of matrix clause from grammatical analysis. In the following cases, the **matrix clause** is in the embedded language, and the **embedded clause** in the matrix language, according to her analysis:

(19) *Mais toi, on dirait que* ozokima te ba*jours* oyo.
'But you, one would say that you do not job these days.'
(Lingala/French; Myers-Scotton 1993b: 132)

(20) *You didn't have to worry* que *somebody* te iba a tirar con cerveza o una botella *or something like that.*
'You didn't have to worry that somebody was going to throw beer or a bottle at you or something like that.'
(Spanish/English; Myers-Scotton 1993b: 128)

(21) *It doesn't mean* ukitembea utakuwa ukishikwa.
'It doesn't mean [that] if you stroll about you will be arrested.'
(Swahili/English; Myers-Scotton 1993b: 131)

Given that genuine matrix/embedded clause asymmetries are generally assumed to have a correlate in sentence planning, it is difficult to conceive of a matrix clause being 'embedded', language-wise, in a complement clause.

To sum up, we see that a generally valid criterion for defining a single matrix language for a sentence or a conversation is hard to find. Nonetheless, in many cases, researchers have no trouble identifying it, using different criteria. I interpret this as evidence that the notion of matrix language is essentially an empirical one – it may be there, or not – rather than a theoretical prime. There is much evidence that indeed in many cases code-mixing is asymmetrical and involves a 'dominant', 'base', or 'matrix' language. However, in other cases it is not.

There is a tension between a structural view of a matrix language and a psycholinguistic view in terms of left-to-right, incremental sentence production, but the two cannot be entirely separate. Myers-Scotton even suggests that the ML could change during a sentence (1993b: 70). While this could be correct, it limits the empirical scope of the notion 'matrix': it may be a notion primarily relevant at the level of constituency. Change, or turnover, in ML is prevalent in changing bilingual communities (pp. 73–4). However, many bilingual communities, particularly migrant communities, are precisely characterized by rapid change. Thus models in terms of this notion may have a limited usefulness.

Borrowing

Code-mixing and borrowing are often distinguished formally, e.g. through morphology, as taking place above and below the word level, respectively. Code-mixing involves inserting alien words or constituents into a clause; borrowing entering alien elements into a lexicon. It is not always the case, however, that borrowing can be seen as a form of simple vocabulary extension, and that code-mixing has a primarily symbolic function, e.g. marking a mixed cultural identity. I will argue that what might be formally characterized as borrowed elements particularly in bilingual discourse take on certain discourse functions of code-mixings. This result perhaps throws some light on the question of why 'nonce borrowings' are so controversial. In the perspective taken here they constitute a class of elements that formally might be grouped with borrowing, and functionally can, in certain circumstances, be grouped with code-mixing, namely when the borrowing primarily has a symbolic function.

I will approach the issue of the relation between code-mixing and borrowing from the perspective of the speaker. Bilinguals dispose of two grammars and lexicons, and the lexicons can be viewed as one large collection that consists of several subsets. Thus lexical borrowing could be termed lexical sharing.

First I will look at the demarcation between borrowing and code-mixing simply in terms of their position with respect to lexical insertion. Then I will consider hierarchies of borrowability and constraints on the process of borrowing. Subsequently I will analyse borrowing from the perspective of morphological theory and the process of lexicalization. I relate the process of borrowing to the three types of code-mixing distinguished in this book: insertion, alternation, congruent lexicalization.

The demarcation between clause level and word level mixing

In the case of word borrowing foreign words are adopted into the lexicon. In the case of code-mixing two grammars and vocabularies are used in producing a sentence or a text. Thus it is easy to chararacterize the French loan *autootje* in (22) as a borrowing into Dutch:

> (22) Wat een te gek autootje. (pronounced: ['əwtotjə])
> 'What a terrific car.'

It is only one word, it is pronounced with a Dutch diphthong, it has the Dutch diminutive suffix and the specifically Dutch neutral gender. It is used very frequently and it is the word used most when referring to cars. It is probably recognized as Dutch by most speakers, and though it has not undergone any semantic changes that could easily have been the case. There is also a more 'French' pronunciation, however, the slightly more posh [o:to:], but that fits perfectly within the Dutch phonological system as well. Borrowing is a quite frequent phenomenon, though Haugen (1956a: 65) suggests that most published accounts of borrowing exaggerate the extent of it, since they are written either to warn against it or to amuse.

Compare in contrast a sentence with code-mixing:

> (23) Ze geven niet ge- uh . . . niet genoeg *pour cette jeun . . . jeunesse.*
> 'They do not give enough for this . . . youth.'   (Treffers-Daller 1994: 213)

The French fragment has not become part of the Dutch lexicon either morphologically, or phonologically, or semantically. While the contrast between (22) and (23) is clear both conceptually and empirically, there turn out to be lots of doubtful cases. Phonological integration is variable with borrowing, and in code-mixing both phonologies are present to some extent. The empirical data (for instance a transcription of recorded bilingual language use) do not always allow us to make a distinction for each single mix. Consider cases such as the following, recorded in French/Dutch bilingual families living in Amsterdam:

> (24) Oh, Micheline, je viens pas au club parce qu'il faut que j'aille au *oogarts*
> [standard French: *chez le* . . .].
> 'Oh, Micheline, I can't come to the club because I have to go to the ophthalmologist.'

> (25) Il y a du *bloot* qui est joli et du *bloot* qui n'est pas joli.
> 'There is /nude/ that is nice and /nude/ that is not nice.'

> (26) Je hebt *bijouteries*, je hebt kleren.
> 'You have /jewellery/, you have clothes.'

Notice that in all these cases and generally speaking, the alien element is not really culture-specific, although it may be so within the family ambience concerned. Furthermore, the words are perfectly integrated syntactically (notice the use of *au* and *du*, as in French, in (24) and (25), and the absence of an article or a preposition in (26), as in Dutch), but not phonologically. We really have no criteria to determine whether it is code-mixing or borrowing. Some people have claimed that because of this it is better to drop the conceptual distinction between borrowing and code-mixing altogether and to speak about 'interference' in general. I will not adopt that position.

Code-mixing can be conceived of as involving words with different language indices, marked with p and q subscripts here, inserted into a phrase structure (27a), where the brackets labelled C mark the clause level, and lexical borrowing as involving formatives (Fr) inserted into a foreign word structure (27b). The word structure is foreign because it behaves externally like an element from the host language and may contain formatives Fr_q from the host language:

(27) a. $[_C$ W_p W_q]   above-word or clause level
      b. $[_W$ Fr_p (Fr_q)]   below-word level

In (27b) the brackets labelled W mark the word level. I will use the term sublexical for mixing below the level of insertion of a word into a syntactic tree; and the term supra-lexical for mixing at the level of insertion in a tree and in the syntactic projection of a word. Thus a word can be inserted into a syntactic tree as, say, English, even though some of its components are French.

Thus we have to take into account whether a particular case occurs at the supra-lexical or sublexical level, in the sense just described; but also whether it involves being listed (DiSciullo and Williams 1989) or not. The dimension of listedness refers to the degree to which a particular element or structure is part of a memorized list which has gained acceptance within a particular speech community. We can arrange linguistic elements on a scale running from essentially creative to essentially reproductive.

Jackendoff (1975) and others have pointed out, of course, that these two dimensions are not entirely separate. The sublexical mode is primarily reproductive (listed), the supra-lexical, syntactic mode primarily creative. Nonetheless, there are many languages, e.g. polysynthetic and agglutinative languages, in which processes of word formation are regularly used to produce novel formations. Similarly, there are phrase structure configurations, most clearly idioms and collocations, which are to some extent reproductive. In the model of Construction Grammar, a much larger set of phrase structure configurations is assumed to be listed (Goldberg 1995). For this reason, it is better to see these dimensions as separate.

When we look at linguistic interference in terms of these dimensions, the following picture emerges:

(28)

	not-listed	listed
supra-lexical	code-mixing (a)	conventionalized code-mixing (b)
sublexical	nonce loans (c)	established loans (d)

Most code-mixings are of course spontaneously formed in discourse, (a). Recall however that there is evidence in the work of Poplack and Sankoff (1988), that certain patterns of mixing are more frequent in one speech community, other patterns in another speech community (the language pair involved being the same). In this case one might speak of conventionalized code-mixing, (b). The phenomenon of nonce loans, (c), was first described by Haugen (1950) and has recently been taken up in the work of Sankoff and Poplack (1984); elements are borrowed on the spur of the moment, without having any status yet in the receiving speech community. Finally, established loans, (d), are a familiar phenomenon.

Taking this set of distinctions into account, we can now return to the problem of the demarcation between borrowing and code-mixing. In Sankoff and Poplack (1984), which summarizes much earlier work, the distinctions shown in table 3.1 were listed between code-mixing and borrowing. Since both involve the dimension of listedness, we can assimilate the phenomena associated with lexical borrowing to those associated with ordinary morphological derivation and lexical coining. It has often been noted that lexical borrowing, in contrast with code-mixing, involves gradual semantic specialization over time, blurring of morpheme boundaries, lexical unpredictability, etc. These strikingly resemble the properties of derivational morphology. Both can be viewed as the consequences of lexicalization typical of sublexical structures. It may be possible to integrate lexicalization into derivation and language contact even further, e.g. if we assume that there is a progressive linking of new forms to established (mono-morphemic) word shapes in both cases. Code-mixing has the ordinary, supra-lexical, productive properties of syntax.

Elements differ in the extent to which they are integrated. In (29a) *guest* functions as an unadapted nonce-borrowing, while *maitre d'*, pronounced [me:təR di:], in some varieties of English is an established loan, though recognizably foreign in pertaining to a particular register of speech. The word *denial* is of course fully integrated, and only recognized as foreign in the sense that it belongs to the 'Romance' lexicon as far as morphological processes are concerned. Finally the fact that the [+ native] affix *-hood* can be

Table 3.1. *Features of code-mixing and borrowing according to Sankoff and Poplack (1984)*

		borrowing	code-mixing
no more than one word		+	–
adaptation:	phonological	±/+	±/–
	morphological	+	–
	syntactic	+	–
frequent use		+	–
replaces own word		+	–
recognized as own word		+	–
semantic change		+	–

attached to *priest*, suggests that the latter has been fully adopted into the core of the English lexicon.

(29)   a.   *Guest* ellaam paattein.
             all see [1sg-PST]
             'I saw guests and all.'   (Tami/English; Sankoff, Poplack, and Vanniarajan 1990: 82)
       b.   The *maitre d'* helped us find a table.
       c.   *denial*
       d.   *priesthood*

The lexicon consists of separate strata or subsets, and this makes the notion of lexical integration all the more complex.

It is an empirical question whether and how quickly nouns brought into a lexicon will adopt the lexical properties of that new lexicon. Budzhak-Jones (1998), in a very detailed study of Ukrainian–English bilingual speech, shows that this is overwhelmingly the case. Single nouns do not behave as switched elements in her study, but as borrowed elements.

Constraints on the process: hierarchies of borrowability
Not all types of borrowing, and not all forms of code-mixing tend to occur with equal frequency, and thus it is possible to formulate grammatical constraints on both processes. In the literature we can find a number of proposals to this effect, but these are generally thought of as being of a very different nature for the two processes.

There is a tradition of trying to establish borrowability hierarchies and implicational universals of borrowing (e.g. Whitney (1881), Haugen (1950); for a summary, cf. van Hout and Muysken 1994). The traditional observation, with deep roots in language contact research, is that different categories can be more or less easily borrowed, or at least, are actually borrowed. This observation, which had a somewhat shaky empirical base until recently, has received massive support from the work reported in Poplack, Sankoff, and Miller (1988). The finding that nouns are the most frequently borrowed element is confirmed for many other language pairs as well (Nortier and Schatz 1992). For borrowing, constraints can then be formulated in terms of a categorial hierarchy: words of one specific lexical category can be borrowed more easily than those of another. An example of such a hierarchy is (30), partly based on Haugen (1950):

> (30) nouns – adjectives – verbs – prepositions – coordinating conjunctions – quantifiers – determiners – free pronouns – clitic pronouns – subordinating conjunctions

Such hierarchies predict that a noun such as French *automobile* can be borrowed more easily into English than a conjunction such as *que*, and this prediction holds reasonably well. The problem, however, with a hierarchy such as (30) is that there is no explanation given for the order of the lexical categories in the hierarchies. In addition, it turns out that there are very striking language-specific deviations from it.

With regard to code-mixing there is much less of a consensus in the literature, as shown in chapter 1. Nonetheless, there is a possibility of greater unification. In chapter 1 I mentioned the possibility of taking a probabilistic approach to code-mixing constraints. Once constraints on code-mixing are given a probabilistic interpretation and mixing types are represented in a mixability hierarchy, there is a possibility of relating the constraints on the two processes – mixing and borrowing – by appealing to the general grammatical notion of coherence.

In Van Hout and Muysken (1994) we explored the possibility of a probabilistic approach to borrowing by comparing two related corpora: a set of Bolivian Quechua folktales collected by Aguiló (1980) and informal Spanish translations of these tales by people from the same villages. The Spanish corpus is taken as the corpus of potentially borrowed elements, the (very numerous) Spanish borrowings in the Quechua folk tales as the actually borrowed corpus. We developed analytical techniques, based on regression analysis, to determine borrowability, the ease with which a category of lexical items can be borrowed. The analysis was based on two assumptions: (a) the distribution of items in the donor language should be taken into account, to explain why certain items are, and others are not, borrowed; (b) the borrowability of a category may result from the interaction of a number of factors. The relevant research question is then to be phrased as follows: given a donor lexicon L_x and a recipient lexicon L_y, what is the chance for an item from L_x to end up in L_y, and what determines this chance? In chapter 6 some of the results of the Van Hout and Muysken (1994) study are presented.

Borrowing and the typology of code-mixing phenomena

Lexical borrowing has been associated with insertional code-mixing, and not without reason. Nouns are the class of elements borrowed par excellence and also the prime example of insertion under categorial equivalence. However, there may also be other kinds of borrowing patterns.

The effort to establish borrowability hierarchies runs into problems in many bilingual settings: in addition to the standard sets of nouns, adjectives, etc. borrowed (which fall under the predicted hierarchies), there is often a recalcitrant set of borrowed conjunctions, prepositions, etc. I argue in chapter 4 that this deviant pattern results from the fact that there is not a single borrowing process, just like there is no single code-mixing process. In addition to the familiar pattern of insertion (producing the Whitney/Haugen borrowability hierarchies), there is a pattern of alternation involving interjections and conjunctions. Insertion is mostly a form of unidirectional language influence, while alternation often goes both ways. Insertion is constituent-internal, alternation is phrase- or clause-peripheral. This alternation-type borrowing will be further studied in the next chapter. Borrowing related to congruent lexicalization is again much less restrained, and can involve all grammatical categories, including functional elements, as shown in chapter 5.

Government and restrictions on borrowing

Recall the perspective on morphological typology given in the previous chapter, which gives much insight into the possibilities of lexical borrowing. These can be described in terms of **government**. We can extend and generalize the government constraint introduced in chapter 1 to cases of lexical borrowing. Recall that code-mixing can be viewed as involving words with different language indices inserted into a phrase structure for a clause C (31a), while lexical borrowing may be seen as involving formatives inserted into an alien word structure (31b):

$$(31) \quad \text{a.} \quad [_C \ W_p \ W_q] \qquad \text{above-word or clause level}$$
$$\qquad \text{b.} \quad [_W \ Fr_p \ (Fr_q)] \qquad \text{below-word level}$$

Here the brackets labelled *W* mark the word level. This conception yields an interesting result for selection.

Selection is a notion derived from the structuralist tradition, e.g. from Harris (1960). It refers to the limitations posed by a given linguistic element on the elements in its environment. Obviously, it can be used as a more general term for government. Here I will explore its meaning in morphology, to account for a frequent type of mixing pattern. Consider examples such as:

(32) **[Indian women]**-e avaa **discriminate** paNNa-ille.
        AC they   do-NEG
        'They don't discriminate (against) Indian women.'
        Tamil/English; Sankoff, Poplack, and Vanniarajan 1990: 80)

(33) **[A las cinco de la tarde]**-ta hamu-saq.
        at the five of the afternoon-AC come-1FU
        'I'll come at five in the afternoon.'   (Quechua/Spanish; Bolivian fieldwork data)

These examples, where a case affix from one language is attached to the nominal constituent from another one, are typical of code-mixing involving agglutinative languages such as Basque, Quechua, Finnish, Tamil, Maori, and Turkish. In these languages morphological elements such as case markers typically have phrasal scope, an invariant form (barring late phonological rules), and no stratal sensitivity.

We may think of agglutinative affixes as being non-selective. Agglutinating languages are defined by the absence of lexical selection by affixes (termed L-marking in chapter 1). Hence there are no conjugation classes, special morphophonemic rules, etc. These affixes are half-way between many Indo-European affixes and clitics, where a clitic may be defined as a phonologically dependent element generated by the phrase structure rules of a language, and an affix is a phonologically dependent element generated by word formation rules. If we think of agglutinative affixes as non-selective, we have a way of dealing with these results, invoking the idea of equivalence. For a non-selective affix, a lexical base in one language is equivalent to one in another language, obviating the constraints imposed by selection.

A more general account of selection in both syntax and morphology will include distinctions such as the following:

(34) a. *semantic selection*
            syntax: theta-marking
            morphology: the effect of an affix as an operator
        b. *lexical selection*
            syntax: subcategorization (*wait for, angry with*)
            morphology: non-productive affixes
                              conjugation class
                              adjacent affix restrictions
        c. *stratal selection*
            syntax: government constraint on code-mixing
            morphology: native/non-native
        d. *morphophonological selection* (Eng *-er* on two heavy syllables)

Agglutination includes only (34a)-type selection.

The empirical effects of the free morpheme constraint can be accounted for by assuming that:

(a) an affix governs its base, and hence should have the same language index as its base;

(b) this restriction can be obviated if the base is equivalent in categorial status to an element from the language of the affix.

This predicts that the free morpheme constraint can be violated where the morphological rules refer to very general categories, such as verb, noun, etc. i.e. in agglutinative languages, but not when the morphology involves rules specified for language-specific categories such as declension class etc.

Consider once again the Finnish example cited in chapter 2:

(35) Misis K. oli housekeeper-*ina*.
Mrs. K. was   ESS
'Mrs. K. was housekeeper.'

Finnish/English: Poplack, Wheeler, and Westwood 1987: 38)

There is L-marking at the phrasal level (assigning an essive case in a predicative construction), which is not problematic because the noun in (35) is Finnish externally, but there is no L-marking between the case affix and the noun.

We predict that fusional languages are highly resistant to borrowing, since the shapes of the formatives in them are highly interdependent. This prediction has some support, as far as known, although recent results by Budzhak-Jones (1998; see also Budzhak-Jones and Poplack 1997) for Ukrainian–English bilingual discourse point in a different direction. In fusional languages we see the extreme noun/verb asymmetries in borrowability: nouns, which can generally occur uninflected, are frequently borrowed, while verbs are not (Nortier and Schatz 1992). In agglutinative languages, we also find such asymmetries, but still a considerable number of verbs are borrowed. The noun is the equivalent category par excellence, and hence easily borrowable.

Before closing this section, a last remark about the Free Morpheme Constraint. In one sense, it holds absolutely and is never obviated by agglutinative morphology: when code-mixing involves alternation and not insertion. All the reported counter-examples to the constraint (Eliasson, Myers-Scotton, Bentahila and Davies, Backus) involve insertion strategies, and there is no reported case where the alternation point is mid-word, that is to say, involving a switch *A [a / b] B*. Some of the cases mentioned by

Clyne come close, but these are problematic as counter-evidence because of the closeness of the languages studied.

Nonce-borrowing = insertion: Tamil/English

With this background we can tackle the issue of nonce-borrowing versus insertion. In a well-known, densely argued, and highly informative study on Tamil/English code-mixing Sankoff, Poplack and Vanniarajan (1990) defend the notion of nonce-borrowing for cases such as:

(36)   Naan pooyi paaḍuvein [*Hindi song*-ei].
       I go.INF sing.1sg.FU Hindi song-AC
       'I will go and sing a Hindi song.'   (Sankoff, Poplack, and Vanniarajan 1990: 79)

(37)   [Oru *seal*] pooṭṭu koḍuppaanga.
       one seal put.INF give.3pl.FU
       'They will put on the seal and give it.'

(Sankoff, Poplack, and Vanniarajan 1990: 80)

Here *Hindi song* and *seal* are basically assumed to have the status of borrowings, even though they may not be established in the Tamil loan lexicon. The reason is that, were they mixes, they would be violations of the equivalence constraint, given the SOV character of Tamil as opposed to English SVO, and (36) would also violate the Free Morpheme Constraint. In fact, there is a sense in which the equivalence constraint, the nonce-borrowing analysis, and the Free Morpheme Constraint form a coherent circle: if there is nonce-borrowing in Tamil, we have no violation of the Free Morpheme Constraint in (36), and also, there is no violation of equivalence. Thus analysing these cases as nonce-borrowings is crucial to Poplack's overall model (Poplack 1980). I want to claim that an alternative, namely that (36) and (37) are N or N' insertions, is equally plausible, and in fact the preferred analysis. I will do this by dissecting the independent arguments given for the analysis of these cases as nonce-borrowings rather than as code-mixes, and adducing some extra arguments against it.

The first argument given is that English **pronouns** are never inserted. Given the type of borrowability hierarchies, this would be indicative of borrowing, since pronouns rank low on these hierarchies. The argument is weakened by the fact that pronouns are rarely inserted in code-mixing settings where equivalence clashes do not play a role. Thus Myers-Scotton (1993b: 15) only reports two English pronouns out of 328 single elements inserted into Swahili (and this excludes borrowings). Nortier (1990: 141) mentions 6 mixed-in pronouns out of 402 single word insertions in Moroccan Arabic/Dutch code-mixing. Treffers-Daller (1994: 99, 100) gives one inserted pronoun among 4,106 single word switched tokens and 1,139 types in French/Dutch mixing.

Poplack (1980) gives zero cases of mixed-in pronouns for Spanish/English mixing in New York, and Nait M'Barek and Sankoff (1988) report no insertions of pronouns for Moroccan Arabic/French mixing. Thus absence of inserted pronouns is hardly an argument for either code-switching or borrowing.

The second argument given is that there are never any English **determiners**, and other prenominal elements such as demonstratives and quantifiers accompanying the English noun. This can either imply borrowing, as assumed by Sankoff, Poplack and Vanniarajan or insertion of a category smaller than a full determiner phrase (DP), such as NP, the analysis I defend. It is a fact that the English elements are mostly lone nouns, but in informal speech complex noun phrases are infrequent in any case, as shown in Hindle's work (1981). This makes the absence of complex inserted nominal groups understandable.

Third, the English nouns follow roughly the same dative and accusative **case marking** patterns, also quantitatively, as Tamil nouns. Again, this observation, the cornerstone of Sankoff, Poplack, and Vanniarajan (1990) in a sense, is compatible either with a nonce-borrowing or with an NP-insertion analysis, since English noun phrases could be inserted into Tamil Case Phrases, the counterpart of determiner phrases in English.

We can assume that both the absence of English determiners and the presence of Tamil case markers are due to the incompatibility of the English determiner system, involving prenominal separate elements, and the Tamil system, which crucially involves case affixes.

Thus, the three arguments given so far are neutral between the two analyses. There are also some arguments that speak specifically against the nonce-borrowing analysis.

First, the 'borrowed nouns' can be **complex**: *snide remarks, serious subjects, educational system, slacks and blouses, Government of India Scholarship, Hindi songs, Indian women, supernatural being, arranged marriage* (Sankoff, Poplack, and Vanniarajan 1990: 80, passim). While some of these combinations could be treated as lexicalized already in English and, as such, liable to be borrowed as wholes, borrowing processes in general do not involve such combinations with the same frequency as they appear to be present in the material presented in the article. These complex nominals are fully compatible, of course, with an NP-insertion analysis.

Second, nouns can be **pluralized** in the Tamil/English nonce-borrowing materials, as in *snide remarks, serious subjects, movies, Indian women*, etc. Again, sometimes elements are borrowed in a plural form, but then the resulting meaning is either singular or generic. The regular possibility of plural nouns with plural meanings is compatible with N' insertion, but not easily with nonce-borrowing.

Third, there is no unambiguous evidence for productive English full noun phrases inserted into the **subject** position of Tamil sentences. Since there is no equivalence clash involving subjects (both languages have the order subject – verb phrase), we have no reason to expect nonce-borrowing here. With subjects we normally get the same pattern as with objects.

> (38) *Professor* enna *mark*-e eṛuti koḍutaar?
> Professor what mark-AC write.INF give.3sg.PST
> 'What marks did the professor write and give?'
> (Sankoff, Poplack, and Vanniarajan 1990: 89)

That is, determiners tend to be absent. This can be explained through the assumption that null nominative case in Tamil blocks a full English noun phrase.

There are also cases of full English noun phrases, but always sentence-initially and there an alternation analysis is clearly possible or even called for, as with (40) and (41):

> (39) *That originality* illave-ille.
> NEG-EMPH-NEG
> 'That originality is just not there.'

> (40) *Especially young widows* kalyaaṇam paṇṇikka paḍaatu.
> marriage do.RE should.NEG
> 'Especially young widows should not marry.'

> (41) *Even the lowest middle class* ellaarum pooyiduvaa.
> all go.3pl.FU
> 'Even the lowest middle class [sic] will all go.'
> (Sankoff, Poplack, and Vanniarajan 1990: 89)

Notice that here we have a clear A – B pattern and sometimes several English constituents, due to the presence of *especially* and *even*. Furthermore, Sankoff, Poplack, and Vanniarajan note that there is frequent switching between Tamil subjects and English predicates, and thus a switch in the other direction:

> (42) *En nyidi* is very clear.
> my principle
> 'My principle is very clear.'

> (43) *Atu vantu* doesn't bother me.
> that (filler)
> 'That doesn't bother me.'   (Sankoff, Poplack, and Vanniarajan 1990: 88)

Since insertional switching patterns are generally asymmetrical (as in the case of direct objects in Tamil/English switching), the cooccurrence of frequent examples such as (42) and (43) alongside (39)–(41) is an argument for alternation in itself.

The pattern which would crucially help decide against the analysis given here and for nonce-borrowing, namely (44), is not mentioned and presumably absent from the data.

> (44) Adverbial Tamil element *full English subject DP* Tamil verb phrase

This pattern would be predicted to occur since the subject position is the same in both languages: pre-verb phrase, and hence no violation of equivalence and regular code-mixing would be allowed. It would be less likely a case of alternation since there is an A – B – A pattern in this case. To be fair, Sankoff, Poplack, and Vanniarajan mention the fact that given the pro-drop characteristics of Tamil, subjects only occur in 60 per cent of the cases, but cases like (44) should still be there.

Sankoff, Poplack, and Vanniarajan mention that there are English clauses inserted through the use of a Tamil complementizing suffix (presumably leading to a violation of the Free Morpheme Constraint):

> (45) [The system has completely changed]-*nu enakku tooNaratu.*
>   that I-DA feel
> 'I feel that the system has completely changed.'
> (Sankoff, Poplack, and Vanniarajan 1990: 91–2)

The inserted clause is simply integrated into Tamil by the addition of -*nu* 'that'. Given the possibility of insertion in these cases, there is no clear reason why insertion would not occur in (some?, all?) nominal constituents as well.

I conclude that a *prima facie* strong case for nonce-borrowing can be best analyzed as involving NP- (rather than DP-) insertion.

DP- versus NP-insertion: Moroccan Arabic/French (MA/Fr) and Moroccan Arabic/Dutch (MA/Du) switching

I now turn to a case which Nait M'Barek and Sankoff (1988) analyze as NP-insertion: Moroccan Arabic/French. Bentahila and Davies (1983) note the following contrast for MA/F switching:

> (46) a. dak *la chemise*
>   that the shirt
>   b. * dak *chemise*

All relevant examples are of the (46a) type; the (46b) type does not occur.

After Arabic demonstratives and *wahed* 'one' the French article is obligatory in mixes. This type of pattern was the basis for Bentahila and Davies' **subcategorization constraint**: since the demonstrative *dak* subcategorizes for a definite article in Arabic, it also needs one in a mixed constituent. Nait M'Barek and Sankoff (1988: 148) show that this pattern also holds for 91 per cent of the cases in their corpus (and claim that the remaining 9 per cent are true nonce-borrowings). The French pattern led Poplack and Sankoff (1988) and Nait M'Barek and Sankoff (1988) to assume that there is a process of constituent insertion going on in French/Moroccan Arabic switching, rather than of single noun switches. They present examples such as (47) and (48):

(47) Žaw *les demandes.*
      have.arrived the requests
      'The requests have arrived.'

In this example the position of *les demandes* is allowed in Arabic, but not in French.

(48) *le charme* walla [hadik *la particularité* dyal *les Clubs Meds*]
      the charm or that the particularity of the Club Meds
      'The charm or rather the specific character of the Club Meds.'
                                          (Nait M'Barek and Sankoff 1988: 149)

This example resembles (46a) in that *la particularité* follows an Arabic demonstrative. In general, the data given by Nait M'Barek and Sankoff (1988) are insertional in nature: mixed-in nouns and noun phrases are always French, verbs tend to be Arabic.

As Nortier (1990: 199) points out, there is a discrepancy between the way French articles are treated in French noun phrases incorporated into Moroccan Arabic (Bentahila and Davies 1983 and other sources), and the way Dutch articles are treated when Dutch nouns occur in Arabic. The opposite pattern is found in MA/Du switching, where we have (data and analysis by Nortier 1990):

(49) a. * dik *het gesprek*
          this the conversation
      b. dik *gesprek*

Here the (49a) type is absent, the (49b) type abundant. After *wahed* 'one' and the Arabic demonstratives such as *dik*, the Dutch article is forbidden. This contrast will make us look at differences between Dutch and French articles in more detail and reconsider the issue of constituent insertion.

The findings for noun phrases in both language pairs after a demonstrative or a preposition can be summarized as follows (Nortier 1990: 201), where # is the switch site:

(50)					MA/Fr	MA/Du
a.	wahed/dem art # N				yes	yes
b.	wahed/dem # art N				yes	no
c.	wahed/dem # [0] N				no	yes
d.	P	art	#	N	?no	yes
e.	P	#	art	N	yes	no
f.	P	#	[0]	N	no	yes
g.	#	art	N	(subj)	yes	yes
h.	#	art	N	(obj)	yes	yes

A number of hypotheses can be formulated to explain the contrast between Moroccan Arabic/French and Moroccan Arabic/Dutch noun phrase insertions:

A   French le/la *resembles Arabic* l, *Dutch* de/het *does not*

In fact, Heath (1989), in his extremely detailed study of borrowing processes in Moroccan Arabic adopts this position without further reservations. Furthermore, Heath argues, French gender resembles Moroccan Arabic gender sufficiently – both have a masculine/feminine distinction in the singular, but generally not in the plural – for the two systems to map onto each other. Finally, Heath treats the Moroccan definite marker as a prefix, an integral part of nominal morphology, and interacting with gender and number markers.

B   French le/la *is proclitic, Dutch* de/het *is not*

Except in certain poetic styles, Dutch articles, even though unaccented, do not cliticize to a following noun: *de overkant* 'the other side' does not become [*doverkant*]. In French, however, we have [*larbre*] rather than [*le arbre*] 'the tree'. There is evidence from French creoles which points in the direction of cliticization. French articles are somehow treated as prenominal clitics (as is the case with the Arabic determiners themselves), and we do not have a real noun phrase inserted in (46a), but rather a (somewhat complex) single noun. In French creoles often the article is incorporated into the lexical element, hence *lamer* 'sea', etc. In any case, there is no trace of the prenominal article as a morpho-syntactic category.

Spanish articles are not pro-clitic, but French and Spanish resemble each other in many respects, e.g. in their gender systems. Compare Spanish *la alberja* to French *l'auberge* 'the inn', or Spanish *la otra* to French *l'autre* 'the other'. Thus Arabic–Spanish contact phenomena would be very informative with respect to a potential explanation in terms of the pro-clitic nature of

French articles. Unfortunately, no systematic data on Spanish/Arabic code-mixing are available so far. We only have indirect evidence from borrowing.

Nortier (1990) has listed the French and Spanish loans in her corpus, and from her data we can conclude that only one out of ten Spanish loans in Moroccan Arabic has a prefixed *l-*, while 10 out of 33 French loans do. Some examples are given in (51):

(51) a. Spanish loans (1 *l-* out of 10) in Moroccan Arabic

e*t*ru, li*t*ru	litro	litre
skwila	escuela	school
lamba	lámpara	lamp
l-maroki	Marroquí	Moroccan

      b. French loans (10 *l-* out of 33) in Moroccan Arabic

l-kar	car	car
'util	hôtel	hotel
le-franat	freins	brakes
l-bulis	police	police

This is confirmed by data from Heath (1989: 185–6) on Spanish borrowings in the Moroccan Arabic in the northern city of Tetouan. Of the 38 nouns listed in common use, only one involved a reinterpreted Spanish article.

Further evidence comes from Rif Berber, where the Spanish influence has been quite strong and similar adaptation patterns exist as in Moroccan Arabic. Belkacem El Jattari (1994) studied borrowings in Rif Berber, and with respect to their phonological adaptation notes that for Spanish elements in Berber, we have four types of adaptation processes:

(52) a. **single vowel**

ipubri*t*	pobres	poor
apinča	pinchar	pinch
abja*h*i	viaje	trip

      b. **/l/ prefixed**

linka*h*i	encaje	insert, lace
lantina	antena	antena
lin_uffi	enchufe	plug

      c. **/ar/ or /al/ prefixed**

arbumbat	bomba	pump
arri*b*ica	rebeca	sweater
arpakijja*t*	paquete	package
arfusina	oficina	office
al bala	bala	bullet

      d. most frequent: no preceding element

There are only three cases of Spanish loans prefixed with *l*. This can be taken as support for my interpretation of Nortier (1990).

Further support for the proclitic argument comes from the fact that prepositions in Moroccan Arabic are proclitic, and cannot be combined with Dutch articles (while they can with French articles), which do not form a phonological word with the following noun and are not a suitable base for procliticization (cf. (50e), where MA = Moroccan Arabic and DU = Dutch):

(53)   * P(MA) DET(DU) N(DU)

   C French le/la *is obligatory in the noun phrase, Dutch* de/het *is not*
As noted by Nortier (1995), French *le/la* does not disappear in telegraphic style (telegrams, headlines), Dutch *de/het* does. Furthermore, the number of contexts in which Dutch nouns occur without an article includes mass nouns and indefinite plurals. In French, articles are necessary in these cases:

(54) | **Dutch** | **French** | |
       |--------|----------|----------|
       | brood | du pain | 'bread' |
       | mensen | des gens | 'people' |

However, we also need to consider the problem of **indefinites**. Heath makes the important point that the use of the French articles is like those in Arabic rather than French (1989: 34):

(55)   Xdəm-t f-wah.əd *la société d'assurances.*
       I-worked in-a the insurance company
       'I worked in an insurance company.'

Even though the noun phrase is indefinite, the French definite article is used. This makes it difficult to talk about constituent insertion here. Heath's analysis does not work for an example such as:

(56)   Ža *un copain* gallik yallah nšarbu *un pot.*
       has.come a friend 2.has.said let's go let's have a drink
       'A friend has come and has told us to go and have a drink.'
       (Nait M'Barek and Sankoff 1988: 146)

According to Heath (1989: 34) the use of *un copain* rather than *wah.ed le copain*, the Moroccan Arabic structure, is not very common. Also problematic is a case such as:

(57)   l wah.ed *une certaine classe* h.ant walla *le luxe*
       to one a certain class since has.become the luxury
       bezzaf f *les hôtels.*
       much in the hotels
       'Especially for a certain class because there is more luxury in the hotels.'
       (Nait M'Barek and Sankoff 1988: 150)

Here Bentahila and Davies' subcategorization constraint is violated, since *wah.ed* selects a **definite** noun, not an indefinite one.

Though we have no quantitative data, I will assume that (55) is the regular pattern, and that (56) and (57) are somewhat exceptional and possibly reinterpretations of the regular pattern as French influence has increased.

Thus there are three aspects of French articles that may be relevant in explaining the contrast between the mixing patterns involving Dutch and French: French articles resemble Moroccan definite markers, French elements are proclitic, and French articles are obligatorily present in French discourse. It seems French definite articles are reinterpreted as Moroccan Arabic elements in a bilingual stratum of the lexicon, and can hence easily become part of borrowings as well.

From a more formal perspective, I will assume that in French and Dutch the article corresponds to an element of the category D (= determiner), but that in Moroccan Arabic the determiner corresponds to elements such as *wah.ed* 'one' and *dak* 'that'. In contrast, the definite marker would possibly correspond to a subordinate functional category of definiteness/number/gender (DNG) and project a DNG-P. Thus a Moroccan Arabic nominal constituent would look like:

(58) [$_{DP}$ wahed/dak,dik/0 [$_{DNG-P}$ 1 [$_{NP}$ noun]]]

Now Bentahila and Davies' (1983) subcategorization constraint can be phrased in terms of the selection by a D of a DNG-P in the language. French articles are D in French but for various reasons listed above reinterpreted as DNG in Moroccan Arabic. Dutch articles cannot be so reinterpreted. Moroccan Arabic prepositions select an appropriate DP, which cannot be the Dutch one (for instance because the Dutch definite articles *de* and *het* are marked for [± neutral], while *wah.ed* and *dak/dik* are marked for [± feminine], if anything), but it can be one in which the D remains empty, a possibility in Moroccan Arabic as well. French article + noun combinations are interpreted as DNG-Ps, and for Dutch an integration strategy is developed, in which null counts as a DNG. When Dutch nouns become the object of a Moroccan Arabic preposition, we have the following structure:

(59) [$_P$ P [$_{DP}$ 0 [$_{DNG-P}$ 0 [$_{NP}$]]]]

Finally, we have to assume that the possibility of indefinite French noun phrases inserted into Arabic structures results from the reinterpretation of French *un/une* as an indefinite DNG, perhaps on the model of Moroccan Arabic *ši* 'some/any', which does not select a definite noun either (Heath 1989: 21).

We thus have an account of the French insertion cases, and a way of explaining the differences with the Dutch cases. The fact that Myers-Scotton, Jake, and Okasha (1996) did not find cases of double determiners in Arabic/ English mixing supports the analysis here.

Wolof/French and Fongbe/French code-mixing

Poplack and Meechan (1995) analyse data from Wolof/French and Fongbe/ French code-mixing in trying to determine the status of French nominals as borrowings, code-switches, or constituent insertions. They tacitly assume that switching under linear equivalence is the zero option; only when there is linear non-equivalence will speakers resort to nonce-borrowing or constituent insertion, in their analysis, which is extremely careful and detailed. The main focus of their paper is on single French nouns in bilingual Wolof and Fongbe discourse. In this type of discourse, the majority of the nouns come from French in their data: 583 French nouns over 265 Wolof nouns, 608 French nouns over 556 Fongbe nouns. After a distributional analysis, Poplack and Meechan argue that these elements behave as nouns from Wolof and Fongbe, respectively, i.e. as inserted elements or borrowings. The multi-word forms in Poplack and Meechan (1995) are analysed as borrowings (with non-equivalent word orders in Wolof) or as switches (when there are equivalent word orders in Wolof). They concern 75 cases, or 11 per cent of the French nominal elements in Wolof. Similarly, French multi-word fragments in Fongbe amount to 7 per cent of the nominal switches. They are analysed as insertions when their distribution does not resemble that of French, i.e. when there are non-equivalent word orders in Fongbe and French. In fact, the large majority of mixed patterns conforms to the matrix language (i.e. Wolof and Fon) rules. Of the 1,310 French elements in Fongbe and Wolof analysed, both single and multi-word, only one may not have conformed to the matrix language rules.

If we want to reanalyse the data in Poplack and Meechan from an insertional perspective, we have to assume different types of inserted elements, in terms of length and complexity:

(60) a. bare French nouns in Wolof and Fon, assumed to be borrowings
        copine 'friend', *science*
    b. **A+N** and **N de N** combinations in Wolof, assumed to be borrowings
        by Poplack and Meechan
        même âge 'same age'
        tête de liste 'head of list'
    c. **N+A**, **N+A**, **N de N**, **Num+N** combinations in Fon, assumed to be
        lexical insertions by Poplack and Meechan

> *mimétisme inconscient* 'unconscious mimicry'
> *autorisation de principe* 'token permission'
> *quatorze ans* 'fourteen years'
> d. **DET+N+PP** sequences in Wolof, assumed to be code-switches
> *egalité entre hommes et femmes* 'equality between men and women'

In the discussion, Poplack and Meechan mention a number of diagnostic features of the three types:

(61)

	borrowing	insertion	switch
lexicalization	+	−	−
AN order	+		
agreement		+	+
complexity	−		+

However, it is not clear whether these features can be applied in absolute terms. Thus some of the multi-word fragments in Wolof appear to be lexicalized, such as *tête de liste* 'head of list', but it is not clear that none of the multi-word fragments in Fongbe are, as in *autorisation de principe* 'token permission'. Similarly, we find gender agreement in the Fongbe fragments, but it is not clear there is none in the Wolof fragments analysed as borrowings. Similarly, there is a difference in maximal complexity of the multi-word fragments at equivalence and non-equivalence sites in Wolof and in Fongbe, but it is not clear how different the average complexity is. Finally, it is suggested that there is one **N+A** combination in the Wolof material, contrary to what is predicted.

The data given are not explicit enough in this respect to see whether the elements analysed as switches (in Wolof/French code-mixing) had other properties reminiscent of alternation, properties that will be discussed in the next chapter. There is one case given as a true code-switch which cannot be analysed as an insertion in the framework presented here:

(62) Am na *parents* yoo xam nak leegi
have it parents that+you know CONJ now
dañuy jənd *le dictionnaire de rap-là pour au moins*
AUX+they buy DEF dictionary of rap for at least
mən a jeli boys yi.
be able PREP understand young the
'There are some people who buy that rap dictionary to at least be able
to understand the young people.'

(Wolof/French; Poplack and Meechan 1995: 214)

Notice that *le dictionnaire de rap-là* and *pour au moins* are not a single constituent, even though they are adjacent French fragments.

To summarize, the assumption of linear equivalence is a sort of economy assumption: operate as much as possible under one system. The data suggest that there are different degrees of complexity of the inserted elements, which may well be related to different degrees of categorial equivalence of French, Wolof, and Fongbe NPs and DPs. In addition, there may be alternation in the Wolof case, as in example (62). However, the difference between borrowing and insertion is not shown to be more than gradual. The role of linear equivalence may well be much less important than suggested by Poplack and Meechan (1995), that of categorial equivalence crucial.

Papiamentu/Dutch code-mixing in noun phrases

Code-mixing data from bilingual parent–child book-reading sessions, involving the creole language Papiamentu and Dutch, show how nouns can be treated as fully equivalent in two languages. The material was studied by Kook (e.g. 1994) and analysed from the perspective of language choice and code-mixing by Vedder, Kook, and Muysken (1996) and Muysken, Kook, and Vedder (1996). The code-mixing in these sessions (around 25 recordings of the reading of three different books) was analysed as highly insertional.

Parent–child interactions play a crucial role in the incorporation of linguistic borrowings. To some extent the highly innovative language use in parent–child interaction throws light on linguistic change in progress, and in this case on the way Dutch linguistic elements are incorporated into Papiamentu (Haugen 1950; Poplack, Sankoff and Miller 1988). From a related perspective, Drapeau (1994) analyses caretaker speech in a small Montagnais-speaking community in Quebec. Montagnais is a member of the Algonquian language family and has been in contact with French for generations. Drapeau notes 'a major decline in Montagnais lexical skills in the younger generation' due to intensive insertional code-mixing by the caretakers: often French noun phrases and prepositional phrases are inserted into Montagnais clause frames.

Animal names are a school-related item. Often we have referential switching to animals outside the Papiamentu domain, for which the language does not even have a word:

(63) Ta un *marmot*.
      'It is a guinea pig.'

However, Dutch words are used as well when Papiamentu words exist and are widespread.

In table 3.2 (based on Muysken, Kook, and Vedder 1996) the words used for animals are represented. The words for animals in our bilingual corpus are drawn from both the Dutch and the Papiamentu lexicon. To fully

appreciate the data in table 3.2, consider the following paradigm for
Papiamentu and Dutch noun phrases:

(64) a. e mucha   'the child'
      b. e mucha-nan   'the children'
      c. dos/tur mucha(*nan)   'two/all children'

(65) a. de muis   'the mouse'
      b. de muiz-en   'the mice'
      c. twee/alle muiz-cn   'two/all mice'
      d. de muis-je-s   'the little mice'

In both languages the definite determiner (*e* in Papiamentu, *de* in Dutch)
precedes the noun, and plural is marked with a suffix (*-nan* in Papiamentu,
-en or *-s* is Dutch). However, as (64c) and (65c) show, plural is marked in
Dutch when there is a quantifier present, but not in Papiamentu. Finally,
(65d) illustrates the use in Dutch of a diminutive suffix, *-je*. Globally many
more Dutch animal names are used than Papiamentu ones: 187 (3.37 per cent
of all Dutch words) versus 98 (0.79 per cent of all Papiamentu words). There
is little difference here between the three settings. Dutch animal nouns are
more frequent in bare form than Papiamentu ones (108 over 83), but
Papiamentu nouns are more frequent with the plural marker *-nan* (35 over
28). This suggests that the Dutch items are still only partially integrated into
the Papiamentu lexicon.

With Papiamentu quantifiers and numerals we never have *-nan* even with
Dutch nouns, and we never have Dutch plurals (*-en* or *-s*) either. The rule in
Papiamentu, blocking nominal plural after a numeral or a quantifier, is
followed here. This is evidence for our earlier claim that the basic structures
are Papiamentu. With Dutch quantifiers (*alle* 'all' in table 3.2) we always
have Dutch plurals, and with Dutch numerals we have Dutch plurals on
Dutch nouns more often than not (23 versus 13 times). Dutch numerals
sometimes occur with Papiamentu nouns (showing they are quite integrated
into Papiamentu) but then they never trigger either *-nan* or Dutch plural
endings on Papiamentu words, which would be the Dutch pattern.

Dutch determiners or demonstratives never occur with Papiamentu nouns,
Papiamentu determiners quite often with Dutch nouns. This suggests again a
basic pattern in which Dutch nouns are inserted into Papiamentu structures,
but not the reverse. Dutch plurals are sometimes (three times) combined with
-nan. Often Dutch unmarked nouns are used with a plural meaning in generic
contexts, which is the Papiamentu pattern. There are a few odd cases where a
Dutch plural is combined with a Papiamentu plural (*muiz-en-nan*), or a

Table 3.2. *Language choice for animal names, differentiated for grammatical context and morphological shape (based on Muysken, Kook, and Vedder 1996)*

N(Du)	46	muis
N(Pap)	30	raton
DE(Du)-N(Du)(sg)	12	de muis
DE(Pap)-N(Du)(sg)	21	e muis
DE(Du)-N(Pap)(sg)	–	* de raton
DE(Pap)-N(Pap)(sg)	6	e raton
e N(Du)-nan	23	e muis*nan*
e N(Pap)-nan	32	e raton*nan*
N(Du)-pl	16	muiz*en*
N(Du)-pl-nan	1	muiz-*en-nan*
DE(Pap) N(Pap)-pl	* (e)	raton-*en*
Q(Pap) N(Du)(pl)	5	tur muis
Q(Pap) N(Pap)(pl)	11	tur raton
Q(Du) N(Du)-pl	4	alle muiz*en*
Q(Du) N(Pap)	–	* alle raton
NU(Pap) N(Du)	10	sinku muis
NU(Du) N(Du)	10	vijf muis
NU(Du) N(Du)-pl	14	vijf muiz*en*
NU(Pap) N(Pap)	22	sinku raton
NU(Du) N(Pap)	2	vijf raton
NU(Du) N(Pap)-nan	–	* vijf raton*nan*
NU(Du) N(Pap)-pl	–	* vijf raton-*en*
N(Du)-dim-pl	7	muis-*je-s*
e N(Du)-dim-nan	1	e muis-*je-nan*
N(Du)-dim-pl-nan	1	muis-*je-s-nan*
N(Pap)-dim	–	* raton-*tje*
other	33	

Note: N = noun, DE = definite determiner, Q = quantifier, NU = number, Du = Dutch, Pap = Papiamentu, dim = diminutive, pl = plural, sg = singular, nan = Papiamentu plural

Dutch diminutive + plural with *-nan*, as in *muis-je-s-nan*. These are exceptional, however.

These results strikingly confirm Myers-Scotton's (1993b) analysis of insertional code-mixing (although she claims it holds for all code-mixing), where it is assumed that function words and particles must be from the matrix language, in this case Papiamentu. All starred options noted in table 3.2 are prohibited in her model, and indeed were not found in our data. One pattern is exceptional from the perspective of Myers-Scotton's model: there are thirteen cases of the pattern *vijf muis* 'five mouse' in which all elements are

Dutch, but still there is no plural marker, as in Papiamentu. The sequence *vijf muis* should be an embedded language island with the rules of Dutch rather than Papiamentu holding in it.

Subject/object asymmetries, word order, and case-marking: Finnish/English code-mixing

In chapter 2 I analysed the phenomenon of equivalence, both from the linear and the categorial perspective. Here I want to consider the relation between categorial and linear equivalence more empirically. Which notion explains the distribution of noun phrases best? This issue will be discussed on the basis of Finnish/English code-mixing data. The reason for this is the following: in many code-mixing settings, there is either both categorial and linear equivalence (e.g. SVO + bare NPs in Spanish/English code-mixing) or both linear and categorial non-equivalence (SOV vs. SVO + case-marking versus bare NPs in Tamil/English code-mixing). While many languages are both SOV and exhibit overt case-marking, and are thus unrevealing mixing partners for the issue I want to raise, Finnish is SVO **and** has overt case-marking, and should thus provide an interesting contrast to English (showing linear, but not categorial, equivalence). Finnish/English code-mixing in an immigrant setting has been studied in several independent projects, notably Lehtinen (1966), Poplack, Wheeler, and Westwood (1987), and Halmari (1993, 1997).

Lehtinen (1966) based her work on a recorded speech sample of over ten hours (consisting mostly of narratives) from only one speaker, a third generation Finnish–English bilingual immigrant from Minnesota, who was a graduate student in linguistics but had no formal training in Finnish. In addition, she had ample fieldwork experience with immigrant Finnish in general. Lehtinen, a Finland-born bilingual, did the recording herself. Poplack, Wheeler, and Westwood (1987) used naturalistic conversations involving eight first generation Finnish–English bilingual immigrants in Canada, who had arrived in the country as adults. Halmari (1993), finally, used eight-and-half hours of material from two Finnish–English bilingual children, eight and nine years of age, who had arrived in California almost two years before, in addition to judgements of bilingual sentences by fluently bilingual first generation immigrants in California. Given these rather different groups of speakers, the findings in these studies are surprisingly similar.

A first result is that most switches are English bare nouns, often though not always accompanied by a Finnish case-marker:

(66) sitte meni . . . *Kansas*sii
      then I went . . . Kansas.ILL
      'then I went to Kansas . . .'   (Lehtinen 1966: 226)

(67) Rupesin pitämään semmosta *rooming house*a.
      started-1pl to keep such-PAR rooming house-PAR
      'I started to keep a rooming house.'
                                    (Poplack, Wheeler, and Westwood 1987: 45)

(68) Mää aina kerron sille *joke*ja.
      I always tell 3sg-ALL joke-PL-PAR
      'I always tell him jokes.'   (Halmari 1993: 1055)

A second common feature of the three studies is the high incidence of flagging and hesitations. This is particularly the case in Lehtinen's corpus, which admittedly was recorded with a non-fluent bilingual, and in the Canadian material. Poplack, Wheeler, and Westwood show that this is particularly frequent with non-case-marked nouns, but it is prevalent throughout. Reumerman (1996) argues that at least in Lehtinen's data (1966) the elements that were flagged, i.e. preceded by either *semmonen* or *eh* were phonologically and morphologically fully integrated loans.

There is also a difference between the three studies, crucial to the issue I want to raise. First of all, Poplack, Wheeler, and Westwood (1987: 41) note that there are 25 cases of an English direct object following a Finnish verb (out of 154 multi-word switches and 1,192 switches in all). An example is:

(69) Mun vanhin on-nyt alkaa *part-time nursing*
      my oldest is-now starts . . .
      in intensive care.
      'My oldest is- is now starts part-time nursing in intensive care.'
                                    (Poplack, Wheeler, and Westwood 1987: 41)

Halmari, in contrast, claims that the following sentence is judged ungrammatical by fluent bilinguals:

(70) * Minä siivos-i-n *the building.*
      I clean-PST-1sg
      'I cleaned the building.'   (Halmari 1993: 1056)

Of course, one difference here is that in the second case there is a determiner present, but I do not know what the implications of this would be.

The data presented by Lehtinen are not much help here. Lehtinen argues that English nouns and adjectives incorporated into Finnish obligatorily carry a stem formant *i* (if they end in a consonant), except where the appropriate Immigrant Finnish case-marker would be null, in which case *i* is optional (1966: 180). Furthermore, objects in Immigrant Finnish are often marked null (1966: 44–6). Thus it would be difficult to see whether the object was case-marked or not. In any case, I could not find an example in Lehtinen's corpus of an object switch without a Finnish determiner. Above, example (67) was given, and here are two more examples:

(71)   . . . ne ne tee.. teki **se** *hospital*
       . . . they they ma.. make that hospital
       '. . . they made the hospital.'   (Lehtinen 1966: 225)

(72)   . . . muttə ko minä teen **semmone** *long sentence* tiäkkö ja . . .
       . . . but when I make such long sentence ya-know and . . .
       '. . . but when I make a long sentence ya-know and . . .'
                                                           (Lehtinen 1966: 225)

Returning now to the issue of categorial versus linear equivalence, there can be little doubt that this evidence favours categorial equivalence as crucial for Finnish/English. The main point of Poplack, Wheeler, and Westwood (1987) is that the Finnish/English case strongly resembles the Tamil/English case, in that in both nonce-borrowing is the dominant pattern. In contrast to Tamil, word order discrepancies cannot be the main factor leading to the adoption of the nonce-borrowing strategy.

I will interpret the Finnish/English case as follows. The typological differences between the languages in terms of case-marking and agreement lead to very limited possibilities for inserting a DP, which is complicated further by the phonological differences between the languages. Nonetheless, case and verb agreement is suffixal and can be added to English nouns/ adjectives and verbs, respectively, once these are morphologically integrated into Finnish. Nouns are often incorporated into Finnish determiner phrases through the use of a Finnish determiner, which carries the case-marking.

Further research will have to establish whether we have adjunction, and hence a form of alternation, internal to the noun phrase here. Consider a case such as:

(73)   . . . se oli semmosen *typical general store* tiäkkö, ja . . .
       . . . it was of-such typical general store ya-know, and . . .
                                                           (Lehtinen 1966: 182)

It may be that the true head of the predicate noun phrase here is Finnish *semosen*, with the English expression *typical general store* simply adjoined, without any evidence that it is integrated into the noun phrase. Recall that in Finnish itself there is agreement between the determiner and the head. This would make some of the Finnish 'dummy determiner' similar to the dummy verb patterns discussed in chapter 7.

There is a tendency towards the exploitation of null marking, where possible. Finally, alternation is frequently relied upon, through the use of pauses and flagging elements. The cases reported by Poplack, Wheeler, and Westwood of true verb/object switches will need to be interpreted as alternations. Evidence for this could come from their being flagged and in a clause-marginal position. However, the data given are not sufficient to determine whether this is indeed the case.

The Finnish/English data suggest that the type of equivalence in the alternation case is much less restrictive than in the insertion case. What we have is probably some kind of semantic compatibility requirement along the lines of selection restrictions, but no syntactic compatibility in terms of case-marking and agreement. Through morphosyntactic restrictions, code-mixing possibilities involving one language pair are more limited than those involving another language pair. One way to circumvent these limitations is through alternation strategies, discussed in the next chapter.

Conclusion and discussion

This concludes a brief survey of patterns of NP-insertion. I hope to have made it plausible that insertion can take place at various levels. Most common are insertions of bare nouns and bare noun phrases. When determiner phrases are mixed, recourse may be taken to alternation, if there is no categorial equivalence at the DP level, as in the case of Finnish/English code-mixing.

Insertional code-mixing is argued to fall under a very general constraint, that can be formalized as:

(74) $*[_{X'} \ldots X \ldots Y \ldots]$, where Y is a sister of X but cannot be licensed by X

Constituent Y cannot be licensed by X if it does not have the appropriate features. This is a general constraint on insertion in syntax, but it is also operative in insertional code-mixing.

4
Alternation

Alternation is very common strategy of mixing, in which the two languages present in the clause remain relatively separate. It can be represented as in:

(1)   A . . . B

However, the precise relation between A and B remains rather undefined, and indeed may not be easily captured in one single principle. I will present various perspectives on the way in which (1) may be achieved, but I will begin by considering the types of alternation we find in French/Dutch code-mixing in Brussels (Treffers-Daller 1994), a data set which is characterized by a high incidence of alternation structures. Then I turn to two general problems: mixing involving conjunctions and prepositions, and the transition point in alternation when the word order of the two languages is parallel. With respect to the functional elements I will argue that these can be incorporated into a language via alternation; thus there is a second path for lexical borrowing, in addition to the insertional path described in chapter 3. With respect to the transition point, I will argue that this must be defined in quite superficial terms.

A first typology of alternation structures: Brussels Dutch/French mixing

French/Dutch code-mixing in Brussels (Treffers-Daller 1994) has a number of features typical of alternational mixing. These I will illustrate one by one.

When we assume that a speaker switches languages or varieties altogether, we can easily expect **several constituents** in sequence to be switched, since sentence planning takes place in an entirely different language after the switch. Treffers-Daller found that 17 out of 141 switches (12 per cent) involved several constituents. Some examples:

(2)   Je dois je dois glisser *[daan vinger] [hier]*.
      'I have to insert/my finger here.'   (Treffers-Daller 1994: 213)

(3) Je téléphone à Chantal, he, *[meestal]* *[voor commieskes te doen]* *[en
eten]*.
'I call Chantal, hm,/mostly to go shopping and eat.'

(Treffers-Daller 1994: 213)

A second feature concerns **non-nested** A . . . B . . . A sequences (where *A*
and *B* refer to languages). Consider mixes of the A . . . B . . . A type. When
the switched string is preceded *and* followed by elements from the other
language, elements structurally related, it is probably a case of insertion, as
was argued in chapter 3. However, when the switched string is preceded *and*
followed by elements from the other language, elements not structurally
related, it is likely to be a case of alternation.

(4) Bij mijn broer *y a un ascenseur* en alles.
'At my brother's place,/there is an elevator/and everything.'

(Treffers-Daller 1994: 204)

(5) Ik heb gehoord van de post he, *que ça pourrait être une histoire* van
racket.
'I have heard of the postal service hm,/that that could be a story/of
blackmail.' (Treffers-Daller 1994: 199)

In these non-nested a b a examples, the two Dutch fragments have no
syntactic relation.

Yet further criteria are **length** and **complexity**. The more words a switched
fragment contains, the more likely that it is alternation. From a psycholinguistic perspective it is plausible that activation of a matrix language
decreases as the number of words in the intrusive language is larger.
Similarly, the more complex structure a switched fragment contains, the
more likely that it is a case of alternation rather than insertion. The fragment
parce que c'est comment dirais-je c'est pas antique c'est classé in (6) is a full
sentence, and hence it would be difficult to treat it like an insertion or a case
of congruent lexicalization.

(6) Ze gaan dat arrangeren van binnen voor appartementen te doen *parce
que c'est comment dirais-je c'est pas antique c'est classé*.
'They are going to arrange that inside to make appartments,/because it
is, how shall I say it, it is not antique it's classified.'

(Treffers-Daller 1994: 204)

Alternational patterns often show some diversity of elements switched.
Content words such as nouns and adjectives are likely to be insertions,
while **discourse particles** and **adverbs** may be alternations. Sentence
Grammar and Discourse Grammar may be relatively autonomous with
respect to each other; there is very frequent language choice disparity
between these systems. In her chapter 7 Treffers-Daller devotes considerable

attention to **syntactically unintegrated discourse markers**. In (7a–c) the relevant paradigm is presented. The borrowed adverb *pertang* 'still' does not trigger verb second when it occurs in initial position, as in (7a). This would be expected if it were inserted into a Dutch structure. Therefore examples such as (7b) do not occur in the corpus. Still, the Dutch equivalent of *pertang*, *toch*, does trigger verb second, in examples such as (7c).

(7) a. *Pertang* **ze hadden** gezeit dat ik die mocht hebben.
   'Still/they had said I could have it.'
   b. * *Pertang* **hadden ze** gezeit dat ik die mocht hebben.
                               [non-occurring]
   c. *Toch* **hadden ze** gezeit dat ik die mocht hebben.
                               [constructed]
                               (Treffers-Daller 1994: 91)

We can argue that the difference between (7a) and (7c) is due to the fact that *toch* in (7c) is inserted, and *pertang* in (7a) simply adjoined.

Parallel to *pertang*, the French discourse marker *donc* 'thus' is used. While generally it does not trigger verb second, as in (8), there are occasional examples where it does, as in (9):

(8) Ge moet gene schrik hebben, maar *donc* **ze hebben** mij gevraagd.
   'You need not be afraid, but so they [have] asked me.'
                               (Treffers-Daller 1994: 178)

(9) Mijnen man is gestorven on veertig jaar *donc* **ha 'k** geen recht voor geen pensioen te krijgen.
   'My husband died when he was forty, so I didn't have the right to get a pension.'   (Treffers-Daller 1994: 177)

In Brussels Dutch, French adverbs such as *donc* 'thus', *d'abord* 'first', *d'ailleurs* 'for the rest', *pertang* 'still' do not trigger verb second (data and analysis from Treffers-Daller 1994):

(10) *D'ailleurs* ik geloof dat alleman daar een bril moeten dragen heeft.
   'For the rest/I believe that everyone had to wear glasses there.'

Dutch initial adverbs such as *nu* 'now' do trigger verb second, in contrast with (10). Thus it may be the case that there is a special kind of syntax in mixed contexts. More likely, however, is that the French-origin adverbs occur 'dangling from' the clause, in a left-dislocated position. We would not have a special kind of syntax, but rather extra-sentential mixing, involving the non-integration of borrowed elements.

Treffers-Daller (1994: 99–104) considers both French mixing in Brussels Dutch and Dutch mixing in Brussels French. Here an asymmetry becomes apparent. In Brussels French only 0.8 per cent of the nouns are of Dutch origin (28 out of 3,419 tokens), while for interjections this is 2.5 per cent (63

Table 4.1. *Number, percentage of total number of borrowings, and type–token ratio (TTR) of French words in Brussels Dutch (Treffers-Daller 1994)*

	#	%	TTR
nouns	2329	58.4	2.9
interjections	496	12.4	15.0
adverbs	388	9.7	14.4
adjectives	362	9.0	4.3
main verbs	353	8.9	2.9
conjunctions	33	0.8	3.3
other	27	0.6	–

out of 2,499 tokens). Interjections are in fact the only type of Dutch element which represents more than 1 per cent of the corresponding category in Brussels French. In Brussels Dutch, the reverse holds. For French single words in Brussels Dutch the token hierarchy in table 4.1 is given. French loans constitute 17.7 per cent of the Brussels Dutch nouns (2,329 out of 13,179), and French interjections 6.8 per cent (496 out of 7,258) of the Brussels Dutch set. So within Brussels there is a tremendous asymmetry (Treffers-Daller 1995): the influence of French on Dutch is much more massive than the reverse. Nonetheless, this asymmetry affects nouns much more than interjections. If we assume that nouns are borrowed through insertion and interjections through alternation, it is clear that insertional mixing is unidirectional and involves a matrix/non-matrix asymmetry, while alternational mixing is bidirectional.

Consider now the phenomenon called **tag**-switching or **extra-sentential** or **emblematic** switching (Poplack 1980). Tags and interjections are often mixed in from another language. An example is *alors* 'well' (similar to *pertang* in this respect):

(11) *Alors*, dat . . . ik zou het niet voor de tweede keer willen doen, hoor.
      'Well,/that . . . I wouldn't want to do it a second time, really.'
      (French/Dutch data recorded in Amsterdam by J. Treffers-Daller)

An example with a Dutch tag is:

(12) Aller à l'hôpital *toch niet*?
      'Going to the hospital,/ you don't mean?'   (Treffers-Daller 1994: 213)

This type is quite frequent in the Brussels corpus.

We can also consider the **structural position** of the switch: if the switch takes place at a major clause boundary, alternation is a plausible option. Treffers-Daller (1994) proposes the following preliminary hierarchy for mixability of constituents, which she then sets out to refine and give an empirical basis, using a probabilistic approach. Of all the possible subjects, relatively few are in a different language from their predicate, etc.:

(13) coordinated NPs/PPs   *switched more*
      dislocated NPs/PPs
      adverbial PPs/NPs
      before subordinate clauses
      predicative NPs/APs/possessive PPs
      subject or object NPs and clauses
      indirect questions   *switched less*

The fact that Treffers-Daller's material conforms to the hierarchy in (13) confirms my analysis of the Brussels bilingual corpus as basically alternational.

The structural position of alternational switches can also be seen in terms of **peripherality**: the distinction between clause-central and clause-peripheral code-mixing. Is the mixing point at the heart of the clause, or rather marginal to the core proposition? When the switched element is at the periphery of a sentence, alternation is a clear possibility. Many examples are given here of peripheral switches. Often, a switch involves a left- or right-dislocated element, or two conjoined clauses. These cases clearly qualify as alternations.

Some examples from Treffers-Daller's study (1994) make it apparent that many cases of mixing involve **adverbial modification**, the use of an alien adverb, (14), or an adverbial phrase, (15):

(14) En *automatiquement* klapte gij ook schoon Vlaams.
      'And/automatically/you would switch to standard Flemish.'
                                                    (Treffers-Daller 1994: 178)

(15) Je suis au balcon *op mijn gemakske zo* en train de regarder les étoiles.
      'I am on the balcony/at my ease thus/watching the stars.'
                                                     (Treffers-Daller 1994: 29)

A second important type of peripheral alternation is **coordination**, either phrasal, (16), or clausal, (17):

(16) Nous on parle français le flamand *en de hele boel.*
      'We speak French, Flemish/and all the rest.'   (Treffers-Daller 1994: 207)

(17) Nadine est née au mois d'avril *en dan in de maand oktober heb ik een winkel opengedaan in ...*
      'Nadine was born in April/and then in October I opened a shop in . . .'
                                                     (Treffers-Daller 1994: 30)

In (18) we have a **clefted** Dutch element, followed by a French clause:

(18) *'T is dat* que j'ai dit à madame.
      'That's/what I told the lady.'   (Treffers-Daller 1994: 30)

In (19) and (20) we have a **fronted** French object, and the remaining Dutch clause contains a verb in second position, the expected word order:

(19) *Le français de Bruxelles* **spreek** ik. [verb second]
'Brussels French/I speak.' (Treffers-Daller 1994: 92)

(20) *Un risque de condensation* **heb** je. [verb second]
'A condensation risk/you have.' (Treffers-Daller 1994: 92)

The occurrence of Dutch word order is indicative of insertion rather than alternation here: overall, Dutch patterns are followed. This contrasts with the cases discussed earlier involving *pertang*. However, the fronting without a pragmatic effect of focussing is suggestive of an alternational pattern. The switch occurs in a clause-peripheral position.

Examples (21) and (22) are two cases of **left-dislocation**. The fronted switched elements are referred to again in the rest of the clause: *ze* 'they' in (21) and *c'est* 'that is' in (22):

(21) *Les étrangers*, ze hebben geen geld, hè?
'The foreigners,/they have no money, huhm?' (Treffers-Daller 1994: 207)

(22) *Awel white spirits*, en français c'est des spirits.
'Well methylated spirits,/in French that is spirit.' (Treffers-Daller 1994: 213)

In (23) there are two switched **right-dislocated** elements, *Tino Rossi* and *moi* 'me', that are anticipated in the main clause with *ik* 'I' and *daarvan* 'of him':

(23) Ik moet daarvan niet hebben, *de Tino Rossi, moi.*
'I don't like him, /Tino Rossi, myself.' (Treffers-Daller 1994: 209)

The following example can also be interpreted as a case of right-dislocation:

(24) D'r zit me hier *une femme qui n'est pas drôle.*
'Here there is/a woman who is not funny.' (Treffers-Daller 1994: 224)

The postposed subject is anticipated by *d'r* 'there'.

An important distinction relevant to alternation mixing is that between **smooth** mixing, in which the transition between the two languages is seamless, as in (24), and **flagged**, specially marked, mixing, as in (25). The latter type characterizes alternation.

(25) Tu sais, l'affuteur de scies **hein**, *daan gink bij die beenhouwers, de zager.*
'You know, the knife-grinder eh,/he went to the butchers, the sawyer.'
(Treffers-Daller 1994: 266)

In this example the discourse marker *hein* 'he' separates the two languages, French and Dutch; in (26) it is *hè* 'huh', in (27) *euh*, and in (28) a pause:

(26) Ze hebben altijd zo'n kop, **hè**, *tête carrée.*
'They have always such a head, huh,/square head.' (Treffers-Daller 1994: 204)

(27) Daar zetten ze **euh** *des barrières.*
'There they put up eh/barriers.' (Treffers-Daller 1994: 204)

(28) Ma ma porte **[PAUSE]** *was in brand.*
      'My my door . . ./was burning.'   (Treffers-Daller 1994: 206)

Similar cases of flagging have been reported for French/English code-mixing in Ottawa in the Poplack (1985) corpus. If the switch is flagged, alternation between codes is a plausible option.

If a switched fragment forms a constituent selected by an element in the fragment in the other language, insertion or congruent lexicalization are good possibilities. If not, i.e. when there is **absence of selection**, alternation is a plausible option. From the high incidence of adverbial elements in the Brussels corpus it is clear that indeed many switches involve non-selected elements.

Many researchers have pointed out that code-mixing sometimes results from **correction** or self-repair:

(29) Et comme ça on est bien eh *perfect tweetalig.*
      'And like that one is really eh/perfectly bilingual.' (Treffers-Daller 1994: 209)

Since the flow of speech is interrupted and the sentence structure is not preserved, there is good reason to assume that we have alternation in these cases.

This concludes the preliminary typology of alternation constructions based on Treffers-Daller's work on Brussels Dutch/French code-mixing. The data in Treffers-Daller (1994) for Brussels show, I have argued, many patterns indicative of alternational code-mixing:

(30) several constituents switched
      non-nested mixing
      long switches
      complex switching
      adverbs and discourse particles switched
      emblematic or tag-switching
      peripheral switches
        adverbial modification
        coordination
        clefting
        fronting
        left-dislocation
        right-dislocation
      non-selected switches
      flagging
      correction and self-repair

Not all mixing in the Brussels corpus is clearly alternational, however. There are several cases that suggest patterns of insertion and congruent lexicalization. Consider first of all cases of insertion in a verb phrase such as:

(31)   Mais non, hij [gaat *au premier*].
      'But no, he goes/to the first.'   (French/Dutch; Treffers-Daller 1994: 223)

(32)   On est en train de [se battre *voor de huishuren af te laten slagen*].
      'We are busy fighting/to lower the rents.'
                                  (French/Dutch; Treffers-Daller 1994: 220)

Treffers-Daller (1994) also gives two examples of mixes between a preposition and a noun phrase:

(33)   en [*malgré* wat al] was er toch plezier.
      'and/in spite of/everything it was fun.'
                                  (French/Dutch; Treffers-Daller 1994: 191)

(34)   Na de match zeggen ze per exempel, [lijk *le premier goal de chose là d'Anderlecht*].
      'After the match they say, for instance, like/the first goal of what's its name, Anderlecht.'   (French/Dutch; Treffers-Daller 1994: 220)

In the Brussels data dislocated switches and switches with hesitation markers are frequent, but no true dummy forms like 'thing' or 'like' (see below) are found.

In two cases it seems there is an inserted verb phrase or small clause: French in (35), and Dutch in (36):

(35)   *Allez*, laat *marcher le bazar alors*.
      'Well, let/it happen.'   (Treffers-Daller 1994 : 112)

(36)   Mon mari a dit que je devais venir ici *een leer halen*.
      'My husband said that I should come here/to get a ladder.'
                                  (Treffers-Daller 1994 : 214)

We find a few cases of ragged mixing, which I will argue in the next chapter to be a diagnostic for congruent lexicalization:

(37)   A la machine je ne connais rien [*er aan*] [*doen*].
      At the machine I not know nothing there to do
      'At the machine I cannot/do anything.'   (Treffers-Daller 1994 : 214)

In (37) the French verb *connaître* 'know a fact or person' is used with the meaning 'be able to', as if it were the Dutch verb *kunnen* 'can'.

(38)   Ik had [de *chou rave*] [*en horreur*].
      I had the kohlrabi in horror
      'I hated kohlrabi.'   (Treffers-Daller 1994 : 214)

In (38) there is the additional complication that the French noun phrase *de chou rave* has a Dutch article, *de*, which is however used in the French way since in Dutch generic nouns do not have an article. Thus the borderline between French and Dutch is fuzzy here. However, evidence such as these two cases for phenomena related to congruent lexicalization is infrequent in this corpus.

Further properties of alternational code-mixing: embedding in discourse, doubling, and dummy insertion

Several properties of alternation cannot be easily illustrated on the basis of the published data from the Brussels corpus.

Embedding in discourse

So far, we have only considered sentence-internal criteria. However, the **embedding in discourse** can also be indicative of the type of mixing. Consider a mixed clause starting in language A and ending in language B. If the preceding utterance is in A, and the following clause is in B, alternation is a plausible analysis, since across the turn boundary a language is maintained. An example that illustrates this line of argumentation is the following interchange from the data collected by Li Wei in the Tyneside Chinese community:

(39) A: Yeo hou do yeo *contact*.
       We have many/contacts.
    G: *We always have opportunities* heu xig kei ta dei fong
       We always have opportunities/to get to know people
       gao wui di yen.
       from other churches.   (Chinese/English; Milroy and Li Wei 1995: 147)

While *contact* in A's line is probably an insertion (it is somewhat integrated in not showing English plural marking), the English stretch at the beginning of G's turn could be thought of as triggered by the earlier English form, and as an alternation with respect to the rest of the turn that follows.

Doubling

There are no cases of true doubling reported by Treffers-Daller (1994), presumably because of the typological similarities between French and Dutch. Below we will see numerous cases of doubling involving other language pairs. Finnish–English adpositions are sometimes **doubled** or repeated in both languages in mixed clauses. An example is:

(40) Mutta se oli *kidney*-sta *to aorta*-**an.**
     but it was kidney-from to aorta-to
     'But it was from the kidney to the aorta.'
          (Finnish/English; Poplack, Wheeler, and Westwood 1987: 54)

Here both the English **pre**position *to* and the Finnish **post**position -*an* occur.

104

Doubling can be best seen as indicative of alternation, since it involves an adjustment in the planning of the sentence.

Nishimura (1986: 139) mentions a number of interesting cases of doubling in Japanese/English code-mixing:

(41) about two pounds *gurai*
                    about
     'about two pounds'

(42) for Sean *ni*
           for
     'for Sean'

(43) become *techi ni narao*
             tight become
     'become tight'

In all cases the construction starts out in English, the VO or right-branching language, and turns into Japanese, the OV or left-branching language. The reverse order does not occur.

Evidence that there must be a syntactic break somewhere comes from doubling examples where the doubled elements are not semantically parallel:

(44) You should see his *karada kinochi warui n da.*
                      body appearance awful-is
     'You should see his bodily appearance, it's awful.'

The stretch *karada kinochi* 'body appearance' functions as the object of *see* and is modified by *his*, but at the same time it is the subject of the Japanese predicate phrase *warui n da* 'is awful'.

Flagging and dummy insertion

Flagging has been analysed as a major strategy in French/English code-mixing by Poplack (1985) and in Finnish/English code-mixing by Poplack, Wheeler, and Westwood (1987). However, flagging is not a unitary notion. In Finnish/English something different appears to be going on: the insertion of dummy elements. An example is:

(45) Oli oikein **niin kuin** *latest.*
     was really like
     'It was really like the latest.'
                              (Finnish/English; Poplack, Wheeler, and Westwood 1987: 45)

The semantically empty element *niin kuin* 'like' signals that there will be a different language.

Semantically empty Finnish nominal dummy determiners, such as *sem-monen* 'such', also occur in:

> (46) me teki semmonen *hay stack* ja . . .
> we made such hay stack and . . .
> 'We made a hay stack and . . .'   (Lehtinen 1966: 225)
>
> (47) Siellä oli semmonen *river*.
> there was such river
> 'There was a river.'   (Halmari 1993: 1062)

In the latter case, Halmari claims, the determiner would be absent in a Finnish monolingual sentence (see also Lehtinen's remarks about the use of *se*; 1966: 175). Halmari interprets such determiners as neutralizers, marking the whole noun phrase as Finnish, while Poplack, Wheeler, and Westwood treat them as a type of flagging device.

While true cases of flagging can be seen as revealing the hesitation of speakers to mix intra-sententially, as in French/English or French/Dutch mixing (perhaps due to strong pressures to produce monolingual, pure sentences or, to use Grosjean's terms, stay in the monolingual mode), the other cases of dummy word insertion, like Finnish/English, can be seen as showing that flagging helps overcome conflicts in linearization patterns: from left to right in English and right to left in Finnish.

Functional elements: discourse-markers, conjunctions, adpositions

Sentence grammar and Discourse grammar (governing the distribution of conversational particles) may be relatively autonomous; there is very frequent language choice disparity between these systems (cf. De Rooij 1996). Here I want to argue that in addition to the insertional route, sketched in the previous chapter, the alternational route words may also allow verbs to be borrowed, initially as adjoined elements similar to discourse markers. Via this route, conjunctions and adpositions may enter a language. Three cases involving an Amerindian language and Spanish will be discussed (see also Suarez 1983 and Stolz and Stolz 1995): the Mexican Otomanguean languages Popoloca and Otomí, and the Andean language Quechua. Then discourse markers in Moroccan Arabic/Dutch code-mixing will be reviewed.

Popoloca

In Veerman-Leichsenring (1991) Popoloca/Spanish code-mixing in Popoloca de Mezontla is illustrated, a group of eleven villages near Tehuacán in the state of Puebla, Mexico. The Spanish elements in the Popoloca texts presented can be split up into the broad categories of content words and function words. The borrowed content words have a quite specific distribution, depending on the topic of the text they occur in.

What is striking, however, is the bare fact that the number of function words borrowed (in tokens) is not much below that of content words (tokens 172 vs. 131; types 79 vs. 42). In general, numbers of function words borrowed are much below content words, as is clear from the borrowability hierarchies discussed in the previous chapter. To take a simple example, Treffers-Daller (1994: 99, 179) shows that in Brussels Dutch (taking the category of function words to include adverbs except for the *-ment* class, *juste* 'precisely', and adverbially used adjectives) the proportion is 3,263/725 (four and a half times as much) on the token level and 1,008/79 (over twelve times as much) on the type level. Facts for Strasbourg (Gardner-Chloros 1991) and Ottawa (Poplack, Sankoff, and Miller 1988) are quite similar to those for Brussels.

The fact that there is this large difference between Popoloca and the other cases cited suggests that the borrowing process itself may have different features in the Popoloca case for some categories. For interjections the language settings may be comparable. The latter are also a frequently borrowed category in the Brussels case: while in the native lexicon interjections constitute only 5 per cent of the tokens, in the borrowed lexicon they constitute over 12 per cent. This may be explained by assuming that interjections are borrowed via alternation, and that this is also a productive route. In the Brussels case conjunctions and prepositions are not borrowed very much (together they constitute 1 per cent of the borrowed tokens); it is here that Popoloca is different with 76 out of a total of 303 borrowed tokens (25 per cent), and I want to propose that the difference lies in the fact that these categories are also borrowed through alternation rather than insertion in Popoloca.

Several arguments may be adduced for this claim. First, of all, sometimes we have **doubling**:

(48) Cùnda nge: thèé ná ngu: karru nà *para iši:* me . . .
     have-1 that PR-look.for-1ex one car for that then . . .
     'We have to look for a car so that then . . .' (Veerman-Leichsenring 1991: 393)

(49) Mé t?àyá-ša: ná nda? khí *para iši:* k?ué-k?iá ná.
     thus cart-INS-1pl water far for that IM-drink-1pl
     'Thus we carted the water from afar in order to drink it.'
     (Veerman-Leichsenring 1991: 400)

Here the Spanish preposition/conjunction *para* 'for' is combined with the Popoloca conjunction *i:ši:* 'that', even though either could have been used (Veerman-Leichsenring 1991). Doubling in itself suggests a paratactic structure.

Second, notice that *para* is **external** to *i:ši:*, with respect to the complement clause. This external doubling is an extra argument for alternation. The

107

Spanish element is simply added or adjoined to the clause here; adjunction is always external to a constituent.

Third, all or most of the borrowed conjunctions and prepositions are **not equivalent** to Popoloca elements, as becomes clear from Veerman-Leichsen-rings grammatical description. Thus, there could not be insertion, since it is not clear what would be the site of insertion, unless the Spanish elements were dramatically restructured.

Otomí/Spanish (Hekking 1995)

Hekking (1995) has done a very detailed study of a language related to Popoloca, within the Otomanguean language family, Otomí, as spoken in the Mexican state of Querétaro. The same arguments can be given for the borrowing of Spanish conjunctions and prepositions in Otomí as for Popoloca. Hekking and Muysken (1995), in a comparative study, show that the proportion of borrowed function words of all borrowings is much higher for Otomí than for Quechua. Furthermore they argue that on the whole the borrowed categories are not present in the same way in Otomí, and it is also clear that there is extensive external doubling with semantically related but structurally dissimilar Otomí elements.

In (50) Spanish *pa* precedes Otomí *dige*, both roughly meaning 'for'; *dige pa* is excluded.

(50) När hyokungú bi hoku 'nar ngú **pa dige** ar nzöyö
DETsg RC-make-house PR3 make Insg INDsg house **for for** DET.
delegate   * **dige pa**
'The mason builds a house for the delegate.'   (Hekking 1995: 159)

In the following examples Spanish *komo* 'like' precedes an Otomí element - *ngu* or *jangu* 'like':

(51) Ya tsoho jwei **komo-ngu** 'nar nhñe.   * **ngu komo**
DETpl star shine like-like INDsg mirror
'The stars shine like a mirror.'   (Hekking 1995: 160)

(52) Yoogo'ä hingi pa kor ntogebojä, ho gi mpefi, **komo jangu** di pöje?
why NEG-PR2 go with-PR2 ride-iron where PR2 work like-like PR1
go-1ex   * **jangu komo**
'Why don't you ride your bicycle to work like we do?' (Hekking 1995: 167)

We also have cases of the temporal conjunctions *asta* 'until' and *kwando* 'when' preceding an Otomí temporal linking element:

(53) **Asta nu'bu** da zor tsi 'ye, ja ga pot'i.   * **nu'bu asta**
until when FU3 RC-arrive-DETsg DIM rain, make FU1 sow
'When the rains come, I will sow.'   (Hekking 1995: 170)

(54) **Kwando nu'bu̱** hinti ja ar 'be̱fi, a bese hñunta ya ndo̱ o ya 'ñoho . . .

                                                * **nu'bu̱ kwando**

when when nothing be DETsg work, sometimes gather DET-PL
husband or DET-PL man
'When there is no work at all, sometimes the husbands or men gather
and . . .'
                                                           (Hekking 1995: 170–1)

Finally, the Spanish complementizer *ke* 'that' is doubled sometimes in
relative clauses:

(55) Ja 'bu̱war sei **ke nä'ä** ngi ödi.   * **nä'ä ke**

       be be-LO.CIS DETsg pulque that that CPR2 ask
       'Here is the *pulque* that you asked for.'   (Hekking 1995: 168)

In all cases, only the order Spanish element–Otomí element occurs, never the
reverse. It should be understood that there are other sentences in which either
the Spanish or the Otomí elements occur, or in which the linkage is understood from the context and not overtly expressed.

Quechua/Spanish

A preliminary analysis of the code-mixes in Spanish/Quechua bilingual songs
showed not unfamiliar patterns of distribution: frequent switches at the
fringe of the clause, including exclamations, quotes, persons adressed. Within
the clause, frequent mixes involving adverbial prepositional phrases. Important from the perspective of this chapter is the phenomenon of doubling,
frequent in Quechua/Spanish code-mixing.

    In three cases Spanish prepositions are borrowed, which may be nearly
impossible in spoken Quechua, which has only postpositions and case
suffixes. Two cases involve doubling. In (56), taken from a bilingual
Quechua–Spanish song from Peru, we find borrowing of *disdi* 'since, from' in
a couplet, and the occurrence of the same preposition *desde* in a mixed line of
the following couplet:

(56) *disdi* warma-**manta**   'from childhood on
       from child-ABL
       yana-yuq ka-na-y-paq   to have a lover
       lover-with be-NOM-1sg-for
       [*desde su palacio*]   from its palace
       gubirnu kamachikamun   the government commands'
                              (Quechua/Spanish; Escobar and Escobar 1981: 123)

In the first line, *disdi* doubles with the Quechua case suffix *-manta* 'from'.
Consider now a similar example, where *para* 'for' doubles with Quechua
benefactive case *-paq*.

(57) sipas kahtan nini, manas kuraqtachu
    'I want the girl, not the oldest daughter'
    para paya-**paq**-qa, wasi-y-pi-pas ka-n-mi
    for old woman-for-TO, house-1sg-LO-INDEF be-3–AF
    'as for old women, those I have at home'

Since the third borrowed preposition, *kuntra* 'against', is used adverbially, it need not concern us here. We can analyse these fragments as cases where the Spanish preposition is simply added onto the Quechua syntactic structure, as a modifier, without creating structure of its own.

Similar issues arise with conjunctions. In Quechua coordination and subordination are generally expressed through enclitics. In addition there are a few sentence-final subordinating particles. In Spanish all sentence-linking is done through sentence-initial elements. As in many Amerindian languages, coordinating conjunctions are borrowed freely. An example of such a borrowed conjunction is *piru* 'but':

(58) hina waqachun, hina ripuchun   'let him cry, let him go
    piru ama nuqaq sutiypichun   **but** not in my name'

In (59), finally, we have the Spanish subordinating conjunction *si* 'if', doubling with the sentence-final Quechua conjunction *chayqa* 'that-TO':

(59) *si*-chus munawanki **chay-qa**   'if you love me
    if-DUB want-1O-2 that-TO
    si-chus waylluwanki **chay-qa**   if you care for me
    if-DUB want-1O-2 that-TO
    en prueba de tu cariño   as proof of your affection
    kay kupata tumay   drink this cup'

The conjunction *si* always occurs with the indefinite enclitic -*chus*.

If coordinating elements can be seen as involving a discourse strategy, then we can summarize that the introduction of Spanish conjunctions is either neutralized through doubling (as with *si*) or involves discourse particles. An interesting issue raised by the Quechua/Spanish data is the grammaticalization of adverbs and parentheticals as discourse markers. A potentially drastic integration into Spanish is constituted by the use of Spanish elements such as sentence-introducing adverbs as conjunctions. In (60) *siguru* 'certain' occurs, and in (61) *akasu* 'perhaps, as if':

(60) *siguru* manaña mamayqa kanchu
    'certain that I have no mother any more?'
    sigura taytayqa manaña kanchu
    'certain that I have no father any more?'

(61) *akasu* nuqapaq mansana phaltanchu
    'as if I lack apples'

> *akasu* nuqapaq sultira phaltanchu
> 'as if I lack girls'

In the final example a Spanish form *awir* (<Sp a ver) 'let's see, lit. to see' is used as a sentence-introducing element:

(62) chukchachaykita t'ipiykukuy
'pull your little hair'
awir manachus nanasunki
'let's see if it does not hurt'

Thus foreign discourse markers are grammaticalized as new conjunctions here.

Moroccan Arabic/Dutch

One of the striking features of the Moroccan Arabic/Dutch mixing analysed in Nortier (1990) is that generally it is Arabic with Dutch elements inserted (cf. chapter 8 for further details). The exception are discourse markers:

(63) Ik ben een dokter *wella* ik ben een ingenieur.
'I am a doctor or I am an engineer.' (Nortier 1990: 142)

The following Arabic conjunctions occur in Dutch sentences:

(64) walakin   'but'
9la-heqq-aš   'because'
wella   'or'
be-l-heqq   'but'

We also have mixed-in interjections, which Nortier (1990: 124) terms extra-sentential mixes:

(65) . . . mineraalwater, *ze9ma*, als cadeau
'. . . mineral water,/so to speak,/as present' (Nortier 1990: 152)

(66) Maar de tijd die gaat toch voorbij, *fhemti?*
'But the time, it still goes by,/understand-2?' (Nortier 1990: 124)

Elements in these extra-sentential mixes include:

(67) fhemti(ni)   'you (PL) understand?'   14
u/wa dak-š-ši   'and/or so'   5
la   'no'   5
iwa   'well'   4   (Nortier 1990: 124)

These cases are mirrored by (not very frequent) Dutch conjunctions in Arabic sentences, as in (68):

(68) Tebgi tefhem eh *terwijl* hadik l-mas'ala ma-tehtaž-š.
2–want 2–understand uh while that DET-question 3-be-not-necessary
'You want to understand uh, while that question is not necessary.'
(Nortier 1990: 153)

Table 4.2. *The use of French discourse markers in Shaba Swahili/French*
bilingual speech

	Fr/bil	Fr/monol	Swahili	
bon 'well'	342	38	–	
non 'no'	88	3	1	(h)apana)
mais 'but'	471	45	16	(lakini)
puisque 'since'	161	22	51	(juu/sababo/maneno)
parce que 'since'	66	12		
donc 'thus'	175	25	65	(tena/kisha/
alors 'then'	99	25		(h)a(la)fu/
et puis 'and then'	63	12		kumbe)
que 'that'	78	8	91	(asema)

Note: (Fr/bil = French markers in bilingual contexts, i.e. preceded and/or followed by
Swahili; Fr/monol = French markers preceded and followed by French; Swahili =
approximate Swahili equivalents (based on De Rooij 1996: 131–59)

Shaba Swahili/French

In his extensive case study of Shaba Swahili/French code-mixing in Lubumbashi, Zaire, De Rooij (1996) devotes considerable attention to both French
and Swahili discourse markers. He notes that French discourse markers
occur in bilingual contexts much more frequently than in French monolingual contexts, and often are used much more than their approximate Swahili
equivalents, if those exist at all. In table 4.2 a quantitative overview is given,
with details of the markers discussed. De Rooij argues that code-mixing has
an important contrastive function and as such functions as a contextualiza-
tion cue. Since discourse markers have the same function, we will often find
code-mixes involving discourse markers. De Rooij illustrates his argument
with a detailed analysis of the alternate use of French *que* 'that' and Swahili
asema 'saying', showing that *que* is used almost as frequently as its Swahili
counterpart in Swahili bilingual discourse, but has been reinterpreted as
syntactically peripheral, parallel to *asema*, and is thus part of alternational
code-mixing. In this way, it escapes being a potential site of code-mixing
constraint violations, which hold for insertional mixing.

Explanations for the use of discourse markers

To the cases already mentioned, we can add Finnish/Swedish code-mixing.
Hyltenstam (1995: 326–7) also has evidence for a pattern in which Swedish
nouns can enter into Finnish structures, and Finnish conjunctions into
Swedish structures, in the speech of bilinguals. Thus we see a frequent

pattern of alternational switching involving discourse markers with the following features:

(69)   unexpected directionality or bidirectionality
       lack of categorial equivalence
       external or peripheral position
       doubling

How can we explain the use of discourse markers, conjunctions and adpositions from another language?

Hamel (1995), analysing Otomí/Spanish bilingualism (but in the Estado de México, instead of Querétaro, as in Hekking's material) claims that language shift affects different domains at different speeds. Hamel distinguishes the domain of cultural patterns and procedures from that of discourse structures and finally from that of linguistic codes and structures (1995: 158). Given that either cultural patterns and procedures or discourse structures could shift first (depending on the circumstance), there is a potential explanation for the frequent occurrence of Spanish discourse markers in Otomí: discourse linkers could belong to a domain (that of discourse structure) affected earlier by language shift than that of the sentence itself. Hence they were in Spanish before the rest of the sentence would have been uttered in that language. However, there are several problems with such an explanation:

(a)   There are cases where the intrusion of discourse markers from a different language does not correspond to language shift, like the case described by Vincent de Rooij involving Shaba Swahili with French discourse markers;

(b)   There are many cases where language shift occurs but discourse organization patterns, even in the language of wider communication, remain modelled on indigenous cultural practices, leading to substrate effects;

(c)   It is not obvious that in the case of e.g. Moroccan Arabic/Dutch bilingualism, the use of discourse markers corresponds to a specific cultural orientation or discourse structure. Recall that the use of alien discourse markers was bidirectional.

Thus differential shifting patterns can at best only provide a partial explanation.

A second type of explanation, given by Hekking and Muysken (1995), likewise lacks sufficient generality. We suggested that Spanish discourse markers in some cases truly fill structural gaps in Otomí, which tends to leave relations between clauses and arguments implicit. Again, this explanation

113

does not get very far with some of the other bilingual settings discussed, and even in Otomí the pattern of borrowing is more pervasive than could be predicted from gap-filling.

A third explanation, given by de Rooij (1996), is more satisfactory. Discourse markers must be highly salient within the discourse which they help structure. There is a pragmatic advantage in taking them from another language, since the foreign character of an element heightens its saliency.

Alternation and word order

At the beginning of this chapter I have defined what is involved in alternation as the simple juxtaposition of elements from different languages:

(70) A . . . B

So far the relation between A and B has been left rather vague, as the absence of a structural connection between *A* and *B*. However, there is the possibility that alternation also can take place under linear equivalence in a connected structure. This is precisely what Poplack (1980) proposes, given her definition of the process of code-mixing as switching between two languages. In fact, the Puerto Rican Spanish/English code-mixing analysed in Poplack (1980) is not like Treffers-Daller's data from Brussels nor like the Amerindian/Spanish cases analysed above. In fact, some of it is much more like the cases of congruent lexicalization discussed in the next chapter: a smooth back and forth between two languages that share a structure. Nonetheless, alternation may be quite frequent in settings where there is word order equivalence. When there is **linear word order equivalence** between the two languages, alternation and congruent lexicalization are a clear possibility (Nait M'Barek and Sankoff 1988; Poplack and Meechan 1995). It is possible that linear equivalence plays a role at the level of sentence processing, allowing for the juxtaposition of languages even when there are grammatical links between the different parts of the sentence.

One important issue is unresolved however: What is the nature of the constituent dominating the top nodes of the constituents from the two languages in an alternation structure? We could assume that it is shared by A and B (as in the congruent lexicalization model), or that it is from either A or B (in which case alternation would be like insertion at the clause-margin), or that it is a non-language-specific node such as 'Utterance' or 'Sentence'.

Word order and phrase structure

While the definition of linear equivalence was left unspecified in Poplack (1980), it was formalized in Sankoff and Poplack (1981) and in Sankoff and

114

Mainville (1986). In the latter work the following formalization of the constraint is presented:

> Given a 'set E of immediate descendants of the node directly above the two constituents', then 'the symbol for any nodes in E to the left of the boundary between the two constituents must precede the symbols for all nodes in E to the right of the boundary, in the right side string of the two rules from the two grammars.' (p. 75)

Thus the formal definition of the word order equivalence constraint is in terms of the immediate daughters of a given phrase structure node. Woolford (1983) gives a similar formulation of Poplack's equivalence constraint in generative terms: when the phrase structure rules (that specify word order) of both languages are identical, switching is possible; otherwise, it is not. An example would be the relation between a verb and a full noun phrase in English and Spanish. In both languages we have a phrase structure rule as in (71):

(71)   VP   →   V   NP

This implies that in (72) it is possible to switch:

(72)   Eng   sees the house
       Sp   ve   la casa

A conceptual problem with the formalization of the linear view of equivalence in terms of a formal rule is that the order of elements in the sentence is expressed in phrase structure configurations, but results from the interaction of a number of independent principles (cf. particularly the work of Stowell (1981), Travis (1984), and Koopman (1984)). Some of these principles include:

(73)   Directionality of government as Case or Theta-role assignment (cf. chapter 2)
       [NP V], * [V NP] under leftward government
       [P NP], * [NP P] under rightward government
(74)   Adjacency or other locality conditions on government
       [V NP X], * [V X NP], since case assignment is local

This principle accounts for the oddness of examples such as:

(75)   a. She sold her dog yesterday.
       b. * She sold yesterday her dog.

These two principles can be supplemented by well-established other sequencing principles:

(76)   Iconicity
       [E1 E2], * [E2 E1], where E1 and E2 are coordinate events and E1 precedes E2 in time

115

This principle regulates narrative sequencing and accounts for the oddness of:

(77)   ?He dried and washed the dishes.

(78)   Considerations of functional sentence perspective: given/new, topic/comment, [given information – new information] etc.

Thus sentences like (79) are odd:

(79)   She went to Paris, as for Mary.

(80)   Prosodic considerations
[short constituent – long constituent]

Prosodic considerations presumably play a role in the contrast between (81a) and (81b), which differ in the length or prosodic weight of the object:

(81)   a. ??I met in Paris her.
b. I met in Paris the most beautiful woman you can ever imagine.

Constituent ordering principles such as these interact to determine word order patterns. These principles do not form a natural class, and derive from different components of linguistic theory in the wide sense. Generally speaking, only the first two, and possibly only the first one, are likely to be language specific and hence pertinent to the equivalence constraint.

Notice now that (73) and (74) are directly determined by government. The equivalence constraint will by accident, as it were, often be pertinent to situations in which there is a government relation as well. Alternatively, the proper formulation of the equivalence constraint involves the notion of government.

Before I turn to this formulation, let us consider the type of situation that distinguishes linear from government accounts. Imagine a language pair of which one member allows sentence-final tags, and the other one does not. Since tags are ungoverned, this could only be some language-specific discourse rule, or a lexical property of the tags in the language where these exist. Now the equivalence constraint as formulated above will block switches involving the tag, while a formulation given in terms of government will not block them. The many cases of discourse markers introduced into peripheral sites not explicitly specified grammatically by the base language would support a restriction in the equivalence constraint to contexts of government.

Governing elements (e.g. verbs and adpositions) and the governed elements (e.g. noun phrases) must be perceived by the speakers as equivalent. Linear equivalence is simply a subcase of categorial equivalence, under the government theory, since the rightward governing verb is not directly equivalent to a leftward governing verb, just like a postposition (governing leftward) is not immediately perceived as the categorial equivalent of a preposition (governing rightward).

What constituent to count

The precise definition of word order equivalence is crucial, as can be seen when we compare Dutch and English word order in the light of the equivalence constraint (Adelmeijer 1991). In simple main clauses, surface strings are similar in the two languages:

(82) a. Mary/eats apples.
         b. Marie/eet appels.

In informal linear terms a switch would be allowed at every point, then, in these sentences. Notice, however, that many grammarians, adhering to different theoretical models, assign rather different structures to these sentences. In some Government and Binding analyses, for instance, the English verb *eats* occupies the auxiliary position (INFL), and the Dutch verb has been moved into the complementizer position (COMP; e.g. Koster 1978). The English subject is in its canonical position, while the Dutch subject has been moved into a sentence-initial position. A switch between subject and verb would not be possible under the more formal configurational definition in terms of sister nodes:

(83) a. NP [$_{INFL}$ eats]
         b. NP [$_{COMP}$ eet]

The opposite result is found when we take main clauses with a fronted adverbial. In English this element will precede the subject, while in Dutch it will occur in preverbal first position instead of the subject:

(84) a. Now / Mary eats an apple.
         b. Nu / eet Marie een appel.

Under a purely linear conception of equivalence, a switch would not be allowed after *now/nu*; the element following differs in the two languages: the subject in English, the finite verb in Dutch. Under the more formal conception of equivalence in terms of sister constituents, there is equivalence between the clausal constituents following the fronted adverbial, and hence switching would be allowed:

(85) a. Now [$_{CLAUSE}$ Mary eats]
         b. Nu [$_{CLAUSE}$ eet Marie]

Although no large-scale systematic studies of Dutch/English code-mixing have been carried out so far, the available evidence points to the possible mixing in the case of (83), but not of (85), and hence to a superficial string-oriented view of mixing.

Word order freedom

Yet another problem in interpreting the linear equivalence constraint lies in defining what the word order of a language is. This problem can be illustrated with Quechua/Spanish code-mixing. Cases in which the direct object is in a different language from the verb are a problem for a linear theory in terms of equivalence. In Quechua the direct object ordinarily precedes the verb and in Spanish vice-versa. (In addition there is a close dependency relation between the two elements, and thus they are also a problem for a structural theory such as government.) The largest group, four cases, involves a Quechua verb followed by a Spanish object:

(86) usqhay, usqhay quykullaway   'quick, quick give me
      el veneno más activo   the strongest poison'

(87) aman urpichallay waqachiwankichu   'don't my little dove make cry
      esa prenda por ser mía   this treasure that is mine'

The way to account for (86) and (87) in a linear theory is by assuming that they are the result of extraposition of a heavy NP to the right, which is possible in many varieties of Quechua. Along the same lines, we can also manage to explain the counter-examples through appealing to requirements of rhythmic structure specific to the genre of bilingual songs. It is clear that in many languages several word orders are possible, some of which are more marked than others. Sankoff, Poplack, and Vanniarajan (1990) crucially rely on this type of explanation to deal with some recalcitrant cases of Tamil/English code-mixing as well.

Deep versus surface structure

Do the restrictions on code-mixing hold at the level of deep structure or surface structure? Do we take the original positions of constituents at deep structure level into account when determining whether a switch involving them is possible, or their position at surface structure level? In other words: do traces of movement rules have a language index? Although some early studies pointed to deep structure level restrictions (e.g. Rivas in unpublished work from 1981), the evidence overwhelmingly supports more surface-oriented constraints.

An example from Poplack supports the surface interpretation of equivalence:

(88) Me iban a *lay off*.
      'They were going to lay me off.'   (Spanish/English; Poplack 1980: 583)

Here *me* is the object of *lay off*, which would be blocked, were it not for the fact that it has been raised to pre-auxiliary position.

The same thing holds for an example from Pfaff:

> (89) Bueno, por qué te hicieron *beat up* ese?
> 'Well, why did they make you beat up that [person]?'
>
> (Spanish/English; Pfaff 1979: 250)

Here the clitic subject of *beat up* has been moved to the left of the Spanish causative. (Notice however, that the sequence causative + infinitive does not occur in English.)

Stretching the pragmatics

An issue that remains to be investigated thoroughly, however, is whether the stylistic and pragmatic effects of different word order arrangements in the two languages are also respected. Do bilingual speakers bend the pragmatic and stylistic rules when aiming for word order equivalence, or should we adopt a strict version which would also include equivalence in pragmatic effect, e.g. of postverbal word order. Language-change data suggest that the latter option would be too strict.

The type of word order equivalence required appears to be quite lax in this respect. Consider cases from Nishmura (1986) on Japanese/English code-mixing cited by Moyer (1995):

> (90) Mannaka ni *they're growing.*
> middle in
> 'They're growing in the middle.' (Nishimura 1986: 132)
>
> (91) Kaeri ni wa *border* de *we got stopped, eh?*'
> return on TO border on
> 'On the way home, we got stopped at the border, eh? (Nishimura 1986: 132)
>
> (92) Asoko *she goes.*
> that place
> 'She goes over there.' (Nishimura 1986: 132)

In all three cases, a curious compromise is reached between Japanese and English. The English subject and verb are in a canonical position (from the perspective of English), adjacent to each other. Japanese constituents are preverbal, as they should be in Japanese, but also presubject. Thus, the relevant syntactic representation of the switch point must be seen as involving a linear sequence rather than a hierarchical structure.

Ellen Prince (1981), cited by Nishimura (1986), discusses the pragmatically marked rule of Yiddish-movement, a type of noun phrase fronting. It may be a source for word order equivalence in contact settings. I will try to explore the theoretical consequences of this observation in more detail, by turning to the relation between word order and phrase structure and then to the requisite level of analysis.

Convergence and linear equivalence

I will illustrate the effects of convergence on linear equivalence with an interesting case where Dutch has been in contact with two languages with different word orders: Sarnami Hindustani (SOV) and Sranan (SVO), and the results have been different. Dutch has SOV (and particle–verb) order in subordinate clauses, but in main clauses without a modal or auxiliary the finite verb moves to second position, thus creating a superficial SVO (and verb–particle) order. In Sarnami Hindustani mixed verbal compounds (involving a helping verb *kare* 'do'), generally the Dutch particle–verb order occurs, as in (93), although there are a few cases like (94) with verb–particle order.

> (93) *uit-leg* kare   [out-lay do]   'explain'
>   *mee-maken* kare   [with-make do]   'experience'
>   *op-geven* kare   [up-give do]   'give up'
>
> (94) *leg uit* kare   [lay out do]   'explain'
>
>   (Sarnami/Dutch; Kishna 1979)

Dutch verbs have also been integrated into Sranan, but always with the verb–particle order, and the particle appears in an adverbial (or serial verb; cf. Seuren's analysis cited in Myers-Scotton 1993b) position following the direct object:

> (95) a. Mi e *leg* i *uit* (*leg uit i).
>   1sg PR lay 2sg out
>   'I explain to you.'
>   b. *druk* en *door* (*druk door en)
>   press 3sg through
>   'push it through'   (Sranan/Dutch; Bolle 1994: 94)

Again, there are cases where a Dutch particle is combined with a Sranan verb (but with Dutch lexical semantics), and these are always verb–particle in order:

> (96) a. Fa Draver o syi *uit* in '92?
>   how Draver FU look out in '92
>   'What will Draver look like in '92?'
>   b. A kranti sa ben gi *uit* na a kop Coroni.
>   the paper FU PST give out with the headline Coroni
>   'The paper would be published with the headline Coroni.'
>   (Sranan/Dutch; Bolle 1994: 93)

The linear equivalence may be the basis for further structural convergence between local varieties of these languages in contact. This is taken up again in chapter 8.

Conclusion

In this chapter I have explored various dimensions of the process of alternation, a form of mixing in which the two languages remain relatively separate. The types of alternation found in French/Dutch mixing in Brussels included adverbial modification, switching at the periphery of the clause (through left-, and right-dislocation and fronting), flagging, tag-switching, and the use of syntactically unintegrated discourse markers. In a brief survey of three Amerindian languages, Moroccan Arabic, and Swahili I showed that functional elements can be incorporated into a language via alternation; thus there is a second path for lexical borrowing. Mixing involving functional elements is a case of alternation. Finally, I looked at the transition point in alternation, and the role of word order. The transition point must be defined in quite superficial terms, it appears.

5
Congruent lexicalization

In addition to insertion and alternation, there is a third type of code-mixing (van Hout and Muysken 1995): congruent lexicalization. As sketched in chapter 1, the structural interpretation of congruent lexicalization is as in (1):

(1)

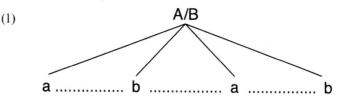

where *A*, *B* are language labels for non-terminal nodes, and *a*, *b* are labels for terminal, i.e. lexical, nodes. The languages share the grammatical structure of the sentence, fully or in part. The vocabulary comes from two or more different languages. When only parts of the grammar are shared by the two languages, it is often the alignment of the major constituents, but not all the internal structure of these constituents. Thus grammatical convergence leads to congruent lexicalization.

The features of congruent lexicalization will be studied in several settings, with a view to answering the question of when to expect it. I will begin by looking at dialect/standard mixing. In this case, generally, very similar varieties are involved. The issues are raised of how different code-mixing is from language variation and style shifting, and whether these phenomena can be studied in the same framework. I will argue that code-mixing is not different, in principle, from variation. I will illustrate the properties of congruent lexicalization with dialect/standard mixing as my reference point.

Then, I will consider Frisian/Dutch and Sranan/Dutch code-mixing, cases where the language varieties involved are progressively less similar. Frisian and Dutch differ in many details but also have overall similarities both in structure and lexicon. Sranan and Dutch differ structurally in many ways, but the varieties of these languages used in the Sranan bilingual community in the Netherlands have tended to converge considerably.

In many bilingual communities code-mixing goes hand in hand with structural convergence. This raises the issue of language change, and the question of whether there is a causal link either way. Does convergence facilitate code-mixing or does code-mixing pave the way for convergence? A further issue to be raised is whether convergence always entails simplification and reduction. Convergence is studied using Moluccan Malay/Dutch code-mixing data.

If congruent lexicalization is frequent in a bilingual setting, it could be due to two things:

(a)   There is an overabundance of homophonous words, **diamorphs**, that serve as bridges or triggers for the code-mix;

(b)   There is a general structural equivalence, both categorial and linear, making code-mixing possible, without there necessarily being any lexical correspondence.

How can we decide between these alternatives? I will contrast examples of linear equivalence with cases where there are many diamorphs, but no general linear equivalence. Code-mixing between English and Spanish exemplifies a case where mixing involves considerable linear equivalence (except for the noun/adjective order) but a largely separate vocabulary, and Dutch and English as languages with an often similar vocabulary (particularly among high frequency words) but some important word order differences, at least at the clause level.

Though congruent lexicalization is mostly a phenomenon occurring at the sentence level, we also find several cases of it in borrowing. These may puzzle language contact researchers if borrowing is only regarded from the perspective of insertional mixing. Examples include hybrid compounds in Germanic languages and the merging of complex verbal morphology in some Andean languages.

Code-mixing and variation: theoretical perspectives

In sociolinguistics a distinction is traditionally made between code-mixing – the alternation of two invariant systems in a single discourse – and variation or style shifting – the realization of different options within one single system. Here I want to argue that this distinction has become less watertight, in the light of developments both in our view of grammatical systems and in our perception of the phenomenon of code-mixing. The phenomenon of style shifting can be seen as one subtype of code-mixing, namely congruent lexicalization. Consider the following (constructed) example:

(2) I've been earn**ing** less than noth**ing**, work**in'** my butt off in the frigg**in'**
bott**ling** plant.

In the paradigm of variation studies, this sentence contains five instances of
the variable (ing), realized twice as [ɪn] and three times as [ɪŋ]. In the corpus
from which this sentence might have been taken, there will be all kinds of
social, phonological, lexical, and syntactic constraints governing the occurrence of either [ɪn] or [ɪŋ]. The sequencing of these variants in utterances and
the covariation with other variables, such as the potential realization of (th)
as [d], is not studied in this paradigm.

In the code-mixing paradigm, the sentence could be analysed as consisting
of an [ɪŋ] part and an [ɪn] part (starting with *workin*), fragments ideally
contrasted in other ways as well. The speaker is assumed to shift to a
different register half-way through the sentence, for whatever reason. Internal variation in a switched fragment is not taken into account.

Abstractly, the research paradigm associated with Labov has the following
representation. An often recorded and transcribed text is viewed as containing a sequence of allomorphic or allophonic realizations of a specific set
of variables under study:

(3) $var_1(a)$ ... $var_2(f)$ ... $var_n(m)$ etc.

The analysis involves determining the frequency of the different variants of a
variable:

(4) var_1 (a, b, ...)
var_2 (f, g, ...)
...
var_n (m, n, ...)

There is no consideration of the relation between $var_1(a)$ and $var_2(f)$.

The dominant paradigm in code-mixing research, in contrast, involves the
study of the linear juxtaposition of elements or sequences of elements
(termed *segments* here) from different codes:

(5) $segm^1$ in code A/$segm^2$ in code B/$segm^3$ in code A ...

The analysis involves the relation between the different segments – words or
constituents:

(6) relation $segm^1$/$segm^2$
relation $segm^2$/$segm^3$
...

Absent is the consideration of the overall frequency of elements in code A, B,
... and of the individual features of elements in $segm^1$, $segm^2$, ...

Variation theory thus takes a **paradigmatic** approach, focussing on differ-

124

ent realizations of a variable; code-mixing research takes a **syntagmatic** approach, focussing on the sequential relation of the elements in the sentence. It is clear, theoretically speaking, that these perspectives constitute radically different ways of looking at the same thing: individual instances of the use of a code can be seen as variants realizing a certain variable. Still, since Labov (1972) they have been studied in rather different ways.

What was the original motivation of Labov for distinguishing code-mixing from variation? Labov (1972: 188–9) wants to demonstrate in *The Study of Language in its Social Context* that a passage such as the following (where two 'codes' are represented in capitals and lower case) cannot be analysed as code-mixing, but should be viewed as variation:

> (7) An' den like IF YOU MISS ONESIES, de OTHuh person shoot to
> skelly; ef he miss, den you go again. An' IF YOU GET IN, YOU
> SHOOT TO TWOSIES. An' IF YOU GET IN TWOSIES, YOU GO
> TO tthreesies. An' IF YOU MISS tthreesies, THEN THE PERSON
> THa' miss skelly shoot THE SKELLIES an' shoot in THE ONESIES:
> an' IF HE MISS, YOU GO f'om tthreesies to foursies.

The reasons he adduces for this are:

> A. 'there is no obvious motivation for him [the speaker – pm] to
> switch 18 times in the course of this short passage'
> B. 'the great majority of the forms are shared by both systems and
> are assigned to one or the other code by the accidents of
> sequencing'

To begin with B, this is not a principled reason, but rather an indication of a practical problem. I will return to it below. As regards A it should be noted that the study of the motivation of code-mixing in bilingual communities had not really advanced very much when Labov wrote this. In work since the early 1970, starting with Gumperz and Hernandez-Chavez (1971: 122), it has become clear that individual switches can not always be motivated through reference to external factors. Rather, there is a much more indirect relation between switches and speakers' motivations: 'What seems to be involved rather is a symbolic process very much like that by which linguistic signs convey sentence information. Code selection, in other words, is meaningful in much the same way that lexical choice is meaningful.' In the work of Pfaff (1976, 1979), Poplack (1980), and Treffers-Daller (1994), among others, it becomes clear that such non-individually motivated switches constitute the rule rather than the exception and that it is rather the frequency and positioning of the switches that carry social meaning and external motivation. Consider an example such as the following mix between Dutch and French from the work of Treffers-Daller in Brussels:

> (8) Bij mijn broer *y a un ascenseur* en alles.
> 'At my brother's/there is an elevator/and everything.'
>
> French/Dutch; Treffers-Daller 1994: 222)

It is not motivation that sets code-mixing apart from variation. Rather, it must be something connected with properties of the grammatical system.

The other problem is the difficulty of studying patterns of covariation. When Labov identified the linguistic variable as the site of variation in linguistic systems, and then proceeded to analyse the behaviour of linguistic variables in isolation, a vision of variation emerged in which individual structural elements: phonemes, grammatical elements, etc. vary independently from one another. This vision, again, reinforces our view of variation (involving isolated, loose elements) as being very different from code-mixing (involving stretches of items from different systems). The non-standard pronunciation of a vowel in one word often goes together with the non-standard pronunciation of another sound in the next word. Many linguistic variables enter into patterns of covariation, however, so that individual cases of variation are closer to code-mixing. The fact that covariation is hard to investigate has made us oblivious to this.

The above plea to collapse the notions of code-mixing and variation is not just a matter of terminology and empty theorizing. It allows us to deal with variation and its quantitative coordinates in terms of variation in lexical insertion. This in turn makes it possible to link up research on variation in speech to psycholinguistic experimentation involving lexical retrieval and sentence production. Ultimately this gives us a better chance to locate linguistic variation in the typology of phenomena of variation in human behaviour. The interaction with theories of grammar involves then mainly the study of constraints on heterogeneous elements inserted in the same structure.

One of the obvious objections to the line of reasoning presented here is: what about the constraints on code-mixing proposed in the literature? Although the empirical details of the various constraints proposed differ, and their conceptual basis is somewhat different, they impose rather strict conditions on where mixing is possible. If code-mixing and variation were the same thing, this would likewise impose conditions on where variation could occur in a structure, something not quite in line with Labov's observation about the passage cited. How can we reconcile the apparently contradictory predictions of this analysis? I will argue that the type of code-mixing involved here, congruent lexicalization, is not constrained in the same way.

Table 5.1. *Examples of two paradigms in sociolinguistic research: the variation paradigm and the code-mixing paradigm*

van Hout	Giesbers
• urban	• semi-rural
• phonology/phonetics	• syntax and discourse
• assumption of gradual transition between varieties	• assumption of two discrete varieties
* individual occurrences of phonetic realizations or word forms	• distribution of words or word sequences within utterances and discourses

Structural dimensions of code-mixing: the properties of congruent lexicalization in Giesbers' Ottersum study

In congruent lexicalization, both languages contribute to the grammatical structure of the sentence, which, in many cases, is fully shared by the languages involved. The vocabulary comes from two or more different languages, but may also be shared.

The contrast between a code-mixing and a variation approach can be illustrated with two studies carried out in and near Nijmegen, in the east of the Netherlands. In the Nijmegen area two detailed studies were done in the 1980s on language variation and dialect/standard use in east Netherlandic dialects. Roeland van Hout (1989) studied variation in the urban dialect of the city of Nijmegen itself, focussing on phonetic variation and adopting the Labovian research paradigm. Herman Giesbers (1989) focussed on mixing between dialect and standard in the small town of Ottersum, and adopted the code-mixing paradigm (established in the 1970s through the work of Pfaff (1976, 1979), Poplack (1980), and others). Their work may be contrasted as in table 5.1. The choices these researchers made are natural ones from the perspective of the research paradigm they are part of, but still the settings of Ottersum and Nijmegen are not dissimilar in many ways, and the question remains of what the relationship is between their choice of paradigm and their findings.

The linguistic situation assumed by Van Hout for Nijmegen can be analysed as an extreme case of code-mixing, given a certain interpretation of the typology of code-mixing settings, and that the code-mixing data described by Giesbers are indicative of a rather similar setting. I will focus here on the material presented by Giesbers in his remarkable study.

Giesbers' study of Ottersum dialect/regional Dutch standard mixing gives sufficient detail to be able to characterize the type of code-mixing occurring.

The Ottersum dialect is part of the northern Limburg dialect cluster (Giesbers 1989: 57–8), related to the pronunciation of Cleve, Germany. The dialect includes the city of Nijmegen and surrounding areas. Differences from the 'southern' pronunciation of standard Dutch include a number of vowel and diphthong pronunciations, the maintenance of [alt] where the standard has the diphthong [owt], and sometimes the deletion of [r] before sonorants. Umlaut is more frequent than in the standard variety. Morphologically, nominal plural is sometimes realized differently, the diminutive is somewhat different, and adjectival and verbal inflection are slightly different. A number of words distinct from the standard forms are also in use. Morphosyntactically, the main difference is the possibility of leaving out the second person pronoun in postverbal position in the Ottersum dialect. For the rest there are no noticeable syntactic differences. Giesbers (1989: 66) concludes that the distance of Ottersum dialect from the standard is mid-range, from the perspective of all Dutch dialects.

Where I differ from Giesbers is in the interpretation of his material. First, Giesbers' own taxonomy of his switches is as either alternational or insertional. In my view his material is mostly illustrative of yet a third type, congruent lexicalization. Second, although Giesbers classifies the utterances or utterance fragments in his corpus as either dialect or standard, it is clear from the actual transcription that often this classification is not based on clear linguistic differences between the two. Third, rather than simply accepting Giesbers' conclusion that the theoretical constraints proposed are indicative that these theories do not work, I want to explore the possibility that this is indicative of a fundamentally different type of code-mixing. Basically anything goes in congruent lexicalization.

The following features are characteristic of congruent lexicalization. In the examples given below I have converted Giesbers' careful transcription of the dialect pronunciations to the standard orthography. Standard Dutch is presented as italic; the elements involved in the mixing are placed between brackets.

Since the varieties are identical, to all intents and purposes, at the syntactic level, there will be **linear and structural equivalence** between them. The only grammatical constraint rarely violated in Giesbers' material is Poplack's equivalence constraint, but then again it is barely relevant since the order of elements is identical in the two varieties (p. 167). A clear example of a smooth switch at a linear equivalence site is:

(9)   *as [wij nou* zegge] da we et anders wille, wa dan
        'If we now / say that we want something else, what then?'

(Giesbers 1989: 76)

The one place where there is a slight difference between the varieties, as noted, involves postverbal second person subject pronouns, and there a potential violation does result:

(10) *maar wat* [kunde *d'r*] *nog aan doen*?
      'But what / can [you] / do about it?'   (Giesbers 1989: 158)

Here in the Dutch standard we would have expected a realized pronoun after the modal, while in Ottersum dialect the pronoun, if anything, is incorporated into the verb form. However, it is not clear that this is not a late morphosyntactic realization difference rather than a true syntactic difference, and hence the status of examples such as this one as counter-examples to the equivalence constraint is unclear. An example of a switch between a verb and a postverbal enclitic pronoun subject is:

(11) ik zei mossele da [mag-*ie*] *toch helemaal nie*
      I said mussels that may-/he though at.all not
      'I said mussels he is not allowed them, is he?'   (Giesbers 1989: 96)

In congruent lexicalization, we can also expect **multi-constituent code-mixing**, not plausibly seen as insertional. This is possible because the syntactic structure is shared by the two codes involved, and hence the switch could be anywhere. In table 5.2 multi-word switches are presented. Although it is impossible to sharply delineate multi-constituent from non-constituent mixing on the basis of Giesbers' quantitative survey, it is quite clear that these categories together constitute an exceptionally high part of Giesbers' data, when compared to other studies, where generally only a handful of these switch types are reported (e.g. Nortier 1990). An example where more than one constituent is switched:

(12) voor gistere hebbe *jullie 't ingedeeld* wa
      for yesterday have / you it subdivided / eh?'
      'For yesterday you have subdivided it eh?'   (Giesbers 1989: 158)

A further feature is **non-constituent mixing** (or 'ragged' mixing, cf. Poplack 1980). This type of mixing cannot be accommodated within theories proposing syntactic constraints on the process, since syntactic theories assume organization in constituents to be an essential component of linguistic structure. Non-constituent code-mixing (or 'ragged' mixing; cf. Poplack 1980) will be expected in congruent lexicalization since the switching involves single words within a shared structure. In Giesbers (1989) a very large number of non-constituent switches was found, something like 543 out of 1,695 cases of intra-sentential switches of more than one word. (There were 1,552 one-word switches in addition.)

There will probably also be **non-nested** *a b a* **structures**, since there is no

Table 5.2. *Multi-word switches in the Ottersum corpus (based on Giesbers'*
tables 4.3.2 and 4.3.5)

	'insertion'	'alternation'
noun phrase	240	19
adverbial phrase	153	7
prepositional phrase	56	18
verb phrase	9	13
clause	5	1765
subordinate clause	3	73
more constituents	104	141
rest of utterance	9	298
incomplete clause	70	419

need for alien *b* elements to correspond to a single well-defined constituent.
No specific analysis is provided by Giesbers for cases in which the two
fragments from variety *a* surrounding a stretch in variety *b* are not related to
each other. In the following example, there is no grammatical connection
either between the dialect fragments or the standard variety fragments:

> (13) ja maar bij *ouwe mensen* komt dat *gauwer tot stilstand als* bij jonge
> mense wa
> 'Yes but with / older people/that comes / to a halt more quickly than
> with younger people eh.' (Giesbers 1989: 147)

All categories can be switched in congruent lexicalization, including
function words, since there is no matrix language determining the language of
the function words (cf. also Giacalone Ramat 1995). To see which categories
are switched in Giesbers' material consider table 5.3, which presents all
single-word switches. This table shows that not only a wide variety of
categories is switched in the Ottersum corpus as single elements, but that
these include a number that would fall under Myers-Scotton's System
Morpheme Principle (boldface in table 5.3). A number of closed-class items
are inserted (bold in (14)–(21); contra Joshi 1985 and other authors, including
Myers-Scotton 1993b). These include 178 pronouns of different categories,
and 75 copulas and auxiliaries:

> (14) allemaal van harte welkom op *deze* avond eh
> 'All heartily welcome on **this** evening eh.' (Giesbers 1989: 154)
>
> (15) *nee* ge *kunt ze zo halen in voorraad gewoon*
> 'No **you** can just get them, just in stock.' (Giesbers 1989: 153)
>
> (16) *sommige elastiekjes* zin *kapot*
> 'Some rubber bands **are** broken.' (Giesbers 1989: 151)

Table 5.3. *Single word switches in the Ottersum corpus (based on Giesbers'*
tables 4.3.2 and 4.3.5)

	'insertion'	'alternation'
noun	459	1
pronoun	178	
finite verb	165	5
infinitive	130	
participle	50	
adjective	149	4
adverb	93	
preposition	82	
interjection, tag	78	1
auxiliary, copula	75	
numeral	53	2
complementizer	12	
article	9	
conjunction	6	

Giesbers also notes that there are 82 separably switched prepositions in his
data (p. 159), 12 subordinators, and 9 articles and numerals:

(17) *dan vind ik 't ook nie zo'n punt om* ene *keer mee te doen*
       then find I it also not such.a point for **one** time with to do
       'Then I do not find it such a major problem to participate **one** time.'
       (Giesbers 1989: 164)

There are 165 cases of finite main verbs in a different language from the rest
of the clause (contra Treffers-Daller 1994):

(18) nou eh dat eh hij ze *bewaart* en dan zedde gij dat nummer
       'Now eh that eh he **saves** them and then you say the number.'
       (Giesbers 1989: 148)

(19) . . . *of we onderweg nog lekkers* kriege
       '. . . whether we **get** a treat while under way'   (Giesbers 1989: 99)

(20) *'t* geet *vaak automatisch bij jou*
       'It often **goes** automatically with you.'   (Giesbers 1989: 149)

(21) ja en dan eh towes as der iets nie *bevalt*, . . .
       'Yes and then eh, by the way, if something does not **suit** [you] . . .'
       (Giesbers 1989: 149)

These occurrences lead to violations of the constraint that a subject pronoun
and a verb must be in the same language, that negation and the verb must be
in the same language, and that the subject and the copula must be in the
same language.

An example from Italian/Sicilian dialect mixing also shows this type of mixing of functional elements:

(22) prima di tutto *u* portiere non c'è, sarà minimo cinque sei anni
first of all **the** porter not there-is, will be minimum five six years
'First of all there has been no porter for at least five or six years.'
(Alfonzetti 1992: 203; cited in Giacalone Ramat 1995)

Here the Sicilian dialect definite article *u* is used in an otherwise Italian sentence, something best interpretable as congruent lexicalization.

Switching of **selected elements** like subcategorized for PPs and objects is expected, since the selection restrictions of the governing elements (e.g. verbs) involved are largely shared. Often the complement is not in the same language as the preposition, contra DiSciullo, Muysten, and Singh (1986):

(23) *vertel* [over *jou] maar effe*
'Tell about/yourself then.' (Giesbers 1989: 59)

(24) ik heb soms snoep [in *die kast*] wa
'I sometimes have candy in / that cupboard / eh.' (Giesbers 1989: 147)

(25) *ze kunnen dus 'n raam maken* [voor *later tegen de tent aan te doen]*
'They can make a window / for / to put against the tent later on' (Giesbers 1989: 96)

Congruent lexicalization often involves **bidirectional code-mixing**, since there is no dominant matrix language. Giesbers claims that of the 5,515 cases of code-mixing, roughly equal amounts are insertional (2,251) and alternational (2,767). A third category, that of intermediate forms, only involves 497 cases (p. 134). Over half of the switches are from dialect to standard (2,971 cases). Particularly for insertions, directionality plays a role (73 per cent dialect>standard and only 27 per cent standard>dialect). For alternations, the direction is almost exactly 50–50 (pp. 138–9). The Giesbers corpus is much more bidirectional than most code-mixing corpora, where almost 100 per cent of insertions are unidirectional, as are roughly 75 per cent of the alternations (see chapter 8).

We often find frequent **back-and-forth switches** in this code-mixing strategy, since there is no dominant matrix language. No systematic data are presented on back-and-forth switching in Giesbers' book, but it is clear both from the high incidence of switches Giesbers terms 'insertional' and from the examples that this is by no means uncommon. Consider examples such as:

(26) . . . nee *onder leiding van jou* gedaan, da gij daor de keuke *kent*, op de Roepaan . . .
'. . . no / under your direction / done, that you know the kitchen there, on the Roepaan . . .' (Giesbers 1989: 249)

(27)   *... maar oa:! oma komt weer nie en ze x had ze al* gezet *op de kaart staat*
       't en daor kwame wij daor onverwachts *aan ...*
       '... but oh! grandma again won't come and she had already said it is on
       the map and / there we arrived there unexpectedly ...'

(Giesbers 1989: 243)

(28)   *De routebeveiliging denk d'r wel* aen dagg ... x as d'r *afgeroepen wordt*
       da jullie *gaan*, da ge ook *gaat*, ...
       'The route safety-measures remember / that you, when it is called that
       you all / go / , that that you / go / then, ...'   (Giesbers 1989: 234)

Another feature that often characterizes congruent lexicalization is the
presence of **homophonous diamorphs**. Clyne (1967) has suggested that it is
possible that the distinction between two codes may be neutralized at the
point where they share a pair of homophonous diamorphs. This concerns the
first problem raised by Labov (1972) against a code-mixing analysis of the
passage cited: that it would be hard to classify all elements unambiguously in
terms of either of the two codes. When two types of speech differ only in a
few items, of course, frequent mixing is possible: a great many elements are
diamorphs.

The notion of homophonous diamorph can be formally represented as
follows. We may mark the fact that a given element belongs to a given
language by assigning it a language index. However, this notion is not
unproblematic; a number of questions arise.

First, is the element limited to terminal nodes, the lexical items, or do we
characterize constituent nodes as having a language index as well – e.g.
through projection from lexical items? The latter is needed if we want to
claim that code-mixing restrictions hold between constituents. However it
may be that not all nodes in a syntactic tree have an index; higher nodes may
be neutral.

A second issue is: how do we know to which language a given word
belongs? This language may be the context in which the word was acquired,
but more clearly the morphophonemic patterns of a language play a role as
algorithms for assigning a word to a given language. Where the languages are
morphophonemically similar, it may not be possible to assign an unambiguous language index.

Third, the lexicon of many languages must be conceived of as stratal,
containing strata with different etymological statuses (e.g. native versus
Romance for English (Aronoff 1976); or Dutch (Booij 1977)) and different
morphophonemic patterning and morphological behaviour. Do these stratal
features affect language indices?

The presence of homophonous diamorphs, given a partly or largely shared

133

lexicon, is also frequently expected in congruent lexicalization because of the close relation between the varieties involved. Obviously, in Giesbers' study a large number of items does not belong to a single variety. Often the dialect word (even though contextually labelled as 'dialect' by Giesbers) is identical to the standard word. On p. 164 Giesbers notes for instance 'it is difficult to establish unambiguous insertions of isolated conjunctions, because only the dialectal variant for *maar* ['but'] diverges sufficiently to come to such a conclusion'. Thus the author (a native of Ottersum himself) has been conservative in labelling the variants in the material, often using contextual 'emic' categories rather than purely linguistic categories.

A frequent feature of congruent lexicalization is the incidence of **morphological integration**, since the morphosyntactic systems are very similar if not identical. There are a considerable number of intermediate forms in Giesbers' Ottersum corpus: over 9 per cent, or 497 cases, of the 5,468 switches analysed by Giesbers involved a form intermediate between the dialect and the standard. Of these intermediate forms 60 per cent was phonological, over 20 per cent morphological, and 18 per cent lexical in nature. There are 63 'word internal' switches (p. 144).

Triggering of code-mixing by words from the other language is also to be expected in congruent lexicalization, since both languages are very close to the activation threshold. Giesbers discusses a number of cases of triggering (pp. 109, 205). Sometimes the use of a specific dialect word, as *knoje* 'grumble' in (29), triggers the continuation in the dialect. The trigger words are given in angled brackets :

(29) *Mijn moeder* <knoje> da'k te loat was.
'My mother **grumbling** that I was late.'   (Giesbers 1989: 109)

Sometimes the trigger is a word identical in the two varieties:

(30) het nog iemand een <barbecue> *thuis*?
'Does someone have a **barbecue** at home?'   (Giesbers 1989: 205)

Mixed collocations and idioms are a final feature of congruent lexicalization, since the structures involved in them are largely shared and the lexicons related. We often find two separable elements (in square brackets) of the same lexicalized combination or idiom in two different languages (contra Poplack's Free Morpheme Constraint). Many of these involve particle + verb combinations:

(31) *Tom, Tom [geef] effe de thee 's* [en]
Tom, Tom **give** just the tea once **to**
'Tom, Tom please pass the tea.'   (cf. aan-geven 'pass'; Giesbers 1989: 47)

(32) ge het nou een hok en dan [goat] er ook maar [*in*]

you have now a cage and then **get** there also just **in**
'You have a cage now and just **get in** then.'

(cf. in-gaan 'enter'; Giesbers 1989: 48)

However, there are others as well:

(33)   . . . *[daar] kun je die namen ook* [mit] *leren kennen.*
there can you those names also **with** learn know
'. . . you can get to know those names **with it** as well.'

(cf. daar-mee 'therewith'; Giesbers 1989: 155)

(34)   da konde toch nie [in de hand] [*houe*]
that can.you though not in the hand keep
'That you cannot really **keep under control.**'

(cf. in de hand houden 'control'; Giesbers 1989: 34)

Discussion

Thus there can be no doubt that the Ottersum corpus fits the characterization of 'congruent lexicalization' to a high degree. Nonetheless, the fact that insertional mixing is still in the majority of cases from dialect to standard and that we have many clearly identified multi-word constituents switched could be interpreted as implying that the Ottersum corpus may be somewhat distinct from the type of material studied by Labov, and possibly van Hout for the Nijmegen dialect. An important factor here are speaker perceptions of distinctness.

The fact that the code-mixing material can be shown to have a great many diagnostic features of congruent lexicalization suggests, however, that the Ottersum corpus may resemble Van Hout's Nijmegen corpus more than it appears at first sight. Still, both data sets should be analysed in strictly comparable ways, following the two paradigms, to reach firm conclusions in this respect.

We can characterize the Nijmegen urban dialect setting as an extreme case of congruent lexicalization: there is one grammatical system into which alternative elements from several varieties can be inserted. In this way we can formalize the Labovian perception of style shifting in terms of options in lexical insertion or phonological specification. The difference that remains concerns the discrete or continuous nature of the variation between the systems involved.

I now turn to cases where the gap between the varieties is progressively wider.

Frisian/Dutch code-mixing

The relation between Frisian and Dutch is quite complex. On the one hand, the two languages are separate branches of West Germanic, and thus cannot

135

be considered to stand in a dialect-standard relation. On the other hand, their coexistence in an asymmetrical dominance relation within the borders of one state has led to considerable convergence, e.g. on the lexical level. Frisian/Dutch code-mixing has so far been studied in monographs from two perspectives: Sjölin (1976) takes a psycholinguistic perspective, studying the relation between transfer and code-mixing in spoken informal conversations, and Gorter (1993) studies the interaction between municipal employees and citizens in an institutional setting from the sociological point of view. In addition, there are a number of shorter papers and occasional remarks in studies on related subjects such as the acquisition of Frisian and Dutch in a bilingual context. Wolf (1995) is studying Frisian from the general perspective that has also been useful for my own research. Since the major research on Frisian/Dutch code-mixing still remains to be done I will limit myself to a brief enumeration of the evidence that we are dealing with for congruent lexicalization here. I will draw on Wolf's work in progress, and give bilingual examples with Dutch and English glosses. Dutch is underlined.

Homophonous diamorphs are found for instance in:

(35) witst noch wol wat se dan seine, wat waar,
     weet je nog wel wat ze dan zeiden? wat voor weer
     know-you still well what they then said, what weather

     [**wat** weer is het bewaarder]?
     wat voor weer is het bewaarder
     what weather is it guard
     'Do you remember what they said then? What weather, what kind of
     weather is it, guard?'

Here *wat* 'what' could be either Frisian or Dutch. Furthermore, the Dutch fragment *weer is het bewaarder?* 'weather is it, guard?' is a non-constituent if we take *wat* to be Frisian. If we take *wat* to be Dutch, we have the anomaly that in Dutch *wat* can only be used prenominally when accompanied by *voor* 'for', as in the Dutch gloss. The same example shows the considerable syntactic and also morphological parallelism of the two languages. Wolf (1995) has shown that one potential locus for linear non-equivalence between the two languages, the order of the infinitival complements, is disappearing due to syntactic change among the younger speakers of Frisian.

The following example shows a similar case of non-constituent mixing introduced by a homophonous diamorph:

(36) en de partij dy't hy derby blaasde,
     en de partij die hij erbij blies
     and the part that he thereby blew

> is net [**foar** <u>herhaling vatbaar</u>]
> is niet voor herhaling vatbaar
> is not for repetition graspable
> 'And 'the song he sang then' is not fit to be repeated.'

Again, Frisian *foar* 'for' is sufficiently similar to Dutch *voor* 'for' to constitute an ambiguous switchpoint, and *herhaling vatbaar* is not a constituent.

There are many cases of **word-internal mixing**. In (37) the lexical element in a Frisian sentence is taken from Dutch, while the diminutive is Frisian, and in the admittedly unusual example (38) the diminutive is taken from Dutch and the lexical base is Frisian. Wolf suggests that the first of these examples is not unusual, but the second rather exceptional:

(37) jo moatte him ris hearre yn dat <u>loo</u>pke yn dy mars
je moet hem eens horen in dat **loop-je** in die mars
'You should hear him in the melody in the march.'

(38) foar in lytsenien kinst wol ta mei in spiker<u>tje</u>
voor een kleine heb je wel genoeg aan een **spijker-tje**
'For a little one you only need a little nail.'

Wolf concludes that word-internal mixing is so frequent that we must assume that there is a process of **conversion** operating, whereby part of a form produced in one language undergoes phonological transformation to yield a form in the other language. A case in point would be:

(39) sneinsskoalle   *Frisian*
sondagskool   *converted form in variety between Frisian and Dutch*
zondagschool   *Dutch*
'Sunday school'

The following example shows evidence of the diversity of lexical elements inserted:

(40) <u>toen</u> eh eh ha we dus de tint wer in bytse makke
toen eh eh hebben we dus de tent weer een beetje gemaakt
then uh uh have we the tent again a bit made

ha we dus eh ien ha we in eh <u>vuilnis</u>sek ha we
hebben we dus een hebben we een eh vuilniszak hebben we
have we thus uh a have we a uh garbage.bag have we

<u>voor</u> in rút <u>ge</u>brocht
voor een raam aangebracht.
before a window brought
'Then uh uh we have the tent again a bit made, we have, we have put a garbage bag in front of the window.'

Not only a noun like *vuilnis* 'garbage' is taken from Dutch, but also *toen* 'then', *voor* 'in front of', and the past participle prefix *ge-*.

An example of a back and forth switch is:

(41) dy lei dea yn 'e hoeke, <u>verroerde</u> gjin <u>vin</u>
      die lag dood in de hoek, verroerde geen vin
      'He lay dead in the corner, did not stir at all.'

A more systematic study of Frisian/Dutch code-mixing will be needed to establish how common the phenomena mentioned here are, and how often there is alternational and insertional mixing. Presumably, the latter two patterns are also quite frequent in Frisian/Dutch bilingual conversations.

Sranan/Dutch code-mixing

Sranan is not related to Dutch, except through its lexifier language, English. However, during centuries of colonial domination lexical and structural elements have entered urban varieties of Sranan in the Republic of Surinam and the process of convergence with Dutch has continued in the large Surinamese migrant community in the Netherlands. Furthermore, the variety of Dutch spoken by many Surinamese also shows structural and semantic features from Sranan. Thus, we may expect congruent lexicalization. The main source for Sranan (Surinam Creole)/Dutch code-mixing is Bolle (1994). Here I will try to show that many bilingual sentences in Bolle's corpus show characteristics of congruent lexicalization.

Contrary to Frisian, Sranan has a constituent order in main and subordinate clauses rather different from Dutch. Some contrastive examples are:

(42) a. bikasi mi e **skribi** en wan brifi   Sranan S V IO DO
      b. omdat ik hem een brief **schrijf**   Dutch S IO DO V
         'because I write him a letter.

(43) a. Tamara **mi e go** na datra   Sranan ADV S V
      b. Morgen **ga ik** naar de dokter   Dutch ADV V S
         'Tomorrow I go to the doctor'

In (42b), a subordinate clause, the Dutch verb occurs at the end. In (43b) a fronted element leads to the order [verb – subject] in Dutch. In Sranan, the order of subject and verb is always quite stable, as in English: [subject – verb]. Thus, congruent lexicalization can never be absolute in Sranan/Dutch code-mixing.

Still, there is ample evidence for it. First, there are a number of different lexical categories from Dutch in Bolle's corpus, individually inserted into Sranan clauses. The first column of table 5.4 gives Dutch words, the second column words Bolle classifies as ambiguous, attested Dutch loans in Sranan which have not been modified by phonological adaptation. It is not surprising that there are far fewer functional elements than lexical elements.

Table 5.4. *Single Dutch elements in the Sranan corpus (based on Bolle's tables 5.2 and 5.11)*

	Dutch	**ambiguous**
nouns	503	1395
verbs	174	75
adjectives	69	33
adverbs	109	633
prepositions	35	11
auxiliaries/copulas	9	109
pronouns/question words/determiners	5	150
conjunctions	135	229
numerals and quantifiers	19	12
exclamatives	20	240
total	1078	2887

Nonetheless, the wide variety of categories from Dutch, and the fact that functional elements are taken at all, are indicative of congruent lexicalization. In addition, the number of exclamatives, typical of alternation, is relatively low.

Table 5.4 also contains information about Dutch words that have already been integrated into Sranan. It is clear that this large group contains many potential homophonous diamorphs, such as the conjunction *dat* 'that', which can be both Dutch and the shortened form of Sranan *dati*.

There are many cases of selected switches, such as the following sentence, where Sranan *habi* 'have' is combined with Dutch *onder controle* 'under control'.

(44) èn ef(u) i no **habi** a pisi dat(i) now *onder controle* hè.
      and if you NEG have the piece that now under control uh
      'And if you (do) not have that part under control now, uh?'

                                                                (Bolle 1994: 73)

Frequent back-and-forth switching is evident in:

(45) wan heri *gedeelte* de ondro *beheer* fu *gewapende machten*
      one whole part COP under control of armed forces
      'One whole part is under control of the armed forces.'   (Bolle 1994: 75)

(46) den man *waardeer* en *heel veel*
      'They appreciate it very much.'   (Bolle 1994: 78)

(47) soort *bijdrage* yu kan *lever op het ogenblik* gi a *opleving* fu a kulturu?
      'Which contribution / can you / make at this moment / for the / revival /
      of culture?'

An example of a non-nested a b a mix is:

(48) mi *rake even kwijt* san mi ben o wan(i) taki
      'I / forget for a moment / what I would want to say.'   (Bolle 1994: 64)

Here there is no direct relation between the Sranan pronoun at the beginning and the Sranan embedded clause. The form *rake* is glossed here as part of the Dutch fragment but the ending *-e* suggests plural agreement or infinitive in Dutch, which is clearly not appropriate (given the 1sg subject); hence *rake* may be a Dutch verb integrated into Sranan.

The next example is particularly complex:

(49) *want* i no mus(u) firgiti [Draver ontstaan [*in* den *tachtiger* yari]]
      for you not must forget Draver emerge in the eightier years
      'For you must not forget Draver came into existence in the eighties.'
                                                                  (Bolle 1994: 80)

In this mostly Sranan sentence there is a Dutch PP in which the Dutch unmarked article *de* has been replaced by the Sranan plural determiner *den*, and Dutch *jaren* 'years' is realized as Sranan *yari*. Furthermore the embedded verb *ontstaan* 'emerge' is a Dutch infinitive or participle form functioning as a past tense main verb.

Examples of switches consisting of several constituents are:

(50) dus dat den sma abi [[*makkelijk ingang*] [*in de politiek*]].
      'So that the people have/easy access in politics.'   (Bolle 1994: 80)

(51) a o wroko [*eerder ondergang*][*voor Suriname [dan vooruitgang*]
      'It will bring/decay for Surinam rather than progress.'   (Bolle 1994: 82)

(52) dus Pom yu *begrijp*, san ben lob(i) tak(i) Kip e kon
      [*op z'n schoot*] [*hield zich koest*].
      'Thus Pom you/understand,/who liked [it] that Kip came/on his lap kept quiet.'
                                                                  (Bolle 1994: 73)

The same holds in the examples presented in (53)–(54), where the language switch is in the middle of the clause:

(53) *verdeeldheid* ben de [*duidelijk merkbaar*] [*tussen*
      division PST COP clearly noticeable between
      hindustani nanga a blakaman]
      Hindustani and the black people
      'Divisions / were / clearly noticeable between / Hindustani and the black people.'
                                                                  (Bolle 1994: 82)

(54) den sten e kon [tapu a *voorgrond*] [*in plaats* fu den dron]
      PL voice PR come to the foreground in stead of PL drums
      'Voices come to the / foreground instead / of drums.'   (Bolle 1994: 82)

Bolle gives a number of examples of non-constituent mixing:

(55) èn eeh precies [so wan *geval*] *bijna*
      'And uh exactly such a / case almost.'   (Bolle 1994: 81)

(56) *ondanks* [*ellende* nanga angri] in(i) Sranan
      'in spite of misery / and hunger in Surinam . . .'   (Bolle 1994: 81)

There are also a number of examples of mixed collocations and idioms. In some, the content words are Dutch, and the frame and function words Sranan:

(57) mi o *pak* a *draad op*
      I FU pick the thread up
      'I will take over.'   (Bolle 1994: 97)

(58) dat un *draag* un *steentje bij*
      that we bring our stone by
      'That we do our share.'   (Bolle 1994: 97)

There are also examples of verb + noun collocations where the noun is in Sranan and the verb a Dutch form:

(59) a man e *lucht* en ati
      the man PR air his heart
      'The man speaks his mind.'   (Bolle 1994: 97)

(60) un mus(u) *gebruik* un(u) ferstan
      we must use our understanding
      'We must use our head.'   (Bolle 1994: 97)

The most frequent type, however, consists of a Sranan verb combined with a Dutch noun:

(61) gi *voorlichting*   'to give information'
      lusu *schot*   'to fire off a shot'
      taki *lering*   'to learn a lesson'

The existence of, but particularly the diversity of, patterns in these mixed collocations provide an argument for congruent lexicalization.

There is no evidence of morphological integration or of word-internal mixing for this language pair, due to the fact that Sranan has little or no morphology, except for compounding.

It is hard to see whether there is a triggering of code-mixing by words from the other language because so many items in the sentence are borrowings or insertions in various stages of phonological adaptation.

Altogether, however, there is strong evidence for congruent lexicalization in this data set, even though there is only partial correspondence of word order patterns.

Something I cannot go into in any detail here, but which surely needs to be investigated further, is the extent to which the varieties of Sranan and Dutch involved in this mixing are themselves the result of convergence. As mentioned above, there is a range of ethnic varieties of Dutch called Surinaams Nederlands, which in the form closest to the standard have a specific lexicon and pronunciation, and in the varieties more distant from the standard have Sranan-like grammatical constructions as well. I will now look at convergence more systematically.

The nature of the languages in contact: convergence and reduction in Moluccan Malay

A notoriously difficult problem in the study of language contact, including code-mixing, is determining the properties of the languages in contact. This is due to the fact that often the bilingual speech community controls not the written standard form of the language (if this exists at all), but a vernacular that is sometimes itself influenced by the other language. This brings in a historical dimension.

Many languages have a long history of contact in various settings. Three possibilities may be involved: (a) several related but clearly different varieties of each language are used; (b) the bilingual discourse is possibly telegraphic in character; (c) it is hard to determine which language a particular element belongs to.

Some languages have a history of both colonial domination and recent migration, e.g. Moroccan Arabic. In this case the colonial languages are French and Spanish, languages spoken in countries of migration include French, English, Dutch, and German. In other cases the same language was the erstwhile colonial language and is the language of the country of recent migration. Examples are Moluccan Malay and Dutch, Hindi/Panjabi and English, Arabic and French.

Hebrew and Spanish in the Sephardic community are yet a third type, because Hebrew has functioned as the language of religion and ritual of the Judezmo-speaking Sephardic Jews in exile in the Balkans and the Levant, and it is of course the official language of Israel, to where many Judezmo-speakers migrated. An interesting example of a bilingual community, already cited in chapter 3, where both languages involved consist of several discrete varieties is the Spanish and Hebrew speaking community in Jerusalem studied by Susan Berk-Seligson (1986). In Hebrew there is both the spoken vernacular and the Biblical language cited, and in Spanish there is both the vernacular, and registers closer to Ladino, which is more closely related to translated Biblical Hebrew. The coexistence of these various registers in the two languages may account for some of the frequent code-mixing 'errors' Berk-Seligson (1986: 328–4) has encountered. A typical example is:

(62) Ni gizár, ni [0] óto, ni . . .
      'Neither cooking, nor [riding in a] car, nor . . .'
      [0] Tefilá, vinir a káza, vizitár prímoz sérka,
      '[saying] Prayer, coming home, visiting cousins nearby,'
      otra vez [0] al kal. [0] Šabat
      'again [going] to the synagogue. [that is] Sabbath.'

The frequent use of Spanish infinitives in this passage can be either interpreted as highly telegraphic or seen as reminiscent of Biblical Hebrew narrative style, where verbal nouns are frequent (Marie Therèse Varol, p.c.), which has influenced Ladino.

Another good example of the methodological problems in determining the nature of the monolingual varieties contributing to bilingual discourse is Moluccan Malay/Dutch code-mixing, as recorded by Huwaë (1992). First there is the huge problem of determining the precise relation of informal spoken Moluccan Malay to the varieties of Malay spoken in Indonesia, both on the Moluccan archipelago itself and in the barracks in Java where the Moluccan troops were quartered in the colonial period. I will not enter into it here, but will focus on the relation between bilingual and monolingual spoken Moluccan Malay. In spoken Moluccan Malay there is often semantic influence from Dutch in code-mixing contexts. There are a number of sentences that sound like translated Dutch, with respect to a specific collocation.

Furthermore we frequently encounter Malay telegraphic speech in code-mixing contexts. Even though Malay initially makes a highly 'telegraphic' impression on speakers of European languages, we do find cases in code-mixing contexts where elements are left out that should have been present in spoken Ambon Malay. The telegraphic character of the code-mixing speech mode affects Malay as well as Dutch, as we will see below.

In one class of examples the Malay verb is in a reduced form:

(63) *en* dek di sini ada tulis *van* eh koé sing boleh
      and then LO here is write PREP eh you NEG may
      bikin *foto's en zo*
      make pictures and so on.
      'And then, it is written here that you may not take pictures.'

In Malay this *tulis* 'write' would have been *ditulis* 'written' or *ada tulisan* 'there is writing'.

Of course the study of telegraphic speech is confronted with at least two methodological problems: (a) it is sometimes hard to reconstruct a unique 'full paraphrase', as in the last example; (b) there is a natural tendency to reconstruct the hypothetical non-bilingual spoken language more fully than it really is perhaps, partly on the basis of intuitions derived from written and decontextualized language use. Of course, we often delete elements. The only thing one can do is try to provide reasonable paraphrases.

Some examples are impossible to reconstruct out of context:

(64) dong mekali su lama su lia ketong su bisa
they maybe PERF long PERF see we PERF can
'Maybe they [have known] already for a long time, [having seen [that]
we have mastered [speaking Dutch].'

The full form would be:

(65) barangkali dong su lama lihat [ketong bisa
maybe they PERF long see [we can
omong (bahasa) Belanda]
speak language Holland]

The following case illustrates the ordinary situation, since it verges on normal colloquial, though highly elliptical, styles of speaking:

(66) *dus* tong pung jang eh Meester Visser
so we POSS REL eh Teacher Visser
'So our [school] is [the one] where Mr. Visser [was the head] teacher'

A fuller paraphrase of what is meant in Ambon Malay would be:

(67) Jodi, tong pung *sekolah* itu *sekolah* di mana
So, we POSS school that school LO where
Meester Visser kepala *sekolah*
Teacher Visser head school

Clearly we can speak of head-teachers in this inexplicit way, referring in fact to the schools they supervise.

In the Dutch fragments of the bilingual recordings we often find reduction as well. One type is absence of the article in either language. In (68) and (69) the absent article is indefinite, part of the Dutch fixed expressions *een keertje* 'once' and *op een gegeven moment* 'at a given moment', respectively:

(68) kej a *keertje* a pi di geredja-nja gereja ini *toh*?
when I occasion I go LO church-DET church DEM though
'When I once went to the church to this church though?'

(69) *op gegeven moment* kué punja sepatu itang *en* kotor
On given moment you POSS shoe black and dirty
'At [a] given moment your shoes are black and dirty.'

This type is frequent in the recorded data. The trouble in interpreting this finding is that the informal Dutch speech of the young Moluccans, and to a lesser extent Dutch informal speech in general, often has no articles. Of the speakers analysed here, only one has frequent Dutch articles in the bilingual conversations, and these are mostly limited to fixed expressions such as *de wijk* 'the quarter' and *de school*. She also sometimes has *de kamp* 'the camp' rather than the correct neuter form *het kamp*, and hypercorrect *het poort* 'the gate' rather than *de poort*, which in native Dutch has a non-neuter article. All other speakers have some, but not many articles.

A third type concerns the absence of a Dutch dummy subject in Dutch fragments (even where they are obligatory in native Dutch).

(70)   Is echt typisch hoor
        '[This] is really typical, you know.'

It is true that the absence of pronominal subjects is characteristic of Indonesian Dutch in general, as well as in Moluccan Dutch, but it should be called to mind that Dutch subject pronouns are present rather often in the recordings, as in:

(71)   Weet ik ik weet niet wat **het** was
        'Know I I don't know what it was.'

(72)   Dus dan eh dat dat dat is **het** echt weer eh
        thus then eh that that that is it really again eh
        'Then that is it again, really.'

In many cases there is no copula present, even where the predicate is straight Dutch. Only the absence of the copula and an occasional Malay functional element betray the Malay character of these sentences:

(73)   En *akan* [0] rose met blauw
        and it pink with blue
        'And it is pink and blue.'

(74)   En *situ* leer [0] goedkoop ja
        and there leather cheap yes
        'And there leather [is] cheap.'

(75)   Makarios [0] eh Aartsbisschop toch?
        Makarios eh archbishop though
        'Makarios [is] archbishop isn't he?'

In this last type of example there is no overt Malay material. Malay has no overt copula in predicative constructions.

There are at least two problems in interpreting these data, which we cannot solve at present. First, it is not always clear whether they show the simplification characteristic of a fossilized interlanguage, a kind of telegraphic style, or Malay influence on Dutch. It could be all three at once in some cases. Second, it is necessary to study in much more detail whether the phenomena are just characteristic of code-mixing discourse or of the informal register in Dutch of young Moluccans. Again it could be both at once, since

145

code-mixing is characteristic of the informal register. What is clear from the recordings as well as from other observations is that these speakers are able to speak Dutch that is grammatically virtually indistinguishable from that of the Dutch of non-Moluccan outsiders.

It should be borne in mind that the Moluccan community has been isolated for a long time in the Netherlands, permitting the development of varieties of Dutch quite different from those of the larger community. Similarly Moluccan Malay has been cut off, for quite some time, from the normative influences of standard Indonesian. Nonetheless, the speakers in this study are by no means marginal with respect to the larger community; all of them can and often do speak something closely approximating the standard language. The interviews contain monolingual fragments which are completely standard Dutch. Similarly, the telegraphic Malay, where it occurs, is limited to code-mixing contexts.

It is possible that the convergence of two grammatical systems by bilingual speakers is furthered by frequent code-mixing but at the same time stimulates it: a case of mutual reinforcement.

Structural and lexical parallels between languages

Many cases of congruent lexicalization involve related and similar languages. There are three logical possibilities:

(a) Both the grammar and the lexicon are similar. This is the case of Dutch/dialect and Dutch/Frisian code-mixing.

(b) The grammar is somewhat similar but not the lexicon. I will illustrate this with Spanish/English code-mixing in Gibraltar (Moyer 1992).

(c) The lexicon is somewhat similar but not the grammar. I will illustrate this with English/Dutch code-mixing.

Spanish/English code-mixing in Gibraltar

From Melissa Moyer's work (1992) on Gibraltar it is clear that many examples of spoken discourse show frequent back and forth switching with a high degree of linear equivalence:

(76) Yo no comprendo como un gobierno *can allow* una cosa así *to happen.*
'I do not understand how a government / can allow / a thing like that / to happen.'
(Moyer 1992: 421)

(77) Any way, *yo creo que las personas* who support *todos estos grupos como los* Friends of the Earth *son personas que* are very close to nature.

146

'Anyway, / I believe that the people / who support / all these groups like the / Friends of the Earth / are people who are very close to nature.'

(Moyer 1992: 437)

In some code-mixing cases it is as if the grammatical switch does not correspond to the lexical switch. Particularly, Moyer's corpus contains many cases where a basically English expression contains a Spanish verb and an English complement. The collocation of two expressions, a verb and a complement, is the site for a code-mix. Often the verb is in the dominant language (boldface in the examples below), and the complement an inserted constituent. Moyer's data from her extensive transcribed corpus in part II of her thesis contain many examples of this:

(78) a. make an appointment
       b. . . . que he **hecho** un / *an appointment and I'll fix everything for her*
          '. . . that I have made an appointment and I'll fix everything for her.'

(Moyer 1992: 341)

The mixed collocation can only be construed if there is a complete equivalence between the two languages. I will assume that these cases are revelatory of congruent lexicalization.

(79) a. take displinary action
       b. El *government* ha dicho que si es necesario **tomarán** *disciplinary action* contra ellos.
          'The government has said that if it is necesary they'll take disciplinary action against them.'   (Moyer 1992: 421)

(80) a. have an ulterior motive
       b. tu te crees que todo el mundo tiene que **tener** *an ulterior motive*?
          'Do you imagine that everybody has to have an ulterior motive?'

(Moyer 1992: 428)

(81) a. be back to square one
       b. Si todavía **estamos a** *back to square one* en verdad en caso de esta mujer.
          'If we are really back to square one in the case of this woman.'

(Moyer 1992: 465)

(82) a. give an appointment
       b. Me puedes **dar** un *appointment*?
          'Can you give me an appointment?'   (Moyer 1992: 524)

Sometimes it is the other way around, with a Spanish expression and a Spanish verb:

(83) a. go on a honeymoon / ir de vacaciones
          'go on a holiday'
       b. Poca gente lo hace pero hay gente que **se van de** *honeymoon*.
          'Few people do it but there are people who go on a honeymoon.'

(Moyer 1992: 311)

(84) a. give a reception
      b. que ya procuraremos los yanitos de **dar**le el *typical friendly reception.*
          'that we will get the Gibraltarians to give him the typical friendly
          reception'   (Moyer 1992: 428)

(85) a. go on strike / ponerse en huelga
      b. Va a ser a los del *income tax office* que **se** han **puesto** *on strike*
          'It will be those of the income tax offices that have gone on strike.'
                                                                       (Moyer 1992: 420)

We do not find English verbs in Spanish expressions (86a) or in English
expressions with a Spanish noun phrase (86b):

(86) a. * They went *de vacaciones.*
          'They went on a holiday.'
      b. * They took *medidas disciplinarias.*
          'They took disciplinary action.'

Some cases correspond to neither a Spanish nor an English expression, as far
as I could ascertain. This is noted by Moyer (1992: 210) for (87):

(87) a. ser flexible / be flexible
      b. Pero tú tienes que tener *flexibility.*
          'But you have to be flexible.'   (Moyer 1992: 473)

(88) Hace *Moslem fast for thirty days* ¿no?
      'He does a Moslem fast for thirty days, doesn't he?'   (Moyer 1992: 352)

English/Dutch code-mixing

For Dutch/English mixing in Australia cases of non-constituent mixing have
been reported as well (Clyne 1987). This makes it possible perhaps to
establish a positive correlation between typological distance and the amount
of non-constituent mixing – indicative of congruent lexicalization – to be
expected. Similar data have been reported for Afrikaans/English code-mixing
in Cape Town (McCormick 1989).

Clyne has demonstrated that switches between closely related languages
are possible in more circumstances than any of the current proposed
constraints would allow, and it is quite possible that this is due to the greater
opportunities for neutralization in these cases.

Applying this idea of Clyne's, Crama and van Gelderen (1984) have
studied Dutch/English code-mixing and found quite a few cases of such
neutralization sites, particularly with the pronunciation of bilinguals:

(89) Je *can it* zondag doen.   (Du *kan*)
      'You can do it on Sunday.'

(90) Met Netty *was it* langer?   (Du *was ət*)
      'Was it longer with Netty?'

(91)   . . . dan zit er een *volunteer there.*   (Du *daar*)
'. . . then there is a volunteer there.'

In cases (89)–(91) the Linear Equivalence Constraint of Poplack (1980) is violated.

(92)   Weet je *where Jenny is?*   (Du *waar*)
'Do you know . . .?'

(93)   Weet je *what she is doing?*   (Du *wat*)
'Do you know . . . ?'

(94)   Would you *even blazen meneer?*   (Du *jə*)
'Would you just blow, sir?'

In (92)–(94) we have a violation of the hierarchical government constraint of DiSciullo, Muysken, and Singh (1986). The reason that these switches occur may be that *where, can,* and *was* are almost homophonous with their Dutch equivalents *waar, kan,* and *was,* while *is* and *it* are also similar to their Dutch counterparts.

Crama and van Gelderen (1984: 6.7) give a list of potential homophonous diamorphs:

(95)

	Dutch	**English**		
verbs	is	is	[ɪs]	[ɪz]
	was	was	[ʋas]	[wɔz]
	kom	come	[kom]	[kʌm]
	kan	can	[kan]	[kæn]
pronouns	je	you	[jə]	[jə, ju]
	hij	he	[hɛɪ]	[hiː]
	we	we	[ʋə]	[wi]
	het	it	[ət]	[ɪt]
determiners	de	the	[də]	[ðə]
wh-words	wat	what	[ʋat]	[wɔt]
	waar	where	[ʋaːr]	[weəʳ]

We need to reflect upon the implications of the notion of homophonous diamorph for our view of the relation between grammar and speech production. Is there no matrix language for the cases involved, or are there inserted elements with lexical neutrality, within a given matrix language?

A comparison

When we compare Spanish/English and Dutch/English code-mixing, both similarities and differences transpire. The main similarity is that code-mixing is relatively free and frequent. However, a difference is that in some Spanish/English code-mixing settings multi-constituent or non-constituent switches are rare. Moyer's material contains many instances like (96), where nominals are inserted:

> (96) . . . comprar *kitchen scales* y *bathroom scales.* Las dos ¿no? . . .
> '. . . to buy kitchen scales and bathroom scales. The two, right?'
>
> (Moyer 1992: 380)

Even cases like (97), which involve a multi-word transition, can be analysed as the insertion of a borrowing and a single verb phrase:

> (97) Y yo no veo ninguno de los *opposition fitting into that category*
> 'And I do not see anyone of the opposition *fitting into that category.*'
>
> (Moyer 1992: 437)

Congruent lexicalization in lexical borrowing

We have discovered patterns of borrowing that are related to insertion and alternation. Are there also cases that resemble congruent lexicalization? It may not be easy to encounter these since congruent lexicalization involves a string of words. Still, there are some word-internal borrowing phenomena that result from shared (word) grammar. I will give two examples, one from English–German mixed compounds (Clyne 1967: 34–5) – and one from Aymara–Quechua affix borrowing (Adelaar 1986, Muysken 1988a, van de Kerke 1996).

In Australia, German immigrants will often form bilingual compounds, headed (Williams 1981) either by a German (most common: 24 types listed) or an English word (7 types listed):

> (98) a. **German head**
>
> | *Beach*landschaft | 'beach landscape' |
> | *Beach*häuser | 'beach houses' |
> | *Country*platz | 'country place' |
> | *Guest*häuser | 'guest houses' |
> | *Gum*baum | 'gum tree' |
> | *Landscape*gärtner | 'landscape gardener' |
>
> b. **English head**
>
> | Eukalyptus*tree* | 'eucalyptus tree' |
> | Grün*grocer* | 'greengrocer' |
> | Ketten*store* | 'chain store' |
> | Les*period* | 'class period' |
> | Schreib[en]*practice* | 'writing practice' |
> | Feuer*brigade* | 'fire brigade' |

The predominance of German headed compounds reflects the fact that German is the matrix language in this bilingual corpus. Several cases of English headed compounds are based on very specific English compounds, like 'greengrocer' and 'chain store'. In any case, it is clear from the examples and their gloss how close German and English are in this respect. The similarity of the compounding pattern in the two languages makes it plausible to regard this as an example of borrowing through congruent lexicalization. The bidirectionality of the process points in the same direction: both German-headed and English-headed compounds occur. Notice that this type of mixed compounds is one step away from loan translations, in which both members of the compound are replaced by elements from another language.

A second example of borrowing through congruent lexicalization comes from the contact between Quechua and Aymara (Adelaar 1986), e.g. in the Quechua of Puno, Peru. These two highly agglutinative Andean languages have been spoken in the same regions for over a thousand years but they present an enigma for genetic and historical linguists in that their basic vocabulary and many of their affixes are clearly distinct, making a common ancestor unlikely. At the same time they have borrowed extensively over time and show an uncanny resemblance in their grammatical structure. In several areas, affixes have been borrowed between them. An example from Chumbivilcas Quechua (Muysken 1988a):

(99) llank'a-*naqa*-yu-ni-n
      work try INT 1sg AF
      'I am certainly trying to work.'

Here the affix -*naqa*- has been borrowed into Quechua from Aymara, but it occupies a slot that is easily available for affixes in either language. The similarity of patterning makes affix borrowing through congruent lexicalization quite easily possible.

Adelaar (1986) shows that the borrowed Aymara affixes -*thapi*- and -*t'a*- trigger deletion of the last vowel of the Quechua base they are attached to:

(100) tiy-*thapi*-chi-   (full form **tiya-**)
       live together CAU
       'permit that they live together'

(101) pas-*t'a*-ku-   (full form **pasa-**)
       pass suddenly RE
       'pass suddenly'

This deletion rule does not exist in Quechua, which underscores the analysis given of these cases as congruent lexicalization. The Aymara morphophonemic system is active at the same time as the Quechua system. Van de Kerke (1996) documents the pervasive influence of the Aymara morphological structuring in Bolivian Quechua.

Conclusions

In this chapter, a third type of code-mixing was introduced, involving related languages. Many authors make a principled distinction between mixing and shifting in terms of the relatedness of the languages or varieties involved. Relatedness can have several interpretations:

(a) Differences in code consciously perceived as such by the speaker. Here there is great variety: sometimes fairly similar dialects are viewed as vastly different and having a different status, while for some groups of bilinguals entirely unrelated languages may be treated as pretty much equivalent (though clearly as distinct), and for other groups, related languages as in conflict with each other.

(b) Structural and phonetic differences as analysed by the linguist. Again, there is considerable variety. Tamil and English are different in most relevant ways, but between Spanish and English there are many structural similarities which are exploited in code-mixing.

(c) Lexical differences are quite visible and are often interpreted as revelatory of distance between speech varieties by speakers (e.g. the case of Media Lengua and Quechua, or of Hindi and Urdu).

Given that there is a gradient both in perceived distance and in analytically established distance, the distance argument as such cannot be the basis for a principled distinction between mixing and shifting.

There is a hierarchy in the degree to which congruent lexicalization occurs in different communities. To just take the case of Dutch in contact with other languages, the one I have most experience with, this hierarchy may take the following form:

(102) dialect/standard Dutch   *frequent congruent lexicalization*
        Frisian/Dutch
        Sranan/Dutch
        Dutch in Australia
        Moluccan Malay/Dutch
        French/Dutch
        Moroccan Arabic/Dutch
        Sarnami/Dutch
        Turkish/Dutch   *infrequent congruent lexicalization*

The upper part of this scalar hierarchy blends into the study of intralinguistic variation.

The plea to link some forms of code-mixing and variation as in congruent lexicalization is not just a matter of terminology and empty theorizing. It makes it possible to deal with variation and its quantitative coordinates in terms of variation in lexical insertion. This in turn enables us to link up research on variation in speech to psycholinguistic experimentation involving lexical retrieval and sentence production. Ultimately this gives us a better chance to locate linguistic variation in the typology of phenomena of variation in human behaviour. The interaction with theories of grammar involves then mainly the study of constraints on heterogeneous elements inserted into the same structure.

6
Function words

This chapter is concerned with the well-known but not unproblematic distinction between lexical and grammatical categories. It is felt by everyone that in dialogue (1) underlined elements like *money* and *parents* have a status different from elements like *you* and *am*:

(1) a. **From** who will you <u>get</u> the <u>money</u>?
    b. I am **going** to <u>ask</u> my <u>parents</u>.

The distinction between the two classes has proven extremely useful in a number of domains, but what is covered by the two terms, lexical and grammatical, and on the basis of which criteria the distinction is made, appears to vary according to the domain involved. Also, some elements appear to have an intermediate status. The preposition *from* is often termed grammatical, but somewhat concrete in its meaning. Similarly, *going* functions as an auxiliary, but has developed from a main verb. In (1) I have classified *get* as lexical, but some of the uses of this verb are grammatical, as in *Let's get started* and *He got hit by a car*. Thus there is good reason to consider the distinction a bit more closely, particularly in the light of theoretical developments.

In many current views of phrase structure the constitution of constituents such as clauses is seen as determined by the selection of complements by a head element within its projection. In most recent generative work the additional assumption is made that head elements do not only include content words such as verb and noun but also **functional elements** such as agreement and tense. Functional elements form the structural backbone of the clause. Differences between languages derive from different characteristics of the functional elements, as sketched in chapter 2.

As pointed out by Aravind Joshi (1985) and Carol Myers-Scotton (1993b), functional elements play a special role in code-mixing as well: they are not often inserted into an alien structure by themselves, and thus tend to come from the base or matrix language. Take a fairly standard case such as:

(2) haukuona a-ki-ni-*buy*-i-a *beer* siku hioy?
     didn't you know 3sg-PR-1sg-buy-BEN-IND beer that day
     'Didn't you know he was buying beer for me that day?'
                                    (Swahili/English; Myers-Scotton 1992b: 6)

Only content words are taken from English and all functional elements, in the form of prefixes and suffixes, are Swahili. The question is how to explain this special role, manifest in the asymmetry of functional elements and content words.

I first give more evidence that there is an asymmetry in code-mixing. Then I discuss the definitions that have been given of functional elements; no sinecure as I already suggested above. Subsequently I provide a survey of some of the domains in which the distinction has played a role, both in language contact and change and in speech production. On the basis of all this, I return to the explanations for the asymmetry at hand.

Function words in code-mixing

To show the generality of the phenomenon of function-word restriction, I will give some examples involving Dutch and a number of minority languages. The bold elements in the glosses are the words from the base languages. These tend to be grammatical elements; for a larger corpus the correct generalization would be that the non-base language elements are lexical.

(3) aku *nog steeds vinden* akan *raar* [kata koe *bellen* aku
     I still find **it** strange **that you** call **I**
     twee keer [*zonder* dapat *gehoor*]]
     twice without **get** hearing
     'I still find it strange that you called me twice without finding anyone
     home.'   (Moluccan Malay/Dutch; Huwaë 1992)

Here all Malay elements, *aku* 'I', *akan* 'it', *kata* 'that', *koe* 'you' and possibly *dapat* 'get' are functional elements, and all Dutch elements are content words.

A similar account can be given of (4)–(7):

(4) wan heri *gedeelte* de ondro *beheer* fu *gewapende machten*
     '**One whole** part **is under** control **of** armed forces.'
                                    (Sranan/Dutch; Bolle 1994: 75)

(5) Ngai yew *krampen in* nga *buik*.
     '**I have** cramps **in my** stomach.'   (Chinese/Dutch; Tjon 1988: 8)

(6) ben *kamer*-Im-I *opruimen* yap-ar-ken
     I room-1sg-AC tidy **while-doing**
     'while tidying my room'   (Turkish/Dutch; Backus 1992)

(7) 9end-na bezzaf bezzaf *moeilijkheden* u *problemen met* . . .
     have-we much much difficulties **and** problems with
     'We have many many difficulties and problems with . . .'
                                            (Moroccan Arabic/Dutch; Nortier 1990: 138)

The type of mixing process illustrated in (4)–(7) is unidirectional: the base language tends to be the community language of the migrant group, the inserted language the dominant national language. While in most of the cases illustrated the distinction between the categories is fairly clear, there are some examples of indeterminacy: while in (4) the preposition *ondro* 'under' is realized in the base language Sranan, in (5) the preposition *in* is realized in the inserted language Dutch.

These examples differ in the morphological nature of the functional elements retained from the base language, but they share the **functional element effect**. This effect may well be related to other differences between lexical and functional categories currently under investigation. I am using the term 'functional elements' as a generic term (rather than 'function words') because words, affixes, and abstract grammatical elements are included in this category and both the term system morpheme employed by Myers-Scotton and the term functional category used by Chomsky (1993) are too theoretically loaded to be suitable at this point.

Two hypotheses will be tested with respect to their special behaviour in code-mixing:

(a) the functional element effect derives from the special status of functional elements within the mental lexicon and speech production, as argued by Myers-Scotton (1993b) and Azuma (1993) on the basis of assumptions made by some psycholinguists

(b) the functional element effect derives from the lack of equivalence of functional elements across different languages, the hypothesis I would like to defend here

Although the evidence is not conclusive, I think a fair case can be made for the second hypothesis.

A third hypothesis, worth exploring in future work, but not taken up here, is that the effect is related to the phonological strength of the elements involved. This theory will hold for the Swahili inflections in (2), but not as well for the Malay words in (3).

Before going on, it is important to recall briefly the special behaviour of adpositions, conjunctions, and interjections discussed in chapter 4 in relation to alternation. The following example of a Dutch sentence with a single Arabic word, illustrates the reverse pattern of (7).

> (8) Ik ben een dokter *wella* ik ben een ingenieur.
>   'I am a doctor **or** I am an engineer.'   (Nortier 1990: 142)

This pattern is found particularly with discourse markers and conjunctions. These elements show a partly divergent behaviour from the other functional elements, since they are involved in alternational rather than insertional mixing.

Definition

A first issue is how to define functional elements. This is by no means easy, and there may not be a single criterion. Traditionally the following external criteria were used for distinguishing the classes of function and content elements (e.g. Emonds 1973; Abney 1987).

Semantically one might distinguish between auto-semantic elements (content words, with a concrete meaning) that have a meaning by themselves, and syn-semantic elements (function words), that have an abstract meaning that depends on the context. However, there may be functional elements that have no evident semantic interpretation at all, not even in conjunction with a content word. Since they have no independent meaning, functional elements cannot be modified (Abney 1987; e.g. *she smiled wickedly* versus * *she has wickedly*).

A second criterion is **open** versus **closed** class. Nouns and verbs typically belong to open classes, pronouns typically to closed ones. Adjectives and adverbs in many languages form an open class, but in some a small closed one. There is often only a limited number of coordinating conjunctions and adpositions in a language, but equally often elements still could be added to these categories. In Dutch, for instance, the prepositional *be-* prefix (found in *binnen* 'inside' from *in*) can be added to the cardinal points 'north' and 'south' to yield the prepositions *benoorden* 'to the north of' and *bezuiden* 'to the south of'. Many more peripheral conjunctions and prepositions can be easily replaced, and may be replaced more rapidly (in terms of types) than content words, in terms of their percentage of the total set of conjunctions or adpositions. Thus the criterium of closedness is not easy to apply in many cases.

A third criterion would be whether a certain class of elements can undergo

derivational morphology, like noun, verb or adjective, or not, like demonstrative and auxiliary (Abney 1987). Since lexical suppletion is characteristic of inflection rather than derivation, functional elements but not content words tend to enter into a suppletive relationship (*walks/walked* < > *is/was*).

A fourth criterion may be **role in structuring the clause**. Some elements, such as subordinating conjunctions and agreement and tense markers, play a central role in the clause; others, such as diminutive markers and degree adverbs, a more peripheral role. It is instructive to take Anderson's (1982) well-known distinction between inflection and derivation into account in distinguishing system and content morphemes. For Anderson inflection is that part of morphology that participates in the rules of syntax. We could extend that by saying that functional elements are those non-content elements that play a syntactic role, and thus exclude derivational elements. Another way of underlining their role in the clause is stating that functional elements have an obligatory complement (Abney 1987) e.g. an auxiliary needs a verb phrase complement.

An often invoked criterion would be whether a given closed class is **paradigmatically** organized, i.e. whether the elements in it are defined in opposition to each other (present versus past, singular versus plural, definite versus indefinite etc.). Particularly pronoun and tense systems tend to be tightly organized paradigmatically, and show a high degree of symmetry. However, we may find tight paradigmatic organization outside the realm of function words, e.g. in kinship terminology. A similar criterion would be to consider grammatical elements as involving an obligatory choice (from the members of a paradigm) and lexical elements as involving a free choice.

Another set of criteria are **phonological** in nature. Grammatical elements do not receive sentential **stress** very easily, and tend to be phonologically weak, **monosyllabic** elements.

An important distinction is that between **bound** and **free** morphemes. In many but not all languages – e.g. the Northwest Coast Amerindian languages form an exception – bound morphemes are functional elements.

Given these different criteria different subclasses can be distinguished in the categorial systems of various languages, in a way that needs to be made more precise. Grammatical elements are not a coherent group. We may distinguish between **relational** elements such as conjunctions, prepositions, and deictic elements, which are often referential or quantificational. Different researchers have noted that languages may differ in the classification of elements as lexical and syntactic. This poses special problems for constraints on code-mixing in terms of the status of elements as functional or not.

As an example, in table 6.1 these criteria are applied to a number of

Table 6.1. *The classification of Dutch elements in terms of a number of the criteria listed*

	ABST	CLOS	DERI	ROLE	PARA	MONO	UNST
articles de, het, een 'the, the, a'	+	+	+	+	+	+	+
negation niet, geen 'not, no'	+	+	+	+	+	+	±
unemphatic pronouns 'k, je, ie, 'm 'I, you, he, him'	+	+	+	+	+	±	+
auxiliaries hebben, worden 'have, be/become'	+	+	+	+	+	−	±
complementizers dat, of, om, te 'that, if, for, to'	+	+	±	+	±	+	+
emphatic pronouns ik, jij, hij 'I, you, he'	+	+	+	+	+	±	±
demonstratives deze, dat 'this, that'	+	+	+	+	+	±	±
abstract prepositions van, aan, door 'of, to, by'	+	+	+	+	−	+	−
modals zullen, moeten 'shall, must'	+	+	+	−	±	±	−
coordinating conjunctions en, of, maar 'and, or, but'	+	+	+	±	±	+	±
quantifiers 1 iets, niets 'something, nothing'	+	+	+	±	+	−	−
question words wie, wat, waar 'who, what, where'	+	+	+	+	−	−	−
quantifiers 2 enkele, sommige 'any, some'	+	+	+	±	−	−	−
subordinating conjunctions als, toen, omdat 'if, when, since'	+	±	±	−	−	±	±

	ABST	CLOS	DERI	ROLE	PARA	MONO	UNST
semi-auxiliaries							
gaan 'go'	±	±	±	−	−	±	±
simple prepositions							
in, op, bij, met 'in, on, at, with'	±	±	−	−	−	−	±
causal coordinators							
want 'because'	+	−	±	−	−	−	±
interjections							
ja, of zo, dus 'yes, or so, thus'	+	−	±	−	−	−	±
abstract adverbs							
bijna, direct 'almost, directly'	+	−	−	−	−	−	−
complex prepositions							
boven, behalve 'above, apart from'	−	−	−	−	−	−	−

ABST	=	abstract meaning
CLOS	=	a closed class
DERI	=	does not participate in derivational morphology
ROLE	=	plays a specific role in the grammar, through its feature specification
PARA	=	paradigmatically organized in terms of opposed values on certain features
MONO	=	monosyllabic
UNST	=	can be without stress

categories in Dutch, yielding a gradient classification rather than an absolute one. It is clear no single unified class can be isolated on the basis of these criteria.

What is worse, sometimes the criteria yield contradictory results. Basing himself particularly on the criteria listed in Abney (1987), Zwarts (1995, 1997) has analysed the Dutch prepositions, which show a quite complex interaction with the pronoun *er* 'there'. Zwarts distinguishes three types of prepositions:

(9) functional: met 'with', naar 'to', te 'at', tot 'until', van 'of'
    simple lexical: aan 'to', binnen 'inside', door 'by, through', bij 'near', in 'in', mee 'with', om 'around', op 'on', etc.
    complex lexical: aangaande 'concerning', benoorden 'to the north of', ongeacht 'disregarding', via 'via', etc.

Only simple lexical prepositions can take the proclitic *er*:

(10) functional: *ermet 'therewith'
     simple lexical: eraan 'thereto'
     complex lexical: *eraangaande 'thereconcerning'

Some prepositions have a lexical form (*mee* 'with'), combinable with *er*, and a functional form (*met* 'with'), which cannot be combined. The lexical form can also be used without a complement:

(11)   a. Hij is mee / *met.   'He is along / *with.'
       b. ermee / *ermet   'therewith'

However, the formal distinction between simple lexical and functional prepositions does not correspond to other criteria. Thus the 'grammatical' prepositions *aan* 'to' and *door* 'by', that play a clearly grammatical role in the dative and passive constructions, respectively, are classified as simple lexical prepositions.

Myers-Scotton's classification

Myers-Scotton formally defines function elements in terms of quantification and theta-theory (1993b: 99–102).

Let us briefly consider Myers-Scotton's criteria for distinguishing between system and content morphemes, which are formulated in terms of two questions: (a) is an element a potential assigner or receiver of a thematic (semantic) role within the clause? (b) does an element quantify over a certain domain (reminding one of Jakobson's shifters; 1971)? Quantifiers are system morphemes in her model, as are elements that are neither theta-role assigners nor theta-role receivers.

These criteria for distinguishing system from content morphemes are problematic for a number of reasons:

- Redundancy: as is clear from table 6.2, the [± Quantifier feature] is not necessary to make the distinction between system and content morphemes, since the features [± θ assigner] and [± θ receiver] make the relevant distinctions.
- It is not easy to see how the classification into system and content morphemes carries across languages. In English the benefactive is expressed by the preposition *for* (thus a theta-role assigning content-morpheme), while in Swahili it is an applicative affix, fully part of the grammatical system, and hence a system morpheme.
- It is not always clear whether an element θ-marks a complement or not. The role of prepositions as thematic role assigners is often not independent from the verb. English *to* θ-marks an object, but often in conjunction with the verb. Compare the contrast between the two Dutch causatives:

Table 6.2. *Myers-Scotton's system for distinguishing between system (s) and content (c) morphemes (1993b: 101).*

	[± θ assigner]	[± θ receiver]	Quantifier	status
Quantifiers		* ±	+	<s>
possessives		* +	+	<s>
tense/aspect			+	s
determiners			+	s
copula	−			s
helping verbs	−			s
poss. 'of'	−			s
dummy pronouns		−		s
parts idioms		−		s
complementizer	−	−		s
agreement	−	−/* ±		<s>
pronouns		+	* +	<c>
nouns		+		c
adjectives		+		c˙
verbs	+			c
prepositions	+	* ±		<c>
?conjunctions				
?adverbs				
?interjections				

Problematic cases (derived from grammatical theory) are marked with a * , and subsequently debatable classifications with < >. Categories not included are listed with ?.

(i) Ik laat het *aan* haar zien.
  'I show it to her.'
(ii) Ik laat het *door* haar maken.
  'I have it made by her.'
Clearly *aan* 'to' introduces an experiencer, and *door* 'by' an agent, but the thematic role of their complement, the Causee, is marked in part by the verbs involved.

- Possessive elements can easily be argued to have the thematic role 'possessor'.
- The criteria conflict with well-established traditional criteria:
  (i) Bound morphemes can be θ-markers, e.g. applicative affixes in Bantu
  (ii) Paradigmatically structured morphemes can be θ-markers, e.g. Finnish case markers
- In the distinctions made by Myers-Scotton, phonology is disregarded. There is a respectable tradition in which content and

system morphemes are distinguished in terms of phonological strength, syllabicity. and feet.

The criteria used by Myers-Scotton are more reminiscent of grammatical models of code-mixing than of the psycholinguistic models that Myers-Scotton draws upon in arguing for the relevance of the distinction (1993b: 54–8). In the latter literature, generally the discussion involves English nominal and verbal inflection, not the whole array of elements defined as system morpheme by Myers-Scotton.

Functional categories and differentiation between languages

In chapter 2 I discussed the issue of lexical differentiation between languages: is it differentiation between major class lexical items, or between any type of lexical item, or is it specific to functional elements and their distribution? We do not know at present whether all differences between languages can be reduced to lexical differences – there are conflicting opinions. Even Borer (1994), one of the main inspirers of the lexicalist learning theory, now believes that some differences do not result from properties of lexical items. I depart here from the assumption that the lexicon, and in particular the function word lexicon, is one of the primary loci of language differentiation.

There is not much clarity yet on the issue of differentiation in the inventory of functional categories across languages. Several possibilities exist:

- All functional categories are defined by universal grammar and exist in all languages. This proposal is attractive in its simplicity, but it forces one either to limit what counts as a functional category to a small set or to postulate many lexically unrealized categories in many different languages. Within this option, language differentiation would be seen in terms of the extent to which functional categories are lexicalized in different languages.
- All categories are potentially available on a list, and their selection in a particular language is triggered by a specific morphosyntax.
- A core list is fixed by universal grammar (containing e.g. tense), and non-core categories (e.g. Focus particles) need to be established on the basis of experience.
- All functional categories need to be triggered on the basis of experience.
- The categories themselves are fixed (tense, number, person, case, etc.), but the values for the categories and the number of the

163

distinctions made (future, dual, inclusive versus exclusive, ablative) need to be established on the basis of experience.

In the minimalist perspective (Chomsky 1993) there are no clear claims for a fixed list of functional categories determined by the grammar as such, but the option is left open that the interface with semantics and phonetics forces certain categories to be present.

A rather different perspective on the inventory of functional elements in different languages is given in cognitive linguistics and grammaticalization research. There it is assumed that there is a fuzzy boundary between function words and content words. The tradition of grammaticalization research has established paths along which content morphemes typically evolve into function words. There is no claim of binary distinctions (e.g. between content and function), nor of absolute universality. To be sure, common trends are noted, though clearly functional elements may be present in one stage in the history of a language but not in another.

Summary

It is not simple either to arrive at a clear definition of functional elements nor to categorize them satisfactorily. In the following discussion I will adopt a rough heuristic distinction between **shifters** (Jakobson 1971), nominal heads that quantify over a certain domain, **functional categories proper**, and **linkers**, that connect constituents and clauses. This distinction is theoretically questionable, at least in part, but it helps structure the data.

(12) shifters:
    pronouns
    demonstratives
    question words
    quantifiers
functional categories proper:
    articles
    tense markers
    agreement
    auxiliaries
    modals
linkers:
    prepositions
    conjunctions
    complementizers
    connectives

The status of functional categories in language change, language contact and creolization

A further domain where the lexical/grammatical distinction plays a role is that of language change, language contact, and creolization. The distinction is relevant here in several respects.

First of all, a certain class of grammatical elements, namely shifters, has proved to be remarkably stable in the process of regular language change (while undergoing a number of more or less regular sound changes). This can be illustrated with the Indo-European proto-form for 'what' and its descendants:

(13)   *'what' in Indo-European* (Delbrück/Brugmann 1911: 349)

Proto-Form	* q^uo- / *q^ue- / *q^ua-
Old Indic	ká-h, ká
Avestic	ko
Old Persian	kaš
Armenian	o
Attic	τίς
Albanian	kuš
Latin	quod
Church Slavonic	čito
Old Irish	cia
Kymric	pwy < k^uei
Gothic	has
Lithuanian	kà

In most branches of the Indo-European language family, the word for 'what' can be directly related to the proto-form. The class of elements which show this stability tend to be the ones that form a tightly organized paradigmatic set, such as the set of pronouns. Grammatical elements that do not belong in this category, notably linkers, such as complementizers and conjunctions, and functional categories such as determiners, tend to be much less stable.

While in regular change we find this pattern of stability at least with one class of grammatical elements, in pidgin and creole genesis there has been a radical restructuring of the overall inventory of grammatical elements. If we take the same element 'what', we find in a few of the creoles with English lexicon forms such as:

(14)   *'what' in some English lexicon pidgins and creoles* (Muysken and Smith 1990)

Chinese Pidgin English	wat-ting
Cameroon Pidgin English	wéting/húskayn/ting
Krio	wât
Sranan	(o) san

Saramaccan	andí
Jamaican Creole	wat/we/wara

These forms contain lexemes derived from *what, thing, kind, something* (Sranan *san*), *where*, as well as a Fon borrowing (Saramaccan *andí*). No doubt these changes are plausible semantically, as has been argued by Seuren and Wekker (1986), but they indicate that the transmission of grammatical elements has been interrupted in the process of creole genesis. The same holds *a fortiori* for other types of grammatical elements such as conjunctions.

Van Hout and Muysken (1994) studied the role of different factors in constraining the borrowing of Spanish lexical and functional elements into Bolivian Quechua. When we consider lexical borrowing, one of the primary motivations for it is to extend the **referential potential** of a language. Since reference is established primarily through nouns, these are the elements borrowed most easily. More generally, content words such as adjectives, nouns, and verbs may be borrowed more easily than function words (articles, pronouns, conjunctions) since the former have a clear link to cultural content and the latter do not. In some cases, borrowing extends beyond cultural content words, however, and there may well be other constraints on borrowing, e.g. distinguishing among different kinds of content words. In addition, there is no unambiguous definition to help us distinguish content words from function words.

In Van Hout and Muysken (1994) a statistical regression analysis was carried out for these factors, as well as for word frequency:

> paradigmaticity
> equivalence between source and recipient language
> inflection in the source language
> inflection in the recipient language
> status as a function word or not
> transitivity
> constituent-peripheral versus -internal

Our main results were the following. Paradigmaticity and inflection in the donor language are revealed to be the strongest structural factors in our regression analysis of the probability of Spanish borrowings in Quechua. Lexical content and equivalence do not play a role independently. Frequency also has a (somewhat weaker) effect, while peripherality has an effect, but opposite to what we originally predicted. Thus it was not an absolute distinction between functional and lexical that proved decisive, but rather a number of factors indirectly related to this distinction.

It should be stressed that the results we obtained for Spanish borrowings in Bolivian Quechua are not meant to be independent of this particular set of languages. In other language pairs quite different factors may turn out to be operant, depending on sociolinguistic factors and different contrasting typological properties. The same holds for the particular factors chosen and the way they are applied to classify the borrowings. The ones we chose relate, in part, to particular properties of Spanish and Quechua, and to our first impressions of which factors may have been steering the borrowing process.

Lexical and functional elements in speech production, agrammatism, language development, foreigner talk

Since code-mixing is a performance phenomenon, both in production and in perception, clearly any grammatical account of code-mixing is only valid insofar as it can be embedded in a psycholinguistic model of speech processing.

Speech production

In psycholinguistic research, a number of features have been found to be characteristic of functional elements. Summarizing a large literature, Butterworth (1989), Levelt (1989), and Shillcock and Bard (1993) list a number of features.

Function words are much more frequent than content words (150 English functional words account for 40 per cent of the tokens in ordinary speech) (Shillcock and Bard 1993: 165). Functional elements can also be set apart by their predictability: since they are chosen from small closed sets, it is much more easy to predict which functional element, e.g. determiner, will come next than which content word, e.g. noun.

A number of their properties are **phonological**. Functional elements are less often preceded by pauses than content words (Levelt 1989: 203). Functional elements that are not phrase final are seldom followed by a break (Levelt 1989: 304). The least pausing should occur between a content word and a function word adjoined to it (Levelt 1989: 391). Closed class words take their accent with them when they shift position (Butterworth 1989: 114).

Functional elements tend to be **destressed** as if they were affixes. Phonologically, they are not really words at all (Levelt 1989: 299). Functional elements do not count as separate elements in motor planning units or stress groups (Levelt 1989: 420).

Function words themselves are only infrequently involved in **speech errors** (Levelt 1989: 339). Elements such as inflectional affixes and determiners have a strong tendency to be stranded in speech errors (Levelt 1989: 249). Closed class items are not accessed independently of syntactic information (Shillcock and Bard 1993).

How can we account for all these differences? The frequency effect may well have a separate explanation, but the psycholinguistic effects are probably related. Maclay and Osgood provide the starting point for much of the thinking in this area in their classic article: 'The evidence as a whole suggests at least two levels of organization in encoding, which we may call lexical (or semantic) and grammatical (or structural)' (1959: 41). In Garrett (1982) a similar distinction is made between a deeper level of **functional** structure in sentences, and a more superficial level of **positional** structure. Garman notes Garrett's treatment of prepositions suggests a sequential two-step approach (Garman 1990: 401–2). Prepositions have the property that they occur in exchange errors: *in* and *to* can interchange positions (see also Butterworth 1989: 115), like other lexical items. They do not undergo sound change errors, unlike true content words. Garrett (1982) explains this by assuming that prepositions are lexical elements in functional structure and subsequently undergo cliticization and appear as grammatical elements in positional structure. Speech errors occur after positional structure has been constituted.

Interestingly, the counterexample to Garrett's model mentioned by Butterworth involves plurals:

> (15)   I'm preparing to fill my air with tyre*s*.

This exchange error should have been, if inflection stays in the place predicted in Garrett's model:

> (16)   I'm preparing to fill my air*s* with tyre.

I will shortly return to this category below.

Agrammatism

A second domain where we find this distinction is with a specific type of aphasic patients, suffering from the syndrome of Broca and showing agrammatism. They can only speak in very short sentences, consisting of lexical elements. They have great difficulty building grammatical structures and using the appropriate grammatical elements, both separate words and inflectional endings.

There is a large literature on agrammatism, and in this literature a number of criteria are suggested to distinguish grammatical from lexical elements. While much research has been done on agrammatic speech, the following remark by Caramazza and Sloan Berndt (1985: 34) remains valid:

> [aside from the work by M.L. Kean] there has not been a formal
> (explicit) distinction drawn between the class of elements omitted and
> those retained in the speech of agrammatics. Most researchers have,

instead, relied on the classical grammatical distinctions among form classes (i.e., function word, noun, adjective, etc.). Whether or not this classical division among lexical items drawn by linguists corresponds to distinctions in a psycholinguistic model of language processing remains to be determined.

No coherent picture emerges with respect to the grammatical elements that are omitted, and indeed Miceli et al. (1989) argue that there is considerable variation between patients in this respect.

I will take the latter study as my point of departure, since it is one of the most detailed studies empirically. The main lexical elements found are nouns, adjectives and main verbs. Adverbs were excluded from the counts of content words because only a few of the patients retained the ability to produce them (ibid. p. 452). Both bound grammatical morphemes such as nominal, adjectival, and verbal inflections, and freestanding grammatical morphemes: prepositions, definite and indefinite articles, clitics, and auxiliaries are absent in various degrees (ibid. p. 453). Only some patients retained the ability to produce subordinate conjunctions. The same holds for indefinite pronouns, possessive pronouns, and quantifiers. Miceli et al. (p. 461) conclude that 'no consistent pattern of impairment in the production of freestanding grammatical morphemes is found in our patient series'.

Caramazza and Sloan Berndt (1985: 34–5) report the following overall hierarchy in omission rates (with descending frequency of omission):

(17) determiners   -ed   verb infl   poss -s/3 sg -s
      auxiliaries   -ing   adj infl   pl -s
      prepositions   -s (pl.) *noun infl
      pronouns
      connectives

Thus linkers and shifters are less frequently omitted than functional elements proper in agrammatical speech.

There is no consensus in the literature on the precise motivation for the omission of elements. One theory, mostly associated with the work of Kean (e.g. 1977), is that the fundamental feature of the missing elements is the possibility for them to be unstressed. Goodglass (1968: 206) reports in an early study 'we find that the omission of function words is primarily correlated with the rhythmic patterning of aphasic speech'.

A second theory assumes that it is the grammatical status of the elements that is crucial. Bennis, Prins and Vermeulen (1983) argue that of the different uses of the Dutch prepositions, the lexical and subcategorized uses are much harder to process than the syntactic uses for Broca patients, and the reverse for Wernicke patients.

Language development

A third area where the distinction has played an important role is in the study of child language development. It has been frequently noted that children use very few grammatical elements while in the one-word and two-word stages. Functional elements are thus **acquired later** than content words in first language acquisition (Shillcock and Bard 1993: 165). There has been considerable discussion in the literature of whether or not children 'know' the grammatical and semantic distinctions implied by grammatical elements at a time that they are not yet using these elements. Particularly functional categories proper are not learned initially; shifters and linkers are acquired relatively early on, but perhaps not yet as functional categories. Certain morphosyntactic distinctions (e.g. [± Tense]) may be present from the beginning.

In the area of second language acquisition it is much less evident that there is a sharp distinction to be made, in terms of acquisition patterns, between the two classes. Indeed, adult second language learners acquire lexical elements first, but start introducing grammatical elements irregularly, in piecemeal fashion, quite early on.

Foreigner talk

The study of foreigner talk – the ways foreigners are addressed in a sometimes telegraphic mode – for quite some time has been occupied with the omission of functional elements (Ferguson 1971; Snow, Muysken, and Van Eeden 1981). In foreigner talk functional categories proper, and to a lesser extent, linkers are omitted, but not shifters.

Functional categories and equivalence in code-mixing

So far, a number of areas have been surveyed where the distinction between two types of elements plays an important role: language mixing, speech production, agrammatic speech, language development, foreigner talk, language change, creolization, and lexical borrowing. Thus the original intuition that the distinction is an important one appears to be correct.

The overview of some of the issues involved in the study of the distinction between lexical and functional elements has shown, I hope, how useful it is to compare and contrast linguistic evidence from widely different sources. The overall distinction is useful, but in different domains different specific dimensions of the distinction, diagnostic criteria, appear to be involved. The criteria point to different factors involved in the behaviour of grammatical elements in different domains. The interesting thing, however, is not so much that there are all these differences, but rather that so often seemingly different

Table 6.3. *Functional elements particularly affected in different linguistic domains*

	shifters	functional categories	linkers
language change	−	+	+
creolization	+	+	+
borrowing	±	+	−
speech errors	−	+	±
agrammatism	±	+	±
L1 development	±	+	±
L2 development	±	±	±
foreigner talk	−	+	±
insertional mixing	−	−	
alternational mixing			+

criteria point in the same direction. Thus in (18), the development through grammaticalization of Sranan *pe* 'where' out of *'which place' involves semantic, syntactic, and phonological changes in parallel:

(18)   which place > uch presi > o presi > o pe > pe

It is this parallelism between at first sight separate dimensions of lexical items, holding at least in an overall statistical sense, which calls for an explanation.

Before returning to the question of how to explain the Functional Element Effect, through speech production or interlinguistic equivalence, I briefly summarize the results so far in table 6.3.

Links between functional elements

If we take differences between languages to be due to differences between lexical and functional elements, we are still faced with a problem in the case of code-mixing research. When one mixes, what leads to the selection from one set? If the functional elements are like lexical items, atomic elements on a list, what then forces the coherence between them? Why are all parameters (linked to specific functional elements) set the same way conjointly? If we think of a language as a collection of lexical items, the perspective on language as a system is lost. This issue has not clearly been dealt with so far. For monolingual utterances, the problem is less apparent: factors relating to identity and communication will impose the choice of either Swahili or English as the language of use (see chapter 2).

What are the relations among the functional elements on the list? One possibility currently discussed is that they are organized in subsystems, like chains. Thus researchers discuss a nominal and a verbal chain, each consisting of a series of distinct but related functional elements:

(19)   Verb . . Aktionsart . . Aspect . . Agreement . . Tense . . Complementizer

(20)   Noun . . Gender . . Number . . Agreement . . Case . . Determiner

Thus, selection of one member of a chain could imply selection of another one. However, what are the relations between these two chains? There are several coselection relations between them. The verb and the tense in (19) are involved in the assignment of the cases in (20), and sometimes also in the choice of the determiner. Finally, there may be agreement across the two categories, as in Swahili. These interdependencies generally secure an overall cohesion of the system of functional categories across the nominal and verbal projections.

It should be mentioned that there is one case of code-mixing precisely between the verbal and the nominal system: the mixture of French and Cree that led to Michif, the language of the Canadian Métis that emerged around 1840 and is still spoken by some older Métis in western Canada and parts of the north-western United States (Bakker 1997).

Equivalence

Clearly, there is an empirical need to distinguish content words from function words in some way, when analysing the mixed sentences. However, the categorization of elements is far from uniform and straightforward, as I have shown. This makes it difficult to appeal to a single principled distinction between content and system morphemes, as in Myers-Scotton (1993b).

I want to propose that the distinction may be given simply in terms of equivalence. Recall the two chains of functional categories given above. Now the only two elements in these chains that receive a universal interpretation are bare nouns and verbs themselves. All other categories are defined in terms of language-specific feature systems, which delimit the paradigm space for e.g. tense and gender in a given language.

The System Morpheme Principle (Myers-Scotton 1993b) can thus be interpreted as a system morpheme or functional element 'effect', a special case of the categorial equivalence constraint. The selection of a tense/complementation system from a specific language triggers a verbal system, which in turn is linked to the nominal agreement and case system.

The development in X-bar theory extending the definition of head to non-lexical, functional elements has new implications for the government and equivalence constraints. Bentahila and Davies (1983) assume that Moroccan

Arabic demonstratives imposed a certain restriction on the noun they modify, namely that it be definite, to account for Arabic/French mixing patterns. Recall that the way to incorporate their idea under the government constraint is to assume that demonstratives are in fact governing heads. This is precisely the claim in the theory of functional heads: not only nouns, verbs, adjectives, and prepositions are heads, but also determiners, auxiliaries, complementizers, etc. These categories impose language-specific restrictions on their syntactic environment, as is the case with Moroccan Arabic demonstratives. This influences their ability to participate in code-mixing.

I will now try to give evidence for the claim that the system morpheme effect is not a principled one, derived from the processing system, but rather the result of equivalence restrictions. I will discuss plural markers, past and present participles, and pronouns.

Plurals

In several code-mixing settings, nominal plural is a counter example to the System Morpheme Principle. Some examples from Swahili/English mixing cited by Myers-Scotton (1993b: 111–12) are:

(21) a. ma stories   'stories'
         NC6
      b. zile trips   'trips'
         NC10

Here the English plural forms are preceded by a Swahili plural noun class marker. As in the Swahili cases cited, in other language pairs as well there is also a plural marker from the matrix language present. The following cases from Papiamentu/Dutch code-mixing were discussed (Muysken, Kook, and Vedder 1996: 501):

(22) a. muizen-nan   'mice'
         mouse-PL-PL
      b. muis-je-s-nan   'little mice'
         mouse-DIM-PL-PL

However, there are also cases with only a plural marker from the embedded language, e.g. in Gardner-Chloros (1991: 165): *photocopies* 'photocopies', *carottes* 'carrots', *exemplaires* 'copies', *articles de bureau* 'office articles'. Admittedly, the French plural marker is inaudible here and only apparent in writing, but the context is clearly plural, and there is no Alsatian German plural marker present. We can assume an equivalence of nominal plural in this case.

Past participles

An interesting case of a violation of the System Morpheme Principle has received little discussion so far. It involves past participles.

Clyne (1967: 48–9) has studied the use of past participle forms of English verbs in Australian immigrant German in the 1960s. Many verbs are integrated into German morphology (23a). In other cases there is both a form with the German prefix *ge-* and one without it (23b). Although Clyne distinguishes between a *-(e)t* and a *-ed* ending in his transcription, this does not reflect pronunciation, which is always [t] due to the German final devoicing rule. It merely reflects the presence of German *ge-*. In (23c) some cases are given where a fully English form is used, and (23d) shows that English verbs are made sensitive to the German rule that already prefixed verbs do not get *-ge*.

(23) a. ge*capture*t, ge*enter*t, ge*line*t, ge*mark*t, ge*mix*t, ge*rescue*t, ge*teach*t, ge*watch*t
      b. ge*bowlt*/*bowled*
         ge*shanghait*/*shanghaied*
      c. Ein Buch *called* 'The Fire Engine' ('A book called . . .')
         Autos sind *parked* an der Strasse ('Cars are parked on the road.')
      d. *adjust*et, *compare*t, *erupt*et, *impress*t

For particle verbs and complex verbs Clyne notes that *mixed up* is somewhat more frequent than *upgemixt*, while less widespread *upgepickt* occurs rather than *picked up*. This suggests adoption of English morphology with more frequent use. Many separable verb forms are only used as infinitives: *babysit*ten. Other instances of use of English verb morphology are limited to lexicalized *-ing*: 'Dann geh' ich *shopping*', 'Ich kann besser *skating* als meine Schwester'.

Interestingly enough, Alsatian/French mixing in Strasbourg, as discussed by Gardner-Chloros (1991: 167–8), also shows this phenomenon. Of the nine single French verbs in the Alsatian material, seven involve a past participle. Some examples are:

(24) Sie sind *condamnés* worre.
      they are convicted been
      'They were convicted.'

(25) Noch schlimmer, wenn de *client recalé* wird am permis.
      still worse, when the client failed is at.the test
      'Even worse, if the client is failed on the test.'

(26) Tee hat er als zamme *mélangé*.
      tea has he always together mixed
      'Tea he has always mixed together.'

(Alsatian/French; Gardner-Chloros 1991: 167–8)

Notice that in the last case, the mixed form *zamme mélangé* 'together mixed' corresponds to an Alsatian particle + verb combination *zammemische* 'mix together'. This underscores the high degree of equivalence required here.

Another set of cases of past participle use which appear to violate the System Morpheme Hypothesis comes from Myers-Scotton's own data:

(27) tu-ko *confused*
'we are confused'

(28) wa-tu wa-ko *trained*
'people are trained'

(29) a-na-ku-w-a *offered* tu
3sg-PR-INF-be-IND offered just
'he was just being offered'   (Swahili/English; Myers-Scotton 1993b: 115)

These data are not discussed in any detail; they appear to be counterexamples to the System Morpheme Hypothesis because the English verb form is inflected and syntactically relevant within the Swahili clause. The English elements function in a passive construction.

Present participles

A similar account can be developed for present participles, as mentioned by Sebba (1998). Often we find English *-ing* participles inserted in places where Spanish would have an *-ndo* participle. At least six cases are documented with the copula *estar* and two with other verbs:

(30) Mi marido está *working on his master's*
'My husband is working on his master's.'   (Lipski 1978: 265)

(31) Siempre está *promising* cosas
'He is always promising things.'   (Poplack 1980: 596)

(32) . . . una vez allí andamos *horseback riding*
'. . . once we went horseback riding there'   (Pfaff 1976: 252)

(33) Si va a ir *shopping* vaya con Mickey
'If you go shopping, go with Mickey.'   (Pfaff 1976: 252)

The opposite pattern, *is trabajando* and *started entrenándose*, is not documented in these sources. This asymmetry may be evidence that as far as these constructions are concerned, we have insertion rather than alternation here. The quantitative data presented for Mexican American Spanish by Pfaff (1979: 299) show the equivalence effect clearly. In the conversion from Spanish to English the question is which stem form to adapt, and in the reverse case, how to transform English stems to fit Spanish conjugations. The pattern can be summarized as in table 6.4. Main verbs are generally adapted

Table 6.4. *English verbs in a Spanish grammatical context (adapted from Pfaff 1979: 299)*

	unadapted	adapted
participles	22	3
infinitives	15	3
main verbs	5	19
unmarked	3	–

to Spanish (by adding a linking vowel and the stem vowel of the first conjugation), while unadapted verbs are either participles or infinitives. Presumably main verb inflection is not considered equivalent by bilingual speakers. It is not, structurally speaking, either, since Spanish inflection allows for null subjects, while English inflection does not.

Discussion

What participles and nominal plurals share is that they are inflectional categories very close to the lexical head, i.e. in terms of selection, they directly select a lexical category (a verb and a noun, respectively), rather than another functional category. The first consequence of this proximity to the head is that they can be reinterpreted as derivational elements. In many languages, nominal plural is in part a derivational category, and past participles are often close to adjectives. The second consequence is that not selecting a potentially non-equivalent functional category (since the categories of noun and verb are universal) by itself increases the chance that a given functional category is interpreted as equivalent to a category in another language. Thus the facts from leaking are often ambiguous between a processing and an equivalence approach. The processing approach will assume lexical retrieval of inflected forms, not containing intermediate foreign elements:

(34) $[[[_x \text{ stem }] [_y \text{ aff }]] [_x \text{ aff}]]$

_____X_____/

Full lexical retrieval would exclude forms such as (34).

However, the equivalence account would not be compatible with the state of affairs in (35), either, since elements that may be equivalent themselves would involve functional elements low in the functional projection rather than higher up (here X is the head and FC is 'functional category'):

(35)

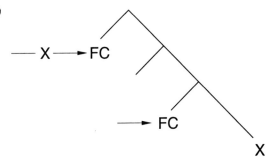

While past participles and plurals may be neutral with respect to the choice between processing and equivalence (since they can often be interpreted as derivational), present participles are much less likely to be seen as derivational, playing an important role in the aspectual system. The possibility of them occurring in code-mixing constitutes an argument for the equivalence approach.

Pronouns

Another area where there are potential problems for a strict interpretation of the System Morpheme Principle involves pronouns. Let us first consider the basic findings, and then the most economic explanation for them. The basic findings in this domain can be summarized as follows:

A   The switching of pronouns is relatively rare.
B   We find strong Arabic, French, and Wolof pronouns in a language different from the following sequence, particularly in left-dislocated position.
C   We find English pronouns in Japanese and Spanish, also frequently in left-dislocated position.
D   Clitic pronouns can only be switched in related varieties, such as dialect and standard in the Netherlands (see chapter 5), and Catalan and Spanish.

The finding in (A) can be related to a hypothesis recently proposed by Backus (1996) in the framework of cognitive grammar: the **specificity hypothesis**. This roughly says that the more culturally or cognitively specific an element is, the more likely it is to be mixed in or switched. One could assume that functional elements like pronouns, in contrast with proper names, are the least specific type of element from the cognitive perspective, and hence the least likely to be mixed in. I will not explore this hypothesis here any further, since it requires a number of extra assumptions pertaining

177

to the framework of cognitive grammar, and these would lead us too far astray.

With respect to (B), Azuma (1993: 1087–8) and Jake (1994: 279–83) cite examples from Eid (1992), which involve a sequence Arabic pronoun/English pronoun:

(36) wi ba?deen ?ihna *we're really struggling.*
 'And then we / we're really struggling.' (Eid 1992: 59)

(37) ya?ni ?ana *I was really lucky*
 'Meaning I, / I was really lucky.' (Eid 1992: 59)

(38) la? hiyya *she started that* la?inn . . .
 No she, / she started that, / because . . .' (Eid 1992: 59)

They go on to cite parallel examples from Bentahila and Davies' (1983) study of Moroccan Arabic/French code-mixing:

(39) nta / *tu vas travailler*
 'You, you are going to work.' (Bentahila and Davies 1983: 312)

(40) huwa / *il s'en fout*
 'Him, he doesn't care.' (Bentahila and Davies 1983: 312)

Jake (1994: 282–3) also cites cases from Nortier's work on Moroccan Arabic/Dutch mixing:

(41) Eh ana *ik heb gewoon ...*
 'Eh I, / I have just . . .' (Nortier 1990: 216)

(42) ḥna ta-šufu bezzaf, ḥna, ḥit *we zijn eigenlijk*
 we we-see much, we, because we are actually

 in de groeitijd
 in the grow.time
 'As for us we see a lot, because / we are actually in our growing years.'
 (Nortier 1990: 163)

The reverse order does not occur, and neither do we get mixed combinations of weak pronouns and predicates (Bentahila and Davies 1983: 312).

(43) *je *ghadi*
 'I go.'
(44) *ana *vais*
 'I go.'

There are also some cases of French strong pronouns, as in:

(45) moi *dxlt*
 'I went in.' (Moroccan Arabic/French; Bentahila and Davies 1983: 313).

Jake (1994: 285) cites two Wolof cases from Swigart (1992) which are quite similar to the Arabic cases just mentioned:

(46) *Man nag*, je crois qu'on a besoin d'une presse qui fait appel . . .
'As for me, I think we need a press that appeals . . .'
(Wolof/French; Swigart 1992: 350)

(47) *Ñoom*, ils parlent français, ils parlent parfaitement le français.
'Them, they speak French, they speak French perfectly.'
(Wolof/French; Swigart 1992: 149)

With respect to (C), Azuma (1993: 1077–8) cites examples from Japanese/English code-mixing in Hawaii (from Higa 1974) in which English pronouns are inserted into Japanese sentences and treated as if they were Japanese-like nouns:

(48) *me* wa *last year Japan* ni itte kita
me TO last year Japan to went came
'I visited Japan last year.' (Higa 1974)

(49) *you* no *number-one boy* wa ima doko ni iru
you GE number-one boy TO now where at exist
'Where is your number-one boy?' (Higa 1974)

Jake (1994: 286) also cites a similar case from Japanese/English code-mixing:

(50) She *wa* took her a month to home *yo*
'Talking about her, it took her a month to home, you know.'
(Nishimura 1986: 136)

This example resembles e.g. (39) in that the English pronoun occurs in the *wa* topic position.

There are also a few cases from Spanish/English code-mixing, cited by Jake (1994: 284):

(51) *You* estás diciéndole la pregunta *in the wrong person.*
'You/are asking the question/to the wrong person.'
(Sankoff and Poplack 1981: 13)

(52) . . . *but you* usates [sic] m'as pa' ir pa'lla
'. . . but you/use more [gas] to go there' (Woolford 1983: 529)

There is one example that is rather difficult to interpret syntactically, in which there is what appears to be an English resumptive subject pronoun in a relative clause:

(53) *There was this guy, you know*, que *he* se montó.
'There was this guy, you know, that **he** got up.'
(Sankoff and Poplack 1981: 11–12)

It is easiest to understand the occurrence of a subject pronoun (in any language) here as a kind of resumption of the topic of the narrative, i.e. as a new main clause subject, and *que* 'that' as a linking device. Seen like this, the example resembles the other two, in involving an emphatic subject.

Class (C) is like class (B), except that English does not have a separately marked class of strong pronouns. Turning finally to class (D), Giesbers (1989: 152) mentions the following type of pronouns in his dialect/standard Dutch mixing:

(54) personal   74
      reflexive   4
      possessive   4
      indefinite   22

Of the inserted personal pronouns, 30 occurred after a preposition. Giesbers does not give details, but it is clear from examples such as the following one that some of the pronouns switched are clitics:

(55)   . . . ik zei mossele da [mag-*ie*] *toch helemaal nie*
      I said mussels that may-/he though at.all not
      '. . . I said mussels he is-not allowed them, is he?'   (Giesbers 1989: 96)

Vila i Moreno (1996), in a study of language use around the school in Catalonia, mentions extensive use of Castillian clitics in Catalan and of Catalan clitics in Castillian. He gives examples like the following:

(56)   això *a el* a ell no li i(m)porta
      this to him to him not him matters
      'this he, he doesn't care'   (Catalan/Spanish; (Vila i Moreno 1996: 393)

(57)   i *el* va taller el cap
      'and he cut his head'   (Catalan/Spanish; (Vila i Moreno 1996: 419)

Jake distinguishes four classes of pronouns:

(58)   • discourse-emphatic pronouns: *Me*, I wouldn't go.
      • dummy pronouns: *It* seems she's ill.
      • indefinite pronouns: *Man* muss arbeiten. 'One has to work.'
      • personal pronouns: *I* wouldn't go

Jake (1994) uses the feature [± thematic] to distinguish system morphemes from content morphemes. Thematic roles can be assigned both by argument structure and by discourse structure. Jake classifies the four classes above as follows:

(59)   • discourse-emphatic pronouns: content
      • dummy pronouns: system
      • indefinite pronouns: content in English/Spanish
                                system in Chinese
      • personal pronouns: content/system

There is a problem in that in many analyses, in a sentence like (60), *moi* is assumed to be non-thematic, but rather a contrastive external element, and *je* thematic:

(60)   Moi, je travaille.
      'Me, I work.'

These interpretations build on work by Jaeggli (1982) and others. Jaeggli argues that subject agreement in Spanish is itself the carrier of a thematic role, as are the object clitics. The elements in canonical subject and object positions are adjuncts. Quite independently of the status of *moi* in (60), which may get a thematic role from the discourse structure, *je* in this account gets the canonical subject role of the verb.

If we make an account in terms of phonological strength, we get the following result:

(61) alguien, someone, etc.   strong
      él, yo; she, me, you   strong
      je, le   weak

This is roughly the right result.

Consider once again the main finding that we find strong Arabic, French, and Wolof pronouns in a language different from the following sequence, particularly in left-dislocated position, as well as English pronouns in Japanese and Spanish, also frequently in left-dislocated position. This finding suggests that pronoun switching is often not insertional, but rather alternational, thus avoiding the equivalence problem.

The fact that clitic pronouns can only be switched in related varieties, such as dialect and standard in the Netherlands (see chapter 5), and Catalan and Spanish, points to the fact that once there is basic equivalence, anything goes.

Towards a differentiated view of function words

In chapter 2 I referred to Sapir's (1921) approach to morphological typology. Sapir distinguished four types of concepts:

- concrete concepts
- derivational concepts: nominal plural, diminutive
- pure relational concepts: subject/object, etc.
- concrete relational concepts: agreement

This four-way distinction has been taken up recently by Myers-Scotton and Jake in a number of papers (e.g. Myers-Scotton 1999) and is labelled the 4M-model. In this model four types of morphemes are distinguished: directly elected content morphemes (cf. Sapir's concrete concepts), indirectly elected morphemes (cf. Sapir's derivational concepts), and two types of structurally assigned morphemes (e.g. agreement elements, cf. Sapir's relational concepts). The distinction between indirect election, direct election, and structural assignment has to do with language production: when we introduce a noun e.g. 'chair', this is part of the meaning representation, i.e. our communicative intention leads us to elect *chair*, as it were. The same holds for nominal plural, which is part of what we elect to say, but only indirectly, namely in relation to the noun. We want to refer to *chairs* (plural). When we introduce a third person singular on a verb, *walks*, the agreement morpheme is seen as triggered by the grammatical context, and hence structurally assigned.

The adoption of these distinctions in the 4M-model is attractive because they help explain part of the results presented so far: nominal plural is a typical indirectly elected morpheme, and this explains its retention on many inserted items. Particularly in lexicalist analyses past and present participle morphemes, *-ed* and *-ing*, can be seen as indirectly elected: participles are then seen as similar to adjectives, derived from verbs through the addition of *-ed* and *-ing*. A more differentiated view of morphology clearly adds to the predictive power of Myers-Scotton and Jake's model.

However, the distinction between indirect election and structural assignment also tends to overpredict. Past tense morphemes like *-ed* in *walked* can be seen as indirectly elected, part of the communicative intention of the speaker. However, past tense is not a morphological category frequently retained in insertional code-mixing.

Another problem lies in the cross-linguistic validity of the distinctions involved. In Cuzco Quechua, the inflected verb can take an overt subject or not:

(62) a. puri-n
          walk 3sg
          '(s)he walks'
      b. pay puri-n
          (s)he walk 3sg
          '(s)he walks'

In fact, the subject is absent more often than not. Thus the communicative intention to refer to a third person may well be expressed mostly through the verb agreement affix rather than through the pronoun (cf. the discussion in the previous section on pronouns). Thus, there may be two kinds of verb agreement, from this perspective: the English type and the Quechua type. However, this difference has not manifested itself in code-mixing data so far.

A similar observation may be made regarding nominal plural. Take again Cuzco Quechua, in contrast with English:

(63) a. tawa wasi
          four house
          'four houses'

   b. wasi-kuna
      house PL
      'houses'
   c. * tawa wasi-kuna
        four house PL

The affix *-kuna* in Quechua clearly expresses the intention to communicate plurality; indeed it cannot be combined with numerals, which in themselves indicate plurality. English plural *-s*, however, does not have this independence. One could argue, from the perspective of Quechua, that in *four houses* the plural *-s* is structurally assigned, rather than indirectly elected. Again, there is no evidence that this difference leads to different switch pattern.

Thus the distinctions made in the 4M-model are a step forward, but raise new issues as well. The functional element effect discussed in this chapter may turn out to be highly pluriform and multi-dimensional, involving both equivalence and processing.

7
Bilingual verbs

This chapter explores the distinction between alternation, insertion and congruent lexicalization for a specific word class, the verb. Verbs play a particularly important role in the code-mixing literature. They function as the core of the clause in their role of case and semantic role assigners, and often subcategorize for specific prepositional phrases. In addition, they are often the flection-bearing elements, marked for person and tense.

In the verbal system, code-mixing is often innovative, leading to structures not present in either of the languages in contact. Basically bilingual verbs come as one of four main types:

(1) a. The new verb is **inserted** into a position corresponding to a native verb, in adapted form or not
      b. The new verb is **adjoined** to a helping verb
      c. The new verb is a **nominalized complement** to a causative helping verb in a compound
      d. The new verb is an **infinitive** and the complement of a native auxiliary

I will illustrate these four types, show how they can be distinguished in a corpus of bilingual speech, and try to determine the factors leading to the choice of one of these four strategies.

In some communities, we find the strategy of attaching inflections to an **imported stem**, either directly, as in the Dutch past participle *ge-zoom-d* (containing English 'zoom') or Quechua *mantini-nki* 'you maintain' (< Sp *mantener*), or to an adapted form (e.g. Dutch *offr-er-en* from French *offr-ir* 'offer'). I argue that here we have **insertion** inside the word: an English stem is treated as the equivalent of a Dutch stem, and a Spanish stem as the equivalent of a Quechua stem. I will assume that the use of bare verbs from Dutch or English in Malay or Chinese (in the case of Dutch either in stem form or infinitive form) is likewise a case of insertion.

In many other bilingual communities there are **bilingual complex verbs**, consisting of an embedded language lexical verb and a matrix language helping verb. A very frequent pattern here is the introduction of a helping verb such as 'make' or 'do'. This is common in the Indic languages, and we see a good example of it in Sarnami (Surinam Hindustani)/Sranan/Dutch/English mixed verbs:

(2)   a. *onti* kare   'to hunt'   Sranan
      b. *train* kare   'to train'   English
      c. *bewijs* kare   'to prove'   Dutch   (Kishna 1979)

You might say that the elements in italics are really borrowings (from Sranan, English, and Dutch, respectively), but the process is completely productive and does not entail phonological or semantic integration into the host language. There is a lexical structure of the type (V *kare*) available to insert alien elements into, in which *kare* 'do' serves as the helping verb. I am using the term 'helping verb' rather than 'auxiliary' to avoid immediate association with AUX, INFL, etc., not excluding that there is such a link. I will argue that these verb complexes can be of three types: adjoined, nominalized complement in a compound, and infinitive complement. In the case of adjunction, we have an **alternation** strategy.

Congruent lexicalization is found, I will argue, in cases where both languages in the contact situation have particle + verb constructions (an example would be Surinam Hindustani/Dutch), and combinations of Dutch particle + Hindustani verb occur in addition to entire Dutch particle + verb combinations that are inserted.

The formation of bilingual verbs may have the function of vocabulary extension, since language contact often also implies culture contact, or a stylistic function. In the latter case the frequent use of alien verbs may serve to underline the speaker's level of education, or perhaps a bicultural identity. Finally, the incorporation of alien verbs may point to lexical loss due to language attrition or language erosion.

Inserted verbs

One way alien verbs are incorporated is by simply inserting them into a position ordinarily reserved for a native verb. In some languages, like Chinese and the Caribbean creole languages, the verb is simply taken in a bare form. Other languages add affixes to alien stems without further adaptation. Yet a third option is that the verb is adapted with a nativizing affix before being inserted.

The borrowing of bare verbs

Languages that lack inflection on their verbs can incorporate alien verbs without further adaptation. I will illustrate this possibility with two groups of migrants in the Netherlands who have two languages spoken in Surinam as their native language: Chinese and Sranan.

Tjon (1988) has carried out a preliminary investigation of Surinamese Chinese migrants (mostly Hakka speaking) in the Netherlands, primarily on the basis of informal recordings of the researcher herself and various acquaintances and family members. In this material Hakka Chinese is the matrix language. Personal pronouns, reflexives, auxiliaries, negation markers, and question words are expressed in that language, and content words can be from Dutch. Notice that this is a good illustration of Myers-Scotton's (1993b) matrix-based code-mixing.

(3) Ngai yew *krampen in* nga *buik*.
    '**I have** cramps in **my** stomach.'   (Chinese/Dutch; Tjon 1988: 8)

(4) Ngi *zetten* ngi *zelf voor schut, man*.
    '**You** put **you** self to shame, man.'   (Tjon 1988: 8)

(5) Ngai *helemaal* m *vinden leuk*.
    I   at all   **not** find nice
    'I don't like it at all.'   (Tjon 1988: 9)

(6) Giesi ya *scriptie af*?
    When you paper finished
    'When will your paper be finished?'   (Tjon 1988: 10)

Tense is not overtly expressed; the Dutch verbs occur in the infinitive form, except when the Chinese resultative suffix *-dao* is added to them. In that case we get a Dutch bare stem:

(7) *Trudy opneem*-dao boen ngai.
    Trudy record-**RES for me**
    'Trudy has recorded it for me.'   (Tjon 1988: 11)

It is clear that verbs are inserted into this structure in the position they would have in Chinese; if there were a true Dutch non-finite verb phrase in (5), we would have the XV order *leuk vinden* 'nice find' rather than the VX order *vinden leuk* actually encountered. Thus Chinese is a clear case of insertion of uninflected alien verbs.

The same holds for the Surinamese creole language Sranan. The main source for data on Sranan/Dutch code-mixing is Bolle (1994). She based herself both on recorded conversations from radio call-in programs and on the extensive transcribed autobiographical texts of Alex Drie (1985). For verbs the main conclusion to be drawn from her data and analysis is that in a minority of the cases (18 per cent) there is an *-e* (pronounced with schwa) ending on the verb (orthographically *-en*). When there should have been

Table 7.1. *Verb particle combinations in Sranan/Dutch code-mixing (based on Bolle 1994: 93)*

	types	tokens
Sranan verb – particle	13	17
Dutch stem – particle	14	20
Dutch stem + *e* – particle	3	3
particle – Dutch stem + *e*	1	1
particle – Dutch stem	–	–
particle – Sranan stem	–	–

(finite) inflection, following Dutch rules, this is 10 per cent, but when the verb is in a non-finite context, this is 42 per cent (1994: 64).

This suggests that the form of the verb is variable, without this having syntactic consequences. Bolle also shows that 61 per cent of the single Dutch verbs have some kind of Sranan preverbal tense/mood/aspect particle or a Sranan modal auxiliary. This does not mean that the other 39 per cent of the verbs are not integrated, since in Sranan discourse itself many verbs occur without any preverbal particles.

(8) Mi gwe go *kampeer gewoon*
      I go.away go camp just
      'I just go away camping.'   (Bolle 1994: 108)

(9) Den man *waardeer* en *heel veel*
      the.PL man appreciate it very much
      'They appreciate it very much.'   (Bolle 1994: 108)

Some verbs in Dutch do not end in *-en* in the infinitive. The Dutch verb *bestaan* 'exist' appears both in its infinitive form (10) and as a bare form (11):

(10) Tu Brook Benton no kan *bestaan*.
       'Two Brook Bentons cannot exist.'   (Bolle 1994: 83)

(11) Now kawna ben *besta altijd*.
       now kawna PST exist always
       'Now, kawna has always existed.'   (Bolle 1994: 83)

Again, the position of these verbs corresponds exactly to that of native Sranan verbs.

Inserted stems with native affixes
Fabian (1982), studying Swahili/French language contact, raises the point that a large part of borrowing is poetic in nature, creating a special stylistic

effect. In this it resembles code-mixing. I will illustrate this with verb doubling in Peruvian Quechua–Spanish bilingual songs, *waynos*. *Waynos* are sung and played both in the towns and in the countryside. It is popular music, and there are radio stations that primarily transmit *waynos*.

Few *waynos* are pure Quechua. In many cases the Quechua contains words borrowed from Spanish, and in a substantial number of them Spanish and Quechua were used in a single couplet. Furthermore many texts contain sentences with such heavy borrowing and so many grammatical irregularities that they cannot be classified unambiguously as Quechua and must be labelled 'mixed'. It is clear that the *waynos* form the expression of a bilingual culture, in which processes of mixing play an important role. The question here is how this mixing occurs in the *waynos*.

The most striking phenomenon in the *waynos* is what Mannheim (1986a, 1986b, 1987) has called 'semantic doubling': the use of Quechua/Spanish doublets through relexification. Here the equivalent Spanish form is preceded by the Quechua form:

> (12) yacharankitaq   if only you knew
>   *sabi*rankitaq   if only you knew   (Escobar and Escobar 1981: 47)

The form *yacha-* is the Quechua word for 'know' and *sabi-* the Spanish word. It is clear here that the Spanish stem *sabi-* 'know' is treated exactly the same as the Quechua stem *yacha-*. Semantic doubling is a kind of semantic rhyme.

Mannheim argues that in Quechua phonological rhyme is trivial given the rich suffixal morphology which allows one to make everything rhyme. Therefore there is semantic rhyme, and it involves nouns as well as verbs. It is in no way limited to Quechua/Spanish pairs; many doublets indeed involve two Quechua nouns or verbs, and some even two Spanish borrowings.

I will focus here on the cases involving a verb. Spanish verbs such as *sabi-* 'know' and *pasa-* 'pass, go away' are quite frequent in the Quechua segments of the *waynos*. To what extent do they participate in semantic doubling? A Spanish verb such as *sabi-* 'know', which occurs in eight *waynos*, is always part of a doublet, with the Quechua verb *yacha-* preceding; it does not occur in spoken Quechua as a loan, in contrast to *pasa-*. For many Spanish verbs which do occur occasionally as loans in Quechua, however, the picture is different: here often no doublet occurs. It is not always clear whether to count Quechua verbs as a doublet; often there is no direct meaning correspondence, not even in the sense that the first item is less specific in meaning than the second item, as Mannheim assumes to be the case. However, it may be that the semantic markedness that Mannheim refers to is but a specific instance of a more general requirement that the second member of the doublet be more marked than the first one, and that being a borrowing is also a marked feature of a lexical item.

Notice that a number of borrowings do not occur as the second member but as the first member of the doublet. If the reasoning given above concerning the marked status of borrowings and Mannheim's assumption about the unmarked status of the first member of the doublet are correct, this should be an indication of integration into Quechua.

The verbs which occur in four *wayno*s or more are frequent enough to be studied quantitatively. As it turns out, they differ considerably in the extent to which they participate in semantic doubling. On the basis of a fairly large corpus of spoken Cuzco Quechua, consisting of the recorded autobiographies of an Indian load-bearer (*cargador*) and his wife, and analysed statistically by Simon van de Kerke (1996), we have some indication of the frequency of specific Spanish verbs in ordinary Quechua discourse. I contrasted this frequency with the occurrence of Spanish verbs as either the second or the first member of a semantic doublet, or by themselves. Four verb classes were distinguished: (A) not loans, (B) low frequency loans, (C) high frequency loans, and (D) the highly frequent but otherwise also exceptional element *pasa-* 'pass'. These four classes are shown in table 7.2. Even a cursory examination reveals significant differences between the four groups. In table 7.3 the group totals are given. These results show that not being a borrowing in ordinary discourse often goes together with being the Spanish second member of a doublet. Being a borrowing often goes together with being in first position or being mentioned independently.

A number of cases have been counted as instances of semantic doubling even though there is very little semantic relation between the verbs involved, as with *maylli-* 'taste' and *tupa-* 'meet'. The reason is that the parallel structure of the verses and the morphology of the verbs concerned imposed such an analysis:

(13)   mayun apamusqa, misk'i naranxata,
                  'the river brought a sweet orange'
         mana *maylli*-yku-spa, warmanayan rayku,
             taste-INT-SUB
                  'not **tasting** it, because of its beloved'
         mana *tupa*-yku-spa, warmanayan rayku.
             meet-INT-SUB
                  'not **meeting** it, because of its beloved'

What is still needed is a much more precise semantic analysis of the verbs involved in terms of semantic features.

Table 7.2. *Detailed analysis of occurrences of doubling with Spanish verbs that occur in four* waynos *or more*

	corpus	2nd	1st	single
(A)				
sabi- 'know'	–	8	–	–
bulta- 'return'	–	13	–	–
tuka- 'play'	–	1	14	–
dispusa- 'betroth'	–	–	1	1
total		*22*	*15*	*1*
(B)				
pasiya- 'stroll'	1	2	1	1
silba- 'whistle'	2	1	5	
ingaña- 'cheat'	2	1	–	4
total		*5*	*2*	*10*
(C)				
gusta- 'please'	7	2	1	3
sirbi- 'serve'	9	1	–	2
tupa- 'meet'	18	5	8	7
phalta- 'lack, miss'	19	1	1	4
kasara- 'marry'	24	–	–	8
tuma- 'drink'	39	5	7	12
total		*14*	*17*	*36*
(D)				
pasa- 'pass'	87	36	7	17

Table 7.3. *Non-loans contrasted with low and high frequency loans; independent occurrences taken together with occurrences in first position of a doublet*

	2nd	1st/independent
non	22	16
low/high	19	65

All verbs discussed are fully integrated morphologically and phonologically. The verb *sabi-* 'know', for instance, which never occurs outside of a semantic doublet, has lost all of its Spanish irregular inflection. It can be identified as etymologically non-Quechua because of the *b*, but Quechua has now many borrowings with that consonant and is quite tolerant of it. The endings of *sabi-* in the texts are always identical to those of its Quechua doublet *yacha-*. The Quechua/Spanish data are a good example of stem insertion and direct affixation of native inflectional and derivational affixes. It should be pointed out that Quechua is a highly agglutinative language.

Van de Kerke (1996) looks at the productivity of Quechua verbal derivational affixes with both Spanish and Quechua roots in a large transcribed Quechua corpus. His analysis is based on the frequency of clusters. A cluster is the set of a root and its derivations, e.g.:

(14) riku-   see   'see'
      riku-chi- see-CAU   'show'
      riku-ku   see-RE   'appear'

This cluster has three members. The average for roots from both languages is 2.33: 433 clusters yield 1,007 types. However, an average cluster with a Spanish root only contains 1.58 members, whereas the average Quechua cluster has 2.95 members. Moreover, only ten Spanish roots participate in clusters with four or more members, while sixty-three Quechua roots do. Most of these ten could be interpreted as reanalysed Quechua roots. Finally, one out of six Spanish types occurs in more than one subcorpus, and one out of three Quechua types does. Van de Kerke's results suggest that most Spanish roots are not fully integrated into the Quechua lexicon.

The *formal* mechanism of morphological incorporation of alien material serves two *functions*: it is both a way to extend the vocabulary and to create bilingual contrasts.

Adapted stems

In some language pairs, the verb can only be inserted in a morphologically integrated form. Thus French verbs can only be introduced into Dutch when the stem is affixed with *-er*:

(15) bless-er-en 'hurt'   (< Fr *blesser*)
      condamn-er-en 'condemn'   (< Fr *condamner*)
      concurrenc-er-en 'compete'   (< Fr *concurrencer*)

(Treffers-Daller 1994: 110–11)

It may be thought that the French infinitive is simply taken as the base form to which the Dutch infinitive ending *-en* is added, but some forms do not derive from French *-er* verbs but rather from *-ir* verbs (16), and others do not derive from French infinitive verbs at all (17):

(16) offr-er-en 'offer'   (< Fr *offrir*)
      farc-er-en 'stuff'   (< Fr *farcir*)

(17) traduct-er-en 'translate'   (< Fr *traduct-ion* 'translation')
      antichambr-er-en 'to be kept waiting'   (< Fr *antichambre* 'antechamber')

191

The addition of *-er* to incorporate alien stems is basically limited to French stems in standard Dutch. With English stems Dutch speakers take the stem and add Dutch inflection to it:

> (18)   ge-*save*-d 'saved (pp)' (of computer files)
>   *interview*-de 'interviewed (past sg)'
>   *crawl*-t '2sg/3sg crawl' (swimming)

Thus we cannot claim that morphophonemic requirements of Dutch verb inflection are responsible for the addition of the *-er* suffix. Rather, they seem to mark the French origin of the stem.

In other cases, there is a need to adapt stems before they can be inflected, e.g. when the matrix language has conjugation classes. Pap (1949) shows that many English verbs are incorporated into the (quite productive) Portuguese *-ar* conjugation class, *bord-ar* 'board, live in a boarding house' and *fris-ar* 'freeze', and that a few receive an *-ear* ending, *raid-ear* 'ride' and *fait-ear* 'fight'. The *-ear* ending is also common with English verbs adopted into Spanish. It is the most productive verbalizing affix in Spanish (see below).

Bautista (1980) and Gerhard (1993) show that the adaptation can be quite radical. Bautista considers the case of English verbs in Tagalog, which can be prefixed (19a), prefixed with a reduplicated prefix (19b), infixed (19c), and suffixed (19d):

> (19)   a. nag-*distribute*
>   b. nag-ga-*graduate*
>   pag-a-*approve*
>   c. *k*-in-*omission*
>   *t*-in-*est*
>   d. *adapt*-in
>   fi-*fill up*-an   (English/Tagalog: Bautista 1980: 34)

In Amharic, English and other alien verbs are made to conform to the native consonant–vowel skeleton (Gerhard 1993):

> (20)   ferrəmə   'he has undersigned' (< It *firmare*)
>   dennəsə   '. . . danced'
>   boqqəsə   '. . . boxed'
>   fottetə   '. . . criticized' (< fault)
>   kotellekə '. . . become catholic'   (Amharic/English; Gerhard 1993)

Summary

In the pure case of verb insertion, no extra structure is created. An affix like Spanish *-ear* also serves as a verbalizer with native Spanish roots, and thus might be thought of as a helping verb as well. The three types I will discuss now contain a native helping verb in addition to the alien verb. The precise nature of the helping verb – alien verb relation is subject to debate.

Bilingual compound verbs: possible analyses

Popoloca is an Otomanguean language, as spoken in Mezontla, in the state of Puebla, Mexico (Veerman-Leichsenring 1991). In this language two types of helping verbs serve to incorporate Spanish elements: one form *č?e:* used with transitive or agentive verbs and another one *tú* used with intransitive or experiential verbs:

(21)	tú	pass, occur
	tú šu:a?	be cured (cf. šu:a? 'medicine')
(22)	tú *yuda*	help (ayudar)
	tú *mantene*	maintain oneself (mantener*se*)
	tú *kompara*	compare (comparar)
(23)	č?e:	cause, make
	č?e: šu:à	cure (cf. šu:a? 'medicine')
(24)	č?e: *pinta*	paint (pintar)
	č?e: *rega*	irrigate (regar)
	č?e: *daniu*	damage (daño 'damage' (n))
	č?e: *kasa*	hunt (cazar)
	č?e: *kompone*	repair (componer)
	č?e: *kompaña*	accompany (acompañar)

(Popoloca/Spanish; Veerman-Leichsenring 1991: 160, 289, 290, 441, 479)

In (21) and (23) the native use of these compound expressions is illustrated: the helping verbs can be combined with nouns to yield more complex verbs. The helping verb for agentives is also causative or active 'make, cause', the helping verb for experientials is also non-agentive 'pass, occur'. In the bilingual use of these verbs the accompanying element is generally, but not always, a verb. The exception is *daniu* 'damage (n)' in (24). The Popoloca pattern illustrated is emblematic for a whole range of cases.

In Navaho bilingual verbs two helping verbs are involved as well (Canfield 1980):

(25)	*swimming*	asht'į		(intransitive verbs)
		1: do/be		
	'I am swimming'			
(26)	*Nancy*	bich'į'	*show*	ánílééh	(transitive verbs)
		3: to		2: make	
	'Nancy shows me.'				

(Navaho/English; Canfield 1980: 219)

Complex bilingual verbs have been noticed in a great many language contact situations, involving matrix languages ranging from Turkish and Greek to

Hindi and Navaho. Many of these cases originate from a large 'linguistic area', in this case stretching from Sri Lanka to Greece (involving the Dravidian and Indo-Iranian languages as well as Turkish and Greek), but it is not limited to this area.

The scholar who has focussed most on the role of the verb in language contact is Edith Moravcsik (1975; 1978). I will take her work as a starting point. Moravcsik (1975: 4) claims on the basis of elements like the ones just described:

> the class of borrowed constituents in a language does not include lexically homolingual constituents that are verbs in both languages . . . borrowed verbs, by internal syntactic composition, are (at least) bimorphemic and [that] they are bilingual, consisting of a generic verb constituent whose form is indigenous, and of a more specific nominal constituent whose form corresponds, by identity or similarity, to the phonetic form of the source verb.

She thus arrives at the following analysis, which she claims to be generalizable to all bilingual verbs:

(27)   COMPLEX VERB
          /   \
    embedded noun   generic matrix verb
          | |
     alien verb   do

This complex verb can take the form of a compound or of a derived verb. In terms of the three-way distinction I am making in this book it would be an insertional pattern. Furthermore, the verb–noun relation would be one of selection, and hence government (cf. chapter 1).

Moravcsik illustrates her analysis with cases such as loans in Hungarian, where alien verbs need to be accompanied by a suffix -*l*:

(28)   a. *gesztikulá*-l-nak   'they gesticulate'
          * gesztikula-nak
       b. *leiszt*-ol   'he accomplishes'
          * leiszt
       c. *menedzs*-el-i   'he manages it'
          * menedzs-i   (Hungarian/English; Moravcsik 1975: 3)

The forms without the suffix are ungrammatical, and the native use of -*l* is that of verbalizer of nouns, often with causative meaning:

(29)   a. Le-por-ol-om az asztalt (< *por* 'dust')
          'I am dusting the table.'
       b. Szeretek zené-l-ni (< *zene* 'music')
          'I like to make music.'   (Hungarian/English)

The same can be said for loans in Russian, where alien verbs need to be affixed with *-ova* (see also Timberlake 1993: 856):

(30) *klassificir*-ova-t′ 'classify'
     abstrahir-ova-t′   'abstract'
     telefonir-ova-t′   'telephone'

Again, the original use of *-ova* is as a verbalizer of native nouns, according to Moravcsik.

Morvacsik mentions a potential counterexample from loans in German:

(31) *draiv*en   'drive'
     *manag*en   'manage'
     *schrink*en   'shrink'   (Moravcsik 1975: 4)

In these cases, the alien verb is simply affixed with German infinitive marking *-en* (but see the discussion above), and there is no verbalizer. Moravcsik notes, however, that in German there is productive null verbalization:

(32) blicken 'glance' (< *Blick* (n) 'glance')
     blitzen 'lighten' (< *Blitz* (n) 'flash')
     arbeiten 'work' (< *Arbeit* (n) 'work')   (Moravcsik 1975: 4)

The German nouns can be verbalized without special affixes.

In other contact situations, the helping verb is not an affix but a separate lexical element, comparable to the Popoloca case, as with complex verbs in American Greek:

(33) O Petros kani *retire*.
     the Petros do retire
     'Petros is retiring.'   (Moravcsik 1975: 5)

In American Portuguese sometimes the embedded verb is nominalized with the Portuguese masculine article *o* (Pap 1949):

(34) fazer o *save*   'save'

(35) fazer o *find out*   'find out'

The Hungarian, Russian, American Greek, and American Portuguese cases are all taken by Moravcsik as evidence for the idea that verbs are incorporated in a nominalized form. The native pattern of verbalization is simply extended to alien verb forms taken in as nominals.

However plausible Moravcsik's analysis is, I will argue against it as an analysis for **all** bilingual compound verbs. There are two other possible analyses. First there is (36), in which the 'helping verb' serves to carry the agreement and tense markers, which cannot be attached to the alien verb stem, presumably for morpho-phonological reasons:

(36)   VERB PHRASE
                           /   \
                 verb phrase   matrix auxiliary verb
                      |
                 . . . embedded verb

Moravcisk mentions three problems with this analysis as the general one for all bilingual complexes. First of all, consider Japanese:

(37)   *operate* su ru   'operate'
       fail su ru   'fail'   (Japanese/English)

Nishimura (1986: 129) describes the case of helping verbs in Japanese as follows: 'this helping verb [su ru] combines with nouns, mostly of Chinese origin, and creates new verbs meaning "to do what the noun refers to". Our informants use this verb with English verbs as in this sentence "grow-SHITARA".' These elements are often analysed as 'light verbs' (Grimshaw and Mester 1988). Their function is to combine with nouns and create complex predicates through the transfer of the thematic properties from the lexical noun to the light verb. Notice that the Japanese helping verb *su ru* does not carry the agreement markers that would be necessary to trigger its insertion, although *su ru* can be inflected for tense.

A second problem is that nominal or adjectival agreement can be put on foreign adjectives and nouns. Moravcsik claims we never have a 'helping noun', and it is not clear what is so special about verbal inflection that would require a special carrier. This claim might not be entirely correct, as we saw with Finnish flagging markers in Finnish/English code-mixing in chapter 3.

A third problem is simply that it is unclear which phonetic restrictions would be involved. Thus indigenous Hungarian *hull-ok* 'I drop' is well formed and corresponds phonologically to the ill-formed loan *pull-ok 'I pull' (correct is *pull-ol-ok*, as in the forms above).

In addition to the three arguments given by Moravcsik against the 'inflection carrier' analysis in (36), there is a fourth problem with taking this as the general analysis for all cases. Recall that in Popoluca and Navaho different matrix verbs are used, depending on the degree of agentivity of the alien verb. Below we will see that this is a frequent pattern. The possibility of several verbs being used, selected on a semantic basis, is hard to reconcile with the idea that there is simple insertion of an inflection carrier (similar to *do* insertion in English). Compare English *did you help her?* and *did you hunt?* to the use of two different helping verbs in Popoloca. Below yet other arguments will be adduced against (36).

Here I want to argue that many cases should be analysed as in (38), in which the alien verb is adjoined to the matrix verb, yielding an alternational pattern:

(38)   COMPLEX VERB
           /   \
      adjoined verb   generic matrix verb

In (38) there is adjunction rather than complementation. In native structures we have the insertion pattern (39a), involving a noun complement, while in many more intense contact varieties we have (39b), involving an adjoined verb (and hence alternation):

(39) a. **native:**   [love(noun) do]   'to perform love'
                        ⇒
      b. **bilingual:** [love(verb) [do]]   'to do something (namely loving)'

The structure I want to argue for is very close to what Richard Wiese (1996) has termed 'quotational' for phrasal compounds (including bilingual ones, such as *die No-future-Jugendlichen* 'the no-future youngsters').

I will use arguments from Sarnami/Dutch and Tamil/English mixing for this last analysis for at least some of the cases, and then turn to the nominalization analysis and the auxiliary verb and infinitive analysis.

There is a conceptual problem with Moravcsik's unitary analysis. While inserting verbs as such may well be problematic for both morphological and syntactic reasons, there is nothing in universal grammar that forces the way they are inserted to be nominal. Thus, postulating a single form of integration as universal is conceptually unjustified, as well as empirically without basis, I want to argue.

Sarnami compound verbs

The bilingual compound construction occurs in many Indian languages: Hindi, Bhojpuri, Panjabi, Hindustani. I will now focus on the Sarnami (Surinam Hindustani) case, drawing particularly on work by Sita Kishna (1979). After the abolition of slavery, 34,304 indentured labourers were taken from northern India to Surinam (the former Dutch colony in the Guyanas in South America), and now there is a community of about 180,000 speakers of Sarnami, mostly living in the Republic of Surinam and in the Netherlands. There are fairly traditional Sarnami communities in the Surinam countryside, but also many speakers in the capital of Paramaribo and in Dutch urban centres, particularly the Hague. The precise relation between Sarnami and northern Indian languages is unclear. Siegel (1988: 4) writes: 'The Hindi spoken by the Indian indentured labourers consisted of many different geographical varieties along with a continuum of a variety used for wider communication [Hindustani].' According to Damsteegt (1988: 109), Eastern Hindi and the Bihari dialects played an important role in the genesis of Sarnami, along with Aqvahi, Bhojpuri, and Magahi.

Dutch words occur, along with borrowings from Sranan, the Surinam coastal creole language, particularly in urban Sarnami, as I have shown before. Cases of regular code-mixing include:

(40) ma ta   *voor de zekerheid*   ham even nihur ke . . .
      but   to be sure   I bent over . . .   (Kishna 1979: 69)

In her study of the Dutch influence on Sarnami, Kishna used nine recorded conversations involving 31 speakers, from her own circle of acquaintances. In the analysed corpus of over 60,000 words, almost exclusively Sarnami conversations, there were over 6,000 Dutch tokens, including both evident code-switchings and lexical borrowings. In addition, there were Sranan (creole) and English borrowings (from neighbouring Guyana).

The qualitative analysis undertaken by Kishna involved 3,000 loanwords, and focussed on semantic fields. In almost all fields there was Dutch lexical influence, even to some extent in the basic vocabulary (measured by the 100–word Swadesh list). Kishna did not want to distinguish between code-switching and borrowing, using the cover term 'lexical interference' to refer to both. The data studied are also difficult to classify: they involve highly productive borrowings, sometimes involving more than a single word.

Here a different focus is taken from Kishna's. I will look at structural rather than lexical semantic features of the borrowing process. Consider some examples of bilingual verbs in Sarnami:

(41) | *mixed compound* | *gloss Dutch stem* | *meaning* |
      | --- | --- | --- |
      | *luk* ho:ve | 'succeed' | 'succeed' |
      | *uit* ja: | 'out' | 'go out' |
      | *over* a:ve | 'over' | 'come over; migrate' |
      | *tegen* rahe | 'against' | 'be against' |
      | *geboren* bhaili | 'born' | 'I am born' |
      | *schoon-maak* kare | 'clean make' | 'clean' |
      | *propaganda* kare | 'propaganda' | 'make propaganda' |
      | *koffer pak* kare | 'suitcase pack' | 'pack a suitcase' |

We notice that the first part of the compound is Dutch and the second part a Sarnami verb. The Sarnami verb can be one of several, although the verb *kare* 'do' is most frequent. The Dutch part may be a verb (*luk*, *schoon-maak*), a prepositional particle (*uit*, *over*, *tegen*), a participle (*geboren*), a noun (*propaganda*), or a verb phrase or another phrase (*koffer pak*).

The number of elements occurring in the left-most position in the

Table 7.4. *The constituency of mixed verbal compounds in Sarnami (based on Kishna 1979)*

	kare	ho:ve	ho:ve ja:i	ho:ve ha	bhaii	ja:	a:ve	rahe	hai	bana:ve	de:ve:
noun											
deverbal	3			1						1	1
simple	3			2				1			
adjective	2	1						2			
adposition	2		1			5	4	1			
verbstem	51	5	2	2	2						
modal									1		
verb+infinitive	5										
2xverb+infinitive			1								
verb+preposition	18										
adjective noun	1										
X+verb stem	13										

compound is quite large. Similarly, a number of different Sarnami verbs occur in the mixed compounds, including *ho:ve* 'be', and forms derived from it, and *kare* 'do':

(42)   ho:ve   be
          ho:ve ja:
          ho:ve hai
        bhail
    ja: go
    a:ve   come
    rahe   stay
    bana:ve   make
    de:ve: make
    kare   make, do

In table 7.4 the different possibilities and their frequencies (in types) in the corpus collected by Kishna (1979) are presented. A natural assumption in the generative literature on compounds is that the head governs the complement (Williams 1981). Since the compounds are right-headed, presumably the Hindi verb would govern the Dutch element, and hence the mixed compounds would constitute a counterexample to the government constraint in DiSciullo, Muysten, and Singh (1986). This point is discussed in Romaine (1995: 134–6), but I do not follow her reasoning on p. 135 where the first element in the compound is assumed to be ungoverned in Romaine's figure 4.1, and without a language index being assigned to it (since it is not a maximal projection). However, I agree with her final conclusions, though for different reasons: I believe that there is no complementation, but adjunction, and hence no government relation here, contrary to what happens in native Hindi structures. Thus the mixed compounds do not necessarily constitute a counterexample to the government constraint for insertional mixing under non-equivalence.

Arguments against assuming government inside of these compound verbs, which would be Moravcsik's analysis, include:

(a) Contrary to Hindi (where only nouns can occur), any type of Dutch element can be the 'object' of the Sarnami verb: not just nouns, but also adjectives, particles, etc.; hence there is no *selection* in this case, a concomitant of government.

(b) Moravcsik's argument would be greatly strengthened if there were strong evidence of nominalization. One might think that perhaps the Dutch 'bare verbs' in the compounds (the dominant pattern as shown in table 7.4) are really nominalized forms. Indeed, Dutch *werk* is both nominal and verbal, as is its English counterpart *work*. Notice, however, that there are many morphologically complex (43a) and learned (43b) stems in the material, which cannot be nominalized in this way in Dutch (this observation is due to R. Singh, p.c.):

(43) a. ver=ken kare   verkennen   'explore'
          be=handel kare   behandelen   'treat'
          ver=wijs kare   verwijzen   'refer'
      b. solliciteer kare   solliciteren   'apply for a job'
          discrimineer kare   discrimineren   'discriminate'
          forceer kare   dwingen   'force'

In addition, the number of verbs which carry the infinitive ending -*en*, which can also function as a nominalizer, for all verbs, is rather limited, as shown in table 7.5.

(c) The object can be a finite verb, as Dutch verb + separable particle combinations show. In Dutch there are particle verbs, which show the order [particle – verb] with infinitives and subordinate finite verbs, and the order [verb – particle] with main clause finite verbs. The latter are assumed to have been moved to the second position in the clause, leaving the particle behind in clause-final position. If we take a principle like the Unlike Category Condition (Hoekstra 1984) or one of its variants seriously, a finite verb cannot govern another finite verb. In the following examples, it is clear from the order [verb – particle], that 'verb second' has applied in verbal compounds, a rule limited to finite verbs:

Table 7.5. *The form of the verb in mixed verbal compounds in Sarnami (based on Kishna 1979)*

	stem	infinitive
simple	32	2
complex	20	3

(44) *leg uit* kare (cf. Du *uit-leggen*)   'explain'
      vraag aan kare (cf. Du *aan-vragen*)   'request'

That this is rare in the data can be explained rather easily: this syntactic process has to take place inside a lexical verbal complex here. First the different options are illustrated, and in table 7.6 the actual findings:

(45) op-geven kare   'give up'   particle + infinitive
      leg uit kare   'explain'   stem + particle
      uit-leg kare   'explain'   particle + stem

   (d) Several Sarnami helping verbs occur. There is congruence in types of verbs, in the sense that *ho:ve* in (46) takes less active verbs than *kare* in (47):

(46) *luk* ho:ve   lukken   'succeed (impersonal)'
      flauw ho:ve   flauw vallen   'faint'
      herstel ho:ve ja: herstellen   'recover'
      verdwaal ho:ve   verdwalen   'get confused'
      vervaag ho:ve hai vervagen   'become vague'
      verbeter ho:ve   verbeteren   'improve (non-causative)'
      verwen ho:ve hai worden verwend   'are spoiled'

(47) *typ* kare   typen   'type'
      regel kare   regelen   'arrange'
      overplaats kare overplaatsen   'transfer'
      schoon-maak kare schoonmaken   'clean'
      solliciteer kare solliciteren   'apply for a job'
      verzuim kare   verzuimen   'neglect'
      verplaats kare   verplaatsen   'remove'
      af-reken kare   afrekenen   'settle the bill'
      handel kare   handelen   'trade, deal'

Singh (p.c.) notes that sometimes the choice of the helping verb brings out subtle meaning nuances. Thus *succeed hona* would be used in a general expression such as 'to succeed is difficult', while *succeed karena* would be used for more intentional 'to succeed in something specific'.

   This congruence relationship is easily compatible with a modification

Table 7.6. *The form of mixed verbal compounds involving a verb + particle combination in Sarnami (based on Kishna 1979)*

	stem	infinitive
particle verb	8	8
verb particle	2	–

structure: 'to X (and more precisely Y)', and does not make much sense in a government relationship, where the lexical verb is the semantic object of the helping verb.

(f) Even *kare* 'do' is not always active or causative, as we would expect if it were a causative-type head:

(48) bijles kare   extra class   'follow extra classes'
      operatie kare   operation   'get operated on'

Notice both compounds could easily have had an active interpretation: 'teach extra classes' and 'operate', respectively. In a grammaticalization perspective, as taken in Backus (1996), this non-active interpretation would be taken as a sign of the gradual loss of the active properties of *kare*.

(g) While the Sarnami verbs *bana:ve* and *de:ve:* take a Dutch noun complement (although both only occur once in the corpus), the verb *kare* takes nouns only infrequently. If it is primarily a noun + helping verb pattern, this is unexpected.

These arguments all suggest that there is a different relationship internal to the compound than government, namely modification, compatible with an adjunction structure. We cannot use extraction facts, a typical argument in the generative syntactic literature, to show that these verbs are in an adjoined position, for two reasons: first, I am assuming that it is adjunction inside a compound, i.e. not in syntax proper, and compounds are islands for extraction. Second, the type of bilingual production data used here do not contain sentences of sufficient complexity to use this line of argumentation consistently.

Veenstra (1996) argues that serial verbs in Saramaccan and other Caribbean Creole languages can best be viewed as adjunction structures: the different verbs in the serial chain function as adverbial modifiers with respect to each other. Even though structurally bilingual mixed compounds and serial verbs are rather different typologically, we can take these two types of verbal complexes as similar on a more abstract level.

Tamil/English compound verbs

I will now turn to Tamil–English bilingual verbs, using data presented in Shanmugan Pillai (1968) and Annamalai (1971). Tamil/English bilingual usage has also been the subject of a recent article by Sankoff, Poplack, and Vanniarajan (1991), but noun phrases, not verbs, were the focus of that publication (see chapter 3). The following example illustrates the use of the bilingual complex verb construction:

(49) oru aambiḷḷainaaka [konjam *discretion*] [*use* paṇṇuvaan]
      one man   if   some   do-3sg-M-FU
      'If he be a man, he will use some discretion.'

(Sankoff, Poplack, and Vanniarajan (1990: 80)

With respect to the categorial status of the embedded element *use* in (49) and its relation to the helping verb, Shanmugan Pillai, summarizing his detailed analysis of mixed Tamil–English verbs, states (1968: 304): 'It seems to be a feature of modern Tamil to only borrow as nouns, whatever may be the class of these loans in the donor.' Thus Shanmugan Pillai also adopts the position taken in Moravcsik (1975).

Indeed, when we consider verbs such as *po:ḍi* 'put' in (50) and *aḍi* 'strike' in (51) this conclusion seems correct. Compounds involving *po:ḍi* have a variety of meanings, often rather lexicalized. In Tamil proper, the embedded element is invariably a noun. Shanmugan Pillai adopts a strict structuralist perspective, and takes the complement to be ambiguous between a noun, verb, and adjective in many cases: 31 mixed compounds with *po:ḍi* listed by him could either have a verbal or a nominal embedded element (NV), etc. Nonetheless, it is clear that all embedded elements in the *po:ḍi* compounds can be interpreted as nominal, and this is semantically by far the most plausible interpretation.

(50) Borrowings involving *po:ḍi*
      a. na:mõ po:ḍi   deceive   N (Tamil)
      b. designation po:ḍi   write down the des.   N 9
      c. sugar po:ḍi   add sugar   NV 31
      d. trunk po:ḍi   put a trunk call through   NA 3
      e. glass po:ḍi   put on glasses   NAV 5

The same holds for the embedded element in *aḍi* compounds, which in monolingual Tamil compounds is always a noun. To assume that the English element is a noun is always possible, and semantically the most plausible analysis:

(51) Borrowings involving *aḍi*
      a. maṇi aḍi   strike the bell   N (Tamil)
         koṭi aḍi   beat the drum

b. lottery aḍi	suffer	N 4
c. tick aḍi	give a tick	NV 21
d. oil aḍi	cajole	NVA 6

The meaning of *aḍi* in the compounds is something like 'hit' or 'strike', but notice again that many of the mixed compounds have acquired a lexicalized meaning.

The compounds with *paṇṇi* are in marked contrast to the ones before. The verb *paṇṇi* in Tamil expresses causation or accomplishment, and in native monolingual compounds, as in (52a), can only be combined with nouns, similar to *po:ḍi* and *aḍi*. Here the similarities stop, however. In his long list of bilingual *paṇṇi* compounds Shanmugan Pillai only gives one example involving an unambigous English embedded noun, (52b). There are three cases of adjectives, (52c), and three of adpositions, (52d). No less than 194 cases can most plausibly be argued to be verbs. Even if an individual case is really an embedded noun rather than a verb, this does not change the overall picture. The vast majority of the bilingual complex verbs in (52e–g) are synonymous with the English embedded verb. The lexicalized meanings in *paṇṇi* compounds occur with adjectives, adpositions, and the noun.

(52)	a.	ke:li paṇṇi	make fun	N (Tamil)
		nage paṇṇi	make earrings	
	b.	idea paṇṇi	give an idea	N 1
	c.	nice paṇṇi	do something to please	A 3
		strict paṇṇi	make things strict	
		tight paṇṇi	make tight	
	d.	in paṇṇi	tuck a shirt in	P 3
		off paṇṇi	switch off	
		on paṇṇi	switch on	
	e.	overtake paṇṇi	overtake	V 60
		fight paṇṇi	fight	
	f.	watch paṇṇi	keep a watch	VN 115
		fight paṇṇi	fight	
	g.	waste paṇṇi	waste	VNA 19

To summarize the discussion so far, we can contrast *po:ḍi* and *aḍi* on the one hand with *paṇṇi* on the other hand along a number of parameters:

- *po:ḍi* and *aḍi* compounds involve an English noun, *paṇṇi* different categories, but productively a verb;
- *po:ḍi* and *aḍi* compounds are often lexicalized in meaning, while only non-verbal *paṇṇi* compounds are;
- *po:ḍi* and *aḍi* compounds and non-verbal *paṇṇi* compounds are less productive than verbal *paṇṇi* compounds;

- verbal *paṇṇi* compounds take the same objects etc. as the embedded element, *po:ḍḍi* and *aḍi* compounds do not.

On the basis of this, I want to propose that the structure of *paṇṇi* compounds, the productive bilingual type, is different for monolingual Tamil compounds.

In the native Tamil case, the nominal element can be seen as the complement of the verb *paṇṇi*. It is selected by it, and receives a thematic role from it. The resulting complex verb becomes intransitive. In the bilingual pattern, the embedded element modifies the helping verb, and the result may easily be transitive. The interpretation is not 'to perform x', but rather 'to do something, namely x'.

In more formal terms, we can state that the government relationship that ordinarily holds in a compound between the verbal head (here the helping verb) and its complement, does not hold in the case of the bilingual *paṇṇi* compounds. The reasons for this are similar to the ones given above for the Sarnami/Dutch bilingual verbs:

(a) *paṇṇi* is not selective: it can be combined with all four major categories. Ordinarily the government relation involves selection of a specific category or set of categories.

(b) There is no absorption of the transitivity properties of *paṇṇi* by the complement. The government relation is one of absorption. Thus in (49) above *use paṇṇi* is transitive; it takes *konjam discretion* as its object. In true incorporation structures (Baker 1988), the transitivity of the matrix verb is absorbed by the incorporated object. If this were *use*, the overall verb would be intransitive.

(c) Semantically, there is no reading of causation or accomplishment, as we would expect in a government relationship.

(d) If there were a government relationship, the productive class of verbal compounds would constitute a violation of the Unlike Category Condition (Hoekstra 1984), or one of its variants.

An issue not discussed so far is that of the inheritance of features of the embedded verb by the overall compound. It is clear that subcategorization follows Tamil, not English rules (Annamalai 1971: 22), as in the following examples:

(53) a. naan *jaan*-e *school*-le *admit*-paṇṇuneen
        I   AC   LO   do-1sg-PST
        '*I admitted John in the school.'
      b. *naan *jaan*-e *school*-ukku *admit*-paṇṇuneen
        I   AC   DAT   do-1sg-PST
        'I admitted John to the school.'

The English verb *admit* subcategorizes for a direct object and a *to* prepositional phrase, not a locative, as in Tamil. Nonetheless, the mixed sentence has Tamil case markings, and the semantics of these do not correspond with the English forms.

Similarly, *discriminate* takes a PP with *against* in English, but in the mixed clause a direct object:

(54) *Indian women*-e avaa *discriminate* paṇṇa-ille
       AC they   do-NEG
      'They don't discriminate (against) Indian women.'

(Sankoff, Poplack, and Vanniarajan 1990: 80)

This can be construed as an argument against the inflection carrier analysis, since under that analysis one would expect the subcategorization patterns and even the material of the alien verb (which is the head of the verb phrase) to prevail.

Nominalization

The Sarnami/Dutch and Tamil/English cases can be best analysed in terms of verb adjunction rather than noun selection. I will now turn to a few cases where nominalization is more plausible. There are some cases of overt nominalization of the embedded verb, either with morphology of the embedded language or of the matrix language. In Catalan we have as an intermediary solution *fer* 'do' + English gerund pattern, as in *fer zap-ping, fer raft-ing, fer foot-ing, fer jog-ging*. It is extended to *fer pont-ing* (from Catalan *pont* 'bridge') for 'jump from bridges' (Xavier Vila i Moreno, p.c.).

Notice that in the nominalization analysis we are dealing with nouns in compounds, not with full noun phrases. This is clear from case marking. Consider the following contrast:

(55) [on *runde*yi] yapanlara
      ten round-AC do-NOM-PL-DA
      'to those who made the ten rounds'

(56) *gratulieren* yapıyo
      congratulate do-PR-3
      's/he congratulates'   (Turkish/German; Carol Pfaff, unpublished data)

In (55) the verb *yap*- selects a noun phrase, marked accusative, and in (56) it occurs with a verb, not marked for case. If the constructions were similar, we would expect case marking in both instances. The 'object of' relation in (55) is truly phrasal. In (56) it is word-internal, and there is no case-marking.

Another potential argument against the nominalization analysis, due to Annamalai, is not valid for a similar reason. Annamalai (1989b: 122) argues against the noun + *kar* analysis on the basis of the fact that the supposedly nominalized verb cannot receive any noun modifiers. However, this is not possible in a compound either.

American Portuguese

Above the case was mentioned of *fazer o save* from American Portuguese, containing the masculine singular definite article *o*. Leo Pap (1949) has analysed the Portuguese of immigrants residing mostly in New England. He gives a number of examples (1949: 114–17) of verbs integrated with *fazer* 'do, make' (in addition to many cases where the verb has been adapted directly to Portuguese inflection):

(57) fazer o chinche   'change (money)'
      fazer o telefone   'telephone'
      fazer o save   'save'
      fazer o find-out   'find out'
      fazer o give up   'give up'
      fazer o fool   'fool'
      fazer o boda   'bother'
      fazer o spoil   'spoil'

Pap does not raise the issue of why sometimes a helping verb is used, and sometimes the verb has Portuguese inflection. It is possible that both syntactic and phonological factors sometimes preclude integration into Portuguese. In the cases of *give up* and *find out* there is no V + particle construction in native Portuguese. In the case of *bother* the final liquid is not a proper base for Portuguese *-ear*. In addition, there are also a few cases of bare verbs used as the complement to *fazer* (1949: 105), as in *fazer box* 'box'. In the Portuguese of this community, *fazer* is also used with nouns, as in *fazer dinheiro* 'make money'. The use of *o* makes a nominalization analysis quite plausible. Also, Pap (1949: 106) notes: 'Since the English word in these combinations appears as a noun, the direct object of a transitive phrase of this kind is preceded by the preposition *de* (of).' Absorption of transitivity (making a preposition necessary) is typical of nominal compounds.

Michif

A rather different example of nominalization is provided by Michif, a Cree/French contact language that emerged in Canada in the nineteenth century. While the predominant feature of this language is that the verbs are derived from Cree and the nouns from French, there are some Michif verb stems derived from either French or English. They are integrated with a prefix *lï* (< the French article *le*) and a suffix *i:* (< the French infinitive *-er*). In (58) we have the verb *bïn* 'bless' (< bénir) and in (59) the verb *selibre:t*.

(58) lï pɛr kiː-**lï-*bïn*-i-w** lï muːd
DET priest PST-DET-bless-INF-TA.3–3′ DET people
'The priest blessed the people.'

(59) lï kat dï žyjet giː-**lï-*sɛlibreːt*-i-naːn**
DET four of July 1PA-DET-celebrate-INF-IA.1pl
'We celebrated the Fourth of July.'   (Cree/French; Bakker 1997: 115–16)

The use of the French nominal determiner to integrate foreign verbs clearly suggests a nominalization strategy. However, the addition of an infinitive marker at the end of the verb may be a verbalizer; notice that it is also added to English-based verbs.

From noun selection to verb adjunction: a developmental perspective

So far, two patterns have been considered: verb + adjoined verb (Tamil, Sarnami) and verb + embedded noun (Portuguese, Michif). I will now look at the evidence for assuming a transition from an earlier verb + noun to a later verb + verb pattern, focussing on different case studies. The possibility of gaining a developmental perspective is hampered by the fact that the scarce historical sources for most of these language contact settings have not been explored yet. The only thing we can do is contrast more or less contemporary settings which can be assumed to reflect different stages of development.

Other varieties of Overseas Hindi

I begin with a more general discussion of varieties of Overseas Hindi. Mixed compounds have been recorded almost everywhere in the Indian diaspora. Siegel (1987, 154–5) provides cases from Fiji:

(60) sāin kar-   sign
     wāiṭ kar-   wait
     mariṭ kar-   marry (in a civil ceremony)   (English/Hindi)

Notice that the case of *mariṭ* in (60) suggests that the first element is not necessarily a verb stem. Notice also that the new mixed compounds often refer to fairly ordinary activities, and do not necessarily constitute cultural borrowings in the sense of Bloomfield (1933: 444).

Meshtrie (1988: 163) gives a few examples of Fanagalo (ultimately Afrikaans)/Bhojpuri compounds from South Africa:

(61) basop kar-   guard, herd (<* pas op)
     bagasha kar-   visit, go on a trip or holiday (<* bagage)

                                                      (Fanagalo/Bhojpuri)

Again, *bagasha* is a noun rather than a verb, while *basop* is a verb + particle combination, at least in the original Afrikaans.

An interesting pattern can be discerned in the Hindi of Guyana (Gambhir 1981) and Trinidad (Mohan 1978; Bhatia 1988). Here the English Creole verb appears with the ending -*am*:

(62) ṭapam kar-   stop
     lāikam kar-   like   (Hindi/Guyanese English Gambhir 1981: 54)

(63) phrāyam kar-   fry
     lāykam kar-   like
     bēgam kar-   beg   (Hindi/Trinidad English; Mohan 1978: 141)

(64) fāitam kar-   fight
     ṭepam kar-   tape
     fonam kar-   phone   (Hindi/Trinidad English; Bhatia 1988: 191)

The -*am* ending occurs in the traditional creoles of both areas, but not much in the current language: 'The termination *am* functions as a third person object pronoun in basilectal Creole English, but is seldom attested [in] Creole English as spoken by its native speakers in Trinidad. In these loan predicates, however, the termination -*am* functions as a predicate marker, and not as a direct object pronoun' (Mohan 1978: 141). It is clear that -*am* does not replace the object in these constructions:

(65) tū māngē ēgō khīsā tēp-am karē
     'do you want to tape-record a folk-tale?'
                 (Hindi/Trinidad English; Mohan 1978: 141)

Here *khīsā* is the direct object. Notice that all examples given involve transitive verbs, so -*am* could be a transitivity marker.

Rajendra Singh (p.c.) suggests that the -*am* suffix could be an older Hindustani or Bhojpuri (compare Sanskrit *satya* 'true'/*satyam* 'truth', and *shiva* 'good'/*shivam* 'goodness') nominalizer. While this analysis requires more thorough historical exploration, keep in mind that the Creole source -*am* does not make particular sense structurally or semantically. What the Trinidad and Guyana examples show is the observation that the left-most member of the compound is an ordinary verb is not always correct; indeed verbs do not occur in these compounds in their canonical form here.

The resultative copula *ho-* (and suppletive forms from the same paradigm) also functions in mixed verbal compounds, in passive-like structures with non-stative predicates in Trinidad, as it did in Sarnami:

(66) tū bōl al, hamār kahānī **tēp-am bhai** gal
     'you speak now, my story has already been recorded'
                 (Hindi/Trinidad English; Mohan 1978: 140)

Another source is Domingue's study of Mauritius (1971), where Bhojpuri and French Creole are mixed. She gives examples such as:

(67) ham diblee plããt karat haĩ
I wheat plant do PRES-PR
'I am planting wheat.' (Bhojpuri/French Creole; Domingue 1971: 101)

In Creole the sentence would be (68), with a different order:

(68) mo plãte dible

Domingue stresses the fact that the overall structure is a Bhojpuri one: 'The pronoun *ham* necessitates the use of the Bhojpuri verbal inflection. When this does not take place, the resulting utterance is perceived as a composite speech production' (1971: 101).

Panjabi and Bhojpuri as spoken in England have received much discussion. Romaine's analysis of Panjabi–English mixed compounds (1989 [1995]) raises the problem of categorial status. Her basic findings are as follows. There are a total of 77 mixed compounds in her data (I assume types, although this is not indicated explicitly). They can be fitted into six categories, according to the English element and the Panjabi helping verb:

(69)

verb hona	12	involve hona
verb + particle	3	cut off hona
noun + verb hona	?2	guilt feel hona
verb kərna	50	appreciate kərna
verb + particle kərna	5	pick up kərna
noun + verb kərna	4	exam pass kərna
gerund	1	lobbying kərna

(Panjabi/English; Romaine 1995: 133)

The helping verb is *hona* or *kərna*, according to Romaine depending on the stativity of the verb (1995: 133), *hona* being generally preferred with statives. Notice examples such as *guilt feel hona*, where the English predicate is clearly stative. In the main text it is claimed there are no combinations of an English noun with a Panjabi helping verb, although in a footnote she reports the case of *translation kərna* (1995: 328).

This is quite a remarkable observation because in Panjabi monolingual verbal compounds the left-most member cannot be a verb, and must be a noun, as we saw above. Also, in the centuries of Arabic and Persian language contact, a great many nouns from these languages have been incorporated into Indian verbal compounds, but no verbs (Rajendra Singh, p.c.). The predominance of verbs in the contact variety is thus an innovation.

Aghinotri (1987: 120) assumes in a study of the bilingual language use of the Sikhs (Panjabi/English) in England that there are four helping verbs: *kərna* 'do', *de* 'give', *le* 'take', and *hona* 'be', with *kərna:* 'as the most frequently used' (p. 121). It is clear from Aghinotri's account that in addition to verbs, nouns and adjectives can also be complements of *kərna:*. Thus we have in addition to *haus we:k kərna:* 'do house work', things like *hɔlidez kərna:* 'go on a holiday', *eksəsaɪz kərna:* 'exercise', and *blek kərna:* 'make black'. It is used more often with English verbs than with English nouns or adjectives. Again, with *hona:* the first element tends to be less active, or stative: *miks hona:* 'get mixed', *lend hona:* 'land', *merid hona:* 'be married'. Since *hona:* is attached to non-agentive intransitives, and *kərna:* to agentives, we can assume that *hona:* is not a complement-taking verb. This is a further argument against government. Given the lexical specificity, we can assume that the helping verb is not without a thematic role of its own.

This concludes my brief survey of bilingual compound verbs in overseas Hindi. The analysis I propose is that there were three steps: introduction of (a) foreign nouns, then (b) nominalized verbs or gerunds, then (c) verbs. The fact that in Guyana and Trinidad the foreign verb needs to be affixed with *-am* – either from older Hindustani, or the older basilectal creole object pronoun, or both – is suggestive of the intermediary stage. If the analysis given above is correct, this shift from nouns to verbs was accompanied by a shift from a government to a modification relationship.

There are a number of unresolved issues, particularly involving the relation between the leftmost verb in the verbal compound and other elements in the sentence. These will be taken up again in chapter 9.

Greek/English compound verbs

Above I briefly alluded to Greek/English cases. The original use of *kani* is that of a verbalizer 'do' used with noun phrases:

(70)   a.   O Petros kani mia prosfora.
            'Petros makes a remark.'
      b.   O Petros kani banyo.
            'Petros takes a bath.'

The Greek/English case is well illustrated in the work of Seaman (1972: 166–169). Seaman's is not a quantitative study of American Greek. Nonetheless, the ample exemplification allows us to compare the frequency of the different patterns. Seaman shows that two verbs participate in the construction: *jino* 'be, become' and *káno* 'do, make', and notes (Seaman 1972: 169): 'This practice of avoiding complex or little known Greek verbal constructions

Table 7.7. *The constituency of mixed verbal compounds in American Greek (based on Seaman 1972)*

	jíno	káno
participle	3	
adjective	2	1
dposition	1	
noun phrase	1	2
noun	2	
verb	21	
verb particle	2	
verb phrase	6	
verb/noun	11	
finite verb	1	
verb mixed noun phrase	3	
verb + ing	3	

by the substitution of hybrid predicates is universal in the Chicago Greek communities, and occurs in the speech of most Greek–American bilingual speakers of all generations.' Some examples of the patterns encountered are:

(71) éxi jíni *stuck*   participle
      ja na jínune *defrost*   verb/participle?

(72) káno *cover up*   verb particle
      káno *delivery work*   noun
      káni *cover her body*   verb phrase
      káni *measure* to *power*   verb + mixed noun phrase
      káni *explains*   finite verb
      kánune *fishing*   verb + ing
      kánune *feast*   verb/noun
      káni *shiny*   adjective

In table 7.7 the distribution of these patterns in the data presented by Seaman is given. It is clear that with *káno* the use of an English verb is the most productive.

Tamis (1986: 169–72) gives the same pattern for Greek in Victoria, Australia. *káno* is used for the 'active voice', and *jínome* for the 'passive'. The latter characterization is not wholly correct, since *jíno* is also used for a verb like *retire*, in addition to passives as in *jínete affect* 'he is not affected'.

Listed with *káno* are:

(73) cover, decorate, enjoy, protect, use, examine, explain

Some nouns are also mentioned as complements of *káno*, as well as gerunds:

Table 7.8. *The use of the Turkish verb* yap- *'do' in three generations of Turkish migrants in the Netherlands (based on data in Backus 1996: 192, table 5.1)*

	1st generation	intermediate generation	2nd generation
Tu noun + *yap-*	16	2	6
Du noun + *yap-*	3	2	0
Tu verb +*yap-*	7	1	1
Du verb + *yap-*	3	4	10

(74) exam, delivery, profit, check

(75) nursing, adjusting, warning, crossing, boasting, starting, freezing

The independent emergence of these bilingual verbs in two separate migration contexts is an argument for the robustness of the pattern involved. Aspessia Hatzidaki (p.c.) suggested that in Brussels bilinguals can combine *kano* with French infinitives as in *kano déménager* 'move house', and in Montreal we find *kano ski*, but also *kano save* and *kano print* (both computer terms), as well as *kano jogging*.

Turkish

It is well known that the productive foreign verb + *yapmak* [do-INF] pattern in bilingual Turkish is matched by a noun + helping verb combination in monolingual Turkish. Türker (1996) notes that *yapmak* constructions are not used with core verbs such as 'go' and 'drive', but only with quite specific non-native verbs. In immigrant Turkish only *yapmak* is found, not *etmek*, unlike in native Turkish verbal complexes, where both forms occur.

A recent study by Backus (1996) discusses these in great detail from the perspective of the grammaticalization of the helping verb. It supports the developmental perspective taken here. Backus has studied several generations of Turkish migrants in the Netherlands, and it is clear from his data that there is a shift in the usage of compound verbs. As is illustrated in table 7.8, with first generation speakers the helping verb *yap-* is primarily used with Turkish nouns, and in the second generation primarily with Dutch verbs; with the intermediate generation (born in Turkey, raised in the Netherlands) it is somewhere in between. The Turkish verbs used with *yap-* are overtly nominalized (either with *-iş* or with *-mε*; Backus 1996: 197–8). The Dutch forms are all infinitives. These could be seen as nominalizations, since the Dutch infinitive can also be used as a nominal, but this is not a necessary conclusion. The interpretation of Dutch infinitives as nominalizations requires an understanding of Dutch grammar beyond the reach of most Turkish learners. This interpretation would not explain the decrease in Dutch noun + *yapmak* and the increase of Dutch verb + *yapmak* patterns across the generations. One could object that the overall numbers involved are too small to draw a definite conclusion. The numbers are small but are completely parallel in the trend to those of other language pairs discussed in the chapter. Finally, many borrowed nouns in *yapmak* constructions get accusative case.

Türker (1993: 99) writes:

> In my opinion, the reason for immigrant Turks' use of Norwegian (or German, Dutch, etc.) verbs in infinitive form and combining them with Turkish verbs to make a verb phrase that functions according to the Turkish grammar rules can be explained by the fact that bilingual immigrant Turkish people tend to accept the 'loan' *infinitive verb* as a *noun* which is already used as a noun in Norwegian.

However, this account cannot easily explain why in (76) there is a *yap*-construction:

(76) *studere* yapmayı isterdim
    study-INF do-INF-AC I would like to
    'I would like to study.'   (Turkish/Norwegian; Türker 1993: 100)

Why not simply take the Norwegian 'noun' *studere* and give it Turkish accusative case?

In an article on Bulgarian Turkish, Rudin and Eminov (1990: 157) show that Bulgarian verbs are generally combined with *yapmak* 'do' in a compound verb construction in their third person singular or first person plural forms. Now this is presumably because Bulgarian has no infinitive, but the choice for the third person singular suggests that what is called for is an unmarked verb form rather than a nominal one; why then a finite form and not a nominalization? Note that in English not all verbs can be simply nominalized in their bare form either.

Malay

For Malay there is no cross-generational evidence available so far, but there are comparative data. Huwaë (1992) contrasts two types of contact between Malay and Dutch: in the Dutch colonial period some Dutch elements were integrated into Malay as nouns in Indonesia, and then verbalized. This is what we see in Bahasa Indonesia as it is spoken now in Indonesia.

In the Moluccan Malay brought to the Netherlands after independence in

1948, leading to a more direct contact with Dutch, these same elements are integrated directly as verbs. Thus we have:

(77) **Bahasa Indonesia**   **Moluccan Malay**
  a. saya tidak me-*reaksi*   a sing *reageren*
     I NEG AG-reaction   I NEG react
                        'I do not react.'
  b. mereka mau meng-*integrasi*-kan   dong mau *integreren*
     they want AG-integration-APPL   they want integrate
     orang Ambon   Ambon
     people Ambon   Ambon
     'They want to integrate the Moluccans.'   (Malay/Dutch; Huwaë 1992)

Again, this difference can be interpreted as a development from a situation where contact between Dutch and Malay was more limited to one where contact was intense.

Tamil

Annamalai (1989a: 50–1) claims that imbalanced bilinguals (whose Tamil is much stronger than their English) will use the (a) pattern in Tamil/English code-mixing, while balanced bilinguals will adopt the (b) pattern:

(78) a. avan enne *confusion*   -paṇṇiṭṭaan   (imbalanced)
     b. avan enne *confuse*   -paṇṇiṭṭaan   (balanced)
        he   me   did
        'He confused me.'

(79) a. onakku oru eDam *reservation*-paṇṇirukeen   (imbalanced)
     b. onakku oru eDam *reserve*-paṇṇirukeen   (balanced)
        'I have reserved a place for you.'

The (a) pattern conforms to what we find in native Tamil [noun – verb] compounds; the (b) pattern is innovative.

To further study possible shifts from verb + embedded noun to helping verb + adjoined verb combinations wide-ranging comparative and diachronic studies are called for.

Auxiliary + infinitive structures

It should be clear that we cannot adopt a single analysis for all the bilingual complex verb constructions. In some languages there is evidence for a clear auxiliary status of the helping verb.

Moroccan Arabic/Dutch

The Moroccan Arabic/Dutch data analysed by Boumans (1995; 1998) contain many cases of the helping verb *der* 'do':

(80) ka-**ndir**-ha *elke keer uitstellen*
　　 1–do-3 every time postpone
　　 'I postpone it every time.'

(81) ma-neqder-sh **ndir** *diepe gesprekken voeren, weet je wel?*
　　 NEG-1sg.can-NEG 1sg.do deep conversations carry on, you know
　　 'I can't carry on deep conversations, you know?'

(Moroccan Arabic/Dutch; Boumans 1995)

In these two examples it is plausible to assume that the Dutch fragments are bare verb phrases that are used as a complement to the Moroccan Arabic helping verb.

In related examples, more than just a Dutch verb phrase is involved:

(82) ana kunt **ndir** *twijfelen of ik ook psychologie ging studeren*
　　 I 1sg.was 1sg.do doubt whether I also psychology would study.
　　 'I doubted whether I would study psychology.'

Here the extraposed embedded complement clause *of ik ook psychologie ging studeren* 'whether I would study psychology' does not form a syntactic constituent with *twijfelen* 'doubt', but is analysed in Dutch grammar as being adjoined to the matrix clause at the highest level.

There are several reasons to distinguish between the Moroccan Arabic/ Dutch case and e.g. the Hindi and Greek cases. First of all, in the Moroccan Arabic case, there is often much more Dutch material than just a verb. This is possible, but rarer, in the other cases studied.

Second, the Moroccan Arabic case involves only one helping verb, *der*. There is no agentivity restriction. A non-agentive verb like *voelen* 'feel' can occur with it freely.

(83) ma ka-t-**dir**-ha š *voelen?*
　　 NEG DUR-2sg-do.IMPF-F NEG feel
　　 'Don't you feel it?'

Third, the Moroccan Arabic verb and the Dutch element need not be adjacent:

(84) ka-t-**dir** mʿa-hum *voetballen?*
　　 DUR-2–do.IMPF with-3pl football
　　 'Do you play football with them?'

All these facts suggest that *der* is an inflection-carrying helping verb in these structures.

Hausa/English

Madaki (1983) contains an analysis of Hausa/English code-mixing in 23 minutes of recordings taken from spontaneous conversations produced by a small group of Nigerian graduate students in the United States (members of Madaki's own circle). There were 29 single English verbs in the corpus, 27 of which had the gerund form, referred to as 'nominalizations' by Madaki (1983: 85). Given that there were only 42 single English nouns in the corpus, this is quite a high number of borrowed verbs. The gerund verbs are either bare, which produces a continuous or habitual interpretation, or they are preceded by a Hausa auxiliary *yi* 'be, become'. In Hausa, *yi* is used with elements Madaki terms nouns denoting quality or state of being (they may also be thought of as predicatively used stative adjectives). An example of a gerund is:

> (85) A'a mun san abin da muka *yi creating* dai
> No we know thing.the which we AUX creating that.is
> 'No, rather we knew what we created.'   (Madaki 1983: 87)

The two verbs that are not in gerund form are exclamative *look* and adjectivally used *scared away*.

What is striking is that English mixed-in verb phrases can have two forms. They are either copular predicates (*is very interesting, was very good*) (eight cases) or they have the gerundive form (five cases): *sharing the same dialect, getting the house organized*. This suggests that a purely lexical nominalization analysis for the *yi* + GERUND combinations is not appropriate. Rather, the English verbs are made fit for the Hausa tense/mood/aspect system through affixation of -*ing*, and *yi* functions as an auxiliary here.

Summary of the argumentation so far

Above I have argued that there are three types of bilingual complex verbs: nominalized verbs in compounds, adjoined verbs, and helping verb + non-finite verb constructions. In table 7.9 I summarize the arguments used so far to distinguish the three models under discussion. These arguments provide one with sufficient criteria, I hope, to determine the precise characteristics of the bilingual complex verb construction involved.

Congruent lexicalization?

In the discussion so far no attention has been given to possible congruence of the languages involved in bilingual verbs. Of special interest is therefore the role of the guest language. Two points come to mind.

First, the number of different structural possibilities for mixed compounds is much larger in the Dutch case recorded by Kishna (1979) than in the material reported on in Romaine (1989, 1995). One possible explanation is that this difference is due to the greater congruence in word order and verb

Table 7.9. *Summary of the arguments given so far, and their implication for the nominalization, inflection-carrier, and adjunction analyses*

	Nominalization	Infinitive	Adjunction
no inflection necessary in helping verb constructions	0	−	0
no helping adjectives/nouns	0	−	0
no obvious phonetic restrictions on inflection	0	−	0
matrix verb			
different verbs	−	−	+
single verb	+	+	0
subcategorization properties			
matrix	+	−	+
alien verb	−	+	−
semantic correspondence	−	−	+
UCC violated	−	−?	+
elements combined with			
single category	+	+	0
different categories	−	−	+
transitivity			
absorbed	+	−	−
not absorbed	−	+	+
nouns			
none	−	+	+
a few	−	−	+
mostly	+	−	−
all	+	−	−
nominalizers			
absent	−	+	+
present	+	−	−
verb/helping verb			
unit	+	−	+
separate	−	+	−

morphology between Dutch and Hindustani than between English and Panjabi. In both Dutch and Hindustani particle + verb combinations are very frequent, and have the same order (at least for Dutch infinitives, verbs in citation form, and subordinate main verbs).

The hypothesis of congruence between Hindustani and Dutch is strengthened by the second point, namely that there are cases where a Dutch particle forms a lexicalized combination (from Dutch) with a Hindustani verb:

(86) voor a:ve   voor-komen   'occur, exist'
     over ho:ve ja: overgaan   'finish the year'
     voor ja: voorgaan   (voor rijbewijs)
     mee a:ve   mee-komen   'come along'
     over a:ve   overkomen   'come over', 'migrate'

Thus the structure of the embedded language, Dutch, plays an important role, even though the group of Sarnami speakers as a whole cannot be termed balanced bilinguals. The similarity of the particle + verb patterns in the two contributing languages gives the possibility of congruent lexicalization.

I will return to this type of mixed compound in chapter 9.

Conclusions

It is unquestionable that in both Panjabi/English and in Hindustani/Dutch mixed compounds the leftmost element can be a verb. It is also uncontroversial that in native Indic varieties it cannot be. Thus the oft-heard remark that the pattern is simply already provided for by the language itself is inaccurate. Is there a special 'bilingual syntax', or can the complex verbs be accounted for by the rules of the matrix language? Is there such a thing as a special bilingual grammar needed, or is the collaboration of the two contributing grammars in accordance with general principles or constraints of mixing sufficient to account for the patterns found? Most researchers, such as Poplack (1980, and later work) and Myers-Scotton (1993b), assume that there is no need for a special grammar.

The Tamil–English data, together with other data sets of bilingual complex verbs, suggest otherwise. The phenomenon at hand is *not* simply using mechanisms already present in Tamil to incorporate alien elements. In most of the cases looked at so far, including Tamil–English, the monolingual compounding strategy is limited to nouns, and the bilingual strategy specifically directed at verbs.

The analysis of the Hindustani and Tamil cases as resulting from a special kind of bilingual syntax is further supported by the fact that in several settings the verbal adjunction strategy appears to have arisen only gradually, out of the noun selection strategy. The frequency with which we find the verb adjunction strategy in different language pairs points to the robustness and universality of adjunction in sentence production.

Foreign verbs are sometimes inserted as finite stems, sometimes as infinitives. The evidence for adjunction, coupled with the presence of

Table 7.10. *Classification of the bilingual verbs in the different settings in terms of the notions insertion (finite (+fin), infinitive (−fin), compound (comp)), alternation, and congruent lexicalization*

	Insertion +fin	−fin	comp	Alternation	Congruent lexicalization
Chinese/Dutch	x				
Sranan/Dutch	x				
Malay/Dutch	x				x
Quechua/Spanish	x				
Tagalog/English	x				
Amharic/English	x				
Popoloca/Spanish				x	
Sarnami/Dutch				x	x
Tamil/English				x	
Portuguese/English	x	x			
Cree/French		x			
Guy Hindi/English		x		x	
Panjabi/English		?		x	
Greek/English				x	
Turkish/Dutch		x		x	
Mor Arabic/Dutch			x		
Hausa/English			x		

congruent lexicalization patterns, suggests that bilingual verbs exhibit the full range of code-mixing strategies. In table 7.10 the results of the analysis in this chapter for the different language pairs discussed are summarized. It is to be hoped that a yet wider typological spectrum of bilingual verbs will be studied in future literature.

One issue that requires more study is how, in a verbal complex created through adjunction, the semantic features associated with the adjoined verbs are combined with the syntactic features determined by the helping verb.

8
Variation in mixing patterns

The previous chapters have presented a fairly complex picture of the processes involved in code-mixing. I have claimed that there are three distinct processes in operation: insertion, alternation, and congruent lexicalization.

Insertion is constrained by requirements imposed by the lexical and functional categories of a matrix language. The borrowing of nouns involves insertion, as does mixing of noun phrases and determiner phrases. Thus insertion concerns constituents of different sizes.

Alternation is constrained, if at all, by surface ordering correspondences and is often characterizable in terms of paratactic adjunction. Conjunctions and adpositions are incorporated through adjunction rather than insertion. Verbs are often incorporated through adjunction to a helping verb.

Congruent lexicalization is akin to language variation and style shifting: switching is grammatically unconstrained and characterizable in terms of alternative lexical insertions. Linguistic convergence feeds into congruent lexicalization, and the two processes may reinforce each other. Some cases of word-internal mixing can be viewed as congruent lexicalization.

It is methodologically desirable to aim for a limited set of universal explanations when looking for grammatical constraints on mixing. It needs to be seen, though, what the relative importance is of structural, social, and psycholinguistic factors in determining whether we find language mixing and of what kind. We need an account that provides a superset of structural possibilities, from which individual communities choose a subset. Different possibilities are chosen with greater frequency in specific language pairs and speech communities. There may be an implicational hierarchy among the structural possibilities, dependent in part on typological similarities and differences of the languages involved.

This chapter attempts to summarize what is known about the relation between mixing patterns and different extra-linguistic factors. Three issues will be addressed successively:

What are the relevant grammatical and extra-linguistic factors influencing the choice of a mixing pattern?

Are we able to differentiate between bilingual corpora in terms of the three-way division proposed here?

What factors explain best why an individual speech community shows one pattern rather than another one?

Code-mixing settings and dimensions of comparison

As a backdrop to the following discussion, consider the variety of settings in which code-mixing occurs.

As to the **social** definition of the bilingual situation on the macro-level, we have to distinguish a great number of different contexts. To name just a few (with illustrative examples in parentheses):

- frontiers between languages or language families (French and Germanic in Brussels and Strasbourg, French and English in Ottawa)
- clusters of multi-lingual tribal groups, the members of which speak each other's languages (Amazonian basin, Australia, New Guinea) (Dixon 1980, Sorensen 1972)
- dialect/standard language relations (Germany, Italy)
- minority language islands (Basque)
- bilingualism of native elites (French and Russian in Tolstoy's Russia)
- colonial language/dominated indigenous language (French in Morocco, English in East Africa)
- migrant communities (Puerto Ricans and Mexicans in the USA, minority communities in Europe)

These communities differ **sociolinguistically** in many ways on the meso-level, including:

- the degree of acceptance in the community of code-mixing
- attitudes towards bilingualism in general
- structures of linguistic domination
- whether it is a transplanted or endogenous bilingual community (e.g. English/Hindi in India or in Great Britain)
- the distribution of patterns of language use, including bilingual speech across generations

Then, the **interactional** setting, on the micro-level, should be taken into account. Contexts investigated so far include:

222

- adolescent peer group informal interactions
- family conversations (mostly caregiver – child interac at mealtimes
- class room interactions
- functionary – citizen interchanges
- market place transactions
- exploratory conversations between relative strangers

A final set of factors that need to be mentioned in this rather hectic catalogue is **duration of the contact**. Long-term contacts may facilitate code-mixing in at least two ways:

- linguistic convergence, leading to increased equivalence
- the emergence of specific bilingual adaptation strategies

In addition, long term contacts may lead to increased tolerance for the mixed forms.

Given the variety of settings on different levels of analysis, a number of perspectives can be used to map the variation in mixing strategies. I will discuss, in sequence, reversed dominance patterns, bilingual proficiency and speaker-type, age-group and generation, and attitudes. Poplack and Sankoff (1988) suggest that there may also be random selection of mixing strategy per community: borrowing versus constituent insertion in Arabic/French mixing in Lebanon and Morocco, respectively.

Reversed dominance patterns

If we want to get a stronger grip on the macro-sociological conditioning of mixing patterns, two possibilities come to mind. One is the case where the same two languages are involved, first in a colonial Third World context and then in the post-colonial West. Examples are Arabic/French in Algeria and in France, Malay/Dutch in Indonesia and in Holland. In this type of comparison, however, it is not only the type of dominance relation that changes, but also the numerical proportion of speakers and the time depth of the language contact.

A second possibility, harder to find, is where the dominance relation between the two languages has been reversed. A case in point is Central American English and Mexican American Spanish (Lipski 1986). English in Central America is the language of the black minorities along the Caribbean coast, and particularly in Costa Rica it has been heavily influenced by Spanish (Herzfeld 1980, 1983), who notes that when bilinguals 'converse informally, languages are alternated constantly' (Herzfeld 1980: 85).

223

An interesting point of comparison between Mexican American Spanish and Central American English involves the incorporation of intrusive verbs. In Limon English Creole mesolect (Costa Rica), Spanish verbs either appear in a frozen form, (1); as an infinitive, (2)–(3); as a spurious English back-formation, (4); or as an infinitive with English -*ing* ending, (5).

(1) ai se *falta* plenti
'I say plenty [of time] is still lacking.'

(2) yu fada kyatch yu/put yu in kana fi tan op/
your father catch you puts you in corner to stand up
kastigar yu
chastize you

(3) an im layk *echar carbon* pan yu, no
'and he likes to get you angry (lit. throw coal upon you)'

(4) konserbyet < Eng conserve, conservation   Sp conservar
fomentyet < Eng foment, fomentation   Sp fomentar
sentralisyet < Eng centralization   Sp centralizar

(5) konfesarin 'confessing'
rechasarin 'rejecting'   (Limon English Creole; Herzfeld 1980, 1983)

The data presented for Mexican American Spanish by Pfaff (1979: 299) show the mirror image. In the conversion from Spanish to English the question is which stem form to adapt, and in the reverse case, how to transform English stems to fit Spanish conjugations. Main verbs are generally adapted to Spanish (by adding a linking vowel and the stem vowel of the first conjugation), while unadapted verbs are either participles or infinitives. Pfaff (1979) gives the following types of examples:

(6) Los están *bussing* pa otra escuela
'They are bussing them to another school.'

(7) Va a *re-enlist*
'He is going to re-enlist.'

(8) Ya no lo *train*iará
'He won't train him any more.'   (Mexican American Spanish; Pfaff 1979: 299)

Thus the shift in sociopolitical dominance relation has a clear linguistic effect on the direction of the insertion found.

The perspective of bilingual proficiency and speaker-type

A set of speaker-related factors which help determine the form of code-mixing in specific situations is **psycholinguistic**, involving factors which may characterize a bilingual situation such as:

- bilingual acquisition
- incipient bilingualism and second language learning
- balanced bilingualism
- Alzheimer syndrome speech (dementia) and aphasia
- language attrition and loss
- age: child/adolescent/adult/old age bilingualism

The aim of a comparison here would be to see to what extent different types of bilingual proficiency influence the mixing process. Such a comparative study is being carried out in the Swedish–Finnish bilingual community in Sweden, where Hyltenstam and Stroud have studied code-mixing among patients with an Alzheimer syndrome (1989, 1993) and where considerable amounts of data are available for other types of bilinguals as well (Boyd, Andersson, and Thornell 1991; Andersson 1990). A first tentative conclusion would be an overall similarity on the structural, though not on the pragmatic level.

Turning to adult bilingualism, Bentahila and Davies (1992) list a number of factors that may distinguish subgroups within a speech community in terms of their code-mixing behaviour. The best researched of these is **bilingual proficiency** (which in itself, of course, results from other social factors on the group level). In some of the literature there is evidence for a relation between the degree of bilingual proficiency and the type of switching that occurs: the more balanced the proficiency, the greater the incidence of intra-sentential switching which nonetheless follows specific patterns (Poplack 1980; Nortier 1990). Poplack (1980), who used self-report measures, and Nortier (1990), who used a variety of measures, though not vocabulary tests, have both argued for a strong relation between bilingual proficiency and the propensity towards intra-sentential code-switching. Poplack showed that Puerto Rican speakers with high levels of proficiency in both Spanish and English in New York demonstrate both emblematic or tag-switching and intra-sentential mixing, while speakers with limited proficiency in English only show emblematic switching. In the latter type, a typical switch consists of an element like *okay?* added to a Spanish sentence. Nortier argues that for the Moroccan Arabic–Dutch bilingual speakers in the Netherlands that she studied 'a high degree of bilingual proficiency is related to the use of relatively many intrasentential and single word switches' (1990: 115). The reason, presumably, for this relation between bilingual proficiency and combining the languages in intricate ways in bilingual speech is that a bilingual needs to know both languages well to combine them within the sentence in rapid speech production. Nonetheless, in other studies no such relation appeared

225

(Berk-Seligson 1986). The fact that Berk-Seligson (1986), who looked at Spanish–Hebrew bilinguals in Jerusalem, found no such relation may be of less consequence, since the group of speakers involved in her research (originating both from the Levant and from Argentina) is rather diverse and the sociohistorical relation between the two languages that she studied is quite complex. The possible relations between syntactic switch patterns and bilingual proficiency remain an important issue.

The results presented in Muysken, Kook, and Vedder (1996), a study of code-mixing in parent–child bilingual book reading sessions, confirm the idea that the overall complexity of the Papiamentu used, by both mother and child, correlates with switching, in a rather systematic fashion, again by both mother and child. The better the Papiamentu, the more switching takes place. No statistically significant correlations were found with the sentence complexity measures for the Dutch portion of the discourses and switching.

When checked for the number of words in both Papiamentu and Dutch spoken by the child during the reading session, there is a reasonable correlation for all three code-switching measures with Papiamentu active vocabulary. In addition, there is a correlation of the less usual type of switch (Papiamentu after Dutch) with the Dutch active vocabulary and the measures for cognitive concepts in both Papiamentu and Dutch in our research (see Vedder, Kook, and Muysken 1996).

Our results confirm the relation between linguistic proficiency and code-switching, but this effect is much stronger for Papiamentu than for Dutch proficiency. The Spanish–English data analysed by Poplack (1980) and the Moroccan Arabic–Dutch data studied by Nortier (1990) show evidence of symmetrical switching, in which both languages in a switching pair play a central role. In contrast, in the type of code-mixing we are confronted with here, one language, Papiamentu, is dominant and functions as the base or matrix language in the switched sentences.

Bentahila and Davies (1992) compare four different code-mixing styles in Moroccan Arabic (MA) – French (Fr) bilingual conversations in Morocco, in speech data from two generations of the educated elite: those schooled primarily in the French colonial period (O), and those schooled afterwards (Y). The styles are the following:

(9) Code-mixing styles in Moroccan Arabic–French bilingual discourse
    (Bentahila and Davies 1992)
    a. Equal Fr and MA, intra-clausal mixing   O, (Y)
    b. Fr dominant, MA discourse-markers   O
    c. MA dominant, a few Fr content words   Y
    d. MA with heavy Fr admixture   Y

An important factor distinguishing the two generations is proficiency: only the older group is capable of and comfortable in informally using French as well as Moroccan Arabic. Style (b) is primarily narrative or descriptive. The younger group knows and uses French, but is Moroccan Arabic-dominant. Their ordinary informal style is (c), while (d) is reserved for specific topics closely tied up with French culture.

More independent variables: age, bilingual proficiency, topic of conversation, level of formality are introduced in Bentahila and Davies (1992) than can be handled at once, given the size and complexity of available bilingual corpora.

The relation between bilingual proficiency and code-mixing is complex. Bilingual proficiency may be closely related to network membership, as in Brussels. It may also be related to prestige in the case of a withdrawing colonial language, as with French in Morocco. Bilingual proficiency may be related, finally, to generational membership in a migrant community. To this I turn next.

The perspective of age group and generation

A second factor is **age group** and **generation**. The strategy of comparing patterns of code-mixing across different generations was taken up by Stölting in earlier work in the German Federal Republic (e.g. 1975), by Gardner-Chloros in the Cypriot community in London, and by Milroy and Li Wei in the Chinese community of Newcastle-upon-Tyne (1995).

For age groups in stable bilingual communities less definite information is available, although it is clear this could be very significant. Pedraza, Attinasia, and Hoffman (1980) state that the Puerto Ricans in New York (Pedraza collaborated with Poplack in her research) primarily engage in code-mixing as adolescents; when they have turned into 'responsible' adults they keep their languages more apart. Adolescent code-mixing has indeed been reported for many communities.

Backus (1996) presents evidence from his research on Turkish/Dutch code-mixing in the Netherlands which tends to lead in the same direction as the research just cited. He discusses two groups of younger Turkish migrants in the Netherlands: a group of male adolescents that is Turkish-dominant and uses a style not unlike Bentahila and Davies' style (d), and a group of more balanced speakers, in terms of proficiency, who produce something like style (a) above. It needs to be seen, however, how precise are the correspondences between Bentahila and Davies' and Backus' findings and which factors are responsible for producing them.

At first glance, Bentahila and Davies' and Backus' results appear to point in a different direction from Poplack's and Nortier's as regards the relation between code-mixing and bilingual proficiency. Recall that the less proficient speakers in Bentahila and Davies' and Backus' research produced a lot of code-mixing. A more detailed analysis suggests that there is no real contradiction. The type of code-mixing analysed by Poplack and Nortier is different from the other two studies. It is much more diverse grammatically, and does not simply involve insertions of single words or simple constituents, as is the case with much of the material in Bentahila and Davies' style (d), as well as in the similar Backus material.

Apparently, it is not simply code-mixing as such that requires considerable bilingual proficiency as the diverse and complex switching back and forth between languages that Poplack (1980) discovered in the New York Puerto Rican community and Nortier (1990) in the Moroccan Arabic community in Utrecht, the Netherlands. This is partly alternational, partly a case of congruent lexicalization.

It may be impossible to achieve this type of symmetric intensive mixing in the case of such typologically dissimilar languages as Turkish and Dutch, so that the step after insertion would be alternation, and separation rather than congruent lexicalization.

Attitude

A third factor is **attitude**. Attitudinal differences have been invoked to explain differences between communities (see below), and they may well play a role as well with respect to subgroups within a community. However, it is difficult to study their role in the type of design needed in code-mixing research independently of other factors.

A preliminary comparison of the data for Brussels collected by Treffers-Daller in recent work and the study of Strasbourg by Gardner-Chloros (1991) yields promising results (cf. Treffers-Daller (1994, 1995), where such a comparison is carried out). French has contributed much more to Germanic, in both cities, than vice versa, and Germanic borrowings into French are mostly interjections. In addition to nouns, interjections constitute a frequently borrowed category from French in both situations, while adjectives, adverbs, and verbs are borrowed somewhat less frequently. There is a similar morphological integration strategy for verbs, involving the suffix *-ieren* (Strasbourg) or *-eren* (Brussels). Verbs occur as infinitives, when not morphologically integrated, but a difference between Strasbourg and Brussels is that in the former French past participles can be used in Germanic clauses:

(10)   Sie sind *condamnés* worre.
       They have been condemned.   (French/Alsatian; Gardner-Chloros 1995: 229)

Treffers-Daller (1994, 1995) attributes the differences between Brussels and Strasbourg to language attitudes in the bilingual community. The grammatical differences between Alsatian German and Brussels Dutch are not large enough to explain the differences in mixing patterns, so that it could be said that structurally the same language pair is involved. In Brussels, there is active competition between the two languages, part of the political struggle between the Flemish and the Walloon communities in Belgium. The code-mixes tend to be rather marginal in the sentence, as shown in chapter 4, involving adverbial constituents and extra-sentential code-mixing. In Strasbourg, where there is a gradual shift from Alsatian to French, but no overt political struggle, a much more intimate type of mixing occurs.

Conclusion

I hope to have made clear the great potential and richness of different comparisons to be made. Some of these possibilities will be explored below, and then I will turn to theoretical models which can account both for the variation encountered and for the recurrent findings from study to study.

Summary of diagnostic criteria

In previous chapters a number of criteria were presented that can be used to distinguish the three code-switching patterns or processes. The three patterns clearly differ in the degree to which the two languages contribute to the grammatical structure of the sentence. The results are summarized in table 8.1.

When we start applying criteria such as these, a complex picture of code-mixing emerges, involving different mixing patterns. However, the patterns are only partly separate, since intermediate cases may exist, as will be discussed below. Furthermore, individual bilingual speech corpora may be characterized by several patterns at once, although in different proportions.

There is alternation between codes, e.g. in intersentential switching, and insertion, e.g. with single borrowed elements. The question is whether we can establish objectively which process we are dealing with in other cases of mixing within the clause. Since for my analysis the difference is an essential one, I have tried to give as detailed criteria as possible for distinguishing them. Embodied in table 8.1 is the empirical claim that these diagnostic properties will **cooccur** in specific settings. Thus the characteristics of the three types would be:

Table 8.1. *Diagnostic features of the three patterns of code-mixing*

	insertion	alternation	congruent lexicalization
constituency			
single constituent	+	0	0
several constituents	−	+	0
non-constituent	−	−	+
nested a b a	+	−	0
non-nested a b a	−	+	+
element switched			
diverse switches	−	0	+
long constituent	−	+	−
complex constituent	−	+	−
content word	+	−	−
function word	−	−	+
adverb, conjunction	−	+	−
selected element	+	−	+
emblematic or tag	−	+	0
switch site			
major clause boundary	0	+	0
peripheral	0	+	0
embedding in discourse	0	+	0
flagging	−	+	−
dummy word insertion	+	0	−
bidirectional switching	−	+	+
properties			
linear equivalence	0	+	+
telegraphic mixing	+	−	−
morphological integration	+	−	+
doubling	−	+	−
homophonous diamorphs	0	−	+
triggering	0	0	+
mixed collocations	0	−	+
self-corrections	−	+	−

+ = indicative of a specific pattern
− = counter-indicative of a specific pattern
0 = neutral with respect to a specific pattern

(11) *insertion*

    single constituent
    nested a b a
    content word
    selected element
    dummy word insertion
    telegraphic mixing
    morphological integration

(12) *alternation*

    several constituents
    non-nested a b a
    long constituents
    complex constituents
    adverb, conjunction
    emblematic/tag
    major clause boundary
    peripheral
    embedding in discourse
    flagging
    linear equivalence
    doubling
    self-corrections

(13) *congruent lexicalization*

    non-constituent
    non-nested a b a
    diverse switches
    function word switches
    selected element
    bidirectionality
    linear equivalence
    morphological adaptation and integration
    homophonous diamorphs
    triggering
    mixed collocations

The prediction of cooccurrence makes it possible to get a grip on different code-mixing patterns. Below I will try to test the predictions implied in these lists.

The modality of the criteria given makes it clear that there will be many undecidable cases in a bilingual corpus. Is a subject in language A followed by a verb phrase in language B a case of alternation, of subject insertion, or of verb phrase insertion? For many language pairs the order of subject and verb phrase will be identical, so that the clause as a whole cannot be assigned to either language with absolute certainty. It is impossible to *prove*, for every

Table 8.2. *Relative proportion of different categories involved in mixes from Spanish to English in Pfaff (1979) and Poplack (1980) (discounting 747 single noun mixes in Pfaff's table 5)*

	Pfaff	%	Poplack	%
determiner	1	–	3	0.7
(single) noun	74	13.6	34	8.8
noun phrase	277	51.2	106	27.4
adjective	4	4.4	3	0.7
predicate adjective	9	5.3	6	1.5
adverb	–	–	14	3.6
preposition	–	–	2	0.5
verb (phrase)	71	13.1	33	8.5
phrases	36	6.7	55	14.2
independent clause	27	5.0	44	11.3
subordinate and relative clauses	2	–	53	13.7
conjunctions	–	–	33	8.5
	n = 541		n = 386	

given case, that it is alternation, insertion, or congruent lexicalization. The best we can do is study patterning at the level of the whole corpus, at this point. I should stress that the result of several competing processing strategies yielding a similar result in individual cases is what we expect in performance data. The undecidability of individual cases is the consequence of a robust and complex model rather than a sign of weakness.

A survey of bilingual speech communities

I will now look at patterns of cooccurrence of diagnostic features of code-mixing types in different bilingual communities, beginning with Spanish/English in the USA.

Spanish/English in the USA

A very rich source of bilingual data is the situation of Spanish/English mixing in various Hispanic communities in the United States. Particularly for Puerto Ricans and Mexican–Americans abundant data are available. It is difficult to compare these studies directly. Consider the quantitative results of the research of Pfaff (1979) on Mexican American bilingual usage in contrast to the data of Poplack (1980) on Puerto Rican code-mixing. The two were calculated in slightly different ways. Nonetheless, some interesting differences emerge. Consider table 8.2, where the proportion of Spanish to English mixes in the two studies is represented. We can see that Pfaff's data show less

Table 8.3. *A quantitative survey of the sample sentences cited in the major*
sources for Spanish/English code-mixing in the USA

single word internal	44
single constituent internal	12
single word external	32
single constituent external	71
exclamations, tags, etc.	(39)
multi-constituent internal	23
multi-constituent external	7

diversity in the type of switched elements found, coupled with a preponderance of noun phrase mixes (over half of the intra-sentential mixes reported). It could be that the data reported on by Pfaff were drawn from a less informal and less varied set of discourse contexts than Poplack's data. Some appear to involve formal meetings. In addition, it may be that some of the elements Pfaff has counted as predicate adjectives were analysed as adverbs by Poplack. Pfaff's Mexican-American Spanish/English code-mixing data appear to be more 'insertion-like' or 'matrix-like' than Poplack's Puerto Rican code-mixing data (recall the preceding discussion with respect to Bentahila's and Davies' results). Pfaff's table 6 (1979: 310) gives an indication of the asymmetry in her conversational data: there were 208 P *NP* mixes from Spanish to English, and none the other way round. Needless to say the whole issue of comparisons between these speech communities deserves a much more exhaustive treatment, both grammatically and sociolinguistically, than was possible here.

I have tried to analyse all the cases of Spanish/English code-mixing, which gave rise to the alternation models in the first place, in a number of published sources. I used the constituency and peripherality criteria to classify the mixes: do they form a single word, one constituent (even if it is a large one), or more constituents? Are they internal to the sentence, i.e. fenced in by fragments from the other language on both sides, or external? Tags etc. were left out of consideration. Of course, these criteria are very rough ones, since they are based on a far from random sample, but they yield an interesting preliminary picture. Of course, these figures should be interpreted with great care: they represent only the published concrete examples from data sets which were collected and interpreted in different ways. Furthermore, certain categories such as single word switches are vastly under-represented in the examples. Nonetheless, they were not selected with the distinctions made here in mind, and correspond with respect to two interesting tendencies:

(a) While for single words no such restriction holds (44 internal, 32 external), switched full constituents tend to occur at the periphery of the sentence (71) rather than internal to it (12). Of course the fact that many sentences are not very long is a bias against switched constituents occurring internally, but still, the contrast is remarkable. Over half of the external constituents (39 out of 71) are clauses; only 2 out of 12 internal constituents are clauses.

(b) While they constitute a minority, there are a fair number of multi-constituent switches, both internal (7) and external (23) in the sentence. Thus, all in all there is good reason to assume that a sizeable portion of the English/Spanish mixes is best analysed as cases of alternation or congruent lexicalization rather than insertion.

In fact, convincing cases of insertion – those where a multi-word constituent (hence not possibly a loan) from one language is surrounded by a syntactically coherent structure from the other language – are rare in these data sets. They may, however, be the dominant pattern in other bilingual communities, as argued by Nait M'Barek and Sankoff (1988), Drapeau (1994), and particularly Myers-Scotton (1993b).

In Sankoff and Poplack (1981), four categories of code-mixing can be distinguished in terms of frequency for the Puerto Rican Spanish–English materials in the Poplack corpus.

(A) Mixes with a frequency of 5 per cent or higher of possible syntactic environments in which they occur include tags (40 per cent), a switch before predicative adjectives (15 per cent), determiner/noun or noun phrase (13 per cent), adverbs and adverbials (5–10 per cent), before coordinating conjunctions (9 per cent). This category is largely alternational, with the exception of the nouns and noun phrases.

(B) Mixes with a frequency of between 2.3 and 3.9 per cent of possible syntactic environments involve a more intimate type: after subordinating conjunctions, between verbs and objects, after coordinating conjunctions, between adjectives and nouns, between subjects and verbs, after prepositions, and between verbs and prepositional phrases. Here congruent lexicalization seems to be dominant.

(C) Mixes with a frequency of 1 per cent or lower of possible syntactic environments include those between auxiliaries or modals and the verb, between prepositional phrases and adjectivals, before subordinating conjunctions, and those involving pronouns. Here and in the next category of non-occurring mixes (D) lack of categorial or linear equivalence probably blocks frequent mixing. Many cases involve functional elements. Thus switches beween clitics and the verb, between Aux and Neg, between Neg and the verb

Table 8.4. *Code-mixes in Spanish/English in New York (based on Poplack 1980: 602), but with the percentages calculated across the switch directions rather than for the categories switched in one direction, as in the original table (percentages over 75 are given in bold). The line separates intra-sentential from other switching.*

	#Eng > Sp	%	#Sp > Eng	%
determiner	3	**100**		
single noun	34	19	141	**81**
subject noun phrase	44	64	25	36
object noun phrase	62	44	78	56
verb	6	31	13	69
verb phrase	27	67	13	33
independent clause	44	56	35	44
subord./rel. clause	53	70	23	30
adjective	3	20	12	**80**
predicate adjective	6	14	37	**86**
adverb	14	30	33	70
preposition	2	**100**		
(adv, adj, prep)phrases	55	58	39	42
conjunctions	33	67	16	33
sentence	201	54	171	46
filler	9	45	11	55
interjection	26	23	89	**77**
idiomatic expressions	8	26	23	74
quotation	20	59	14	41
tag	9	2	403	**98**
TOTAL	659		1176	1835

or modal, and between the verb and a following subject do not occur in the material.

We also learn quite a lot if we consider the **directionality** of the mixing patterns in more detail. Table 8.4 contains a detailed division along these lines. It is remarkable for how many categories there is a bidirectional pattern suggesting congruent lexicalization. Included are frequent switches of syntactically deeply embedded categories such as direct objects. To some extent Spanish functions as a matrix language: there were more English single nouns than Spanish nouns inserted (81 per cent versus 19 per cent), and more English interjections (77 per cent versus 23 per cent) and especially tags (98 per cent versus 2 per cent) than Spanish ones. In the other direction, there is a less clear dominance pattern: only function words are occasionally inserted from Spanish into English, indicative of congruent lexicalization

Table 8.5. *Directionality of multi-word switches in Moroccan Arabic (MA)/Dutch (Du) code-switching (based on Nortier's table 7.4, 1990: 126)*

	N	% MA > Du	% Du > MA
(a) insertion			
V/NP	40	100	
subject NP/ . . .	23	100	
P/NP	15	100	
inside NP	22	95.5	4.5
(b) alternation			
apposition/dislocation	29	79.3	20.7
around adverbs	42	78.6	21.4
. . . /PP	25	72.0	28.0
main/subordinate S	37	70.3	29.7
(c) discourse			
between coordinate S	42	35.7	64.3

again. Interesting is also the dominance of English adjectives over Spanish ones: this may have to do with their being non-inflected, and hence easier to fit in.

Moroccan Arabic/Dutch

I will now illustrate the criteria developed above in more detail using the Moroccan Arabic/Dutch corpus described by Nortier (1990). It reveals itself to be fairly similar to the materials described by Poplack (1980) for New York and by Gardner-Chloros for Strasbourg: all processes occur, although insertional patterns dominate.

Let us begin by analysing the directionality of switching in Nortier's material, since it yields further insights into the types of code-switching in the corpus. Consider tables 8.5 and 8.6. In table 8.5 I have interpreted the switching of noun phrases as insertional, identified a number of alternational switch types, and finally looked at alternational switches at the discourse level (between coordinate clauses; Nortier did not quantify switches between turns in her study).

Table 8.5 shows that insertional mixing is unidirectional, with Moroccan Arabic as the matrix language and Dutch as the intruding language. For all categories, the direction from Moroccan Arabic to Dutch is over 95 per cent. In contrast, alternational mixing is bidirectional in this corpus, even though still over 70 per cent is from Moroccan Arabic to Dutch. In discourse-level alternations, the dominant direction is from Dutch to Moroccan Arabic.

The data from single word switches confirm these findings independently.

Table 8.6. *Directionality of single word switches in Moroccan Arabic (MA)/*
Dutch (Du) code-switching (based on Nortier's table 7.15, 1990: 141)

	N	% MA > Du	% Du > MA
(a) **major**			
adjectives	26	100	
verbs	11	100	
numerals	4	100	
nouns	286	99.7	.3
(b) **minor**			
pronouns	6	83.3	16.7
adverbs	41	70.7	29.3
prepositions	8	62.5	37.5
(c) **discourse**			
conjunctions	20	30	70

Table 8.6 shows that for single word switches, major categories follow the insertional pattern (almost 100 per cent from Moroccan Arabic to Dutch), while minor categories (a much more limited group) are switched in both directions (though mostly again from Moroccan Arabic to Dutch). This may be partly alternational, for adverbs, but for pronouns and prepositions it must be due to congruent lexicalization. With conjunctions, the reverse order predominates (except for subordinating conjunctions).

Data which look like congruent lexicalization have been reported on for Moroccan Arabic/Dutch code-mixing. In Nortier (1990: 140) a number of examples are mentioned (five, to be precise), in which the item mixed-in does not correspond to a constituent, as discussed in chapter 5.

> (14) xeṣṣ-na m9a *bestuur praten*
> we-must with board speak
> 'We must speak with the board.'

> (15) baġi   nešri   dik s - *smurfen voor de auto*
> wanting I-bought that the smurfs for the car
> 'I wanted to buy those smurfs for the car.'   (Nortier 1990: 140)

In (14) the transition occurs internal to a PP but the noun mixed-in is followed by the verb governing the PP as a whole. In (15) the noun mixed-in and the PP following it do not form a constituent either.

On the basis of the criteria given, Nortier's corpus can be characterized as in table 8.7. All in all, it is a corpus in which all three patterns play an important role.

Table 8.7. *Features of the corpus of Moroccan Arabic-Dutch switching (based on Nortier 1990)*

single constituent	frequent
several constituents	some cases
non-constituent	few cases
peripheral	often
nested a b a	frequent
non-nested a b a	few cases
selected element	often
linear equivalence	frequent
length	long fragments occur
complexity	complex fragments occur
bidirectionality	infrequent
embedding in discourse	not known
major clause boundary	frequent
flagging	infrequent
lexical category	many
function word	few
adverb, conjunction	quite a few
integration	frequent through omitted articles

Turkish/Dutch

Data from Turkish/Dutch code-mixing reported on in Boeschoten (1990) and based on data from Backus (1992) suggest that here an insertional pattern is dominant. However, in more recent work by Backus based on another Turkish peer group (Backus 1996), alternation patterns occur as well. The rough picture sketched by Backus (1996) shows that first generation immigrants have limited insertions from Dutch, mostly a few content words. Intermediate generation speakers have more extensive insertions from Dutch into Turkish sentences as well as considerable alternation. Finally, for second generation speakers there is still an asymmetry: Turkish utterances are more likely to contain Dutch elements than vice versa. There is a considerable amount of alternational switching.

Swahili/English in the Nairobi corpus

An important bilingual corpus in code-mixing research was gathered by students and assistants of Carol Myers-Scotton (1993b) in the 1970s. It consists of about 20 hours of informal conversations audio-recorded in an urban context. The main language is Swahili, but English and occasionally another Kenyan language also appear. Swahili is the lingua franca of Kenya (as well as of much of East Africa in general), and an official language

Table 8.8. *Single word mixes in the Nairobi corpus (based on Myers-Scotton 1993b)*

	types	tokens	% tokens
nouns	141	174	0.46
verbs			
finite	91	91	0.24
infinitive	37	37	0.10
past participle	13	15	0.04
adjectives	27	36	0.09
adverbs	11	11	0.03
interjections	4	4	0.01
conjunctions	2	2	
pronouns	1	1	
possessive pronouns	1	3	0.01
	328	374	

Table 8.9. *EL Islands (multi-word mixes) in the Nairobi corpus (based on Myers-Scotton 1993b)*

	#	% of total #
copula VP complements	31	26
prepositional phrases	24	20
time adverbials	20	16.5
non-copula VP complements	16	13
set expressions	12	10
main clauses with CP	5	4
complement clause[s]	5	4
possessive pronouns	2	
subject NPs	2	
conditional clauses	2	
copula + complement	1	
interjection	1	

together with English. The latter has a role in education, business, and authority and is 'linked with high socio-economic prestige' (Myers-Scotton 1993b: 11). Swahili has no particular prestige, but is associated with urban values. The conversations show what Myers-Scotton (1993a: 14) has called 'code-switching as an unmarked choice.'

Myers-Scotton provides two tables with a quantitative overview of the mixes in her material. In the first table (1993b: 15), given here as table 8.8, the single word mixes are presented. The large number of nonce mixes in the corpus is indicative of very productive borrowing. Established borrowings, occurring in at least three conversations, and cultural borrowings, were excluded from the analysis, but figures are not given for these categories. As Myers-Scotton notes (p. 14), there is a high proportion of verbs (N = 141) in the switched material, when compared with other corpora. However, this may be because of the way the material was analysed (as I will argue below).

The second table, given here as table 8.9, presents the multi-word mixes. The largest category is represented by complements of a copula such as *very surprised*, and prepositional phrases and temporal expressions are quite frequent. Complements of other verbs than copulas are also often present in the data. The frequency of English adverbial elements and prepositional phrases may suggest that recourse is often taken to alternation.

A striking feature of the Swahili material are examples such as the following. However, their status in the MLF model is not clear because of the uncertain morphological status of the prefixes involved.

>　(16)　ni-ka-*wash all the clothing*
>　　　　1sg-CONSEC-wash all the clothing
>　　　　'I washed all the clothing.'　　　　　　　　　　(Myers-Scotton 1993b: 80)

Here one would tend to treat the whole verb phrase as a unit, prefixed by two Swahili morphemes. This is in accordance with the tree that Myers-Scotton presents (1993b: 79) for Swahili sentences, in which tense and agreement prefixes are represented as a separate INFL-node. However, what is the nature of the Swahili prefixes on English verbs? Schultink (1988) discusses Swahili affixation, and shows that all categorial information, the domain of morphology proper, is encoded in the suffix system. The prefixes pertain to tense, aspect, and agreement. This makes an analysis in which the prefixes are really proclitics quite plausible. In code-mixing, they are retained and simply added onto the verb phrase.

However plausible this analysis is for (16), it is not automatically transferable to cases like (17a), in which the object of the English verb *taste* is also expressed by a proclitic, since we would expect the alternative (17b), where the object is contained in the verb phrase:

>　(17)　a.　ni-ka-i-*taste*
>　　　　　　1sg-CONSEC-O.NC9–taste
>　　　　　　'then I tasted it'　　　　　　　　　　　　(Myers-Scotton 1993b: 29)
>
>　　　　b.　*ni-ka-*taste* it

Myers-Scotton (1993b: 78) analyses *all the clothing* in (16) as an EL island separate from *wash*. There are other examples of the same kind:

240

(18) . . . niende ni-ka-*check for you*
     so that 1sg-CONSEC-check for you
     '. . . so that I go and check for you' (Myers-Scotton 1993b: 124)

(19) . . . yaani ku-*set good examples* . . .
     '. . . that is, to set good examples . . .' (Myers-Scotton 1992b: 6)

This example is acknowledged by Myers-Scotton as containing an EL-island *set good examples*. In (20) there is only a person prefix, and no aspect or mood prefixes:

(20) Ni-*check all that particular day's constructions*
     1sg
     'I should check all that particular day's constructions.'
     (Myers-Scotton 1993b: 146)

Compare the form *ni-ka-i-taste* in (17a) with (21), where the object pronoun is in English:

(21) a-na-*clear them*
     3sg-NON-PST-clear them
     'he clears them' (Myers-Scotton 1993b: 127)

This is a counterexample to Myers-Scotton's System Morpheme Principle, unless one assumes that *clear them* is one unit. It is not necessary to reinterpret *them* here as a content morpheme.

While generally Myers-Scotton assumes that the Swahili prefixes are attached to a single word, on p. 130 she appears to adopt the position that they are attached to a phrase:

(22) *It's only essential services* amba-zo zi-na-*function right now.*
                            that-NC10 NC10–PRES
     'It's only essential services that function right now.'
     (Myers-Scotton 1993b: 130)

It is not quite clear how Myers-Scotton analyses this example; from the text it appears that the complementizer *amba-zo* 'occurs in one island', presumably also including *zi-na-function*. In that case *zi-na-* must be part of the island.

However, the Adjacency Principle (see chapter 3) cannot always be invoked. It seems particularly suited when there is a link of government or selection between the adjacent inserted elements. This link is not there in:

(23) ni-li-m-*grab last week*
     1s-PST-O-grab last week
     'I grabbed him last week.' (Myers-Scotton 1993b: 92)

The latter example is problematic for the analysis just given since one would expect *grab him last week*. However, the direct object of *grab* is part of the prefixed agreement complex.

There is some evidence that in addition to insertion, there may be congruent lexicalization and alternation in the Swahili/English materials. Consider the following example:

(24) Mbona hawa *workers* wa *East Africa Power and Lightning*
Why
wa-ka-end-a *strike* . . .
3pl-CONSEC-go-IND strike . . .
'Why did the East Africa Power and Lightning [sic] workers go on strike . . . ?'

(Myers-Scotton 1993b: 96)

Here the issue is whether the English idiom *go on strike* is partly realized with the Swahili verb *end* 'go'. This would suggest evidence for a congruent lexicalization approach.

Violations of the system morpheme principle mentioned in chapter 6 point in the same direction:

(25) wa-tu wa-ko *trained*
3pl-person 3pl-be trained
'people are trained'   (Myers-Scotton 1993b: 115)

Instead of Swahili passive morphology, an English passive form with a (Swahili) copula is used.

(26) tukutane *[this evening] [at the usual place]*
let us meet   (Myers-Scotton 1993b: 140)

Here Myers-Scotton assumes two separate EL islands, while the Adjacency Principle would assume that they belong together. Again, multiple constituent switches are indicative of alternation or congruent lexicalization.

(27) Mimi ni-ta-*try* kuwa nyumbani / *throughout*
EMPH 1sg-FU-try to be home / throughout
the day. I'm sure / hi-zo sherehe . . .
the day. I'm sure / these-NC10 celebrations . . .   (Myers-Scotton 1993b: 146)

This example is interesting because there is a mixed-in fragment across the sentence boundary, best analysed as alternation.

(28) au ni hizi nyingine ambazo *no ordinary* mbuzi?
'or are they the ones which [are] no ordinary goats?'

(Myers-Scotton 1993b: 236)

Myers-Scotton treats this example as problematic for the Morpheme Order Principle since *ordinary* should follow *mbuzi* 'goats' in Swahili rather than precede it. However, it also contains a non-constituent mix, since presumably *no* modifies the whole expression *ordinary mbuzi*. Thus there is a bidirectional mix: [ₛ . . . ambazo [ₑ no ordinary [ₛ mbuzi]]]. A Swahili element is inserted into an English constituent which is inserted into a Swahili constituent. This pattern suggests a stronger role for English in the last part of the clause.

Another example of the quite intricate relations between the two languages is the following:

(29)   i-me-*turn black* sana
        3sg-PERF-turn black very
        'It had turned very black.'   (Myers-Scotton 1992b: 5)

This example is quite interesting because it contains two potential bracketing paradoxes, assuming that *turn black* is a single expression in English. The first one is that *turn* is prefixed with Swahili elements, and the second one that *black* is modified by Swahili *sana*. This type of example will come up again in chapter 9 in the context of simultaneous representations. The same thing is going on in:

(30)   haukuona a-ki-ni-*buy*-i-a *beer* siku hioy?
        didn't you know 3sg-PROG-1sg-buy-BEN-INḍiC beer that day
        'Didn't you know he was buying beer for me that day?'
                                                                  (Myers-Scotton 1992b: 6)

Here the expression *buy [someone a] beer* is fully embedded in a Swahili structure, involving an applicative as well as aspect and person marking.

(31)   ha-tu-end-i *college Saturday* asubuhi
        NEG-1pl-go-APPL
        'We don't go to college Saturday mornings.'   (Myers-Scotton 1992b: 10)

Myers-Scotton analyses this example as having a Swahili ML since *hatuendi* contains Swahili system morphemes. However, the expression *Saturday asubuhi* is modelled on the English *Saturday mornings* rather than on a Swahili expression, and hence has English as its basic structure.

I hope to have shown that there is sufficient evidence to indicate that it is not possible to analyse Swahili/English code-mixing as purely insertional. There are phenomena suggestive of congruent lexicalization and the frequency of syntactically peripheral mixed-in elements such as adverbials suggests alternation as well.

French/Alsatian in Strasbourg

If we contrast the material in Treffers-Daller (1994) for Brussels, analysed in chapter 4, with that of Gardner-Chloros collected in Strasbourg, we notice that the latter also contains many cases of paratactic mixing (1991: 166):

(32)   *La cassette*, wie lang ass se geht?
'The cassette, how long does it run for?'

(33)   . . . diss haw i jetz zufallig g'sähn, *le remboursement.*
'. . . I just happened to see that, the repayment.'

(34)   *A l'époque*, 's isch nitt wild g'sinn.
At the time, it wasn't so hot.   (French/Alsatian; Gardner-Chloros 1991: 160)

Nonetheless, I argued in chapter 6 that the pattern of German auxiliary + French past participles suggests fundamental equivalence, and congruent lexicalization. For single word switches an insertional pattern is quite clear: 90 French lexical elements are inserted into Alsatian sentences, and only 8 Alsatian elements into French sentences. For greetings, interjections, tags, phatic markers etc. there is more of a balance between the languages. For multi-word switches the data are not sufficient to establish a clear pattern. It is clear that some of the cases are intimate switches:

(35)   On a un tas de problèmes *wiriklisch demit, ne.*
'We have a heap of problems / really with him, you know.'
(French/Alsatian; Gardner-Chloros 1991: 174)

Notice that *demit* 'with him' is directly selected by *problèmes*, but that a sentence adverb, *wiriklisch* 'really', intervenes.

Moluccan Malay/Dutch code-mixing

Moluccan Malay/Dutch code-mixing as reported on by Huwaë (1992) suggests broadly an insertional pattern:

(36)   [*volgens mij*]   a su [*verslaafd aan die pijnstillers*]
according-to me   I PERF addicted to those painkillers
'I think I have become addicted to those painkillers.'

(37)   ini tong [*nog*] ada [*bedanken*]
DET we still be/have give thanks
'That is we are still saying thanks here.'   (Huwaë 1992)

In the Matrix Language Frame model proposed by Carol Myers-Scotton the grammatical morphemes have to be from the base language, and notice that the subject pronouns, the copula, and the perfective marker are indeed from Malay, even if most of the lexical material is Dutch. The convergence facts discussed for Moluccan Malay/Dutch code-mixing in chapter 5 also point to tendencies towards congruent lexicalization in this material, but most of the switches are insertional.

Summary and general analysis

I have summarized some studies that have appeared so far and tried to

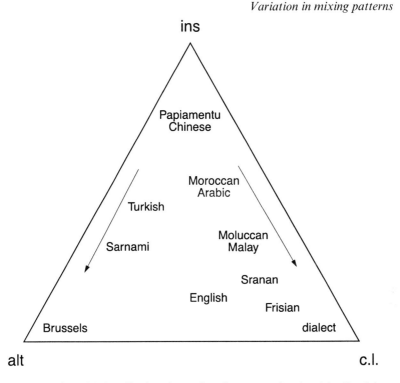

Figure 8.1 Localization of a number of contact settings involving Dutch in the triangle alternation, insertion, congruent lexicalization.

interpret them in terms of their choice of strategy. In earlier chapters I have also discussed a number of bilingual settings. It is time to see whether an overall picture emerges. Given the preliminary state of findings in this area, I will try to present this information graphically, separating the various migrant groups in the Netherlands treated in this study (figure 8.1) from the other major bilingual corpora (figure 8.2). Recent and fairly closed-off migrant groups show insertional patterns, while for other groups there is a shift according to the generations. Turkish and Sarnami speakers may shift towards more alternational patterns, as documented by Backus (1996), while Moroccan Arabic and Moluccan Malay speakers shift towards more congruent lexicalization. Speakers of Sranan, English, Frisian, and various dialects show patterns closer to the congruent lexicalization point of the imaginary triangle.

A similar picture emerges for other bilingual corpora, as illustrated by figure 8.2. Myers-Scotton's Swahili material shows a predominantly insertional pattern, Treffers-Daller's Brussels data a more alternational pattern.

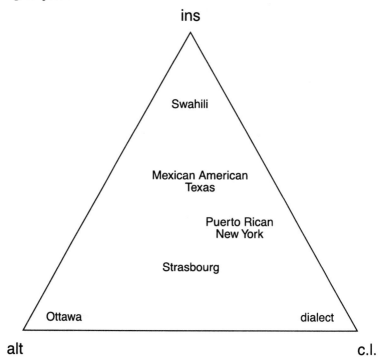

Figure 8.2 Localization of a number of contact settings in the triangle alternation, insertion, congruent lexicalization.

Gardner-Chloros' Strasbourg data have characteristics of various patterns, as do Poplack's New York data. The data reported on by Pfaff are more insertional in character.

When we attempt to generalize these findings in terms of theoretical models, the following problem emerges. Researchers assume a main pattern and subsidiary pattern, but what is assumed to be the main pattern appears to differ considerably for different researchers.

Poplack and Sankoff, as becomes clear from Nait M'Barek and Sankoff (1988) and Sankoff, Poplack, and Vanniarajan (1990) appear to consider alternation under linear equivalence and nonce-borrowing to be the unmarked options, and constituent insertion a special case.

Myers-Scotton (1993b: 144)) assumes insertion as the major pattern, coupled with an implicational hierarchy of EL islands, which runs as follows:

(38)   a. Formulaic expressions and idioms (in VP complements and adverbials)

       b. Other time and manner expressions

    c. Quantifier expressions
    d. Non-quantifier, non-time NPs
    e. Agent NPs
    f. Main finite verbs

This hierarchy is similar to the one proposed by Treffers-Daller (1994) cited above. Finally, Myers-Scotton assumes ML Turnover, once one matrix language gives ground to another one in a shift process.

Backus (1996) basically assumes the following hierarchy across the generations in a shift process:

(39)   a. simple insertions
       b. more complex insertions
       c. alternations
       d. insertions in the other direction

It is fairly clear that no single dimension is involved in accounting for the variation in mixing patterns. A number of factors interact:

(a) **Structural factors**. Structural factors play a role in helping to define different options available in bilingual communities, in two respects. When typologically similar languages are being spoken linear equivalence often plays an important role; thus congruent lexicalization becomes an easily available option. Morphological encapsulation occurs most frequently when at least one of the languages involved has a complex agglutinative morphology: thus the viability and stability of insertional patterns is promoted by agglutinative morphology. Since categorial equivalence is not a purely objective notion, both diachronic and sociolinguistic factors determine the extent to which this strategy is involved.

(b) **Dominance in use**. It is clear from work by Bentahila and Davies (1992), Backus (1996) and others that styles of code-mixing, in a process of language shift e.g. in a migrant community, will develop from insertion to alternation to possibly congruent lexicalization (depending on structural factors). This development is embedded in an overall shift from one matrix language to another one, across the generations.

(c) **Bilingual proficiency**. Parallel to the generational shift just mentioned there is a distinction between less fluent bilinguals with a primarily alternational and small insertional pattern, and more fluent bilinguals with a pattern tending towards congruent lexicalization and more complex insertion.

(d) **Attitudes**. While all communities where code-mixing occurs allow alternation, a juxtaposition strategy, insertion and congruent lexicalization are characteristic of communities with intense language contact and no strong attitudinal barriers against mixing.

(e) **Norms**. Transplanted varieties with weak links to matrix communities

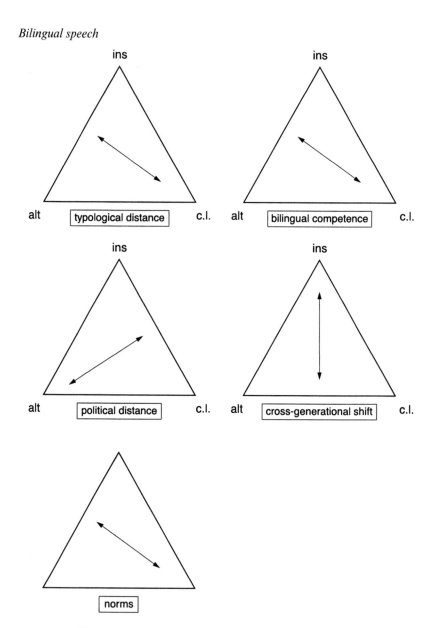

Figure 8.3 Factors governing the choice of a particular code-mixing strategy in different communities.

will show stronger patterns of adaptation than those with strong links (and cyclic migration patterns), and also than native varieties.

(f) Different transfer or incorporation strategies may be **conventionalized** as part of a lexical rule similar to a word formation rule. Conventionalization may well be limited to local mixing processes. The contribution of these factors may be represented as in figure 8.3.

We need a probabilistic model to account for the patterns encountered. Communities differ in their choice of strategy, but the difference is rarely absolute: what we find is (sometimes strong) quantitative tendencies towards particular patterns. Speech communities in which mixing often involves morphological encapsulation also show juxtaposition and occasionally equivalence matching, etc. This state of affairs calls for a probabilistic model, in which various factors, structural equivalence, dominance, and atittudes, are introduced as weighted constraints. Of course, this is only possible in the abstract at present, since bilingual corpora are not sufficiently comparable. Still, outcomes such as those impressionistically presented in figure 8.1 could be viewed in this light.

As the extent of language contact grows the type of mixing will shift from insertional to either alternation or congruent lexicalization. This can be presented in the following model:

(40)

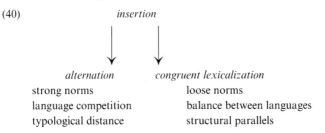

insertion

alternation
strong norms
language competition
typological distance

congruent lexicalization
loose norms
balance between languages
structural parallels

From the sociolinguistic perspective likewise the three processes may carry specific social meanings, although we should avoid assuming a one-to-one relationship. The reason for this caution is that social meaning is carried mostly by the external aspects of language: **lexical choices** and **pronunciations**. Apart from this caveat, we may think of alternation as being associated with a greater separateness of the two languages, of insertion as linked to the primacy of one language over the other, and of congruent lexicalization as entailing links with two languages at the same time.

9
Code-mixing, bilingual speech, language change

The field of code-mixing research so far has found itself in the exploratory and taxonomic stage, explainable perhaps in terms of its origins as a response to the bewildering variety of forms of language use found in the many bilingual communities that Western countries have within their borders. A good example is the Mexican American community in the United States in the 1970s. Bilingual settings were studied and explored, and research objects were selected on the basis of the settings encountered. Research methodology was fairly uniform: naturalistic recordings of in-group conversations.

However, when we start to investigate the relation between the three types of code-mixing described and other phenomena of language interaction, the methodological limitations of this approach become evident. I think we have reached the limits of what can be learned about the phenomenon of code-mixing itself using the Labovian techniques introduced in the 1960s. Limitations of the subfield of code-mixing and the research community engaged in its study include:

- Relatively little time-depth was involved in the studies. In addition, historical research in this area has not fully developed.
- There were few links to other concerns in bilingualism research: bilingual proficiency, interference, etc.
- Little attention was being paid to phonology, phonetics, and intonation. We often find the reduction of the data to typed transcripts (as in this study).
- The lexicon, and lexical semantics have remained underdeveloped as a research topic.
- There is a strong reliance on corpora of spontaneous bilingual speech, and no strongly developed experimental tradition.

The next stage of the research in this domain may involve more experimental techniques, as well as a stronger historical and typological focus. Indeed, we have learned a tremendous amount, but the questions that remain now may

250

require a more precise and directed research effort, incorporating more typological variation into the research design, taking a historical perspective, adopting experimental techniques, and relating code-mixing more directly to other contact phenomena.

In this chapter I will try to outline some of the consequences of the work on code-mixing for a general perspective on processes of contact-induced language change and bilingual language use. Particularly important in this respect is the realization that many instances of code-mixing do not involve the simple linear juxtaposition of elements from two languages, but a more complex structural dependency and simultaneous presence. This opens up the way for a more fruitful and direct dialogue between code-mixing researchers and scholars working on language change and bilingual processing than would be the case if we interpreted code-mixing purely as sequential juxtaposition. I will begin by discussing further directions in the study of bilingual processing. Then I will turn to different language contact phenomena in sequence, using the work of Thomason and Kaufmann (1988) as my point of departure. For a number of phenomena I try to present the way they interact with code-mixing, properties they have in common with code-mixing, and the line of demarcation, if there is one.

As the study of language contact has progressed since the pioneering work of Haugen and Weinreich in the 1940s and 1950s, the set of analytic distinctions and concepts has multiplied. While these authors centred their work around a single concept – Haugen (1950, 1956b) used **borrowing**; Weinreich (1953) **interference** –, it is clear we need to keep a number of phenomena separate. This is what recent studies, such as the work of Poplack and D. Sankoff, have tended to do, and for very good reasons. Still, there is a dilemma.

In many situations of intense language contact, a number of phenomena involving mixing are going on at the same time: lexical borrowing, code-mixing, interference, calquing, relexification, semantic borrowing, L1 transfer in L2 learning, possibly convergence. It is not always possible to decide beforehand what is what and therefore it is important to have a set of clear cases as a base, abstracting away from the others, and setting up models which will divide, perhaps artificially, the domain of study into distinct sets of phenomena (e.g. borrowing and code-mixing, or syntactic convergence and code-mixing).

Simultaneous access to both languages

Most recent models accounting for intra-sentential code-mixing (Poplack 1980; Myers-Scotton 1993b; DiSciullo, Muysken, and Singh 1986) are based on an on/off view of the languages participating in the mix: at any one point one language is active or the other. In none of these models are the two languages represented at the same time. This is formulated most clearly by Sridhar and Sridhar (1980) as the 'Dual Structure Principle'.

In this section I want to argue that in many cases at least of insertion and congruent lexicalization, components of the two languages are not active in sequence, but simultaneously. There are several reasons why the on/off view is somewhat unsatisfactory. I will mention three potential problems with it.

First of all, the relation with **other types of language contact** is lost, where there is no on/off syntagmatic relation between the two languages, but rather a coexistence. These types include (see also Haugen 1950):

(1)   L1 transfer
      bilingual interference in different components
      calquing, as in *Wolkenkratzer* etc. for 'sky scraper';
      relexification

Since these phenomena cooccur with code-mixing in bilingual speech, it is important to develop models in which they can be related to it.

Second, psycholinguistic research has produced evidence for what Grosjean (1995, 1996) calls the **bilingual mode** of speech production during code-mixing, in which both languages are active at the same time.

Third, mixed speech has always been admitted to require simultaneous representations for **phonology**: the sentence fragments in the two languages are not always pronounced with two separate phonological systems.

I will present three different types of evidence that the separate systems view needs to be revised and replaced by a simultaneous access model:

(a) **Idioms and collocations** from one language occurring in verbal compounds from the other language, simultaneous representations in mixed verbal complexes. Crucial cases involve the presence of an idiom from one language in a morphosyntactic frame from another language. Thus *kick the bucket* can be present in Hindi/English bilingual speech as *bucket kick kare*.

(b) Mixes sometimes occur at **arbitrary points** in the middle of a constituent, as in ragged code-mixing. This may be termed delayed lexicalization. Sentences may switch matrix grammar half-way through.

(c) Syntactic phenomena in mixed clauses characteristic of language *q* occur in the middle of a fragment in language *p*. An example is given from **pro-drop** phenomena.

I will end by preliminarily sketching a chamber orchestra model of bilingual behaviour, to use an expression coined by François Grosjean (p.c.).

Crucial in this discussion will be modularity. Both languages are accessed, but different modules of each.

Idioms and collocations in verbal compounds and other incorporated verbal structures

I will first discuss a number of cases where there is both a noun or an adverb and a verb from language B inserted into a frame from language A. I will mainly focus on Sarnami Hindustani/{Dutch, Sranan}, and Panjabi/English. In her work on verbal compounds in Panjabi/English mixing Romaine (1989, 1995) encountered a number of expressions of the following type:

(2)   *guilt feel* hona   (Panjabi/English; Romaine 1995: 133)

Romaine concludes that all cases fit into a single pattern:

(3) $NP_{Eng/Pan}$ V_{Eng}+particle/-ing   hona/kərna

The cases where there is a preceding noun, as in (2), are analysed as consisting of two separate main constituents: the object noun phrase, and the verb + verb compound. The reason for this analysis would appear to be straightforward. If *guilt feel* were an English predicate, the order should be the inverse. Notice we do not get **off cut hona* or **up pick kərna*, but rather *cut off hona* and *pick up kərna*; this is predicted by Romaine's analysis, where the particle is part of a cluster with its verb. Notice, however, that there is an alternative analysis: *guilt feel* is a unit fitted into a morpholexical or morphosyntactic (depending on one's analysis of verbal compounds as primarily a lexical or a syntactic phenomenon) Panjabi frame.

This will not work very well at first sight in cases where the English noun is part of a Panjabi noun phrase or prepositional phrase structure, as discussed by Romaine (1995: 141):

(4)   [Mə apni *language*] [*learn* kərni]
      'I want to learn my own language.'   (Panjabi/English; Romaine 1995: 140)

Here *language* is modified by a Panjabi element, and hence part of a Panjabi constituent.

Another argument for treating the object and the verb as two separate syntactic constituents derives from cases where the verb has been passivized (Kachru 1978):

(5)   Tīsre din [kuch zarūri *Drāphṭ*] [*tāyp* karvāne]
      third day some important draft type do-were
      'On the third day some important drafts were typed.'

                                              (Hindi/English; Kachru 1978: 201)

If the object were part of the same constituent as the verb, they could not behave as separate units.

There is something unsatisfactory, however, about separating combinations like *guilt* and *feel* entirely, for two reasons. First, the cooccurrence of the two ends up being coincidental: there are two separate mixes in two separate constituents. This goes against the Adjacency Principle, which suggests if you have two adjacent intruding elements in a mixed sentence, you should try to analyse them as part of a single mixed-in fragment, other things being equal. Still, the phenomenon is not infrequent.

Second, although *feel guilt* is not an idiom, it is a relatively fixed expression and may represent a single entry in the mental lexicon. Romaine (1995: 133) writes: 'There does not seem to be any semantic reason for taking the noun + verb as a unit.' Nonetheless, often the two elements are closely linked, as in some of the other examples given by Romaine (*time waste, exams pass*).

The Sarnami/Dutch material studied by Kishna (1979) contains some of these paradoxical structures as well. An example is (6), where the Sranan idiom *boro plafond* 'hit the ceiling' occurs in a mixed compound:

(6) *plafond boro* kare
    ceiling bore.through do
    'hit the ceiling'   (Sarnami/Dutch; Kishna 1979)

Again, analysing *plafond* as the object of the compound verb *boro kare* does not do justice to the idiomatic nature of the noun + verb construction *boro plafond* 'hit the ceiling' in Sranan. However, analysing *plafond boro* as a Sranan constituent of the mixed compound does not explain why the elements are in a Hindustani OV order rather than a Sranan VO order.

A similar dilemma emerges with (7). In Dutch *platen draaien* 'play (lit. 'turn') records' is a fixed combination, which one would expect to be embedded as a single constituent. In (7), however, the verb is part of the compound, and the Dutch noun *plaat* has undergone a Sarnami reduplication rule whereby the element is repeated with an initial /v/, to mean 'ENTITY, etc.', and is hence part of a Sarnami noun phrase:

(7) *plaat*-va:t *draai* kare   'play records etc. (i.e. cassettes, compact disks)'

The paradox thus seems unresolvable unless one admits of the possibility of simultaneous access to components of the two languages, something incompatible with most current analyses of code-switching as an off/on phenomenon.

Some further examples from Sarnami/Dutch code-mixing illustrate the same problem. In each case the relation between the two parts of the inserted element is collocational.

(8)   *nuchter bekijk* kare   'consider soberly'
       prijs verhoog kare   'raise the price'
       mogelijkheid bieden kare   'offer the opportunity'

In these cases, however, the order of a Dutch and a Hindustani verb phrase would be similar, so that we cannot establish the constituency of these cases.

The same holds for many Turkish/Dutch (Backus 1992, 1996) and Turkish/German (Treffers-Daller and Daller 1995a,b) cases:

(9)   *politiek* essahtan *reet interesseren* yapı-yor
       'Politics really does[not] interest [me] [a] bit.'

(Turkish/Dutch; Boeschoten 1990: 90)

In (9) we find the Turkish verb *yap(mak)*, preceded by a Dutch fragment. This fragment is at the same time a verb phrase idiom, which suggests that it is a constituent, and highly telegraphic – the negator *geen* 'not a' and the indirect object *me* are lacking – which suggests that it is perhaps inserted into a Turkish frame that includes more than the *yap(mak)* phrase. The Dutch verb is an infinitive, and the OV order in the Dutch fragment is characteristic of Dutch infinitival structures.

The following cases from Backus' recordings illustrate the same point: the inserted verb and its single noun object are syntactically part of separate (Turkish) constituents, but form a lexical unit:

(10) [Bir bisürü *taal*-lar-ı]   [*beheersen* yap-ıyorken] . . .
       a range language-PL-AC   know-INF do-PR-while
       'While he knows a lot of languages . . .'

(11) Türk-ler alsa,   [*klant*-lar]   [*wegjagen* yap-ıyor]
       Turk-PL taking,   customer-PL   chase-away do-PR=3sg
       'If he were to take Turks, he chases away customers.'

(12) Baba-m-a   [bir *smoes*]   [*verzinnen* yap-tık]
       father-1sg-DA   one excuse   make-up do-PR=1pl
       'We made up an excuse for my father'.

(13) . . . ama ben bir *leeftijd*-in-i *schatten* yap-tım
       but I one age-3sg-AC estimate do-PR-1sg
       '. . . but I estimated her age.'   (Turkish/Dutch; Backus 1996: 104–14, 230–50)

While some of these cases could be seen as accidental double switches, there can be no doubt that others are specific idiomatic combinations, such as (10) [*taal*] and (12) [*smoes*].

In a few of the sentences given as examples in the work on Tamil/English (Sankoff, Poplack, and Vanniarajan 1990) on nonce-borrowing in Tamil we also find some examples of the paradoxical pattern at hand:

(14) oru aambiḷḷainaaka [konjam *discretion*] [*use* paṇṇuvaan]
      one man   if   some   do-3sg-M-FU
      'If he be a man, he will use some discretion.'

(Tamil/English; Sankoff, Poplack, and Vanniarajan 1990: 80)

Here *konjam discretion* is a Tamil noun phrase containing an English loan, in
the analysis of Sankoff, Poplack, and Vanniarajan (1990), and *use paṇṇuvaan*
constitutes a separate complex Tamil verb, again containing an English loan.
However, *to use discretion* is a fixed expression, stored as such in the mental
lexicon. This raises further doubts about the appropriateness of the concept
of nonce-borrowing to describe these cases (cf. chapter 3).

Similarly, in (15) there is a relation between *create* and *belief* which does
not correspond directly to a constituency relation. In (16) the relation
between *phone* and *pick up* (with the specific collocational meaning of
'answer the call') is atrophied in that the particle *up* is absent from the
bilingual expression.

(15) *Religion*-uDaya *main purpose* vantu [oru *supernatural*
      religion-GE main purpose FILLER a supernatural
      being-la [oru *belief*] [*create* paṇṇaratu]
      being-LO a belief create do-INF
      'Religion's main purpose is to create a belief in a supernatural being.'

(16) *phone pick* paṇṇareeḷaa
             do.2pl.request
      'Will you pick up the phone?'

(Tamil/English; Sankoff, Poplack, and Vanniarajan 1990: 83)

The case of Moluccan Malay/Dutch code-mixing (Huwaë 1992) requires a bit
more explanation. In Moluccan Malay Dutch verbs are incorporated in their
infinitive form. They occupy a fixed position in the sentence, between the
auxiliary/aspectual adverb complex and the direct object, given that Malay is
an SAuxVO language. In the following example, the Dutch verb *happen* 'bite'
thus occupies the Malay position. At the same time, however, it is used
figuratively, as part of a Dutch expression, together with *als een gek* 'like
crazy':

(17) *want* aku djuga tukan [*happen*] [*heel vaak als een gek*]
      for I also HAB bite very often as a crazy person
      'For I am used to biting very often, as crazy, as well.'

(Moluccan Malay/Dutch; Huwaë 1992)

The same occurs in another example:

(18) akan [*brengen*] [*geluk*]
      it bring good fortune
      'It brings [you] luck.'   (Moluccan Malay/Dutch; Huwaë 1992)

256

There are also a number of Moluccan Malay sentences that sound like translated Dutch, with respect to a specific collocation. Two involve the verb *bikin* 'do':

(19) aku bikin *heel dom*
      I do very dumb
      'I act very dumb.' (compare Du *dom doen* 'act dumb')

(20) kue bisa bikin *wens*
      you may do wish
      'You may make a wish.' (compare Du *een wens doen* 'make a wish')
                                    (Moluccan Malay/Dutch; fieldwork data Huwaë 1992)

The following example shows a similar complex relation between the languages:

(21) aku *nog steeds vinden* akan *raar* [kata koe *bellen* aku
      I   still   find   it strange that you call I
      twee keer [*zonder* dapat *gehoor*]]
      twice without   get hearing
      'I still find it strange that you called me twice without finding anyone
      home.'   (Moluccan Malay/Dutch; Huwaë 1992)

Notice that the Dutch collocation *gehoor krijgen* 'finding someone home' (lit. 'get hearing') is partly represented in Malay, where *krijgen* has been replaced by *dapat* 'get'. Also the Dutch expression (*iets*) *raar vinden* 'find (something) strange' has been reordered and made to fit into a Malay frame.

In examples from Shaba Swahili/French switching, from fieldwork data collected in Lubumbashi (Zaire) by Vincent de Rooij (1996), the paradoxical pattern is quite frequent. In (22) the French infinitive is part of a Swahili verb *ku-satisfaire* and the French noun in *ma-besoins* receives a Swahili plural prefix:

(22) Mwanaume eko-na-tafuta mwanamuke njo
      man 3sg-PR-look-for woman TO
      ku-*satisfaire* ma-*besoins*
      INF-satisfy PL-needs
      'A man looks for a woman to satisfy [his] needs.'

At the same time, of course, the two French elements form a fixed expression, stored as such in the lexicon. The other examples illustrate the same pattern:

(23) Mbele [tu. . tu-*mettre*] [*situation* iko (h)apa sasa]
      first . . . 1pl-put situation is here now
      'First let us take the situation that exists right now.'

(24) bon chunga r'i-*poser* [*question* moya] eh?
      good wait=IM 1sg-put question one
      'Good, wait, let me just ask one question.'

(25) (h)ai-na Mungu eko-na-*permettre souffrance*
 NEG-COP God 3sg-PR-permit suffering
 'It is not God who tolerates suffering.'

(26) Shetani njo ku. . a-na-tu-*utiliser* njo tu-ji-*détourner*
 Satan TO . . . NC1–PR-1pl-use TO 1pl-RE-turn.away
 [*pouvoir* ya Mungu]
 power of God
 'It is Satan who uses us that we might turn away from the power of
 God.'

(27) kila mu-ntu a-na-*concevoir Bible* . .aye. . *de sa façon*
 each NC1–man NC1–PR-understand Bible . . . in his way
 'Everyone understands the Bible in his own way.'

As in Turkish, some examples are integrated morphosyntactically into the matrix language ((22) *satisfaire . . . besoins*, (23) *mettre . . . situation*, (23) *poser . . . question*, (26) *utiliser . . . détourner . . . pouvoir*), and some are not ((24) *poser . . . question*, (23) *permettre . . . souffrance*, (27) *concevoir . . . Bible*). The examples closely resemble Myers-Scotton's *ni-ka-wash the clothes* example cited in chapters 3 and 8.

A final set of examples comes from one of the styles of Moroccan Arabic/French code-mixing described in Bentahila and Davies (1992) on variation in mixing patterns. As in the case of Swahili, French verbs are integrated in infinitival form, and are the base for Arabic inflections. Once again, however, these French verbs can be part of French lexicalized expressions involving a French object, often, but not always embedded in an Arabic noun phrase:

(28) . . . hija lli ta-t-*secréter*-na *les hormones*
 that which DUR-3Fsg-secrete-1pl.O the hormones
 'It is that which secretes the hormones.'

(29) dak *la femme* ta-t-*lancer* dak *l'ovule*
 DEM the woman DUR-3Fsg-emit DEM the ovum
 'That woman emits the ovum.'

(30) huma Yadi j-*transmi*-w *les ordres*
 '. . . transmit . . . the orders'

(31) huma kaj-*executi*-w *l'ordre* djal *le chef*
 '. . . execute the order of the boss'
 (Moroccan Arabic/French; Bentahila and Davies 1992: 388–9)

There are also some cases in the examples presented by Bentahila and Davies (1992) of an action nominalization involving a fixed expression:

(32) dak *la régulation* djal *les naissances*
 DEM the control of the births
 'that birth control'

258

(33)   dak *le rôle* djal *la transmission* djal *les ordres*
       'that role of the transmission of the orders'

I have presented six language pairs with mixed sentences involving a bilingual complex verb with an object also partly or wholly inserted. What all these cases have in common is the semantic relation, idiomatic or collocational, between the lexical verb and the lexical head noun of its object. At the same time, the two intruding elements, lexical head noun and lexical verb, cannot be said to form an embedded language constituent apart from the surrounding matrix language material. Thus we have a bracketing paradox roughly as in:

(34)   MORPHOSYNTAX
           /   \
       noun   verb   helping verb/affix/shape
               \   /
       SEMANTICS/MENTAL LEXICON

This bracketing paradox constitutes the first bit of evidence for a dual representation view of code-mixing. It should be kept in mind, however, that in the large majority of the cases, the noun and verb are not very far apart in the speech string, even if they can be separated by affixes and functional elements from the other language.

Even though my argument is based on a handful of examples per language pair, it should be kept in mind that none of the material cited was collected with this particular construction in mind. In all cases, I could only draw on small subsets of data arbitrarily taken from much larger corpora.

Thus, the fact that many cases were found at all is indicative of the regularity of the phenomenon at hand.

Delayed lexicalization

A second phenomenon that may be used to argue for a dual representation involves what may be termed delayed lexicalization, involving shared structure. Consider the following mixed sentence:

(35)   ka-yxeṣṣ [[bezzaf dyal *generaties*] *voorbijgaan*]
       it must   much of generations   pass
       'Much of a generation must pass.'

(Moroccan Arabic/Dutch; Nortier 1990: 140)

If we adopt the Adjacency Criterion, *generaties voorbijgaan* 'generations pass' may be considered to constitute a single embedded constituent. In addition, this is a frequent combination. However, the Dutch plural noun *generaties* is modified by *bezzaf dyal* 'much of', and thus is part of an Arabic noun phrase. Therefore, in this sentence, the transition between Arabic and

Dutch may be said to take place after the Moroccan Arabic modal *ka-yxess* from a structural point of view. Nonetheless, lexically the transition takes place after *dyal*. Thus there seems to be an asynchrony between the syntax and the lexicon, again best explained in terms of a dual representation:

(36) MORPHOSYNTAX
```
          /      \
element  element  element
          \      /
       LEXICON
```

A similar example is:

(37) xeṣṣ-na [[m9a *bestuur*] *praten*]
      we-must with board   talk
      'We must speak to the board.'

Here Arabic *m9a* 'with' occurs in an otherwise Dutch verb phrase. Other examples include:

(38) 9refti   [[shal men *Marokkaanse liedjes*] *zingen*]
      you-know how many of Moroccan songs   sing
      'How many Moroccan songs can you sing?'

(39) baġi   [nešri [dik s-*smurfen*] [*voor de auto*]]
      wanting I-bought that the smurfs for the car
      'I wanted to buy those smurfs for the car.'   (Nortier 1990: 140)

There is almost no useful published material on these delayed lexicalizations because they have so far resisted any systematic treatment. In interesting work on Gibraltar Spanish/English code-mixing Moyer (1992) does analyse relevant cases in a slightly different way. Examples in her work include:

(40) He is going to [[tell *a un tal ensalada que acepte el* [British interpretation of the airport deal]] (. . . some nitwit to accept the . . .) (Moyer 1992: 127)

In this example there is a verb phrase which starts with the English verb *tell* and contains two other constituents: *a un tal ensalada* and *que acepte el [British . . .* However, the particular form these complements take: a noun phrase marked with *a* and a finite subjunctive complement, would go together with the Spanish verb *decir*, not with the equivalent English *tell* that we actually encounter. Thus we have to assume that something like the Spanish verb *decir* was intended, but that the lexical form chosen (through delayed lexicalization again) is from the preceding English fragment. Similarly in the next example:

(41) He accused *a Mister Bigote de doble lenguaje*
      Mister Bigote of double talk   (Moyer 1992: 128)

Here the Adjacency Criterion coupled with the fact that we get the Spanish prepositions *a* and *de* suggests once again that in fact the whole verb phrase is Spanish, including the verb *accused*, which replaces Spanish *acusó*.

Non-sequential interaction of the two grammatical systems: pro-drop

Yet a third area that could be explored with respect to the issue of simultaneous representations is that of sentence-level interference. Here the two grammars are not interacting sequentially, but are intersecting in a more complicated way. Clause fragments sometimes appear to be governed by the syntax from one language, but have lexica from the other language. I will briefly explore the case of pro-drop, the possibility for mixed sentences to occur without a lexical subject. In Spanish–English code-mixing there are many examples with null subjects [0], provided the finite verb is Spanish (see the discussion in Klavans 1985):

(42) No creo que [0] son *fifty-dollar suede ones.*
      '[I] don't think that [they] are . . .'   (Spanish/English; Poplack 1980: 598)

(43) [0] Pegó *right here.*
      '[(S)he] hit [me] right here.'   (Spanish/English; McClure 1977: 107)

Presumably in these clauses the Spanish inflection on the verb 'identifies' and 'licenses' the empty subject (see e.g. Rizzi 1989) under government. Thus we minimally have a structure as in:

(44) $[[0]_i \quad V–INFL_i \ldots]$

Since the subject is in the domain of the inflection, the overall structure is Spanish, and the English elements in (42)–(43) are inserted or embedded into a Spanish verb phrase. Presumably the null-subject is also in some sense 'Spanish', although this is arguable.

Since in Spanish these null-subjects are adjacent to the inflected verb, there is no problem in just assuming a Spanish structure up to the elements *fifty* and *right there*. Turkish cannot be explained the same way. Consider the following two examples from Turkish/Dutch switching:

(45) ja, zie je dat [0] donker *ol-muş?*
      yes, see you that dark become-PRET
      'Yes, did you see that it got dark?'

(46) waarom [0] *san-a* dof *gel-iyor?*
      why you-DAT dull come-PR-3sg
      'Why does it come out so dull on you?'   (Backus 1996: 183)

Turkish allows null-subjects in the same way as Spanish, but the inflected

261

verb tends to be at the end of the verb phrase, as in (45) and (46). Thus the place of the 'Turkish' null expletive subject (Dutch would have *het*, pronounced [ət]) occurs in an otherwise Dutch structure, on the surface. To understand these cases, the syntax and lexicon of Turkish and Dutch have to be viewed as interacting in other ways than just sequentially.

Admittedly, these are only a few instances, and the subject needs to be explored both empirically and theoretically in much greater depth, but still the argument seems pretty straightforward.

The following cases are all from the Moluccan Malay-influenced Dutch in the Netherlands (Huwaë 1992). We find null subjects quite frequently in Malay-style Dutch; they can marginally occur in native Dutch as well, but only in specific discourse contexts, not the ones in (47) and (48). I will just present some examples here:

(47) [0] Is een kerk ook.
      '[This] is a church as well.'

(48) [0] Is echt typisch hoor.
      '[This] is really typical, you know.'

(Moluccan Malay-influenced Dutch; data R. Huwaë 1992)

These cases are different from the Turkish–Dutch ones presented by Backus in lacking an overt inflection to license the null subject. In fact, Malay is a pro-drop language more like Chinese in allowing null subjects without an overt inflection (which is absent in the language). The Dutch copula *is* in these examples must be seen as an invariant verb form imbued with the Malay qualities that allow it to have no subject. Notice that the subjects are not expletive here, but recoverable from the discourse. This is quite frequent in Malay as well.

Summary

Moluccan Malay/Dutch code-mixing points to the simultaneous presence of Malay grammar and Dutch lexicon; at the same time, Malay lexicon and (mostly lexicalized) bits of Dutch grammar are operant. The simultaneous presence of two languages in the representation may be realized in different ways: (a) both languages are fully present; (b) any one module can be selected from either language, but not from both. The first option would resemble the idea of simultaneously available multiple trees proposed by Moyer (1992), the second is more like the 'chamber orchestra' suggested by Grosjean (p.c.), where different languages play different instruments, as it were, in the chamber orchestra of sentence-production. Often there is something like the division of labour given below:

(49)   syntax
      function words
      phonology

      ――――――

      lexicon
      semantics

Division of labour for different modules, a more restrictive option, would appear to be characteristic of insertional code-mixing and the process of language intertwining (Bakker 1997). The first option calls for a more wholesale cooperation between the two languages and is akin to congruent lexicalization styles of code-mixing. It may well be of course, that option (b) is too restrictive. To give but one example, it is not possible to neatly separate the phonology from the lexicon: with the lexical forms associated with lemmas, specific sounds are introduced. These may well be transformed in the bilingual representation, but are still present. Similarly, syntax and semantics cannot be separated.

Language contact and language change

One of the reasons why so little agreement has been reached with respect to the question of what can be borrowed in language contact is that the focus has been on the supposed **outcome**, i.e. the elements borrowed and the directionality of borrowing, and not as much on the **processes** of borrowing, determined by the type of contact situation. This makes all the difference in the world, and therefore we need to discuss different scenarios for linguistic borrowing.

The best-known recent treatment of contact-induced language change is Thomason and Kaufman (1988), who have provided a comprehensive framework for genetic linguistics as it relates to language contact. Thomason and Kaufmann stress the asymmetry involved in contact-induced language change: we find either interference from the dominant language within the subordinate language, or retention of features of the subordinate language while shifting to the dominant language.

A similar asymmetrical pattern is found in Myers-Scotton's (1993b) work in the distinction between matrix and embedded language. From my perspective here the most important conclusions from the work of Thomason and Kaufmann are:

(a) Structural conditions on language contact phenomena can only be valid when embedded in specific socially conditioned contact processes.

(b) The two most important contact processes are borrowing and shift.

(c) Within each process the structural conditions on language contact phenomena take the form of implicational hierarchies.

Rooted in historical linguistics and basing themselves on historical material, Thomason and Kaufmann attempt to explain what has happened in linguistic systems rather than what is happening right now in patterns of language use. Nonetheless, they do not deny the potential implications for present day contact situations. I think the greatest value of their work lies in explicitly distinguishing the two processes of borrowing and shift and their structural properties.

As to outcomes of borrowing, there is a distinction, at least in principle, between **convergence**, the result of bidirectional influence, and **grammatical borrowing**, generally seen as a unidirectional result. There are a number of ways in which grammatical borrowing could potentially take place.

The phenomena of language interaction (a cover term for all forms of language contact) can be divided into lexical, grammatical, and phonetic phenomena. We can perhaps assume that the lexical phenomena belong to a separate module: within the bilingual lexicon, words from different lexical sets entertain all kinds of complex relationships, on the semantic, the morphological and the phonological level.

The core idea I want to suggest here as an avenue for further research is to link Thomason and Kaufmann's 1988 model for contact-induced language to recent synchronic models for bilingual behaviour, such as the one defended here. Their account suffers from being monodimensional and not taking into account the different strategies of bilingual language use; the bilingual speech accounts suffer from being rather static and not taking into account the outcomes of language change. If we project the two types of models on top of each other, there are some interesting results.

In the Thomason and Kaufmann model (ignoring pidgin and creole formation for now), there are two dominant scenarios for contact-induced language change: borrowing under maintenance of L1, and interference under shift to L2. In the code-mixing model proposed here a three-way distinction between insertion, alternation, and congruent lexicalization is made. Each of these has a different diachronic dimension, sketched in rough terms in figure 9.1. We saw already in earlier chapters that different patterns of borrowing are associated with different mixing strategies. In the next sections I will comment on other relevant diachronic aspects of language contact research.

264

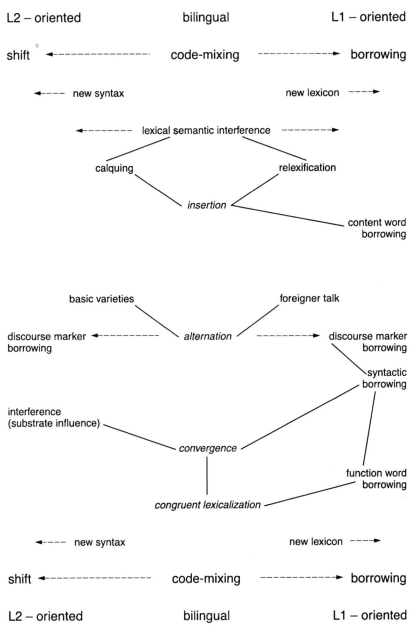

Figure 9.1 Typology of language contact phenomena

Relexification and intertwining

The renewed focus on insertional code-mixing as involving a single matrix language (Myers-Scotton 1993b) has made it possible to once more compare code-mixing to other matrix language-based phenomena discussed in creole studies, such as relexification (Muysken 1981a, 1988b, 1996) and intertwining (Bakker 1997, forthcoming). Undoubtedly, insertional code-mixing and relexification are different phenomena, but there are enough common features to make a much more detailed comparison, and hence a more comprehensive view, possible.

Generally relexification is used to refer to a process of lexical borrowing which (a) involves a large part of the vocabulary, and (b) involves the replacement of native items, rather than the mere addition of vocabulary. The way the term is used in Muysken (1981a) and subsequent work goes one step further: in fact the new relexified forms do not enter as full lexical entries, but as phonological shapes which are grafted onto the original lexical entries. Thus the original entry is not replaced, but merely altered in its outer shape. Take the French verb *embrasser* which means 'embrace' as well as 'kiss' (the original French verb meaning 'kiss', *baiser*, now often means 'sleep with'). One could imagine a French relexified with German vocabulary where *küssen* also has the double meaning and corresponding range of uses of the French original. Since the grammatical properties of the original element are maintained, this type of language contact has the effect of pairing the lexical shapes of one language with the syntax of another one.

The different components of a lexical entry function so independently of each other that (apparently) a phonological representation can be substituted into an entry without affecting the other sets of features (syntactic, subcategorization, semantic, selectional). A language which emerges through relexification has the same lexical, morphosyntactic and syntactic categories as its source. An example from Media Lengua, Quechua relexified with Spanish (Muysken 1981a; 1996), is (where SD = sudden discovery tense):

(50)   a.   ubixa-buk yirba nuwabi-shka   (MeL)
            sheep for grass there is not SD
            'There turns out to be no grass for the sheep.'
       b.   llama-buk k'iwa illa-shka   (Qe)
       c.   No hay hierba para las ovejas   (Sp)
                                          (Muysken 1981a)

Relexification necessarily must take place on the basis of meaning correspondences. In Media Lengua, a Spanish stem as close as possible in meaning to the Quechua original is used to replace it. The question now is how closeness in meaning is determined. It is necessary to distinguish here between lexical meaning and grammatical meaning. The former can be determined by reference to some extralinguistic entity, the latter only by reference to the language system itself. When the Quechua verb *riku-* 'see' is relexified as *bi-* (from Spanish *ver*), this is possible because there is a large shared element of meaning. Relexification is feasible, with all the difficulties mentioned, for lexical items, but operates in a very incomplete manner for grammatical items. In the latter case, there is drastic restructuring of the system. Function words do not **have** a meaning outside the linguistic system that they are part of, since their meanings are paradigmatically defined within that linguistic system. So when you relexify a system of paradigmatically organized function words, automatically the semantic organization of the target language comes in, and the result is at best a compromise between source and target language systems.

Sometimes it is not quite possible to maintain the original grammar in the process of relexification, particularly if function words from the new language are introduced as well. In Media Lengua, some changes have occurred due to this. An example is first person reflexive. In Quechua reflexive is generally marked with a suffix *-ku* on the verb. Since Media Lengua has formed a non-subject first person pronoun *ami* 'me' (from Spanish *a mi* '(to) me'), it is possible to form first person reflexives in Media Lengua without the Quechua suffix *-ku-*, by simply adding *-lla-di* 'self' to the object pronoun.

> (51) *ami*-lla-(da)-di *bi*-ni
>   me-self-AC-EMPH see-1sg
>   'I see myself.'

In the light of Media Lengua, consider now examples involving Swahili/English mixing, e.g. from work by Myers-Scotton (1992b):

> (52) i-me-*turn black* sana
>   3-PERF-   very
>   'It had turned very black.'   (Swahili/English; Myers-Scotton 1992b: 5)

We must ask ourselves whether in fact we do not have a (possibly less extensive) form of relexification here, similar to the phenomena encountered in Ecuadorian Quechua mentioned above.

To determine what is going on, consider an example from Tamil/English mixing (Sankoff, Poplack, and Vanniarajan 1990), where we have:

> (53) [*Indian women*]-e avaa *discriminate* paṇṇa-ille
>   AC they   do-NEG
>   They don't discriminate (against) Indian women.
>   (Tamil/English; Sankoff, Poplack, and Vanniarajan 1990: 80)

267

Do the imported lexical elements behave as in the matrix language or as in the embedded language? In the latter case, relexification is not impossible. In chapter 7 I discussed example (53) and argued that the subcategorization properties of *discriminate* (taking *against*) have been lost. This would make some of the Tamil/English data very similar to relexification (cf. Annamalai 1971).

Consider also a case like the following:

> (54) watashi wa Waseda (o) *graduate* shimashita
> I TO Waseda [University] AC graduate did
> 'I graduated from Waseda University.' (Japanese/English; Azuma 1993: 1080)

Here the use of the English verb *graduate* does not impose the subcategorization requirements of this verb ([. . . from]) at all, if we assume that a variety of English is involved in which *graduate* takes *from*. Rather those of the corresponding Japanese verb *sotsugyoo* are met, namely accusative. The probability of this occurring may be enhanced by the fact that for some English speakers *graduate* can be used without the preposition *from*. Thus (53) and (54) differ from (52) in that in the latter the evidence for Swahili subcategorization features in the English verb is lacking, making an analysis in terms of relexification less likely.

A hierarchy can be established in the embedding of forms according to the amount of material imported, with relexification as the importation (Haugen 1950) purely of form, and other types of mixing involving progressively more material. It goes from phonetic word shapes (as in Media Lengua) to full single words (as in nonce-borrowing) to the lexical core of idioms to full constituents (as in noun phrase insertion). In some sense, any insertional model assumes by definition that some part of the host or matrix language is represented at the same time as the inserted element:

> (55) **importation hierarchy**
> relexification   form
> borrowing   + meaning
> embedding   + lexical environment
> insertion   + syntactic environment
> alternation   + language mode

The case of embedding of collocational verb + object combinations is presented here as an intermediary step between borrowing and constituent insertion.

Language genesis

Pidgins and creoles are a case of drastic language change due to contact, with far-reaching syntactic consequences. **Contact pidgins**, which involve a somewhat symmetrical relationship of often only two ethnolinguistic groups, are different from **L2 pidgins**, which result from the attempt by different groups to communicate on the basis of an imperfectly mastered dominant language. **Creoles** result from adoption of L2 pidgins as community languages.

Syntactic issues in the study of contact pidgins are the nature of the **convergent structural adaptations** to reach a common medium of communication and the factor of **markedness** in steering the adaptations towards an unmarked system. Thus Kouwenberg (1992) argues that the SVO-character of Berbice Dutch Creole (spoken in Guyana) resulted from a compromise between surface SVO patterns in spoken colonial Dutch and surface word order patterns in Ijo, the language spoken by most slaves. Remarkably, both contributing languages are underlyingly SOV. It is clear that the kind of linear convergence we often see in alternation and congruent lexicalization resembles this convergence. Similarly the patterns of deletion of determiners, copulas, and subject pronouns encountered e.g. in the Moluccan Malay/ Dutch case could be seen as leading to an unmarked system.

For L2 pidgins the relevant issues are the types of grammatical **simplification** that characterize stabilized interlanguage systems, and the consequences of the loss of inflectional morphology for the grammatical system as a whole: fixed word order, emergence of **grammaticalized auxiliary particles**, etc.

For creoles the main issue concerns **substrate influence**, something that remains as hotly disputed as grammatical borrowing, since we do not know much about the way language can be mixed. Mixing implies that elements of one language are put together with elements of another one, and this in turn calls into question the cohesion of the grammatical systems involved. The tighter a particular subsystem (e.g. the vowel system, or the system of referential expressions) is organized, the less amenable it will be to restructuring.

Rarely do bilingual varieties of the code-mixing type develop into new languages. There is some discussion on this matter with respect to the origin of Michif, the Cree/French mixed language of western Canada. Bakker (1997) argues that Michif emerged through a process of **intertwining**, akin to relexification, in the nineteenth century. The process produced different results in the case of Michif than of Media Lengua due to characteristic features of Algonquian verb morphology in Cree. However, Drapeau (1994) showed that code-mixing in present day Cree communities produces sentences very similar to Michif.

Lexical borrowing
Sometimes **lexical borrowing** will lead to syntactic borrowing, e.g. when a language with case-suffixes and/or post-positions borrows prepositions from a

prestige language under alternation. In this case the [P–NP] syntactic pattern will be borrowed as well, but I noted in chapter 4 that the prepositions at least initially have the status of adjuncts. Sometimes the borrowing is limited to a frozen pattern as in Ecuadorian Quechua *sin . . . -r* pattern borrowed from Spanish: e.g. *sin miku-r* 'without eating' modelled on Spanish *sin comer*.

In other cases, the construction may retain a grammatically peripheral status, e.g. the introduction of a Persian complementizer into Turkish. Turkish has undergone extensive lexical influence, from Arabic and Persian successively, and at the Ottoman court a very complex and flexible form of Turkish was spoken, full of Arabic and Persian expressions and phrases. One element introduced was the Persian particle *ki*, somewhat like English 'that', which created the possibility of having Indo-European-like relative clauses such as (56b) in addition to original Turkish patterns such as (56a):

(56) a. kapıyı kapamıyan bir cocuk
          door not-shutting a child
      b. bir cocuk *ki* kapıyı kapamaz
          a child REL door not-shuts
          'a child who does not shut the door'   (Turkish; Lewis 1972)

In (56a) the relative clause is formed with a participial form of the verb, and in (56b) with the particle *ki* and a fully inflected verb. Furthermore, the original type of relative clause precedes the head noun, and the 'Persian' type follows the head noun.

This would seem to be a clear example of syntactic borrowing, in this case through cultural influence and lexical borrowing: the introduction into Turkish of the element *ki* opened the way, for new types not only of relative clauses, but also of complement clauses, just as with English 'that'. Lewis (1972) notes, however, that there is an old Turkish interrogative element *kim*, which through its phonetic similarity may have paved the way for the extension in syntactic use of *ki*. Second, there is some doubt that constructions of type (b) ever really became part of Turkish. Lewis suggests that this construction 'is regarded as alien and is increasingly rare in modern Turkish.' While the latter is not borne out by recent recordings, the use of *ki* may still be a peculiar type of alternational code-mixing, triggering a non-Turkish syntactic pattern in speech production, without this pattern really entering the grammar. This would be similar to the way Spanish complementizers and prepositions enter Otomí.

Second language learning and substrate
Another type of syntactic borrowing may occur in **massive second language learning**: semantic distinctions, pragmatically relevant ordering patterns,

ways of marking causality and conditionality, etc. may be taken over into the new language. Transfer and substratal influence often involve lexical characteristics of content words.

In order to explain how daughter languages came to diverge widely from the mother language some scholars have appealed to **substrate** influence. When a language is brought into another region than the one of its original use, and when speakers of other languages in that region adopt that language as their second one, because of its cultural and political prestige, then the original language of these speakers may influence the new language in various ways. Schematically:

(57)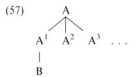

Thus Romance scholars have sometimes argued that French is derived from Vulgar Latin not only through a series of linguistic changes internal to the system, but also because of Celtic influence on Vulgar Latin in the late Roman era. This type of influence would explain a number of the differences between French, Spanish (Basque substrate), Portuguese (Celtic substrate?), Roumanian (Thracian substrate), etc.

Presumably this type of substrate influence would occur because the Celts learned Vulgar Latin as a second language, but only imperfectly, and introduced many elements from their own language into it. The process requires three steps:

(a) One or more features of language **B** (cf. the schema above) are transferred into the **B/A interlanguage**, i.e. the result of the attempts by speakers of **B** to learn **A**.

(b) These features remain in the interlanguage, even when speakers of **B** learn **A** rather well.

(c) The features, originally characteristic of **B**, are adopted by native speakers of **A** in successive generations, sometimes as a stylistic variant of the original corresponding feature of **A**, sometimes as the only variant.

Again, some of the concrete cases of this type of substrate influence suggest superficial convergence rather than deep structural influence. Muysken (1984a) analyses Quechua SOV patterns in the Andean Spanish of central Ecuador, and notes a statistical predominance of object – verb sequences among Quechua – Spanish bilinguals when compared with Spanish monolinguals. Nonetheless, cases of true SOV orders (with a subject present) did not occur in the corpus analysed. Rather, OSV, OV, and OVS patterns occurred, suggesting that the predominance of OV patterns among bilinguals results from the quantitative overextension of object fronting among bilinguals. Recall from chapter 4 that this overextension of object fronting was also found in Japanese/English code-mixing.

Gradual convergence due to prolonged coexistence

Similar, but perhaps more intensive, are the effects of **interference** in **long-term and massive bilingualism**. The latter has been the source for the remarkable phenomena of **convergence** and drastic **syntactic restructuring** in the Balkan and Indian subcontinent. Sometimes it seems more appropriate perhaps to speak of one syntax with different lexica attached to it (the different languages), than of syntactic systems which have converged. Again, more studies are needed of contemporary communities where the apparent convergence is taking place.

An apparently rather clear case of this type of syntactic influence involves some dialects of Konkani, an Indo-European language related to Marathi spoken in central India. Some centuries ago a group of Konkani speakers moved into an area where Kannada, a Dravidian language, is spoken, and they were forced by the circumstances to become bilingual: Konkani inside the home, Kannada outside. That their bilingualism was maintained and shows no sign of disappearing is perhaps due to the rigid ethnic, religious, and caste divisions that cut through Indian society: the Konkani speakers were Brahmans and kept themselves separate socially. Nadkarni (1975) claims that the structure of the Konkani dialects involved was directly affected, becoming very much like the structure of Kannada.

The original Konkani relative clause, formed with a relative particle as in (58), was gradually replaced by a Kannada-type relative clause, formed with a question word and a yes/no interrogation element as in (59):

(58) **jo** mhantaro pepar vaccat assa, to daktaru assa
      REL old-man paper reading is that doctor is

(59) **khanco** mhantaro pepar vaccat assa-**ki**, to daktaru assa
      which old-man paper reading is-Y/N, that doctor is
      'The old man that is reading the newspaper is the doctor.'

(Konkani; Nadkarni 1975: 675)

This replacement can only be explained through the postulation of Kannada influence; it is not motivated structurally. On the whole the case presented by Nadkarni is very strong and hard to explain otherwise. An alternative

explanation could involve two observations: (a) In (59) there is no replacement of one type of relative clause by another one, but rather the loss of the
possibility to relativize, and its replacement by a question-like structure,
which functions somewhat like a relative clause. (b) Konkani grammar is
not undergoing some change, but Konkani grammar is replaced by
Kannada grammar, while maintaining Konkani vocabulary. This may be
called **resyntacticization** (as opposed to relexification). Centuries of coexistence and massive bilingualism have led to the convergence of the
grammars of the Indian languages, but the existing social divisions called
for pluriformity. Therefore the languages remained as separate as possible on
the lexical level.

Roman Jakobson has described a number of cases of phonological
convergence, in terms of the notion 'phonological **Sprachbund**' (1931), a
notion derived from earlier work of Trubetzkoy. In several cases, for
instance, unrelated languages spoken in the same area have developed a tone
system. Chinese and Tibetan are one example, and another example is
formed by the languages of the Baltic sea. The situation is a little different in
the Balkan and in Northern India, regions for which extensive convergence
of complete grammatical systems has been claimed.

Why did this type of convergence take place? In the work of Poplack and
her associates, there is a frequent implicit appeal to economy principles,
based on equivalence, in bilingual language use (1980). A principle such as
the following seems to be in operation:

(60)   When there is equivalence in a switching context, make use of it.

Thus there is a pressure towards congruent lexicalization in bilingual settings.

Calquing and imitation of prestige patterns

Some prestige languages, e.g. Latin in Renaissance Europe or French in
eighteenth-century Europe, have been involved in syntactic borrowing
through **calquing** and **imitation of prestige patterns**. Here the effect of the
syntactic borrowing is mostly limited to the (extended) lexicon: set phrases
and expressions (cf. Du 'als 't u belieft', Eng 'if you please' < Fr *s'il vous
plaît*). This type of calquing can be viewed in terms of the simultaneous
access models and the frequent switching of idioms in bilingual language use.
It is only one step away from lexically embedding an idiom to translating it
literally:

(61)   a. s'il vous plait
       b. *?als 't u *plaisier*t
       c. als 't u belieft

Table 9.1. *The relation of the three mixing strategies to the processes of contact-induced language change*

	insertion	alternation	congruent lexicalization
borrowing	+	–	–
relexification	+	–	+
calquing	+	–	–
genesis	–	+	+
shift	–	+	+
convergence	–	+	+

In (61b) an intermediate form is suggested in which the French verb is used in a hypothetical form derived from the noun *plaisir* 'pleasure'.

Conclusion

It is clear that many of the phenomena in contact-induced language change are better understood under a model which allows simultaneous access to (modules of) two different languages. Furthermore, there is frequent recourse to alternational strategies, particularly adjunction, on the clausal level. We can characterize the processes of contact-induced language change in terms of the three notions of insertion, alternation, and congruent lexicalization, as in table 9.1. It would appear that they fall into two main classes: (a) **lexical** phenomena, which rely primarily on insertion, and (b) **clausal** phenomena, which rely primarily on alternation and congruent lexicalization.

Avenues of research in bilingual processing

In the last section of this concluding chapter I will sketch some lines of research in the area of bilingual processing that arise from the work in code-mixing so far. Three themes will be broached, roughly corresponding to the three main types of code-mixing – the role of the **lexicon** (insertion), the role of **adjunction** (alternation), and the role of **processing economy** (congruent lexicalization).

Content words and functional elements in bilingual processing

At several points in this book, the matter of different roles of content words and functional elements in bilingual processing has come up. However, the implications for speech production models of this research are not clear yet. To clarify some of the aspects of this problem, I will take as an example the speech production model presented in Levelt (1989), following Kempen and

Hoenkamp (1987). In this model Levelt makes the assumption that speech production is not syntactically, but rather lexically driven: the need to express concepts leads to the choice of particular lexical items, which impose certain requirements on their environment, hence syntax. This model matches with the view of phrase structure in Government and Binding theory starting with the work inspired by Stowell (1981). As is cogently argued by Myers-Scotton (1993b), the code-mixing data are partly in line with recent work in speech production research: lexical selection takes place independently of syntactic processing.

For code-mixing constraints this model has the implication that mixing is possible as long as the requirements of the relation between individual lexical items and their syntactic environment, expressed in subcategorization frames or a licensing mechanism, are satisfied. So if a verb takes a dative object there needs to be one, i.e. the language switched to must have dative case-marking as an option for noun phrases. Within this view, categorial equivalence is required where specific categories are lexically specified in the subcategorization frame of a lexical item.

Let us assume for the moment, as Myers-Scotton (1993b) does, with Levelt (1989), that sentence production is 'lexically driven'. It is not clear what this means, exactly. Are we talking about the content morphemes (such as the predicate) that drive production, not the function morphemes? Why then should the latter impose the matrix language? Why are specialized morpho-syntactic procedures triggered by lemmas? Myers-Scotton writes (1993b: 118): 'Either ML or EL content morphemes may be "called" by ML or EL lemma's respectively, but they both appear in slots prepared by ML lemma's.' Now take an example like:

(62) Tajziw tajdiru dak *la regulation* [sic] djal *les naissances* . . .
      'They come and do that-[the limitation] of [(the) births] . . . .'
      (Moroccan Arabic/French; Bentahila and Davies 1992: 106)

What Myers-Scotton would have to propose here is that the French elements are replacing abstract Arabic lemmas, which trigger the Arabic sentence frame. This then leads to the selection of Arabic system morphemes such as *dak* 'that' and *dyal* 'of'. Now that latter assumption seems correct, but the assumption that the medical discourse is regulated by abstract Arabic lemmas is implausible. If one examines the fragment from which the sentence is taken, from the work of Bentahila and Davies (1992), it is clear that the Moroccan doctors or interns are talking **in Arabic** about the **French** medical universe, implying the complete European medical vocabulary, set of concepts, etc. that they have learned in their training. This type of example, which is not uncharacteristic, suggests that selection of a morphosyntactic frame is not linked directly to lemma-selection, but is a separate process, and not necessarily one that follows lemma-selection.

The same question can be broached by looking at the precise definition of **lemma**. It is not clear exactly what Myers-Scotton's (1993b) view is on the lemma in relation to the bilingual. In figure 4.3 on p. 116 of that work lemma selection triggers the calling of specialized morphosyntactic procedures. Hence one would assume that lemmas are language-specific. However, further down in the same figure, we notice that the lexemes called by lemmas are realized. Where is congruency tested in the process of speech production? The notion of lemma fluctuates: sometimes it is abstract, as in Garrett's perspective (1993b: 48), and sometimes it is language specific. If we take lemmas to be abstract, language-independent entities, congruency matching could take place quite early on. In that case, it is hard to see how lemmas could trigger language-specific morphosyntactic procedures by themselves. If we take lemmas to be language-specific entities, it is not clear where and how congruency can be defined. Thus I diverge from Myers-Scotton in terms of the priority given to the two kinds of processing: the code-mixing data suggest that syntactic (including the function words) and lexical processing proceed on an equal footing.

It is important to stress that the content-word and the function-word approaches to lexical triggering correspond to two aspects of the sentence-planning process: linear planning (how am I going to put the words in a string) and content-word planning (which main content words is my clause going to contain).

Adjunction as a fall back strategy in language processing

One of the conclusions of the research reported on here concerns the role of adjunction in language processing. We have seen that in many bilingual communities language mixing takes the form of the fairly loose association of fragments from different languages. In structural terms, this loose association can be analysed as a case of adjunction.

This adjunction has been argued to play an important role in language use in several very different strands of linguistic research. Talmy Givón (1979) has distinguished between the syntactic and the paratactic mode in language, arguing that paratactic constructions are grammaticalized as syntactic constructions, before finally entering the morphology. Kenneth Hale (1975) has argued that in certain Australian native languages 'gaps' in the grammar, *in casu* concerning relative clauses, are filled with adjoined structures. Charles Ferguson (1971) has developed the idea that there is telegraphic speech in certain registers such as foreigner talk, and that similar phenomena can be found in emerging pidgins. Foreigner talk can be seen as a form of adjunction-steered speech.

Finally, there is a tradition in child-language research of assuming fall back options of this type (Goodluck 1992: 177), based on research reported on in Goodluck and Tavakolian (1982): 'It is possible that a conjoined or adjoined structure is a very early form of embedding for the child and is reverted to when other factors . . . make the relative clause difficult . . . Errors are also potentially revealing, laying bare non-adult rules that may be part of an immature grammar.' However, these fall back structures may be potentially available to the adult user as well at moments when the grammar fails. This is one of the ways bilinguals can bend the rules of their system.

Language contact frequently involves the adjunctional, paratactic mode. As I argued in chapter 7, examples include bilingual verbs. We have also encountered a number of telegraphic or null constructions in this work; they could be construed as the result of adjunction. We thus may have suspension of true syntax (and recourse to paratax) rather than zero syntax in these cases.

Separateness and processing economy in interference
A potential paradox is coming to the fore in bilingual processing research. It appears that speakers can and often do keep their languages separate. Why then don't they always do this? The answer may lie in what was discussed at the beginning of this chapter: simultaneous access. It is precisely the simultaneous presence of both languages that favours the searching for parallels between them, and hence the striving towards congruent lexicalization.

One area only briefly touched upon in this book is the discrepancy between the grammar and the processing system. Suppose we have two separate grammars that have to be processed by one system. It is conceivable that there is a uniformizing tendency resulting from the processing system, tending towards one superficial word order for both languages, etc.

Ironically, it would seem that we have come full circle in bilingualism research, and will go back to Weinreich's **interference** as a core subject for study, after a long period in which separateness was stressed. However, the researcher will come armed with a great many insights from the code-mixing research of the last twenty years, insights both theoretical and methodological. Interference may take several forms, two of which are sharing and conversion. **Sharing** may involve categories (as discussed in the section on equivalence) rules, i.e. shared subcategorization frames of functional categories, and components of the production system, e.g. linearization.

Conversion may involve the lexicon (**faux amis**) and the syntax (**transfer**). There may also be phonological conversion and interlingual identification. Sharing is symmetrical, conversion asymmetrical, with respect to the language subsystems involved.

In fact, the type of research I propose is quite close to the one which Lars Johanson has been proposing (1992, 1993; see also Backus 1996 and Boeschoten 1996), and has elaborated in his book on Turkish in contact with other languages (1992): the **code-copying model**. The crucial property of this model is that we cannot only take lexically filled-in constituents or word sequences from another language (material copying or, as it is termed in this study, code-mixing), but also patterns and skeletons.

To conclude

I hope to have conveyed here some of the excitement of working in a field that is moving quite rapidly and is located at the cross-roads of structural analysis, sociolinguistics, and psycholinguistics. Many questions remain, but at least some of these can and will get an answer in coming years. Code-mixing provides bilingual speakers with a means to drastically extend their verbal repertoire, and there is evidence that many bilingual speakers take the opportunity. However, for both speakers and hearers there is a cost, in terms of more complex processing, and the strategies we find can be seen as ways of reducing this cost.

References

Abney, Steven 1987, 'The English noun phrase in its sentential aspect', Unpublished doctoral dissertation, MIT.

Adelaar, Willem F. 1986, 'Aymarismos en el quechua de Puno', *Indiana* 11: 223–31.

Adelmeyer, Liesbeth 1991, 'The level of code-switching', MA thesis in linguistics, Universiteit van Amsterdam.

Aghinotri, R.K. 1987, *Crisis of identity. The Sikhs in England*, New Delhi: Bahri.

Aguiló S.J., Federico 1980, *Los cuentos. ¿Tradiciones o vivencias?*, Cochabamba: Editorial Amigos del Libro.

Akers, Glenn A. 1981, *Phonological variation in the Jamaican continuum*, Ann Arbor, Mich.: Karoma.

Alfonzetti, Giovanna 1992, 'Il discorso bilingue. Italiano e dialetto a Catania', *Materiali Linguistici* 8, Milan: F. Angeli.

Anderson, Stephen A. 1982, 'Where's morphology?', *Linguistic Inquiry* 13: 571–612.

　1985, 'Typological distinctions in word formation', in Timothy Shopen (ed.), *Language Typology and Language Description*, Vol. III: *Lexicon*, Cambridge University Press, pp. 3–50.

　1992, *A-morphous morphology*, Cambridge University Press.

Andersson, Paula 1990, 'Finns and Americans in Sweden: patterns of linguistic incorporation from Swedish', International Workshop on Ethnic Minority Languages in Europe, Tilburg, Netherlands.

Annamalai, E. 1971, Lexical insertion in a mixed language, *Papers from the Seventh Regional Meeting*, Chicago Linguistic Society, pp. 20–7.

　1989a, 'The language factor in code mixing', *International Journal of the Sociology of Language* 75: 47–54.

　1989b, 'Review of Ira Pandit, Hindi–English code-switching: mixed Hindi–English', *Indian Linguistics* 48 [1987]: 121–3.

Aoun, Josef and Sportiche, Dominique 1983, 'The formal theory of government', *The Linguistic Review* 2: 211–36.

Appel, René and Muysken, Pieter 1987, *Language contact and bilingualism*, London: Edward Arnold.

Aronoff, Mark 1976, *Word formation in Generative Grammar*, Cambridge, Mass.: MIT Press.

References

Auer, Peter 1995, 'The pragmatics of code-switching: a sequential approach', in Milroy and Muysken, pp. 115–35.

Azuma, Shoji 1993, 'The frame-content hypothesis in speech production: evidence from intrasentential code switching', *Linguistics* 31: 1071–94.

Backus, Ad 1992, *Patterns of language mixing: a study in Turkish–Dutch bilingualism*, Wiesbaden: Otto Harassowitz.

1996, *Two in one: bilingual speech of Turkish immigrants in the Netherlands*, doctoral dissertation, Katholieke Universiteit Brabant, Tilburg, Studies in Multilingualism 1, Tilburg University Press.

Bailey, Beryl J. 1966, *Jamaican creole syntax*, Cambridge University Press.

Baker, Mark C. 1988, *Incorporation*, Chicago University Press.

1995, *The polysynthesis parameter*, Oxford University Press.

Bakker, Peter 1997, *A language of our own. The genesis of Michif. The mixed Cree–French language of the Canadian Métis*, Oxford University Press.

in prep., *Language mixing*, Ms., University of Aarhus.

Barkow, J.H., Cosmides, L. and Tooby, J. (eds.) 1992, *The adapted mind: evolutionary psychology and the generation of culture*, Oxford University Press.

Barz, R.K. and Siegel, Jeffrey (eds.) 1988, *Language transplanted: the development of Overseas Hindi*, Wiesbaden: Otto Harrassowitz.

Bautista, M.L.S. 1980, *The Filipino bilingual's competence: a model based on an analysis of Tagalog–English code switching*, The Australian National University: Pacific Linguistics, Series C, No. 59.

Belazi, Hedi M., Rubin, Edward J. and Toribio, Almeida Jacqueline 1994, 'Code-switching and X-bar theory: the Functional Head Constraint', *Linguistic Inquiry* 25: 221–38.

Bennis, H., Prins, R.S. and Vermeulen, J. 1983, 'Lexical–semantic versus syntactic disorders in aphasia: the processing of prepositions', Ms., Universiteit van Amsterdam.

Bentahila, Abdelâli 1983a, *Language attitudes among Arabic–French bilinguals in Morocco*, Clevedon, Avon: Multilingual Matters.

1983b, 'Motivations for code-switching among Arabic–French bilinguals in Morocco', *Language and Communication* 3: 233–43.

Bentahila, Abdelâli and Davies, Eileen D. 1983, 'The syntax of Arabic–French code-switching', *Lingua* 59: 301–30.

1992, 'Code-switching and language dominance', in R.J. Harris (ed.) *Cognitive processing in bilinguals*, Amsterdam: Elsevier, pp. 443–58.

Berk-Seligson, Susan 1986, 'Linguistic constraints on intra-sentential code-switching: a study of Spanish/Hebrew bilingualism', *Language in Society* 15: 313–48.

Bhatia, Tej K. 1988, 'Trinidad Hindi: its genesis and generational profile', in Barz and Siegel, pp. 179–96.

Bhatia, Tej K. and Ritchie, William C. 1996, 'Bilingual language mixing, universal grammar, and second language acquisition. In William C. Ritchie and Tej K.

Bhatia (eds.) *Handbook of second language acquisition.* New York: Academic Press, pp. 627–88.

Bickerton, Derek 1975, *Dynamics of a creole system,* Cambridge University Press.

1981, *Roots of Language,* Ann Arbor, Mich.: Karoma.

Bittner, Maria and Hale, Kenneth L. 1996, 'Ergativity: towards a theory of a heterogeneous class', *Linguistic Inquiry* 27: 531–604.

Bloomfield, Leonard 1933, *Language,* New York: Houghton.

Boeschoten, Hendrik E. 1990, 'Asymmetrical code-switching in immigrant communities', *Papers for the workshop on Constraints, Conditions, and Models, London, 1990,* Network on code-switching and language contact, Strasbourg: European Science Foundation, pp. 85–100.

1996, 'Zur Charakterisierung des Kodekopierens', in Á. Berta, B. Brendemoen, C. Schönig (eds.) *Symbolae Turcologicae,* Swedish Research Institute in Istanbul, Transactions, vol. VI. Uppsala, Sweden, pp. 31–9.

Boeschoten, Hendrik E. and Huybregts, Riny 1997, 'Code switching without switching codes', TULP workshop on code switching and language change, Tilburg University, 15–16 May, 1997.

Bolle, Jette 1994, 'Sranan Tongo – Nederlands. Code-wisseling en ontlening', MA thesis in linguistics, Universiteit van Amsterdam.

Booij, Geert E. 1977, *Dutch Morphology,* Lisse: Peter de Ridder.

Borer, Hagit 1983, *Parametric syntax: case studies in Semitic and Romance languages,* Dordrecht: Foris.

1994, 'The projection of arguments', in E. Benedicto and J. Runner (eds.) *Functional projections,* University of Massachussetts Occasional Papers 17, GSLA, University of Massachusetts, Amherst, pp. 19–49.

Borer, Hagit and Wexler, Kenneth 1987, 'The maturation of syntax', in Tom Roeper and Edwin Williams (eds.) *Parameter setting,* Dordrecht: Kluwer Academic, pp. 123–72.

Bot, Kees de and Schreuder, Robert 1993, 'Word production and the bilingual lexicon', in Robert Schreuder and Bert Weltens (eds.) *The bilingual lexicon,* Amsterdam: Benjamins, pp. 191–214.

Boumans, Louis 1995, 'The integration of verbs in code-switching', *Summer School – Code-Switching and Language Contact. Ljouwert/Leeuwarden, 14–17 September 1994,* Ljouwert/Leeuwarden: Fryske Akademy, pp. 294–9.

1998, *The syntax of code switching: analysing Moroccan Arabic/Dutch conversation,* doctoral dissertation, Nijmegen University, Studies in Multilingualism 12, Tilburg University Press.

Boyd, Sally, Andersson, Paula and Thornell, Christa 1991, 'Patterns of incorporations of lexemes in language contact: language typology or sociolinguistics?' *Papers for the symposium on code-switching and language contact: theory, significance and perspectives, Barcelona, March 21–23, 1991,* vol. II. Network on Code-Switching and Language Contact, Strasbourg: European Science Foundation, pp. 463–88.

References

Brugmann, Karl and Delbrück, Berthold 1893–1900, *Grundriss der vergleichenden Grammatik der indogermanischen Sprachen*. Strasbourg: Trübner.

Bruyn, Adrienne 1995, 'Grammaticalization in creole: developments in the Sranan noun phrase', doctoral dissertation, Universiteit van Amsterdam/IFOTT.

Budzhak-Jones, Svitlana 1998, 'Against word-internal codeswitching: Evidence from Ukrainian – English bilingualism', *International Journal of Bilingualism* 2: 161–82.

Budzhak-Jones, Svitlana and Shana Poplack 1997, 'Two generations, two strategies: the fate of bare English-origin nouns in Ukrainian', *Journal of Sociolinguistics* 1: 225–58.

Butterworth, Brian 1989, 'Lexical access in speech production', in William Marslen-Wilson (ed.) *Lexical representation and process*, Cambridge, Mass.: MIT Press, pp. 108–35.

Canfield, Kip 1980, 'Navaho–English code-mixing', *Anthropological Linguistics* 22: 218–20.

Caramazza, A. and R. Sloan Berndt (1985) 'A multi-component deficit view of agrammatic Broca's aphasia'. In Mary-Louise Kean (ed.) *Agrammatism*, New York: Academic Press, pp. 27–63.

Cavalli-Sforza, L.L., Piazza, A., Menozzi, P. and Mountain, J. 1988, 'Reconstruction of human evolution: bringing together genetic, archeological, and linguistic data', *Pro. Nat. Ac. Sc. USA* 85: 6002–6.

Chambers, J.K. 1995, *Sociolinguistic theory: language variation and its social significance*, Oxford: Blackwell.

Chana, Urmi and Romaine, Suzanne 1984, 'Evaluative reactions to Panjabi/English code-switching', *Journal of Multilingual and Multicultural Development* 5: 447–73.

Cheshire, Jenny and Gardner-Chloros, Penelope 1997, 'Code-switching and the sociolinguistic gender pattern', in B. Hill and S. Ide (eds.) *International Journal of the Sociology of Language*, Special issue on Gender.

Chomsky, Noam 1981, *Lectures on government and binding*, Dordrecht: Foris.

1986a, *Barriers*, Cambridge, Mass.: MIT Press.

1986b, *Knowledge of language: its nature, origin, and use*, New York: Praeger.

1993, 'A minimalist program for linguistic theory', in Kenneth Hale and S. Jay Keyser (eds.) *The view from Building 20: essays in linguistics in honor of Sylvain Bromberger*, Cambridge, Mass.: MIT Press, pp. 1–52.

1995, *The minimalist program*, Cambridge, Mass.: MIT Press.

Clyne, Michael 1967, *Transference and triggering: observations on the language assimilation of postwar German-speaking migrants in Australia*, the Hague: Martinus Nijhoff.

1972, *Perspectives on language contact: based on a study of German in Australia*, Melbourne: Hawthorn.

1987, 'Constraints on code-switching: how universal are they?' *Linguistics*, 25: 739–64.

Collins, J.T. 1987, *Ambonese Malay and creolization theory*, Kuala Lumpur: Dewan Bahasa dan Pustaka Kementerian Pelajaran Malaysia.

Comrie, Bernard 1987, 'Holistic and partial typologies', Plenary lecture at the XIV International Congress of Linguists, Berlin, *Preprints of the Plenary Session Papers*, 213–32.

Crama, Rob and Gelderen, Heleen van 1984, 'Structural constraints on code-mixing', MA thesis in linguistics, Universiteit van Amsterdam.

Croft, William 1993, *Language typology*, Cambridge University Press.

Dabène, Louise 1991, 'Quelques aspects du rôle de l'environnement familial dans un contexte multilingue', *Revue Enfances* 4: 159–69.

Dabène, Louise and Moore, Danièle 1995, 'Bilingual speech of migrant people', in Milroy and Muysken, pp. 17–44.

Damsteegt, Theo 1988, 'Sarnami: a living language', in Barz and Siegel, pp. 95–120.

DeCamp, David 1971, 'The structure of a creole continuum', in Dell Hymes, pp. 68–93.

De Houwer, Annick 1995, 'Structural aspects of young bilingual children's mixed utterances: a unified analysis', Ms., Universitaire Instelling Antwerpen.

Dijkhoff, Marta B. 1993, 'Papiamentu word formation', doctoral dissertation, Universiteit van Amsterdam.

DiSciullo, Anne-Marie, Muysken, Pieter and Singh, Rajendra 1986, 'Code-mixing and government', *Journal of Linguistics* 22: 1–24.

DiSciullo, Anne-Marie and Williams, Edwin 1989, *On the definition of word*, Cambridge, Mass.: MIT Press.

Dixon, Robert M.W. 1980, *The languages of Australia*, Cambridge University Press.

Domingue, Nicole M.Z. 1971, 'Bhojpuri and creole in Mauritius: a study of linguistic interference and its consequences in regard to synchronic variation and language change', doctoral dissertation, University of Texas.

Doron, Edit 1983, 'On a formal model of code-switching', *Texas Linguistic Forum* 22: 35–59.

Drapeau, Lynne 1994, 'Code-switching in caretaker speech: a case-study in an enclave indigenous group', *International Journal of the Sociology of Language* 113: 157–64.

Drie, Alex 1985, *Sye! Arki tori!* Paramaribo, Surinam: Drukkerij Aktua.

Eid, Mushira 1992, 'Directionality in Arabic–English code-switching', in Aleya Rouchdy (ed.) *The Arabic language in America: a sociolinguistic study of a growing bilingual community*, Detroit: Wayne State University Press, pp. 50–71.

El Jattari, Belkacem 1994, 'Les emprunts espagnols dans le dialecte berbère de Nador', Ms., Universiteit van Amsterdam.

Eliasson, Stig 1995, 'Grammatical and lexical switching in Maori–English "Grasshopper speech"', *Summer school in code-switching and language contact*, 45–7.

Emonds, Joseph E. 1973, *A transformational grammar of English*, New York: Academic Press.

Escobar, Gabriel and Escobar, Gloria 1981, *Huaynos del Cusco*, Cusco: Garcilaso.

References

Extra, Guus and Verhoeven, Ludo (eds.) 1993, *Community languages in the Netherlands*, Amsterdam: Swets and Zeitlinger.

Fabian, Johannes 1982, 'Scratching the surface: observations on the poetics of lexical borrowing in Shaba Swahili', *Anthropological Linguistics* 24: 14–50.

Ferguson, Charles A. 1971, 'Absence of copula and the notion of simplicity: a study of normal speech, baby talk, foreigner talk, and pidgins', in Dell Hymes, pp. 141–50.

Fishman, Joshua 1964, 'Language maintenance and language shift as a field of inquiry: a definition of the field and suggestions for its further development', *Linguistics* 9: 32–70.

Flege, J.E. 1988, 'The production and perception of foreign speech sounds', in H. Winitz (ed.) *Human communication and its disorders: a review 1988*, New Jersey: Ablex, pp. 244–401.

Frazier, Lyn 1989, 'Against lexical generation of syntax', in William Marslen-Wilson (ed.) *Lexical representation and process*, Cambridge, Mass.: MIT Press, pp. 505–28.

Fries, Charles C. 1952, *The structure of English*, New York: Harcourt Brace.

Gambhir, Surendra Kumar 1981, 'The East Indian speech community in Guyana: a sociolinguistic study with special reference to koine formation', doctoral dissertation, University of Pennsylvania.

Gardner-Chloros, Penelope 1990, 'Codeswitching and child language', in Rodolfo Jacobson (ed.) *Codeswitching as a worldwide phenomenon*, New York: Peter Lang, pp. 169–84.

1991, *Language selection and switching in Strasbourg*, Oxford: Clarendon.

1995, 'Code-switching in community, regional and national repertoires: the myth of the discreteness of linguistic systems', in Milroy and Muysken, pp. 68–89.

Garman, Michael 1990, *Psycholinguistics*, Cambridge University Press.

Garrett, M.F. 1982, 'Production of speech: observations from normal and pathological language use', in A.W. Ellis (ed.) *Normality and pathology in cognitive functions*, London: Academic Press.

Gerhard W., 1993, 'Borrowings in Amharic', paper presented at the Second Symposium on Bilingualism, University of Amhaburg, September 1993.

Giacalone Ramat, Anna 1995, 'Code-switching in the context of dialect-standard language relations', in Milroy and Muysken (eds.), pp. 45–67.

Giesbers, Herman 1989, *Code-switching tussen dialect en standaardtaal*, Amsterdam: Publicaties van het P.J. Meertens Instituut 14.

Givón, Talmy 1979, *On understanding grammar*, New York: Academic Press.

Goldberg, Adèle E. 1995, *Constructions: a construction grammar approach to grammatical structure*, University of Chicago Press,

Goodglass, H. 1968, 'Studies on the grammar of aphasics', in S. Rosenberg and J.H. Kaplan (eds.), *Developments in applied psycholinguistic research*, New York: Macmillan, pp. 177–208.

Goodluck, Helen 1992, *Language acquisition: a linguistic introduction*, Oxford: Blackwell.

Goodluck, Helen and Susan Tavakolian 1982, 'Competence and processing in children's grammar of relative clauses', *Cognition* 11: 1–27.

Gorter, Durk 1993, *Taal fan klerken en klanten*, doctoral dissertation, Universiteit van Amsterdam, Ljouwert: Fryske Akademy.

Green, D.W. 1986, 'Control, activation, and resource: a framework and a model for the control of speech in bilinguals', *Brain and Language* 27: 210–23.

1993, 'Towards a model of L2 comprehension and production', in Rob Schreuder and Bert Weltens (eds.) *The bilingual lexicon*, Amsterdam: Benjamins, pp. 249–77.

Greenberg, Joseph E., Turner II, Christy G. and Zegura, Stephen L. 1986, 'The settlement of the Americas: a comparison of the linguistic, dental, and genetic evidence', *Current Anthropology* 27: 477–88.

Grimshaw, Jane and Armin Mester 1988, 'Light verbs and θ-marking', *Linguistic Inquiry* 19: 205–32.

Grosjean, François 1995, 'A psycholinguistic approach to codeswitching', in Milroy and Muysken, pp. 259–75.

1996, 'Processing mixed language: issues, findings, models', in Annet de Groot and Judith Kroll (eds.) *Tutorials in bilingualism: psycholinguistic perspectives*, Hillsdale, N.J: Lawrence Erlbaum, pp. 225–54.

Gumperz, John J. 1982, *Discourse strategies*, Cambridge University Press.

Gumperz, John J. and Hernandez-Chavez, Eduardo 1971, 'Cognitive aspects of bilingual communication', in W.H. Whiteley (ed.) *Language use and social change*, Oxford University Press, pp. 111–25.

Gumperz, John J. and Wilson, Robert 1971, Convergence and creolization: a case from the Indo-Aryan/Dravidian border, in Dell Hymes, pp. 151–68.

Hale, Kenneth L. 1975, *Gaps in Grammar and Culture*, Lisse, the Netherlands: The Peter de Ridder.

1983, 'Warlpiri and the grammar of non-configurational languages', *Natural Language and Linguistic Theory* 1: 5–48.

Halmari, Helena 1993, 'Structural relations and Finnish–English code switching', *Linguistics* 31: 1043–70.

1997, *Government and code-switching: explaining American Finnish*. Amsterdam and Philadelphia: Benjamins.

Hamel, Rainer E. 1995, 'Indigenous language loss in Mexico: the process of language displacement in verbal interaction', in Willem Fase, Koen Jaspaert and Sjaak Kroon (eds.) *The state of minority languages: international perspectives on survival and decline*, European Studies on multilingualism, Lisse and Exton, Pa.: Swets and Zeitlinger, pp. 153–72.

Harris, Zellig 1960 [1951], *Structural linguistics*, University of Chicago Press.

Hart-Gonzalez, Lucinda 1979, 'The Huaynito: a multilingual, multi-channel event', Ms., Georgetown University.

Haspelmath, Martin, König, Ekkehard, Oesterreicher, Wulf and Raible, Wolfgang (eds.) forthcoming, *Language typology and language universals: an international handbook*, Berlin and New York: Walter de Gruyter.

References

Haugen, Einar 1950, 'The analysis of linguistic borrowing', *Language* 26: 210–31.

1956a, *Bilingualism in the Americas: a bibliography and research guide*, Publication 26 of the American Dialect Society, Birmingham, Ala.: University of Alabama Press.

1956b, *The Norwegian language in America: a study in bilingual America*, Philadelphia: University of Pennsylvania Press.

Heath, Jeffrey 1989, *From code-switching to borrowing: a case study of Moroccan Arabic*, Library of Arabic Linguistics, Monograph 9, London: Kegan Paul International.

Hekking, Ewald 1995, 'El otomí de Santiago Mexquititlán: desplazamiento lingüístico, préstamos y cambios gramaticales', doctoral dissertation, Universiteit van Amsterdam/IFOTT.

Hekking, Ewald and Muysken, Pieter 1995, 'Otomí y Quechua: una comparación de los elementos gramaticales prestados del español', in Klaus Zimmermann (ed.) *Lenguas en contacto en Hispanoamérica. Nuevos enfoques*, Frankfurt: Verveurt/ Iberoamericana, 101–18.

Hengeveld, Kees forthcoming, *A hierarchy of categories*, Universiteit van Amsterdam.

Herzfeld, Anita 1980, 'Creoles and standard languages: contact and conflict', in Peter H. Nelde (ed.) Sprachkontakt und Sprachkonflikt. *ZDL Zeitschrift für Dialektologie und Linguistik. Beihefte* 32: 83–90.

1983, 'The creoles of Costa Rica and Panama', in J. Holm (ed.) *Central American English*, Heidelberg: Groos, pp. 131–56.

Higa, Masanori 1974: 'Hawai no Nihongo', *Genda no Espri* 85: 178–97, Tokyo: Ikubundo.

Hill, Jane H. and Hill, Kenneth C. 1986, *Speaking Mexicano*, Tucson, Ariz.: University of Arizona Press.

Hindle, Donald 1981, 'A probabilistic grammar of noun phrases in spoken and written English', in David Sankoff (ed.) *Variation omnibus*, Edmonton: Linguistic Research, pp. 369–78.

Hinnenkamp, Volkert 1984, 'Eye-witnessing pidginization? Structural and sociolinguistic aspects of German and Turkish foreigner talk', *York Papers in Linguistics* 11: 153–66.

Hinton, G.E. and S.J. Nowlan 1987, 'How learning can guide evolution', *Complex Systems* 1: 495–502.

Hoekstra, Teun 1984, 'Transitivity: grammatical relations in government–binding theory', doctoral dissertation, Rijksuniversiteit Leiden.

Hout, Roeland van 1984, 'The need for a theory of choice in sociolinguistics', *Linguistische Berichte* 90: 39–57.

1989, *De structuur van taalvariatie: Een sociolinguïstisch onderzoek naar het stadsdialect van Nijmegen*, Dordrecht: Foris.

Hout, Roeland van and Muysken, Pieter 1994, 'Modelling lexical borrowability', *Language Variation and Change* 6: 39–62.

1995, 'Insertion, alternation, congruent lexicalization, corpus-based approaches to bilingual speech', *Summer School Code-Switching and Language Contact. Ljou-*

wert/Leeuwarden, 14–17 September 1994, Ljouwert/Leeuwarden: Fryske Akademy, pp. 302–06.

Huang, C.-T. James 1982, 'Logical relations in Chinese and the theory of grammar', doctoral dissertation, MIT.

Huls, Erica 1989, 'Interactienetwerken in Turkse gezinnen'. Ms., Tilburg University.

Humboldt, Wilhelm von 1949, *Über die Verscheidenheit des menschlichen Sprachbaues*, Darmstadt.

Huwaë, Rosita 1992, 'Tweetaligheid in Wierden: het taalgebruik van jongeren uit een Molukse gemeenschap', MA thesis in linguistics, Universiteit van Amsterdam.

Hyltenstam, Kenneth 1995, 'The code-switching behaviour of adults with language-disorders – with special reference to aphasia and dementia', in Milroy and Muysken, pp. 302–43.

Hyltenstam, Kenneth and Obler, K. Loraine (eds.) 1989, *Bilingualism across the lifespan: aspects of acquisition, maturity, and loss*, Cambridge University Press.

Hyltenstam, Kenneth and Stroud, Christopher 1989, 'Bilingualism in Alzheimer's dementia: two case studies', in Hyltenstam and Obler, pp. 202–26.

1993, 'Second language regression in Alzheimer's dementia', in Kenneth Hyltenstam and A. Viberg (eds.) *Progression and regression in language: Sociocultural, neuropsychological, and linguistic perspectives*, Cambridge University Press, pp. 222–42.

Hymes, Dell (ed.) 1971, *Pidginization and Creolization of Language*, Cambridge University Press.

Jackendoff, Ray 1975, 'Morphological and semantic regularities in the lexicon', *Language* 51: 639–71.

Jaeggli, Oswaldo 1982, *Topics in Romance syntax*, Dordrecht: Foris.

Jake, Janice 1994, 'Intrasentential codeswitching and pronouns: on the categorial status of functional elements', *Linguistics* 32: 271–98.

Jake, Janice and Myers-Scotton, Carol 1997, 'Codeswitching and compromise strategies: Implications for lexical structure', *International Journal of Bilingualism* 1: 25–40.

Jakobson, Roman 1962 [1931] 'Über die Phonologischen Sprachbünde', [Orig. publ. in *TCLP* IV], *Selected Writings* I, The Hague: Mouton, pp. 137–43.

1971 [1957] 'Shifters, verbal categories, and the Russian verb', *Selected Writings* II, The Hague: Mouton, pp. 130–47.

Johanson, Lars 1992, *Strukturelle Faktoren in türkischen Sprachkontakten*, Sitzungsberichte der Wissenschaflichen Gesellschaft an der Johann Wolfgang Goethe-Universität Frankfurt am Main, Band XXIX/5.

1993, 'Code-copying in immigrant Turkish', in Guus Extra and Ludo Verhoeven (eds.) *Immigrant languages in Europe*, Clevedon: Multilingual Matters, pp. 197–221.

Joshi, Aravind 1985, 'Processing sentences with intra-sentential code-switching', in David Dowty, Lauri Karttunen and Arnold Zwicky (eds.) *Natural language parsing*, New York: Academic Press, pp. 190–205.

References

Kachru, Braj B. 1977, 'Towards structuring code-mixing: an Indian perspective', in P. Gopal Sharma and Suresh Kumar (eds.) *Indian bilingualism*, Delhi: Kendriya Hindi Sansthan, pp. 188–209.

Kean, Mary Louise 1977, 'The linguistic interpretation of aphasic syndromes: agrammatism in Broca's aphasia, an example', *Cognition* 5, 9–46.

Kempen, Gerard and Hoenkamp, E. 1987, 'An incremental procedural grammar for sentence formulation', *Cognitive Science* 11: 201–58.

Kerke, Simon C. van de 1996, 'Affix order and interpretation in Bolivian Quechua', doctoral dissertation, Universiteit van Amsterdam.

Kishna, Sita 1979, 'Lexicale interferentie in het Sarnami', MA thesis in linguistics, Universiteit van Amsterdam.

Kiss, Katalin É. 1995, *Discourse-configurational languages*, Oxford University Press.

Klavans, Judith L. 1985, 'The syntax of code-switching: Spanish and English', *Proceedings of the Linguistic Symposium on Romance Languages*, Amsterdam: Benjamins, pp. 213–31.

Kook, Hetty 1994, 'De ontwikkeling van het lezen en schrijven in een tweetalige context', doctoral dissertation, Universiteit van Amsterdam.

Kook, Hetty and Narain, Goretti 1993, 'Papiamento', in Guus Extra and Ludo Verhoeven (eds.) *Community languages in the Netherlands*, Amsterdam: Swets and Zeitlinger, pp. 69–92.

Koopman, Hilda 1984, *The syntax of verbs*, Dordrecht: Foris.

Koster, Jan 1978, *Locality principles in syntax*, Dordrecht: Foris.

Kouwenberg, Silvia 1992, 'From OV to VO: Linguistic negotiation in the development of Berbice Dutch Creole', *Lingua* 88: 263–300.

Krishnamurti, B. 1968, *Studies in Indian Linguistics*, Deccan College, Poona, India.

Labov, Willam 1972, *Sociolinguistic patterns*, Philadelphia: University of Pennsylvania Press.

Lance, D.M. 1975, 'Spanish–English code-switching', in Eduardo Hernández-Chavez et al. (eds.) *El lenguaje de los chicanos*, Arlington, Va.: Center for Applied Linguistics, pp. 138–52.

Lehtinen, Meri K.T. 1966, 'An analysis of a Finnish–English bilingual corpus', doctoral dissertation, Indiana University, Bloomington, Ind.

Leopold, Werner F. 1939–1949, *Speech development of a bilingual child: a linguist's record*, 4 vols., Evanston, Ill.: Northwestern University Press.

LePage, Robert B. and Tabouret-Keller, Andrée 1986, *Acts of identity*, Cambridge University Press.

Levelt, Willem J.M. 1989, *Speaking: from intention to articulation*, Cambridge, Mass.: MIT Press.

Lewis, G.L. 1972, *Turkish Grammar*, Oxford University Press.

Li Wei 1994, *Three generations, two languages, one family: language choice and language shift in a Chinese community in Britain*, Clevedon, Oh.: Multilingual Matters.

Li Wei, Milroy, Lesley, and Pong Sin Ching 1992, 'A two step sociolinguistic analysis of code-switching and language choice: the example of a bilingual Chinese community in Britain', *International Journal of Applied Linguistics* 2: 63–86.

Lieber, Rochelle 1981, *On the organization of the lexicon*, Bloomington, Ind.: Indiana University Linguistics Club.

Lipski, John M. 1978, 'Code-switching and the problem of bilingual competence', in Paradis, pp. 250–64.

1986, 'English–Spanish contact in the United States and Central America: sociolinguistic mirror images?', in M. Görlach and J. Holm (eds.) *Focus on the Caribbean*, Amsterdam: Benjamins, pp. 191–208.

Ludérus, Suzanne 1995, 'Language choice and language separation in bilingual Alzheimer patients', doctoral dissertation, Universiteit van Amsterdam/IFOTT.

Maclay, Howard and Osgood, Charles E. 1959, 'Hesitation phenomena in spontaneous English speech', *Word* 15: 19–44.

MacSwan, Jeffrey 1997, 'A minimalist approach to intrasentential code switching: Spanish–Nahuatl bilingualism in central Mexico', doctoral dissertation, University of Caligornia, Los Angeles, to be published by Garland.

Madaki, R. 1983, 'A linguistic and pragmatic analysis of Hausa–English code-switching', doctoral dissertation, University of Michigan.

Mahootian, Shahrzad 1993, 'A null theory of codeswitching', doctoral dissertation, Northwestern University.

Mahootian, Shahrzad and Santorini, Beatrice 1996, 'Code switching and the complement/adjunct distinction', *Linguistic Inquiry* 27: 464–79.

Mannheim, Bruce 1986a, 'Popular song and popular grammar, poetry and metalanguage', *Word* 37: 45–75.

1986b, 'Poetic form in Guaman Poma's *Wariqsa Arawi*', *Amerindia* 11: 41–57.

1987, 'Couplets and oblique contexts: the social organization of a folksong', *Text* 7: 265–88.

Martin-Jones, Marilyn 1995, 'Code-switching in the classroom: two decades of research', in Milroy and Muysken, pp. 90–112.

Matthews, Peter H. 1972, *Inflectional morphology: a theoretical study based on aspects of Latin verb conjugation*, Cambridge University Press.

McClure, Erica 1977, 'Aspects of code switching among Mexican–American children', in Muriel Saville-Troike (ed.) *Linguistics and anthropology*, Washington, D.C.: Georgetown University Press, pp. 93–115.

McCormick, Kay 1989, 'Unfiltered talk – a challenge to categories', in P. Livesey and M. Verma (eds.) *Festschrift R.B. LePage. York Papers in Linguistics* 13: 203–14.

Meechan, Marjory and Poplack, Shana 1995, 'Orphan categories in bilingual discourse: adjectivization strategies in Wolof–French and Fongbe–French', *Language Variation and Change* 7: 169–94.

Meshtrie, R. 1988, 'Lexical change in a transplanted language: the case of Bhojpuri in South Africa', in Barz and Siegel, pp. 151–77.

Miceli, G., Silveri, M.C., Romani, C., and A. Caramazza 1989, 'Variation in the pattern of omissions and substitutions of grammatical morphemes in the spontaneous speech of so-called a-grammatic patients', *Brain and Language* 36: 447–92.

Milroy, Lesley and Muysken, Pieter (eds.) 1995, *One speaker, two languages, cross-disciplinary perspectives on code-switching*, Cambridge University Press.

Milroy, Lesley and Li Wei 1995, 'A social network approach to code-switching: the example of a bilingual community in Britain', in Milroy and Muysken, pp. 136–57.

Mohan, Peggy Ramesar 1978, 'Trinidad Bhojpuri: a morphological study', doctoral dissertation, University of Michigan.

Moravcsik, Edith 1975, 'Verb borrowing', *Wiener Linguistische Gazette* 8: 3–31.

1978, 'Language contact', in Joseph E. Greenberg (ed.) *Universals of Human Language* I, Stanford University Press, pp. 95–122.

Moyer, Melissa 1992, 'Analysis of code-switching in Gibraltar', doctoral dissertation, Universitat Autònoma de Barcelona.

1995, 'On defining matrix language in sentential code-switching: a syntactic approach', *Summer School Code-Switching and Language Contact. Ljouwert/Leeuwarden, 14–17 September 1994*, Ljouwert/Leeuwarden: Fryske Akademy, pp. 192–204.

Muysken, Pieter 1981a, 'Halfway between Quechua and Spanish: the case for relexification', in Albert Valdman and Arnold Highfield (eds.) *Historicity and variation in creole studies*, Ann Arbor: Karoma, pp. 52–78.

1981b, 'Quechua Word Structure', in Frank Heny (ed.) *Binding and Filters*, London: Croom Helm, Cambridge: MIT Press, pp. 279–327.

1981c, 'Spaans en Quechua in Ecuador', *Tijdschrift voor Taal- en Tekstwetenschap* 1: 124–38.

1984a, 'The Spanish that Quechua speakers learn: L2 learning as norm-governed behaviour', in Roger W. Andersen (ed.) *Second languages: a cross-linguistic perspective*, Rowley, Mass.: Newbury House, pp. 101–24

1984b, 'Linguistic dimensions of language contact: the state of the art in interlinguistics', *Revue québecoise de linguistique* 14: 49–76.

1986, 'Contactos entre Quichua y Castellano en el Ecuador', in Segundo E. Moreno Yanez (ed.) *Memorias del Primer Simposio Europeo sobre Antropología del Ecuador*, Quito: Ediciones Abya Yala, pp. 377–451.

1987, 'Neutrality in code-mixing', *Eigen en Vreemd. Handelingen van het 39e Nederlandse Filologencongres*, Amsterdam: VU Boekhandel/Uitgeverij, pp. 359–74.

1988a, 'Quechua affix order and interpretation', in Martin Everaert and Mieke Trommelen (eds.) *Morphology and modularity*, Dordrecht: Foris, pp. 259–80.

1988b, 'Lexical restructuring and creole genesis', in Norbert Boretzky, Werner Enninger and Thomas Stolz (eds.) *Beiträge zum 4. Essener Kolloquium über 'Sprachkontakt, Sprachwandel, Sprachwechsel, Sprachtod' vom 9.10.-10.10.1987 an der Universität Essen*, Bochum: Studienverlag Dr. N. Brockmeyer, pp. 193–210.

1989a, 'Media Lengua and linguistic theory', *Canadian Journal of Linguistics* 33: 409–22.

1989b, 'A unified theory of local coherence in language contact', in P. Nelde (ed.) *Language contact and conflict*, Brussels: Center for the Study of Multilingualism, pp. 123–29.

1989c, 'Waarom zijn er verschillen tussen de talen: het Babelprobleem', *Tijdschrift voor Taal- en Tekstwetenschap* 9, 131–42, Inaugural lecture, Universiteit van Amsterdam, 20 November 1989.

1995, 'Grammatical concepts in code-switching', in Milroy and Muysken, pp. 177–98.

1996, 'Media Lengua', in Sarah G. Thomason (ed.) *Non-Indo-European-based pidgins and creoles*, Amsterdam: Benjamins, pp. 365–426.

Muysken, Pieter, Kook, Hetty and Vedder, Paul 1996, 'Papiamento/Dutch code-switching in bilingual parent-child reading', *Applied Psycholinguistics* 17: 485–505.

Muysken, Pieter and Norval Smith 1990, 'Question words in pidgin and creole languages', *Linguistics* 28: 883–903.

Myers-Scotton, Carol 1992a, 'Constructing the frame in intrasentential code-switching', *Multilingua* 11: 101–27.

1992b, 'Codeswitching as a mechanism of deep borrowing, language shift, and language death', in Matthias Brenzinger (ed.) *Language death in East Africa*, Berlin: Mouton de Gruyter, pp. 31–58.

1993a, *Social motivations for code-switching: evidence from Africa*, Oxford: Clarendon.

1993b, *Duelling Languages: grammatical structure in codeswitching*, Oxford: Clarendon.

1995, 'A lexically based model of code-switching', in Milroy and Muysken, pp. 233–56.

Myers-Scotton, Carol 1999, 'Putting it all together: The matrix language and more', in Brent Brendemoen, Elizabeth Lanza and Else Ryen (eds.) *Language encounters across time and space*. Oslo: Novus Press, pp. 13–28.

Myers-Scotton, Carol and Jake, Janice L. 1995, 'Matching lemmas in bilingual language competence and production model: evidence from intrasentential code-switching', *Linguistics* 33: 991–1024.

Myers-Scotton, Carol, Jake, Janice L. and Okasha, Maha 1996, 'Arabic and constraints on codeswitching', in Mushira Eid and Dilworth Parkinson (eds.) *Perspectives on Arabic linguistics* IX, Amsterdam: Benjamins, pp. 9–43.

Nadkarni, Mangesh V. 1975, 'Bilingualism and syntactic change in Konkani', *Language* 51: 672–83.

Nait M'Barek, Mohamed and Sankoff, David 1988, 'Le discours mixte arabe/français: des emprunts ou alternances de langue?', *Canadian Journal of Linguistics/Revue canadienne de linguistique* 33: 143–54.

Nartey, Jonas N.A. 1982, 'Code-switching, interference or faddism? language use among educated Ghanians', *Anthropological Linguistics* 24: 183–92.

Nishimura, Miwa 1985, 'Intrasentential code-switching in Japanese and English', doctoral dissertation, University of Pennsylvania.

1986, 'Intra-sentential code-switching: the case of language assignment', in J. Vaid (ed.), pp. 123–43.

1995, 'A functional analysis of Japanese/English code-switching', *Journal of Pragmatics* 23: 157–81.

Nortier, Jacomien 1990, *Dutch–Moroccan Arabic code-switching among young Moroccans in the Netherlands*, Dordrecht: Foris.

1995, 'Code-switching in Moroccan Arabic/Dutch versus Moroccan Arabic/French language contact', *International Journal of the Sociology of Language* 112: 81–95.

Nortier, Jacomien and Schatz, Henriette 1992, 'From one-word switch to loan: a comparison of between language-pairs', *Multilingua* 11: 173–94.

Ouhala, Jamal 1989, *Functional categories and parametric variation*, London: Routledge.

Pandit, Ira 1990, 'Grammaticality in code-switching', in Rodolfo Jacobson (ed.) *Code-switching as a world-wide phenomenon*, New York: Peter Lang, pp. 33–69.

Pap, Leo 1949, *Portuguese American speech: an outline of speech conditions among Portuguese immigrants in New England and elsewhere in the United States*, New York, Columbia University: King's Crown. [Distributed by University Microfilms International. Ann Arbor, Mich., 1979.]

Paradis, Michel (1978) (ed.) *Aspects of bilingualism*, Columbia, S.C.: Hornbeam.

Paradis, Michel 1987, *The assessment of bilingual aphasia* (with the collaboration of Gary Libben), Hillsdale, N.J.: Lawrence Erlbaum Associates.

Pedraza, Pedro, Attinasi, John, and Hoffman, Gerhard 1980, 'Rethinking diglossia', in Raymond V. Padilla (ed.) *Ethnoperspectives in bilingual education research: theory in Bilingual education*, Eastern Michigan University: Bilingual Bicultural Education Programs, pp. 75–97.

Peñalosa, F. 1980, *Chicano sociolinguistics: a brief introduction*, Rowley, Mass.: Newbury House.

Pfaff, Carol 1976, 'Functional and syntactic constraints on syntactic variation in code-mixing', in B. Steever et al. (eds.) *Papers from the parasession on diachronic syntax*, Chicago Linguistic Society, pp. 248–59.

1979, 'Constraints on language–mixing: Intrasentential code-switching and borrowing in Spanish/English', *Language* 55: 291–318.

Piatelli-Palmarini, Massimo 1989, 'Evolution, selection and cognition: from "learning" to parameter setting and selection in biology and the study of language', *Cognition* 31: 1–44.

Pinker, Steven and Bloom, Paul 1992 [1990] 'Natural language and natural selection', in Barkow et al., pp. 451–95.

Poplack, Shana 1980, 'Sometimes I'll start a sentence in Spanish Y TERMINO EN ESPAÑOL', *Linguistics* 18: 581–618.

1985, 'Contrasting patterns of code-switching in two communities', in H.J. Warkentyne (ed.) *Methods* V: *Papers from the fifth international conference on methods in dialectology*, University of Victoria Press, pp. 363–86.

1993, 'Variation theory and language contact', in David Preston (ed.) *American dialect research: an anthology celebrating the 100th anniversary of the American Dialect Society*, Amsterdam: Benjamins, pp. 251–86.

Poplack, Shana and Meechan, Marjory 1995, 'Patterns of language mixture: nominal structure in Wolof–French and Fongbe–French bilingual discourse', in Milroy and Muysken, pp. 199–232.

Poplack, Shana and Sankoff, David 1988, 'A variationist approach to languages in contact' [updated version of 'Code-switching'], in Ulrich Ammon, Norbert Dittmar and Klaus J. Mattheier (eds.) *Sociolinguistics: an international handbook of the science of language and society*, Berlin: Mouton de Gruyter, pp. 1174–80.

Poplack, Shana, Sankoff, David, and Miller, Christopher 1988, 'The social correlates and linguistic processes of lexical borrowing and assimilation', *Linguistics* 26: 47–104.

Poplack, Shana, Wheeler, Susan and Westwood, Anneli 1987, 'Distinguishing language-contact phenomena: evidence from Finnish–English bilingualism', in Pirkko Lilius and Mirja Saari (eds.) *The Nordic Languages and Modern Linguistics* 6, Proceedings of the Sixth International Conference of Nordic and General Linguistics in Helsinki, August 18–22, 1986, Helsinki, pp. 33–56.

Prince, Ellen 1981, 'Topicalization, focus-movement, and Yiddish-movement', in D. Alford et al. (eds.) *Proceedings of the Seventh Annual Meeting of the Berkeley Linguistic Society*, Berkeley: University of California, pp. 249–64.

Reumerman, Roland 1996, 'Code-switching: Fins in Amerika', Seminar paper, Universiteit van Amsterdam.

Rickford, John R. 1987, *Dimensions of a creole continuum: history, exts, and linguistic analysis of Guyanese creole*, Pasadena, Calif.: Stanford University Press.

Rivas, Alberto 1981, 'On the application of transformations to bilingual sentences', Ms., University of Massachusetts, Amherst.

Rizzi, Luigi 1982, *Italian Syntax*, Dordrecht: Foris.

1989, 'Null objects in Italian and the theory of *pro*', *Linguistic Inquiry* 17: 501–57.

Romaine, Suzanne 1986, 'The syntax and semantics of the code-mixed compound verb in Panjabi/English bilingual discourse', in Deborah Tannen and J.E. Alatis (eds.) *Languages and linguistics: the interdependence of theory, data, and application*, Washington, D.C.: Georgetown University Press, pp. 35–50.

1989 [1995], *Bilingualism*, Oxford: Blackwell.

Ronjat, Jules 1913, *Le développement du langage observé chez un enfant bilingue*, Paris: Champion.

Rooij, Vincent de 1996, 'Cohesion through contrast. French–Swahili code-switching and Swahili style shifting in Shaba Swahili', doctoral dissertation, Universiteit van Amsterdam/IFOTT.

Rudin, Catherine and Eminov, A. 1990, 'Bulgarian Turkish: the linguistic effects of a recent nationality policy', *Anthropological Linguistics* 32: 149–62.

References

Sankoff, David and Mainville, Sylvie 1986, 'Code-switching of context-free grammars,' *Theoretical Linguistics* 13: 75–90.

Sankoff, David and Poplack, Shana 1981, 'A formal grammar for code switching', *Papers in linguistics* 14: 3–46.

1984, 'Borrowing: the synchrony of integration', *Linguistics* 22: 99–136.

Sankoff, David, Poplack, Shana and Vanniarajan, Swathi 1990, 'The case of the nonce loan in Tamil', *Language variation and change* 2: 71–101.

Santorini, Beatrice and Mahootian, Shahrzad 1995, 'Codeswitching and the syntactic status of adnominal adjectives', *Lingua* 96: 1–27.

Sapir, Edward 1921, *Language*, New York: Harcourt Brace.

Schultink, Henk 1988, 'Morphological heads: evidence from Swahili', in G.E. Booij and J. van Marle (eds.) *Yearbook of morphology* I, Dordrecht: Kluwer Academic, pp. 247–58.

Scotton, Carol 1983, 'The negotiation of identities in code-switching: a theory of markedness and code-choice', *International Journal of the Sociology of Language* 44: 115–36.

Seaman, P.D. 1972, *Modern Greek and American English*, The Hague: Mouton.

Sebba, Mark 1998, 'A congruence approach to the syntax of code-switching', *International Journal of Bilingualism* 2: 1–20.

Seuren, Pieter and Herman Wekker 1986, 'Semantic transparency as a factor in creole genesis', in Pieter Muysken and Norval Smith (eds.) *Substrata versus universals in creole genesis*, Amsterdam, Benjamins: pp. 57–70.

Shaffer, D. 1978, 'The place of code-switching in linguistic contacts', in Paradis, pp. 265–74.

Shanmugan Pillai, M. 1968, 'English borrowings in educated Tamil', in Krishnamurti, pp. 296–306.

Shillcock, Richard C. and Ellen G. Bard 1993, 'Modularity and the processing of closed-class words', in Gerry Altmann and Richard Shillock (eds.) *Cognitive models of speech processing: the second Sperlonga meeting*, Hove, UK and Hillsdale, N.J., Lawrence Erlbaum, pp. 163–85.

Siegel, Jeffrey 1987, *Language contact in a plantation environment: a sociolinguistic perspective*, Cambridge University Press.

1988, 'Introduction', in Barz and Siegel, 1–22.

Sjölin, B. 1976, *Min Frysk; een onderzoek naar het ontstaan van transfer en 'code-switching' in het gesproken Fries*. Bijdragen en mededelingen der dialectencommissie van de KNAW, Amsterdam: Noord-Hollandsche Uitgeversmaatschappij.

Snow, Catherine E., Muysken, Pieter, and Eeden, Roos van, 1981, 'The interactional origins of foreigner talk: municipal employees and foreign workers', *International Journal of the Sociology of Language* 28: 81–91

Sobin, Nicholas 1984, 'Word order constraints on code mixing', *Journal of Applied Psycholinguistics* 5: 293–303.

Sorensen jr., A.P. 1972, 'Multilingualism in the northwest Amazon', in J.B. Pride and J. Holmes (eds.) *Sociolinguistics*, Harmondsworth: Penguin, 78–94.

Sridhar, S.N. and K. Sridhar 1980, 'The syntax and psycholinguistics of bilingual code-mixing', *Canadian Journal of Psychology* 34: 407–16.

Steele, Susan, with Adrian Akmajian, Richard Demers, Eloise Jellinek, Chisato Kitagawa, Richard Oehrle, Thomas Wasow 1981, *An encyclopedia of AUX: a study in cross-linguistic equivalence*, Cambridge, Mass.: MIT Press.

Stölting, W. 1975, 'Wie die Ausländer sprechen: Eine jugoslawische Familie', *Zeitschrift für Literaturwissenschaft und Linguistik* 18: 52–67.

Stolz, Cristel and Thomas Stolz 1995, 'Funktionswortentlehnung in Meso-Amerika. Spanisch-amerindischer Sprachkontakt (Hispanoindiana II)', *Sprachtypologie und Universalienforschung (STUF)* 47: 86–123.

Stowell, Timothy A. 1981, 'The origins of phrase structure', doctoral dissertation, MIT.

Suárez, Jorge A. 1983, *The Mesoamerican languages*, Cambridge University Press.

Swigart, L. 1992, 'Practice and perception: language use and attitudes in Dakar', doctoral dissertation, University of Washington, Seattle.

Tamis, A. 1986, 'The state of modern Greek language as spoken in Victoria', doctoral dissertation, University of Melbourne.

Thomason, Sarah G. (ed.) 1996, *Contact languages: a wider perspective*, Amsterdam: Benjamins.

Thomason, Sarah G. and Kaufmann, Terence 1988, *Language Contact, creolization, and genetic linguistics*, Berkeley: University of California Press.

Timberlake, Alan 1993, 'Russian', in Bernard Comrie and Granville G. Corbett (eds.) *The Slavonic Languages*, London: Routledge, 827–86.

Timm, Lenora A. 1975, 'Spanish–English code-switching: el porqué [sic] and how-not-to', *Romance Philology* 28: 473–82.

1978, 'Code-switching in *War and Peace*', in Paradis, pp. 302–15.

Tjon, S. 1988, 'Conversationele Codewisseling bij Chinese jongeren', seminar paper, Chinese Department, Rijksuniversiteit, Leiden.

Travis, Lisa 1984, 'Parameters and effects of word order variation', doctoral dissertation, MIT.

Treffers-Daller, Jeanine 1994, *Mixing two languages, French–Dutch contact in a comparative perspective*, Berlin: Mouton de Gruyter.

1995, 'Les effets contrastants de l'emprunt et de l'interférence: similitudes et dissimilitudes entre Bruxelles et Strasbourg', *Plurilinguismes* 9/10, Les Emprunts: Paris, Université René Descartes, CERPL, 101–24.

Treffers-Daller, Jeanine and Daller, Helmut (eds.) 1995a, *Zwischen den Sprachen: Sprachgebrauch, Sprachmischung und Sprachfähigkeiten türkischer Rückkehrer aus Deutschland*, Band 1, Language Center, Bogaziçi University, Istanbul.

1995b, *Zwischen den Sprachen: Sprachgebrauch, Sprachmischung und Sprachfähigkeiten türkischer Rückkehrer aus Deutschland*, Band 2, Language Center, Bogaziçi University, Istanbul.

Treffers-Daller, Jeanine and Yalçin, K. 1995, 'Variabilität türkisch-deutscher Sprachmischung', Germanistensymposium, Eskiyehir, June 1995.

References

Trudgill, Peter 1986, *Dialects in contact*, Oxford: Blackwell.

Türker, Emel 1993, "Fremmedord bilmiyom': a sociolinguistic study of second generation immigrant Turkish in Norway', MA thesis in linguistics, University of Oslo.

1996, 'Semantic triggering in codeswitching', Paper presented at the Norwegian Institute Seminar on Language Contact, Rome, November 4–8, 1996.

Urioste, Jorge L. 1966, *Transcripciones quechuas*, Cochabamba: Instituto de Cultura Indígena.

Vaid, Jyotsna (ed.) 1986, *Language processing in bilinguals: psycholinguistic and neuropsychological perspectives*, Hillsdale, N.J.: Lawrence Erlbaum.

Vedder, Paul, Kook, Hetty, and Muysken, Pieter 1996, 'Language choice and functional differentiation of languages in bilingual parent–child reading', *Applied Psycholinguistics* 17: 461–84.

Veenstra, Tonjes 1996, 'Serial verbs in Saramaccan: predication and creole genesis', doctoral dissertation, Universiteit van Amsterdam/HIL.

Veerman-Leichsenring, Annette 1991, *Gramática del Popoloca de Mezontla (con vocabulario y textos)*, Amsterdam/Atlanta, Ga.: Rodopi.

Vila i Moreno, Xavier 1996, 'When classes are over. Language choice and language contact in bilingual education in Catalonia', doctoral dissertation, Vrije Universiteit Brussel.

Vincent, Nigel 1993, 'Grammaticalization and functional categories', address delivered at the Il Ciocco Meeting of the European Science Foundation Network on Language Typology, September 1993.

Voigt, Herman A. 1994, 'Code-wisseling, taalverschuiving en taalverandering in het Melaju Sini', MA thesis, Katholieke Universiteit Brabant, Tilburg.

Weinreich, Uriel 1953, *Languages in contact*, the Hague: Mouton.

Weinreich, Uriel, Marvin Herzog, and William Labov 1968, 'Empirical foundations for a theory of language change', in Winfred P. Lehmann and Yakov Malkiel (eds.) *Directions for historical linguistics*, Austin: Texas University Press, pp. 95–188.

Whitney, W.D. 1881, 'On mixture in language', *TAPA* 12, 5–26.

Wiese, Richard 1996, 'Phrasal compounds and the theory of word-syntax', *Linguistic Inquiry* 27: 183–93.

Williams, Edwin 1981, 'On the notions "lexically related" and "head of a word"', *Linguistic Inquiry* 12: 245–74.

Wode, Henning 1990, 'But Grandpa always goes like this . . or: The ontogenesis of code-switching', *Papers from the workshop on impact and consequences: broader considerations. Brussels 22–24 November 1990*, Network on code-switching and language contact, Strasbourg: European Science Foundation, pp. 17–50.

Wolf, Henk 1995, 'Fries-Nederlandse Code-wisseling', Seminar paper, University of Utrecht.

Woolford, Ellen 1983, 'Bilingual code-switching and syntactic theory', *Linguistic Inquiry* 14: 520–36.

1984, 'On the application of wh-movement and inversion in code-switching sentences', *Revue québecoise de linguistique* 14: 77–86.

Zwartjes, Otto 1993/4, 'La alternancia de código como recurso estilístico en las *xarja*-s andalusíes', *La Corónica* 22: 1–5.

Zwarts, Joost 1995, 'Lexical and functional direction in Dutch', in Marcel den Dikken and Kees Hengeveld (eds.) *Linguistics in the Netherlands 1995*, Amsterdam: Benjamins, pp. 227–38.

1997, 'Complex prepositions and P-stranding in Dutch', *Linguistics* 35, 1091–111.

Author index

Subject and language index

Printed in the United Kingdom
by Lightning Source UK Ltd.
131511UK00002B/36/A